The Schneider
Trophy Story

The Schneider Trophy Story

EDWARD EVES

Edited by L.F.E. Coombs MPhil, AMRAeS, FRSA

MBI Publishing Company

This edition first published in 2001 by MBI Publishing Company
Galtier Plaza, Suite 200, 380 Jackson Street, St. Paul,
MN 55101-3885 USA

Previously published by Airlife Publishing Ltd., Shrewsbury, England.

MBI Publishing Company books are also available at discounts in
bulk quantity for industrial or sales-promotional use. For details write
to Special Sales Manager at Motorbooks International Wholesalers &
Distributors, Galtier Plaza, Suite 200, 380 Jackson Street, St. Paul,
MN 55101-3885 USA

Library of Congress Cataloging-in-Publication Data Available.

ISBN 0-7603-1118-8

Printed in England.

Dedication

In 1964 my late husband Ted Eves founded the Thursday Club, an informal monthly meeting of the technical leaders of the UK motor industry. This unique gathering provided Ted with invaluable material that he was able to use in his professional activities as author and journalist.

Inevitably, figures from the aviation industry also became involved in Thursday Club meetings, and on one occasion members were privileged to meet the legendary Air Commodore Rodwell Banks, q.v., supported by his right-hand man, Wing Commander Harry Mundy, then of Jaguar Cars. Another memorable club night saw Klaus von Reuker, a very senior figure in BMW's second world war aero engine division, revealing the problems that BMW experienced in identifying a durable jet-blade material.

The Thursday Club also became involved in the support of the motor industry's own charity – The Motor and Allied Trades Benevolent Fund – known affectionately as BEN. It is my wish that all royalties accruing from the sale of *The Schneider Trophy Story* be donated to BEN, in recognition of the fine work they carry out for the dependants of motor industry employees.

Finally, my personal thanks to Keith Douglas, who succeeded Ted as Thursday Club organiser and who assisted the publishers in bringing *The Schneider Trophy Story* to print.

Doreen Eves

Acknowledgement

The publishers would like to thank Leslie Coombs for his invaluable assistance during the preparation of this book.

Edward Eves would also have wished to thank the following for their help during the research for this book – Derek N. James, Philip Jarrett, Brian L. Riddle: Librarian, Royal Aeronautical Society, Richard Haigh and Mike Evans: Rolls-Royce Heritage Trust, Alec Lumsden, Alan Vessey: Napier Power Heritage Trust and Sandy Skinner. Also C. Deventhery-Lewis, The United States Naval Institute via P.M. Maddocks, T.R. Chilvers, Stato Maggiori Aeronautica and Musée de l'Air.

Contents

Introduction

The Sporting Setting

It is difficult to imagine the excitement and novelty of aviation in the early 1900s. While the politicians, strategists and industrialists pulled the strings, the flying enthusiasts of the first decade of the century revelled in the excitement of the new sport. The man in the street was entranced by the spectacle it provided. In the first decade of the twentieth century, mastery of the air had much in common with the conquest of space today, with the big difference that participation was open to ordinary people who had the necessary means and were imbued with the spirit of adventure.

The Schneider Trophy. Won outright in 1931 by the RAF High Speed Flight's Supermarine S.6B flown by Flight Lieutenant J.N. Boothman. The Trophy is in the custody of the Royal Aero Club in London.

In common with the motor car the main development area was destined to be that of competition. The only difference was that the automobile was already established as a serious means of travel. In 1910 touring aircraft, airlines and regular passenger services were ten years into the future. The stimulus of a major war was needed to develop large, load-carrying aeroplanes. But the commercial possibilities of the aeroplane were already being foreseen and wise men were smoothing the way by putting up prizes for contests designed to develop the fledgling heavier-than-air machines.

A typical example of this was in England, where Lord Rothermere, proprietor of the *Daily Mail* offered a whole series of large prizes to encourage the development of practical aviation. They included the sum of £5,000 for the first British flight of more than 1 mile, and £10,000 – a huge sum in those days – for the winner of a race from London to Manchester.

One of Rothermere's most significant primes was a £1,000 prize for the first man to cross the English Channel. On 25 July 1909, in the course of winning this particular prize with a momentous flight in his Blériot-Anzani monoplane, Louis Blériot made aviation history while at the same time causing uneasy stirrings in the heart of the British naval establishment. France, then in the throes of the *belle epoque*, was at the forefront of aviation progress as it was in automobilism. Blériot's flight was just one confirmation of the work being done by a myriad of Gallic experimenters. It could not even be said that the Wrights had shown the French the way, because men of the calibre of Santos-Dumont and Maurice Farman, in aircraft built by the brothers Voisin, had made successful flights with unassisted take-off before the Wright brothers' work at Kitty Hawk was made public.

In France the Gordon Bennett Aviation Cup, donated by James Gordon Bennett, the expatriot owner of the *New York Herald*, was presented as the award for an international speed event for land planes. It was first contested at the momentous Rheims aviation meeting of 1909 where appropriately enough it was won by the American pioneer, Glenn Curtiss, flying a machine of his own construction. His average speed was 75.49 km/h (46.92 mph) over two laps of a 10 kilometre circuit.

In the USA, too, the nation which had produced the first practical, powered, heavier-than-air machine, aviation was beginning to stretch its wings although progress was slow compared with Europe. In that country prizes were small to begin with and aviators complained that for every $50 offered in the United States, the equivalent of $1,000 was being put up in Europe. This was handsomely rectified in 1910 when a sum of $80,000 (£20,000) in prize money was put up at the Los Angeles Aeronautical Tournament. Here again Glenn H. Curtiss won the speed event, confirming his success at Rheims.

It was a measure of progress in aviation that the Englishman Claude Grahame-White, in the course of winning the Gordon Bennett Aviation Cup from the Americans in 1910, covered twenty laps of a 5 kilometre circuit located at the New York Belmont Park Race Course, in 1 hr 1 min 4.72 sec. His mount was a

Gnome-engined clipped-wing Blériot XIbis and his average speed 98.55 km/h (61.25 mph). Grahame-White won the race from Le Blanc, who set a new World Air Speed Record of 70 mph during the course of the race before crashing sensationally as a result of shortage of fuel. This Belmont Park event gave the Americans their first, and rather startling, insight into the progress being made in Europe.

Charles Terres Weymann regained the Gordon Bennett Cup for the USA in 1911 with a speed of 125.6 km/h (78.1 mph). This was hardly an American success. The aircraft was a French-built Nieuport-Gnome and Weymann, although an American citizen, had been born in Haiti and brought up in France. The venue in this case was Eastchurch, in Britain, on the Isle of Sheppey to the east of London where the Royal Aero Club had its flying grounds. The race distance by this time had been extended to 94 statute miles.

Such was the pace of progress, forged in the white heat of competition, that just one year later, in November 1912, a tiny Deperdussin monoplane, one of a team of three shipped from France by Armand Deperdussin to challenge for the Gordon Bennett Trophy, and flown by Jules Védrines, shattered the Americans by winning at over 100 mph, 105.47 mph (169.7 km/h) to be exact. Another Deperdussin, flown by Maurice Prévost, was second.

The Deperdussin monoplane was a pointer to the future of aircraft design. The creation of Louis Béchereau, it had the tiny span of 7 m, an overall length of 6.250 m and a wing area of 12 sq m. It was powered by a 160 hp, double-bank, 14-cylinder Gnome rotary engine. Béchereau gave it a laminated-wood, monocoque fuselage, based on vestigial longerons, a braced monoplane wing and an engine cowling which would not be out of place today. Earlier in 1912, on 22 February, Jules Védrines had exceeded 100 mph for the first time with one of the team aircraft establishing a new World Air Speed Record of 110.48 mph (177.77 km/h).

One of the wealthy Frenchmen who visited America to attend the Gordon Bennett races and to cheer on his compatriots was the French sportsman, scion of a great industrial family, Jacques Schneider. A close friend of Louis Blériot, Schneider had been a high-speed motorboat pilot of some standing before a motorboat crash handicapped him with an arm injury. In March 1911, some time before this accident, he had joined the Aéro-Club de France and gained pilot's licence no. 409 on aeroplanes and no. 181 qualifying him to fly free balloons. Inevitably he attended the 1912 hydro-aeroplane meeting at Monaco to see the two loves of his life, motorboats and seaplanes, perform. It was there that he conceived the idea of a series of contests for seaplanes on the lines of the Gordon Bennett Cup for landplanes.

Legend has it that an American friend of Schneider's, Henry Woodhouse, persuaded him of the future of hydro-aeroplanes and suggested that he should institute a series to improve the breed. It seems certain that Schneider had decided to instigate the Cup long before he left for America and chose to announce his intentions at the dinner which followed the 1912 Gordon Bennett race. While landplane design was sweeping on like wildfire, the development of aeroplanes designed to fly off water was slowly forging ahead after a poor start. A number of very early pioneers, before the Wrights, had chosen to make their early attempts to become airborne off water, perhaps because it appeared nice and soft to have an accident into. Many of them were destined to find it was otherwise. In one such demonstration, in 1904, at the Crystal Palace in London, Major B. Baden-Powell made a series of glides off a special staging in a Lilienthal-type glider wing mounted on a lightweight pontoon. These flights were more like semi-controlled crashes. But a box-kite glider on floats, built and flown by Gabriel Voisin was much more successful on 6 June 1905. He made a number of flights towed by the fast launch, *La Rapière*, between the Billancourt and Sèvres bridges on the Seine.

It was left to a Frenchman, Henri Fabre, to make the

Jacques Schneider.

The hydroplane that started it all. Fabre's seaplane *Goeland*, the first to take off from water, lying in the harbour at Monaco, where it gave a series of demonstrations in 1912. In the background is a hangar constructed for Santos-Dumont's airship. This is now used as a garage in Roquebrune.

first powered flight off water, on the Étang de Berre, which was later to play a historic role in the development of French Schneider Trophy machines. His quaint craft, the *Goeland*, was described at the time as half hydroplane, half aeroplane. It rested on three floats with literally flat, plane-surface, bottoms and curved upper surfaces which produced lift when the machine became airborne. It was a canard – it flew 'tail first' – and the wings were covered with artificial silk which could be furled like sails when the craft was at rest. Its main asset, and the main reason it eventually became airborne, was that the original four 12 hp Anzani engines with which it was first fitted were replaced by a rear-mounted 50 hp Gnome engine. Weighing a mere 172 lb and giving its genuine rated horsepower, this engine lifted the *Goeland* off the sea at Martigues on 28 March 1910.

In America Glenn Curtiss started experimenting with his June Bug, mounted on floats and christened *Loon*, on Lake Keuka in 1908. Although somewhat delayed by other flying commitments he finally got off the water on 26 January 1911 flying a biplane – not the *Loon* – of his own design. It was fitted with tandem floats and a 6 ft hydrofoil mounted below the forward elevator. The tandem float and hydrofoil were later replaced by a single, 12 ft swim-bow pontoon to produce the forerunner of the Curtiss Navy flying-boats. Incidentally, the Curtiss boat, having the tail mounted on booms, should be regarded as a distinct type from the classic Donnet-Leveque type of 1912 which had its tail surfaces mounted on an extension of the hull.

As the pre-eminent sea-going nation Britain was not lagging behind and numerous experiments were taking place all over the country. The first successful flight was a truly naval affair. Intent on upholding the tradition of his service, Commander Oliver Schwann of the Royal Navy airship tender HMS *Hermione*, urged on by Captain Murray Seuter, acquired an Avro D seaplane and fitted it with a series of pairs of floats of his own design. After months of experiments he finally got airborne from Cavendish Dock, Barrow-in-Furness, on 18 November 1911 using stepped floats with air bleeds to the aft side of the steps. Only seven months later, on 9 May 1912, Commander Samson flew a Short S.27 fitted with airbag floats off staging erected on the foredeck of the old battleship HMS *Hibernian*. He was not the first to perform the feat; Eugene Ely had flown a land plane off the American cruiser USS *Birmingham* as early as 14 November 1910.

In Italy too, there were great goings-on with beautiful, but abortive designs from Gabardini and Caproni. Much pioneer work was done on the hydrofoils by Professor Forlanini and Crocco. An eminent practical worker was Guidoni, who later, as General A. Guidoni, was a driving force behind Italy's Schneider Cup involvement. Progress in France had been rapid too. The French had already built up a sizeable air force by the standards of the day. In 1912 they were able to muster at least 200 military aircraft, not to mention a number of airships. Gabriel Voisin had also supplied the French navy with its first hydro-aeroplane, a canard biplane of the Fabre type which was meant to be housed in a hangar built aboard the cruiser FS *Foudre*, the world's first aircraft-carrier.

The sporting element flourished alongside the growth of the military branch. In many ways it was part and parcel of it because, without the stimulus of sporting aviation, the aeroplane would have been a slow developer indeed. Authority, both civil and military had actively encouraged races and rallies for landplanes for some years, and watched the results with professional interest. With the advent of the hydro-aeroplane and its possibilities as a naval weapon it, too, received its due share of encouragement from those, amateur and professional, whose object was to foster the new science through sport.

Which brings us to the principality of Monaco which, at that time, was in strong competition – 'battle-royal' would be a better description – with Biarritz as a social centre for the *haut-monde*. So far as the promoters of both these watering places were concerned the rewards were not in the pockets of the hoteliers, nor even the shopkeepers, but in the coffers of the casino operators. In Monaco this organisation was innocently styled the Société de Bains de Mer. Through the International Sporting Club (ISC), M. Camille Blanc, head of the Société, was prepared to promote any spectacle of consequence, backing it with profits from the casino where huge fortunes were being lost and won.

The annual motorboat races established in 1903 were a very rich man's sport and were a typical example, ready made for Monaco. The royalty, nobility and gentry of Europe made their way to the Côte d'Azure in their steam yachts, bringing with them their fast launches as deck cargo, to compete against each other for big prizes and even bigger personal wagers. It was a sport almost as new as aviation, packed with technical interest. Many famous automobile racing engines, too powerful for existing test-beds at their makers' works, had their first run in motorboats at Monaco. And many of these valuable prototypes lie at the bottom of the bay to this day.

One result of the display by the *Goeland* at Martigues was to implant in some Monégasque brain, or perhaps in the mind of Monsieur Georges Prade of the journal *Les Sports*, the idea of combining hydro-aeroplane races with the annual motorboat affair. Thus, in 1912, it was a logical development to organise competitions for the latest thing in sporting flying, flight off water, alongside competitions between skimming boats. To be cynical it also padded out the period of the meeting from two weeks to four at the end of the season, to the ultimate benefit of the natives.

Certainly the Aéro-Club de France was ready with a set of regulations early in 1912 in preparation for a seaplane meeting at Monaco in April of the same year. Georges Prade was prevailed upon to act as clerk of the course. Georges, apart from his outstanding reportage of motoring and aviation sport, was the man who had been despatched to America to investigate the Wrights' claims and who had sent back some very cynical reports.

He was destined to organise all the Monaco seaplane meetings both before and after World War One.

The 1912 experiment was so successful that for 1913 two aviation events were scheduled to take place following the motorboat races and occupying no less than a fortnight. Presumably this was to allow for weather and the repair of breakages. The main event, the Grand Prix de Monaco, was to be an ambitious series of events embracing all aspects of seaplane operation including a 500 km, non-stop race. The other was Jacques Schneider's Coupe d'Aviation Maritime.

This first Schneider Trophy race was scheduled to take place during the last week of the fourteen-day meeting. It appears to have been of little consequence to international observers, who probably regarded it as a ruse to keep them in the principality for a further week. Many journalists went home immediately after the Grand Prix and didn't even bother to report the Schneider race.

The rules for the Grand Prix were not greeted with universal approval. A crew of two had to be carried, and fuel and oil for 500 km non-stop called for special machines to carry the weight. Moreover, the whole week of tests, towing, long-distance 'taxying', hoisting by cranes and flying ability necessitated specially constructed aircraft. The race would require a duration of at least five hours if the machines were to go the whole distance without refuelling. But the rewards would be great for it was well known that the burgeoning French air arm would be keeping a watchful eye on the results.

In contrast, the deed of gift of the Coupe d'Aviation Maritime Jacques Schneider called for an entirely different type of machine. For one thing they could be single-seaters while the Grand Prix rules called for two-place aircraft. They set out to encourage the production of as rational and practical a hydro-aeroplane as possible with the accent on speed. History went on to prove that the first two attributes gradually faded into the background as the pursuit of the last requirement took over. Comparing the two events, the Grand Prix tended to produce bomber types while the Schneider races became the forcing ground of fighter development.

In more detail Jacques Schneider, through the Aéro Club, was presenting to the Fédération Aéronautique Internationale (FAI) a trophy in the form of an object of art worth 25,000 francs (roughly equivalent to £1,000), as an aviation challenge trophy between national clubs. Its correct title was to be 'La Coupe d'Aviation Maritime'. Schneider modestly omitted his own name. He also agreed to award the sum of 25,000 francs to the pilot of the winning aircraft in the first three events.

The essential ingredients were that the contest should be between national aeronautical clubs, as with the Gordon Bennett Cup, that it should take place annually, and that any country which won three times in a period of five years, or failed to attract a challenge for a period of five consecutive years, would retain the cup and the contest would end. That it was a seaplane event is implicit in the title of the cup. Seaworthiness is not dwelt upon specifically although it is covered in the requirement that the regulations should aim to produce the ideal type of seaplane. It was left to the organising club to specify any seaworthiness tests, presumably on the thesis that as the art of flying off water progressed they would have to become more stringent, which was the case. However, speed was specifically mentioned and speed became the keynote of the Schneider Trophy, at times to the exclusion of other qualities. In later years, the Schneider races were criticised because it was felt that they were departing from Schneider's original intentions. When one rereads the rules it is clear that this is not so. The only unambiguous stipulation was the one that it should be a speed event.

Monaco 1913

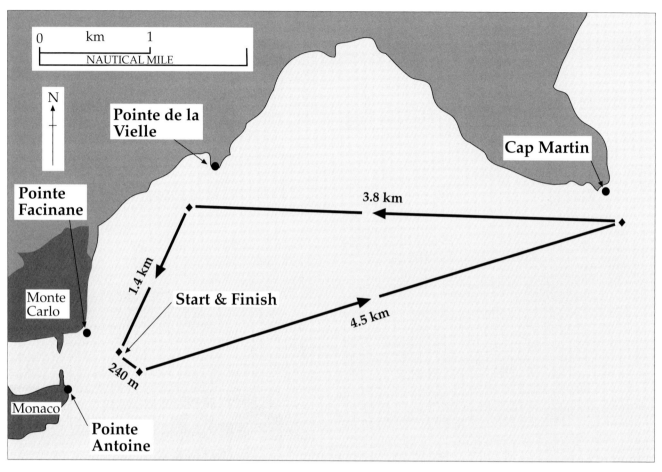

Schneider Trophy Contest Course: Monaco 1913 and 1914.

Preliminaries

The regulations for the 1913 Schneider races were formulated at almost the last moment, as late as January of that year, giving manufacturers little time to build special aircraft. They were the product of a small but noble committee of the Aéro-Club de France. In the chair was prince Roland Bonaparte, president of the club with comte Castilon de St Victor as secretary: the comte de la Vaulx, and baron de Zuylen were also present.

The rules were quite simple. As required by the deed of gift each competing nation would be represented by a team of three aircraft to be selected by national trials. The French trials were arranged to take place at Monaco as part of the spectacle and also to give their constructors the maximum time to get their creations *au point*. On arrival at Monaco they would be required to cover four laps of a 10 km polygonal course with a proportion of the distance on the surface. For the race the same circuit was to be used and the regulations were much the same except that the race distance was longer. The chosen aircraft had to set off at intervals, the order being decided by drawing lots, and were called on to taxi 2 nautical miles before taking off and completing twenty-eight laps, a total distance of 151.09 nm. Competitors could take off at any time between 8 am and legal sunset but only one start was permitted and before that could take place the competitor was required to hand to the race commissioners a duplicate set of regulations, signed by himself, as a declaration of his intention to race.

The importance of the Grand Prix was the part it played in bringing entries for the Schneider Trophy. All of them, with the exception of Roland Garros, were participants in it. And it certainly taught all the pilots a lot about seaplane handling, being an event cursed with particularly bad weather. Weymann, for example, badly

Competing aircraft for the 1913 race moored in Monaco harbour.

damaged his Nieuport when a gust of wind caused it to do a back somersault during a compulsory alighting off the harbour of Beaulieu-sur-Mer. And on the very first day of the meeting, 4 April, all three of the new big Deperdussin IIs entered for the Grand Prix were damaged on alighting by striking their tailfloats too hard on the water. Prévost's aircraft broke its back and as a result was late in starting the compulsory tests.

The whole of the first week of the hydro-aeroplane meeting was taken up with the various starting, towing and hoisting trials for the Grand Prix. The qualifying trials for the Schneider Trophy had to wait until Monday 11 April, halfway through the meeting. As already stated they were a French domestic affair arranged by the Aéro-Club de France for the five French entrants. Weymann, as the US contestant and only foreign entrant, did not have to be interested although,

enigmatically, as a French entry in the Grand Prix he was fully occupied with that event and his qualification for the Grand Prix final speed event was announced on the day of the Schneider eliminators. In the Schneider race he was the essential international ingredient.

Charles Terres Weymann, as already related, had been born in Haiti, Port-au-Prince, to be exact, on 2 August 1889 of a French mother and American father. He had trained in France on Henry Farmans and held one of the earliest Aero Club of America licences, no. 24, granted in 1909 by proxy. Henry Farman aircraft were his first love and as early as 1910 he was attempting a flight over the Simplon pass at the same time as the successful flight by Chavez. He changed to Nieuport tractor machines in May 1911 and only two months later won the Gordon Bennett Cup at Eastchurch with his new machine. The following year he changed over to

Charles Weymann, the charming Franco-American pilot of Nieuport No. 5, made the first Schneider Trophy an international event. In the motoring world he is best known for his patent fabric for bodies which graced many fine cars in the interwar years. Prior to World War I he was most famous as an aviator, holding many records in France. He never flew in America and spoke only poor English. (*Musée de l'Air*)

Garros's Morane-Saulnier is handled down the slipway at Monaco in 1913. (*Musée de l'Air*)

Charles Weymann's Nieuport being prepared for the 1913 race. (*Musée de l'Air*)

Chemet's Astra, powered by a 160 hp Gnome engine, taxying off the harbour entrance at Monaco. It was eliminated in the 1913 pre-race trials. (*Musée de l'Air*)

float planes and competed successfully at St Malo in 1912 as well as setting up long-distance records. He was a man of many parts, with interests in the motor trade as well as aviation. He was an agent for Hispano-Suiza cars with premises in Rue Thoyron in Paris, designed and had built a pusher monoplane with the propeller behind the rudder in 1916 and supplied many manufacturers, including Bugatti, with instruments. He was also responsible for the method of coachbuilding for which his name is renowned among collectors of old automobiles.

The French entrants were Bregi, in a Salmson-engined Breguet biplane, Roland Garros, in his Morane-Saulnier monoplane specially fitted with an 80 hp 7-cylinder Gnome engine. Normally it would have been powered by a Le Rhône of the same horsepower. Dr

Espanet was in a Nieuport-Gnome 100 hp, Chemet in a Borel (Gnome 80 hp) and Maurice Prévost in a Deperdussin which is variously described in French reports of the meeting as being powered by either a 100 hp or 160 hp Gnome rotary.

Of these five only three presented themselves on 11 April: Prévost, Garros and Dr Espanet. Chemet had damaged his Borel in one of the early Grand Prix tests, being forced to continue that event in an Astra. Bregi, an outstanding pilot, was presumably saving his machine for the 500 km race to be held the day before the Schneider race, for which he was one of the favourites.

As mentioned earlier the French qualifying test was quite simple. It consisted of four laps of a 10 km triangular course which had been buoyed out in the bay for the Prix de l'International Sporting Club. The first five

The Deperdussin Schneider Special that could not be used in the 1913 race because its engine overheated. (*Musée de l'Air*)

kilometres had to be covered taxying on the surface of the water; the remainder was in the air. Conditions were not ideal. There was a long cross-swell which did not help Garros, whose Morane was not at all happy, mainly because the pilot, although a virtuoso, was new to float planes.

Prévost was fastest, spending 9 minutes 18 seconds on the water, and 22 minutes 9 seconds in the air, a total time of 31 min 27 sec. Prévost's speed for the 35 km of flying, including take-off was 94.80 km/h, slow by Deperdussin landplane standards but fast for a floatplane of the period. Garros spent an interminable time on the water – 13 min 2 sec in all – before getting airborne to cover the remainder of the course in 27 min 10.4 sec (77.28 km/h). Dr Espanet, who had been a local dental surgeon and knew local conditions better than most, spent a mere 6 min 34 sec on the water although his airborne time was a lengthy 36 min 2 sec (58.28 km/h). His slow time must be attributed to the fact that his Nieuport was the 100 hp model and slower than the others. These speeds, with the exception of Prévost's, were substantially lower than those achieved in the race, possibly because of a head wind on one of the long legs.

Prévost's high speed in relation to the other competitors could possibly be explained by the fact that he was flying a special racing single-seat Deperdussin with the 160 hp, two-row, Gnome engine and not the two-seater Grand Prix machine which he used in the

This Deperdussin single-seater should have flown. Powered by a 160 hp Gnome, it was 'cleaner' than the winning aircraft of 1913 but was less well-tried. (*Musée de l'Air*)

race. This machine, bearing the same number 19 as the Deperdussin II two-seater, was much in evidence during the week and there are photographs of it in flight and in the harbour. It is difficult to ascertain just what befell this practice machine. One report said that it seized a piston in practice, presumably during another

Early in the Monaco fortnight Prévost's Grand Prix Deperdussin was badly damaged when landing, breaking its back. It was repaired in time to take part in the Schneider Trophy, superseding the unsuccessful Schneider Special built specially for the occasion. It can be seen from this photograph that this aircraft was far from being a racer. The drag inherent in the float structure must have been a great disadvantage. (*Flight*)

Prévost in his 1913 winning 'military' Deperdussin. (*Musée de l'Air*)

flight, and was unable to take part in the race. It is difficult to believe that a piston seizure in a two-row Gnome could have been the reason. It was a too common occurrence, and a good mechanic would have changed the cylinder and piston in a few hours. Maybe the single-seater did not have sufficient duration to cover the 280 km of the race without refuelling. Or perhaps the wily Armand Deperdussin had brought it along to put in fast times which would be attributed to the two-seater.

What we do know is that, for the Schneider race, Prévost had to make do with the heavy Deperdussin II Grand Prix machine. With an all-up weight of 1,350 kg (2,970 lb) and fitted to carry 375 ltr (82 gal) of fuel and 70 ltr (15 gal) of oil to last the 500 km duration of the Grand Prix, it was hardly the machine for a 150 km speed event. The actual aircraft was one which had broken its back on 4 April and had been hurriedly repaired in time to participate in the Schneider Cup race and the Prix de l'International Sporting Club on 12 April, when it flew a few laps and then retired.

Whatever the problem Maurice Prévost would be loyal to any decisions made, if he didn't make them himself. Born in Rheims in 1887 he had been a fascinated spectator of the historic Rheims meeting. Inspired by what he saw there he went along to the Deperdussin School at Conroy Betheny, gaining his brevet in 1911. He was soon breaking records, always with Deperdussin. The first Paris to London flight with a passenger was by Prévost and there were second places in the Gordon Bennett and the British Military Trials that year. Late in 1913, after the Coupe Maritime, he went on to win the Gordon Bennett Cup at the record speed of 200.3 km/h (124.36 mph), a fantastic speed at that time. After a brilliant career in aviation he went into the oil business and was for many years a representative of Esso on the aviation side. He died in 1969 at the age of eighty-two.

Louis Béchereau had designed the Deperdussin II, as it was designated, very much with military contracts in mind. Armand Deperdussin needed them badly at the time. Starting his working life as a shop assistant he had made a big fortune out of silk-broking during the Russo-Japanese war. Unfortunately he had the gift for spending money much more rapidly than he could make it. It could be said that one of his better extravagances was to start the Deperdussin company, very appropriately located in the Rue des Entrepreneurs in Paris, after meeting the brilliant young Louis Béchereau in 1910.

Louis Béchereau, who was responsible for the first Schneider winner, and the most famous designer of high-speed aircraft prior to World War I. He was responsible for all the racing Deperdussins and later the SPAD fighters and seaplanes. He even influenced the design of the Bernard record-breaking aircraft. (*Musée de l'Air*)

He spent a small fortune building the winning team of aircraft for the Gordon Bennett cup races in Amsterdam in 1912, sending them and their pilots across the Atlantic at his own expense. It is to his eternal credit that he recognised Béchereau as the genius he was, gave him his head and allowed him to build a number of special-purpose aircraft. Such were the Gordon Bennett racers which held the world airspeed record right up to the beginning of World War One.

The monoplace Schneider Special floatplane was one such special, a typical lightweight, purpose-built racer with the touch of the master. But the team of three two-seat Deperdussin II floatplanes for the Grand Prix, which must have been immensely costly to construct, were a different story. They were a last fling in an attempt to gain military orders and divert financial disaster for Armand Deperdussin personally, not for Appareils Deperdussin, which was financially sound. It was too late. Only four months later, in August, Deperdussin was arrested on fraud charges involving the equivalent of more than £1m sterling.

Alongside the Deperdussin, the Nieuports of Weymann and Espanet appeared square and homely. Deceptively so because, despite their plain box-section fuselages they had far less parasitic drag built into them in the way of wires and struts than their elegant looking adversaries. Designed by the Nieuport brothers – their real family name was de Niéport – they had already won a number of hydro-aeroplane events, mainly in the hands of Charles Weymann and Gabriel Espanet. Before the 1913 meeting both the Nieuport brothers, Édouard and Charles had been tragically killed in flying accidents. Édouard, who had been a noted cyclist, was a born engineer and designed the ignition systems for both the Santos-Dumont and Farman first flights. He started building aeroplanes and engines in 1911 and was killed on 15 September that year. Charles took over the company on his death, learnt to fly, and was killed demonstrating a triplane on 24 January 1913.

It is doubtful if the American's Nieuport with the 160 hp engine could get anywhere near the single-seat Deperdussin Schneider Special in terms of speed. But on paper at least it had the legs of the heavy Deperdussin II with the same engine which weighed 200 kg (440 lb) more and was of larger span. Espanet's Nieuport with the 100 hp Gnome would appear hardly to have been in the running unless he had succeeded in obtaining one of the new monosoupape type then in the process of development.

Compared with its competitors, Garros's Morane-Saulnier monoplane was diminutive, both in size and power. Although Raymond Saulnier had designed and build a specialist water-plane, it was a large, 17-m-span biplane. Garros preferred to take the much handier, standard, single-place monoplane, with which he was very familiar, and fit it with floats. The diminutive Morane was a great favourite with the experts and Garros was at that time one of the best, if not the best, Morane exponents. That year he had been nominated the French equivalent of the British Sportsman of the

Roland Garros was the prototype of the French airman; neat, dark and dapper, he was a superb aviator. His apparently daring and adventurous flights stemmed from a proper appreciation of the mechanics of the machine he was flying. (*Musée de l'Air*)

Garros, with his Morane-Saulnier hydroplane in the main harbour of Monaco. In the background can be seen the Tir aux Pigeons with its colonnade pillars. Garros flew across the Mediterranean for the first time in a similar machine. It was the lowest-powered entry in 1913 with an 80 hp single-row engine. (*Musée de l'Air*)

Year. In honour of this he had been given race number 1. He was certainly as popular in France as Gustav Hamel, who also flew Moranes, was in England. Both were first-class aerobatic pilots. Garros amused the Monaco crowd with several displays flying his landplane during the period of the meeting. When war came his ability to weigh up a risk stood him in good stead. He flight tested Raymond Saulnier's idea of hardened steel deflectors on the propeller blades to deflect any bullets which might hit them. His was the distinction of being the first pilot to shoot down an enemy aircraft with a gun firing through the propeller disc.

As an aside it is noteworthy that both Espanet and Garros were very satisfied Bugatti owners and had become personal friends of Ettore Bugatti, the car designer, as a result. Louis Blériot and the French pioneer Archdeacon were also cronies of Bugatti, which may explain his ventures into aero-engine construction. Espanet gave up medicine in 1907 to devote all his time to flying.

It may be a measure of the initial lack of enthusiasm for the Coupe d'Aviation Maritime, or the manner in which it was overshadowed by the Grand Prix, that the Schneider field was so small, consisting of only three distinct types of aircraft, all of them French. It might have been more if Grahame-White, from England, had sent in his entry in time to be included on the list. However, the pilots were the best that France could muster. I would include Weymann in this despite his American citizenship.

In 1913, bearing in mind that the third anniversary of Fabre's first water take-off had only just been celebrated, the art of the hydro-aeroplane had advanced tremendously. Float design was not all that it might have been. The short, punt-shaped floats of the Deperdussin and Morane-Saulnier did not support the tail of the aircraft. A tail float was called in to do that. As a result, until the aircraft attained sufficient forward speed for the elevators to become effective and lift the tail float off the water, the main floats ploughed along literally dragging their heels. When they did eventually get on the plane the pilots had to hold them there until flying speed was gained with the flat bottoms of the floats banging on the waves and putting such loads into the float chassis that some designers built springs into the float struts.

Alighting on the water, *amerrissage,* the French called it, was also a hazard. These men had no instructors to teach them the tricks of handling a water plane. They were the pioneers. Even the best of them found it difficult to judge height above water whether it be calm or rough. Consequently the machine would often hit the sea with a terrific bang, bending or breaking the float struts, or even fracturing the rear fuselage, in the process. It was much later that vee-bottomed floats came in with their inherent shock-absorbing effect.

Once the aircraft was on the water it was at the mercy of the elements. It was literally like a sailing boat in stays without a rudder. If engines had been more flexible it would have been a help. But the Gnome especially, for all its virtues, would not run slowly, having to be controlled by an ignition on-off switch on the control column. For this reason, and because the tail surfaces were so small, the aircraft had to be taxied fast, almost at flying speed. Often a gust of wind would come along, provide an extra bit of lift and flip them over.

None the less the design problems were being tackled one by one as experience grew. At least more of the machines at Monaco in 1913 were specifically designed as hydro-aeroplanes rather than being adapted landplanes, as most of the French machines at the 1912 meeting had been. For this we had to thank the Grand Prix regulations, which focused attention on seaworthiness, even calling for towing attachments, an anchor and a lifebuoy as well as sufficient fuel to cover 310 miles (500 km) without alighting.

On the score of handling, however, the French hydro-aeroplanes were no match for their landplane equivalents. The effect of the side area of the floats was considerable. Even the best pilots rounded the markers in a wide sweep with hardly enough bank on to overcome the outward forces. Design was one reason. Another was that pilots of good calibre were so much in demand that they tended to move quickly from one type to another, never getting familiar with any one of them. It is doubtful if Prévost, for example, had flown more than four or five hours on the Deperdussin II before the 1913 race. It was a new type and he was new to it. He was hardly likely to put it to extremes of handling. Moreover, it could not have been nearly so pleasant to fly as the short 22-ft-span Deperdussin racers with which he was so familiar. On these aircraft the mechanical forces necessary to warp the wings were finger-tip light; lighter than, say, the aileron controls of a Tiger Moth. The big Dep. with its 44-ft-span wing and maze of warping wires must have felt like a bus in comparison.

The Race

The circuit specially laid out for the race in the Baie de Roquebrune was a roughly triangular one of 10 km. It was, in fact, four-sided because the corner outside the harbour of Monaco was chopped off to act as a start line 240 m long, both ends of the line acting as markers once the machines were airborne. The start line was in full view of the Tir aux Pigeons of the International Sporting Club. The course was to be flown anticlockwise, the first turning point being a marker boat anchored off Cap Martin, a distance of 4.49 km on a bearing of 073 deg. Aircraft then headed due west for 3.87 km to round a further marker boat stationed off the Pointe de la Vieille before flying the final 1.4 km leg back to the start line. The rules called for the aircraft to taxi on the surface for a distance of 2.5 nm, take off and then fly a further 150 nm, about 278 km, a nautical mile taken as being 1.852 km. This made the race distance twenty-eight laps of the 10 km circuit. The taxying, or navigating on the surface rule meant that entrants had to cross the start line opposite the Tir aux Pigeons and remain on the surface in the open waters of the bay, as far as the Cap Martin marker boat, before getting airborne.

The race was scheduled to take place on Wednesday 16 April. Well before then the gales which had raged during the Grand Prix had blown themselves out. Even the swell that had made the French eliminators difficult had subsided. The only wind was a light westerly which would not help the hydro-aeroplanes on their navigation test to Cap Martin. It is never fun taxying with the wind on your tail, but it did mean that the take-off run would be in the direction of the course.

Monaco on a morning like this has a magic all its own and the mechanics were up at dawn in the hangars erected in the corner of the harbour by the gasworks, preparing the aircraft, draining the cylinders of the Gnomes and running them up with onlookers hanging onto the floats. Polishing propellers and wings, filling up

The Garros aircraft being carried out of the hangar to the quayside for launching. Manpower was cheaper in those days and cheaper than trolleys. (*Musée de l'Air*)

with the right amount of fuel and oil were other pre-race devotions. The rule about fuel in air racing is not too much and not too little. Excess weight creates drag. Oil was a critical factor with the Gnome engines. They were capable of consuming vast quantities of it, about one gallon to every five gallons of petrol, to prevent their steel pistons picking up on the steel cylinders. And it had to be castor oil to stop it combining with the fuel and forming a mixture in the crankcase which would be a poor lubricant and an even worse fuel.

Every pilot knows that perfect weather conditions can deteriorate quickly, especially when they happen in the morning. So the pilots were down at the harbour early to take advantage of the rule which allowed starts from 8 am, remembering that the race was to be run as a time trial, with the aircraft starting at intervals to avoid crowding at the turns, although in a long race some conflict was inevitable.

Prévost won the draw. He handed in his starting papers, the starting maroon was fired and he ploughed across the starting line just 3 minutes and 55 seconds after eight o'clock. Quickly he got the aircraft up on the heels of the floats and skimmed off in the direction of Cap Martin. His taxying time was a commendable 6 min 50 sec to the first marker boat, where he turned into wind and took off, flying low over the water to complete his first lap in 11 min 15 sec including taxying time.

Next away was Garros in the Morane at 16 minutes

Garros taxying his Morane-Saulnier into the entrance of Monaco harbour. (*Musée de l'Air*)

and 34 seconds after the hour. In contrast with the Deperdussin the little hydro-aeroplane was unhappy on its long legs and short floats, not helped by the tail wind. Garros was trying to taxi fast and the little Morane-Saulnier pitched badly, throwing up so much spray that after four kilometres the magneto was drowned (the official reason was a broken magneto switch). He

Swinging the propeller of Garros's Morane on the quayside. In the background is the Bessonneau-type hangar in which the Moranes were housed. Behind the hangar is the famous gas works. The rowing boat partly visible in the background with the ISC flag is one of the marker boats. (*Musée de l'Air*)

Garros turning round the start line marker boat and heading for Cap Martin in the background. Note the modest angle of bank of these early hydroplanes when 'cornering'. (*Musée de l'Air*)

signalled for a tow back to harbour, losing one and a half hours there before the trouble was put right and he could complete his taxying test and hoist the Morane into its natural element. He got going well, flying quickly and precisely for fifteen laps before he was seen to alight and again signal for a tow. This time the trouble was more fundamental; a pushrod had broken and it was almost midday, three hours after his start, when he rejoined the race. Eventually he did finish in a total time of 5 hr 4 min 7.6 sec.

Meanwhile Prévost and the two Nieuports were battling it out on the circuit. Prévost, an experienced racing pilot who was well aware that the engine of Weymann's Nieuport had been carefully prepared for this one race, was lapping with great regularity at around 102 km/h (63 mph) taking the turns neatly, offsetting drift on the crosswind leg and putting all he knew into getting the best out of his aircraft. The bay was alive to the soft whirr of the Gnome engines as the aircraft drifted round the circuit at speeds only a little higher than those of the motorboats that had raced earlier. One of these boats was out there piloted by Jacques Schneider, at the helm of his *Je t'en Veux* patrolling the bay ready to go to the assistance of any seaplane that should be in trouble.

Prévost knew that Weymann's Nieuport had the legs of the unwieldy Deperdussin. The French-American started last, and took eight minutes longer than Prévost in taxying across to Cap Martin, almost fifteen minutes. But once airborne he quickly made up time, covering the first airborne 100 km in fifty-eight minutes and turning in some laps at 69 mph. His first lap time had been 18 min 24 sec, a gift of seven minutes to Prévost, who was lapping at slightly better than seven minutes per lap. But when the times for the first five laps were given out it was seen that Weymann had already taken back 105 seconds of his seven minutes. Even more significant was

The scene on the quayside during the 1913 race. In the foreground the Deperdussin Équipe with the packing cases in which the aircraft arrived arranged to form a barrier against the onlookers. The work was done inside the Hervieu tent on the extreme right. In the background is the Morane-Saulnier camp, while further back devotees of Monaco will notice the famous gasholder. The line of buildings along the back of the harbour no longer exists, having been replaced by a promenade. Poking up behind it can be seen the Bristol Hotel where the winning Sopwith team stayed in 1914.

the way that this more powerful of the two Nieuports drew away from the Deperdussin when they coincided on the circuit. Weymann was lapping at 69 mph and despite immaculate flying in the turns and holding accurate headings on the legs Prévost could do no better than 63 mph.

At the end of fifteen laps Weymann had moved just three minutes ahead of Prévost on speed although, of

Espanet's Nieuport of 100 hp in the main harbour of Monaco. With him in the cockpit is Charles Weymann, who flew a similar but more powerful aircraft as the 1913 entry from the USA. The bomb-shaped *'flotteur derriere'* can be clearly seen, as well as the tiny hydrofoils on the tips of the well-shaped floats. (*Musée de l'Air*)

course, the Deperdussin was far ahead on distance, 9 hr 14 min 34 sec to be exact, the Franco-American pilot having delayed his start until 9.14 am. However, by the time that Weymann had completed twenty laps it was clear that the race was his, if he could finish. And it was likely that he would because his engine was fresh for the race and the aircraft had been rebuilt after its ducking at Beaulieu. Gabriel Espanet had started 50 minutes and 25 seconds after eight o'clock. His taxying time had been slower than Prévost's. When he did get into the air it became apparent that his small, 100 hp engine could not get him along as fast as the Deperdussin. After five laps he was 75 seconds behind the air-racing champion and dropping back on time with every lap. Nevertheless he pushed on calmly, no doubt contemplating the eternal truth that no time trial is won until the last machine has crossed the line. He was certain of third place because of the time that Garros had spent in the harbour. But after only seven laps his engine started to misfire and at the end of the Cap Martin-Monaco leg he was forced to put his Nieuport down on the water and taxi into the harbour and retire with fuel feed problems. Garros was still there having his engine repaired when Espanet taxied in. After 100 km and 58 minutes of racing Weymann had a clear lead over Prévost, who had taken 1 hr 3 min 42 sec to cover the same distance. At 200 km the relative times were 1 hr 59 min 23 sec and

1913; Weymann's Nieuport leading the race prior to being eliminated by engine trouble. (*Musée de l'Air*)

2 hr 2 min 29 sec. But the American representative was slowing. However, before this could be known Prévost, who himself was slowing – his speed over the last three laps had dropped to 93.9 km/h (58.4 mph) – had finished twenty-seven laps and came round on his ultimate circuit. But instead of turning at the Tir aux Pigeons marker to cross the line in full flight he landed 500 metres before the marker boat and proceeded to taxi into the harbour. Despite remonstration and exhortation

Espanet's Nieuport in Monaco harbour. (*Musée de l'Air*)

The Aircraft

The Deperdussins

As recounted in the race report Prévost's very fast time in the trials may be explained by the fact that Armand Deperdussin and Louis Béchereau had built what was historically the first Schneider Special for this first race of the series. It was a clean little single-place monoplane in the best Béchereau tradition with diagonal-planked front monocoque, close-cowled engine and a rear fuselage based on four longerons encased in a light plywood fairing. The wing span was almost certainly of the order of 8.60 m and the overall length 6.20 m. A fourteen-cylinder, 160 hp Gnome engine provided the motive power. Contemporary reports mentioned a Gordon Bennett machine mounted on floats. This was certainly not the machine, if it existed.

From photographs the Schneider single-seater appears to have been halfway between the Deperdussin landplane racer and the Grand Prix, military-style Deperdussin. However, it was very much cleaner than the latter machine. In the float area there were only two bracing wires between the edge of each float and the root of the strut. This compared with the four steel-tube braces and four bracing wires of the bigger aircraft. Float bracing was different too. The front float spreader was an ash, streamlined section strut. The rear spreader was a steel tube carrying the wing-warping rocker. However, the main float struts were similar to those of the bigger aircraft and still carried the knuckles, halfway up the float struts, to which the crowfoot, tubular steel braces would be attached. Wing bracing was simplified, each wing being braced by three upper landing wires and three lift wires. The outer wires were duplicated front and rear. The wing-warping arrangements, utilising the float chassis to achieve advantageous control wire angles, prove that it was designed from the start as a seaplane. A look at the control arrangement showed the lower wing-warping wires coming together at a ring joint just outboard of the floats. A single wire, passing under a pulley in the bottom of the strut picked up with wires from a central quadrant lever mounted on the steel tube rear float spreader. The central cabane structure was also simplified compared with the Grand Prix seaplane, having two struts per side instead of three. The tiny rear float was a Fabre type with a flat bottom and a curved, airfoil top.

The Deperdussin II was an entirely different machine, an intriguing cocktail of the best and the worst in aerodynamic design. If anything it went to prove that Béchereau's forte was single-seater machines, as history was to prove. In common with his Gordon Bennett racers it was a braced mid-wing monoplane with monocoque front fuselage and fully cowled engine. It was the largest aeroplane he had designed embodying these features. The constant-chord wings had a span of 13.5 m and a chord of 2.1 m giving an area of 27 sq m. Overall length was 8.9 metres. Designed all-up weight was 1,350 kg with a payload of 450 kg, which included a pilot, passenger and fuel. For the Grand Prix race,

from the crew of his tender he just shrugged his shoulders and carried on. The story is that he was so convinced that Weymann had the race in the bag he reckoned that it was just not worth the trouble of flying across the line and finishing the race properly. Despite the prospect of substantial prize money he was apparently not prepared to be classified a certain second. He would know this because he could see both Garros and Espanet in the harbour.

This behaviour is so untypical of the trustworthy Prévost that one is tempted to hypothesise that the real reason for his alighting may have been some mechanical failure or shortage of fuel, which was rectified while he was in the port. His engine had played up the previous day when he had completed only a few laps of the Prix de l'International Sporting Club before being forced to give up because of engine trouble. The fact that he was relinquishing one third of the 25,000 francs prize money as the second of two finishers was unusual behaviour for any Frenchman. Moreover, Armand Deperdussin was his friend and he would surely know how much depended on a good showing.

However, Weymann's time at the 200 km point showed that he was losing speed. He had already lost some of the time that he had gained at the 100 km mark. Obviously his engine was tightening. He was just about to complete his twenty-fifth lap and it stopped altogether. He had run out of oil – one report says that an oil pipe had broken – and a piston had seized.

By this time Prévost had been in harbour for more than half an hour. When he saw the Nieuport come in on the end of a tow rope he jerked out of his doldrums and called the mechanics to fire up his engine. Taxying out of the harbour he took off and in minutes had crossed the line to become the first winner of the Coupe d'Aviation Maritime and the owner of not one third of 25,000 francs, but the whole of it.

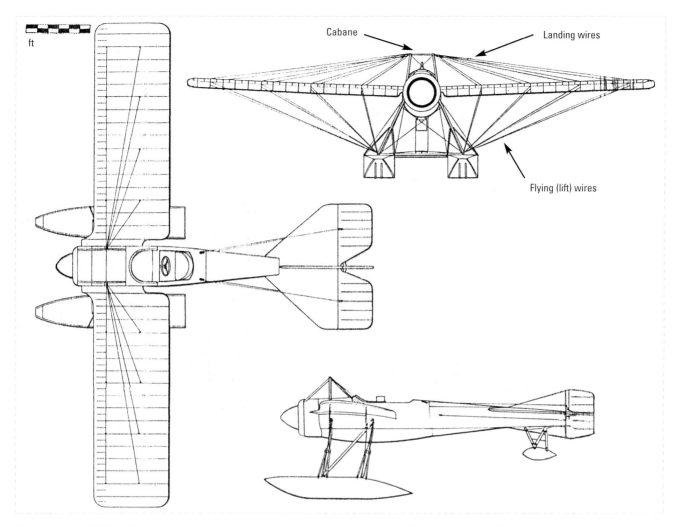

Cabane

Landing wires

Flying (lift) wires

ft

Deperdussin (1913): Wing Span: 44 ft 3 in (13.49 m). Length Overall: 29 ft 6 in (8.99 m). Wing Area: 301 sq. ft (27.96 m^2).
Weight Empty: 2,095 lb (950 kg). T-O Weight: 2,645 lb (1,200 kg). Max Wing Loading: 8.79 lb/sq. ft (42.92 kg/m^2). Gnome rotary of 160 hp.

375 ltr (82 gal) of petrol and 70 ltr (15 gal) of castor oil could be carried.

Power units mentioned in reports of the Grand Prix refer to both 100 hp 14-cylinder Gnome and 160 hp 14-cylinder Gnome engines being installed in the Deperdussin II. Both had roughly the same installation dimensions, although the more powerful unit weighed 80 lb more. Judging by the speeds achieved in the Schneider Race the 160 hp engine was fitted. However the lighter and more economical 100 hp engine could have been used for the Grand Prix to extend the duration to 500 km.

The crew of two were arranged in tandem with the petrol tank between them. A passenger-cum-mechanic sat up forward, where he could attend to engine requirements, and crank the engine with the manual starting device required by the Grand Prix regulations, but not by the Schneider rules. The mechanic's seat was on the centre of gravity of the aircraft, in the position which became traditional for open-cockpit aeroplanes. In this location the trim of the aircraft was not adversely affected when being flown solo. And the controls, being roughly in line with the rear main spar, lent themselves

to an easy mechanical connection to the wing-warping wires.

Undoubtedly the outstanding feature of Béchereau's designs was the fuselage. For the front fuselage he used a diagonal-planked monocoque built from either cypress or tulip-wood, glued and then riveted with tiny copper rivets. It made for a commodious and uncluttered cockpit. The cockpit openings of the Deperdussin II were a metre wide and two metres long. The whole forward monocoque was faired into the circular cowling which completely enclosed the engine.

The Deperdussin cowling was the forerunner of the pressure cowling as we know it today. Air was admitted through an annual opening between the front edge of the cowl and a large spinner and extracted through a slot formed between the rear, bottom end of the cowling and the flat bottom of the fuselage. This cowling, as with all Gnome-engined machines did double duty as a catcher for the enormous amount of castor oil these engines threw off.

Aft of the front fuselage, from a point about three feet behind the pilot, the fuselage was based on ash longerons, wire-braced, and covered with a light

Prévost in his Deperdussin. How on earth did it fly with all that drag from the float struts and bracing wires? This is the Grand Prix machine, which had to be used in the 1913 race after engine trouble in the Schneider Special. (*Musée de l'Air*)

Prévost in his Deperdussin being towed. His mechanic stands on the port float. (*Musée de l'Air*)

plywood fairing to simulate a monocoque. It was carefully faired into triangular fixed tail and fin surfaces. The empennage control surfaces were roughly rectangular in shape and were operated by cables from a rudder-bar and elevator cross-shaft located inside the fuselage and out of the airstream. The aerodynamic cleanliness of these fuselages would have been admirable twenty years later.

The fabric-covered wings were equally clean, rectangular in plan and with a hollow profile typical of the period. Construction was in wood, the main spars being of composite construction. Hickory and ash were used because of their high modulus, making up for the small spar depth dictated by the thin wing section. These materials were also suitably flexible to allow for wing-warping. The ribs were fabricated from spruce with ash cappings.

From this point on the design lapsed into aerodynamic chaos. Béchereau was obviously unsure of the water loads imposed on the floats during alighting and take-off and adopted a belt-and-braces design policy in this area. The two Tellier box-section main floats, each 4 m long and 1.1 m beam, were supported on four streamlined ash struts, each side being braced by a diagonal strut of the same section. Tubular steel spreaders maintained the 'track' of 2.4 m.

Most designers would have been happy with this arrangement. But Béchereau went one step further by adding a series of steel tubular struts placed between the edges of the floats and a kind of knuckle halfway up the leg. There were four of these per leg, sixteen in all. They were backed up by forked wire braces stretched between the edges of the floats and the roots of the water chassis legs. Add to this the transverse diagonal bracing wires, the wing-warping quadrant lever and its associated rods on the rear float spreader, the warping and bracing wires and you are left with an aerodynamicist's nightmare. Just for good measure the forward

wing-bracing wires, four per side, and the wing-warping wires, four per side, led to the front and rear strut attachment points respectively. In all more than seventy wires, rods or struts sprouted from the floats, and most successfully offset all the aerodynamic cleanliness of the beautiful fuselage.

It is said that because bracing wires were very much a way of life with the early aviators, and because these wires were of small section, the pioneers really believed that they produced very little drag. However, used in profusion as they were by Béchereau, with many wires sprouting from a single attachment point they must have made very effective airbrakes because of the interference effect between the wires.

An unusual application of wire bracing was a radial-spoked steady for the front of the engine cowling. Made up of a series of 1 mm radial spokes connecting the rim of the cowling to a bearing floating on the propeller shaft, it stabilised the annular slot between the cowling and spinner.

The Nieuport II

The Nieuport II seaplane was virtually the Nieuport brothers' last design and a considerable tribute to their engineering ability. In general configuration it was a taper-wing monoplane with a span of 12.9 m (39 ft 7 in) and an overall length of 9 m (29 ft 6 in). Wing area was 31 sq m (334.4 sq ft) for a total all-up weight of 1,100 kg (2,425 lb) in normal trim. The fuselage was constructed from ash as a straightforward lattice girder box with piano-wire bracing. A special and very sound feature was that the 40 × 28 mm longerons were extended forward beyond the engine bulkhead and carried a bridge-piece supporting a supplementary outboard bearing for the propeller shaft of the Gnome engine.

Each wing, which had a mean chord of 3 m (10 ft) was based on a pair of ash, box-section spars picking up with tubular steel sockets on the upper longerons. A fine point of the design was the forward socket fixed rigidly to the fuselage and the rear one articulated in its seating to assist wing-warping. Ribs were cut from plywood with glued ash flanges. The wing was braced with stranded steel wire of 5 mm circumference for the landing wires and 6 mm for the flying wires.

In contrast with the Deperdussin the wing-bracing was simple, there being only two lift wires and two landing wires per side. In the interests of safety and at the expense of slightly increased drag, the outer wires were duplicated, held parallel with small cleats, and attached to closely spaced attachment points on the wing. The upper and lower warping wires doubled the number of wires disturbing the airflow over the wings, but the result was clean by contemporary standards. The landing wires fed their loads into a trestle-pylon mounted above the main longerons while the flying wires picked up with a similar structure, inverted, mounted below the front fuselage. Loads from the float chassis were also fed into this structure.

This interesting structure was made up of three inverted V-strut assemblies with their spaces joined by what is best described as a tubular steel ridge pole which formed the backbone of the float chassis. At the front the float spreaders and leg struts, in combination with the V-struts, formed a triangulated bracing of great strength. At the rear the spreaders picked up with the backbone midway between the mid and rear pairs of V-struts, forming what was virtually a flexible Warren truss, if this were possible. It was arranged so that alighting loads tended to bend the backbone tube and provide a certain degree of shock absorption. Just to get the maximum value out of this long-suffering tube, the wing-warping trimmers were mounted on its rearmost extremity. The net result was far less complex than the description and was a first-class piece of engineering carried out in welded steel tube, streamlined where it was set across the airstream.

Setting a trend which persists to this day in some American light aircraft, the empennage was framed in steel tube and fabric-covered. It was of flat section with no great aerodynamic pretensions. Total tail area was 4.27 sq m (46 sq ft).

Tellier, a renowned power-boat builder of the era, built the main floats. Having an overall length of 3.2 m (10 ft 6 in) and a beam of 1.1 m (3 ft 7 in), their total volume was 1,850 ltr (112,850 cu in). Much comment was attracted by the unusual underwater shape which consisted of a wide keel with three steps in it flanked by flat bilges sloping gently upwards to the chines. The bows were swim-shaped with tiny hydrofoils, like ears, sprouting out of them as a precaution against nose-over. Construction was mainly of plywood, the bottoms being three-ply and the sides two-ply with canvas decks. The tail float, an aluminium, bomb-shaped device with a capacity of 150 l (9,154 cu in) created an equal amount of interest. It and the main floats were the trademark of Nieuport hydro-aeroplanes and seaplanes for many years afterwards, right into the early twenties. The main float

Two of the 1913 Nieuport entries on the quay at Monaco. (*Musée de l'Air*)

shape was certainly effective. The Nieuports were notably free from the prevalent accident of the time, which was to bounce off the water before flying speed had been gained and to drop a wing on the ensuing flop back.

Power for the Nieuport was provided by either a 100 hp or 160 hp 14-cylinder Gnome rotary engine driving a 2.55 m (8 ft 5 in) Chauvière propeller of 2.10 m (6 ft 11 in) pitch. As mentioned earlier a particularly good design feature was to sling the engine between two mounting points, the normal one on the front bulkhead and an outrigged bearing on a bridge-piece spanning forward extensions of the fuselage. It was far more mechanically sound than the normal Gnome overhung mounting planted on the front fuselage bulkhead. The cowling was a simple, beaten, curved panel clipped to the longerons. Its main function was to protect the pilot from the fine spray of castor oil for which Gnomes were notorious.

The Morane-Saulnier

The Morane-Saulnier was the creation of the Morane brothers, Léon and Robert, and Raymond Saulnier. It was an extremely simple and efficient midwing monoplane with a box-section fuselage and 'all flying' tail surfaces. The front fuselage was a steel cage welded up from light-gauge angle section steel with the spruce rear fuselage longerons socketed into it. In elevation the sides of the fuselage tapered down to a point leaving a horizontal edge on which the balanced elevator pivoted. The rudder hinged on a small vertical king-post. Spruce or poplar main spars with plywood and spruce ribs provided the framework of the deeply arched wings. They were braced in the usual way with stranded wire, three lift and three landing wires per side and the same number of warping wires. All the upper wires came together at a steel tube bipod. The lower warping wires terminated at another streamlined bipod underneath the fuselage, a reminder of the hasty conversion from a land-plane.

In the short time available Morane had built a sturdy, long-legged float chassis built up from streamlined section steel tube. In design it was a cross between the Deperdussin and Nieuport chassis, having the inverted 'W', Warren truss configuration of the latter and the triangulated, crow's-feet float edge bracing of the former. Fore and aft bracing was by diagonal wires. As ever the floats were by Tellier; they were simple punt-shaped affairs made of plywood and were devoid of steps or any other hydrodynamic niceties to help them up off the water. The small tail float was of similar design and was supported on four braced struts.

The main dimensions of Garros's Morane were 9.8 m (32 ft 2 in) span, chord 1.7 m (5 ft 6 in), wing area 14 sq m (150 sq ft). All-up weight of the landplane was 855 kg (1,887 lb) with a useful load of 279.9 kg (617 lb). The extra weight of the float gear would reduce the payload by about 150 lb, taking into account the weight of the landplane undercarriage.

With its 80 hp, 7-cylinder Gnome engine the Morane did not stand much chance against the more powerful machines of Prévost and Weymann. Its main assets would be the skill of the pilot, and manoeuvrability, which would enable it to pick up seconds at the acute turning point of the 10 km triangular circuit which had been laid out in the Baie de Roquebrune. Garros hoped, too, that his relatively simple, single-row Gnome would stay the course. The others, with their two-row engines, were highly likely to suffer from piston seizures, which was the Achilles' heel of the big Laurent Seguin motors.

Monaco 1914

Third from left is Jacques Schneider and sixth from left, is the organiser of the 1914 event, Georges Prade. (*Musée de l'Air*)

Preliminaries

Thanks to Prévost's reluctant victory in 1913 the honour of staging the Coupe d'Aviation Maritime once again fell to the Aéro-Club de France. And once again Georges Prade got the job. The 1913 race had been successful enough (probably because it was less drawn out than the interminable Monaco Grand Prix of 1913) for there to be contenders for the distinction of holding the event. Both Biarritz and Deauville put in bids to hold the event at their particular gambling centres.

But Monaco had a prior claim apart from the experience of having successfully staged two major hydro-aeroplane meetings. This was that 1914 was the twenty-fifth anniversary of the accession of Prince Albert I to the throne of the principality. To mark the occasion there was to be a ceremonial visit by the President of the Republic, M. Poincaré.

From the practical aspect of organising a seaplane meeting there was the physical advantage of Monaco's sheltered harbour combined with favourable meteorological conditions in April when the event was scheduled to be held in conjunction with the eleventh motorboat meeting, the Concours des Canots Automobiles, to give the affair its French title. Moreover, the ever-obliging Société de Bains de Mer offered to provide hotel accommodation for the teams and financial backing for the organisation. The two alternative venues had nothing like this to offer. Add to this the fact that at this time of the year sea conditions on the French Atlantic coast tend to be inhospitable so it would seem that Biarritz and Deauville were really not in the running from the moment the date for the contest was fixed.

The date proposed by the Aéro-Club de France was 20 April. It was the culminating event of a great manifestation organised by the International Sporting Club of Monaco whose published programme of seaplane and power-boat events stretched from 1 April until the date of the race. The French eliminating trials were scheduled for the 18th.

Although the Schneider race had gained in status since the preceding year it was still a subsidiary event to a Grand Rallye Aerien which was intended to be the aerial counterpart of the Monte Carlo Rally for automobiles established four years earlier, in 1910. In common with the automotive event the Rallye Aerien had a number of starting points as far afield as London, Paris, Brussels, Gotha, Milan, Madrid and Vienna. The entrants were intended to converge on Marseilles, at the Parc Borely, where they would change their landplane undercarriages for flotation gear and fly along the coast to Monaco.

It is apparent that Georges Prade did not do things by halves when one realises that in addition to the aeronautical activity a motorboat exhibition was scheduled for the 5th and motorboat trials and racing were to take place almost continually from the 6th to the 19th. However, just to get the whole thing into perspective, in the calendar of the Côte d'Azure this momentous aviation affair had to be sandwiched between a Concours des Chiens at Monaco and a Concours des Chats at Nice.

It was intended to hold the Schneider race over the same 10 km circuit as the previous year and for the same number of laps. The only difference was that although the aircraft were required to cross the start line on the surface as before, they were expected to get airborne immediately afterwards and to alight briefly and take off twice during the first lap at points indicated by marker boats. The exact wording for these alightings was, '*deux amerrissages très nets...*'. In this context *net* is interpreted as distinct or clear. In other words the competitors had to put their machines positively on the water before taking off again. As an indication of intent to compete, there was also the requirement for pilots to hand signed copies of the regulations and the latest changes to the regulations, to the commissioners immediately before leaving the harbour.

Anticipating a healthy entry from their nationals, the Aéro-Club de France had brought forward the date of their national eliminating trials to 8 April, twenty-eight allocating the whole day to this activity. This would give participants twelve days to repair any damage in time for the race. The trials were almost a race rehearsal, being conducted over the race circuit with the two *amerrissages très nets* on the first lap but only four instead of twenty-eight laps to fly. A rather complex regulation was woven round the fuel load for these trials. It was obviously meant to ensure that each aircraft was capable of finishing the race without a refuelling stop although the 1914 regulations specifically allowed them to do so. To this end each pilot was called on to declare the amount of fuel and oil in his tanks before taking off for the trial. He was then required to add ballast of four times the weight of this fuel and oil on the basis of 750 grams per litre.

A final clause allowed the alightings to be omitted if conditions of wind and sea made this procedure too hazardous.

The Entry

The 1913 meeting at Monaco was probably the biggest gathering of seaplanes that had ever been held, and evoked worldwide interest. This was reflected in the entries for the 1914 Rallye Aerien and the Coupe d'Aviation Maritime Jacques Schneider. Whereas the previous year the only justification for giving the Coupe Maritime the 'international' tag was the entry of a French machine piloted by an American born in Haiti whose only language was French, for 1914 there were firm entries from the national aero clubs of Germany, Great Britain, Switzerland and, at the last moment, the USA. Moreover, British, German and American aircraft were included in the entry although the one American aircraft, William Thaw's Curtiss flying-boat, eventually turned out to be uncompetitive.

Naturally the highest number of entries came from France with eight aircraft entered for the eliminating trials on 8 April. Two of these were Deperdussins, one for Prévost the other for Emile Janoir. There were three Nieuports, pilots Dr Espanet, Levasseur and Bertin, two Morane-Saulniers to be flown by Roland Garros and Brindejonc de Moulinais and a sole Breguet for Moineau, winner of the 1913 Grand Prix.

Challenging the best three of these champions of France were a team of two aircraft from the USA comprising the inexorable Weymann in his Nieuport now re-engined with a Le Rhône engine, and William Thaw, a real American flying a real Yankee aeroplane, a Curtiss flying-boat. As a reserve the Americans were fielding Lawrence Sperry fresh from his gyroscopic display flights.

The Royal Aero Club of Great Britain had also entered two machines; one of British construction, the Sopwith Baby, notified on 7 February, and the other a Nieuport II for the notable British racing driver, pilot and sporting gentleman, Lord Carbery.

In common with Britain, Switzerland would be represented for the first time. Their champion was the

Aircraft at Monaco 1914: (L–R) The FBA of Burri, the Morane-Saulnier of Brindejonc de Moulinais and a Nieuport. (*Musée de l'Air*)

Monaco 1914: competing aircraft, small boats, mechanics and spectators. On the left a Morane-Saulnier, on the right a Deperdussin. (*Musée de l'Air*)

popular and extremely competent Burri, flying a French-built FBA. FBA signified Franco-British Aviation of Bezons, Seine and the machine was entirely of French construction. A Swiss pilot, Parmelin, flying a Deperdussin of unspecified type was nominated as Swiss reserve.

Finally there was a single entry from Germany, an Aviatik Flêche biplane powered by a Mercédès engine and piloted by Stoeffler, which was taking part in the Rallye Aerien and would participate in the Coupe Maritime if it survived.

Despite the jailing of Armand Deperdussin for financial irregularities – he received the result of the 1914 Gordon Bennett race in his prison cell – the company of Appareils Armand Deperdussin continued to prosper with Louis Béchereau as chief designer and Louis Blériot as financial adviser. Later in 1914, Blériot formed the Société pour Avions et ses Dérivés, SPAD for short, to exploit fully the genius of Béchereau, whom he not only admired but saw as an ally in his business interests. In acquiring the Deperdussin designer, he also acquired the design team, including a nucleus of skilled workmen at 19 Rue des Entrepreneurs, who had produced the Gordon Bennett racers.

For these reasons and with the blessing of Louis Blériot, Béchereau was able to field two special aircraft

Monaco 1914: the Morane-Saulniers of Brindejonc de Moulinais and Roland Garros on the slipway. (*Musée de l'Air*)

for the 1914 race. Although there were Deperdussin entries for the Monaco Aerial Rally, they failed to materialise. This was a long-distance event and although the

Monaco 1914: Janoir's Deperdussin moored off the quay. (*Musée de l'Air*)

company had ambitions to produce military machines, all the available competition Deperdussins were short-circuit racers. Lack of preparation was another good reason. From 1914 onwards the story of Deperdussin and their unreadiness was to typify French participation in the Schneider Trophy series.

It hardly comes as a surprise that Prévost's aircraft, the most interesting of the two Deperdussins entered for the 1914 race, was scarcely ready for the French eliminating trials a week before the race proper. None the less, this floatplane, bearing race no. 1 in photographs, had the engine been reliable and the airframe seaworthy, could have been a real factor in the race. Unfortunately, it was not ready in time to undertake full sea trials and these were more than important to the pilots because the racing Deperdussins were enough of a handful on land chassis without the complication of floats. They touched down at the then unheard-of speed of 60 mph at a time when most contemporary aircraft could barely reach that velocity.

Béchereau had limited experience of water gear – he did not enter works machines for any of the other French seaplane meetings – and he leaned heavily on the racing motorboat builder Tellier for advice in this area of design. By all reports this no. 1 racer, while being sleek

and beautiful, was not pleasant to handle on the water. This could have been due to what appears to be rather unusual float design which threw up spray in the slightest sea, either breaking the propeller or dousing the motor. One has the feeling, too, that Prévost, a farmer's son from the Marne valley, was not enamoured of these nautical goings-on. His sole appearances in hydro-aeroplanes seem to have been at the 1913 and 1914 Monaco meetings. Maybe his reluctance to return to the race in 1913 was due to this distaste for seafaring. Incidentally this exotic-looking, advance Schneider Special must have been almost the last of the Deperdussin monoplanes. Even as the Schneider event was being run Béchereau was drawing biplanes, influenced by the trend of military thinking towards that configuration for fighters which led to the immortal SPAD. Sopwith was within a few days of confirming this thinking. That fateful August of 1914 was only three months away; there was already the scent of gunsmoke in the air.

Although it was hardly recognised by the French, who were so besotted by the lead they had gained in aviation development in the early days that they could scarcely believe that anything of consequence in aviation could happen elsewhere, aviation was developing apace in the UK. In France the trend was for fighters to be built as pusher biplanes on the Voisin/Farman model – the British had them too – and for the scout type of tractor machine to be generally of monoplane construction. The British had turned against the monoplane – there was a War Office ban on them – as a result of accidents; thus the main line of development was in biplanes which, at the speeds of the time, was perfectly logical because of their greater structural integrity. The result was a series of outstanding tractor biplanes; typical examples were the Avro 504, the BE series of machines designed by Geoffrey de Havilland, the Short seaplanes and, late in the day but coming up fast, brilliant designs from the Sopwith Aviation Company.

The Sopwith Company had been founded in 1912 at a disused roller-skating rink in Canbury Park Road in Kingston-upon-Thames by Thomas Octave Murdoch Sopwith, affectionately known as Tom Sopwith, who was the son of a wealthy civil engineer, and an avid experimenter. His closest associates were Fred Sigrist, an intuitive engineer who had been the engineer on his yacht, and Harry Hawker, a fine test pilot whose gift for design was fundamental to the success of the company. Backing them up were R.J. Ashfield as chief draughtsman, Victor Mahl in charge of metal-work construction and Sid Burgoyne, scion of a notable family of Thamesside boatbuilders, who looked after the design of the floats and hulls of the seaplanes and flying-boats which were Sopwith's early speciality. One of these had been the only seaplane to make any kind of showing in the *Daily Mail* Circuit of Britain seaplane race; it had been followed by a three-seat landplane, shown at Olympia in 1913, which set new standards of performance and established a British height record of 12,900 ft for a machine with a passenger.

The sale of his first biplane, the Hybrid, to the Royal Navy had encouraged Sopwith to go ahead with the formation of his company. More orders followed the success of the three-seater. At the end of 1913 he had orders for nine of the Olympia machines, a seaplane version of it and also for a larger torpedo-carrying machine, the first in the world. By the end of 1914, from the nucleus of Sopwith, Sigrist, Hawker and Ashfield the organisation had grown into one employing a well-staffed design office with a number of project teams. The rink had been transformed into a fully equipped works with ample wood and metal-working machinery and 150 employees, mainly woodworkers, on the shop floor.

In the middle of all this Harry Hawker was due to visit his family in Australia. With an eye to business he suggested to Sopwith that it might be a good idea to combine the visit with a sales tour. Obviously space would be at a premium in the ship to Australia and Hawker suggested that they should build the smallest practical two-seater biplane to save shipping costs. Both Sopwith and Sigrist liked the idea and, led by Hawker, all three set to and chalked out the outline of the aeroplane on the wooden floor of the rink. This would have been in July or August of 1913. Within two months the machine, a side-by-side, two-seat, biplane with equal

spans of 25 ft 6 in and an overall length of 20 ft, had been built and was test-flown in early November by Hawker. Flight trials took place at Farnborough on 19 November 1913 when the machine, powered by an 80 hp Gnome rotary and with an all-up weight of 1,230 lb, could climb at 1,200 fpm, had a top speed of 92 mph and stalled at 36 mph. Officially designated the SS but referred to by all and sundry as the Tabloid after Burroughs and Wellcome's compressed pills, it was a sensation and Ministry orders followed almost immediately.

The last machine out of the order for nine 80 hp standard Sopwith three-seater biplanes was delivered by one Howard Pixton, who had taken on Hawker's test-flying duties while Hawker was in Australia, on the third Wednesday in January 1914. Only a week later the Royal Aero Club of Great Britain received an entry for the Schneider Trophy from the Sopwith Aviation Company.

Sopwith's decision to enter a machine for the Schneider race is an interesting one. Many flying buffs will not know that Sopwith, apart from his aviation interests, was one of the world's leading high-speed motorboat racers and had twice won the International Motorboat Trophy, the second time in 1913, from the Americans with his *Maple Leaf IV*. Tommy Sopwith was a sportsman to his fingertips and against this background the temptation to enter what promised to be Europe's biggest motorboat and seaplane meeting, and to do with a seaplane version of the Tabloid what he had already achieved with *Maple Leaf IV* must have been well-nigh irresistible.

The decision left the company just six weeks to build, prepare, test and have a machine transported to Monaco by rail. A complication was that as a result of Hawker's demonstration at Farnborough in November, military orders had been forthcoming and a production line for the SS was being brought into existence at Kingston. It was only with the collusion of Brigadier-General Sir David Henderson, head of the new Military Aircraft Directorate, that one of the War Department machines was taken off the line and diverted to the Schneider project.

One of the main jobs was to increase the fin and rudder area to offset the increase in forward area brought about by fitting floats. The other modification was to re-engine it with one of the new Gnome Monosoupape engines which Sopwith had brought back in his baggage from Paris after visiting the Paris Air Show at the Grand Palais in February. He had a good excuse for acquiring one of these engines, for one was required to power an enlarged version of the Tabloid, officially designated the Sociable but nicknamed the 'Tweeny', which was on order from the Navy for Mr Winston Churchill at the Admiralty. In a letter to the writer Sir Tom Sopwith remarked that the Monosoupape in the Schneider machine was the only one in the UK at the time so it seems likely that Sir David Henderson gave permission for it to be borrowed from the Tweeny for the occasion.

Howard Pixton, the pilot of the Sopwith, was typical

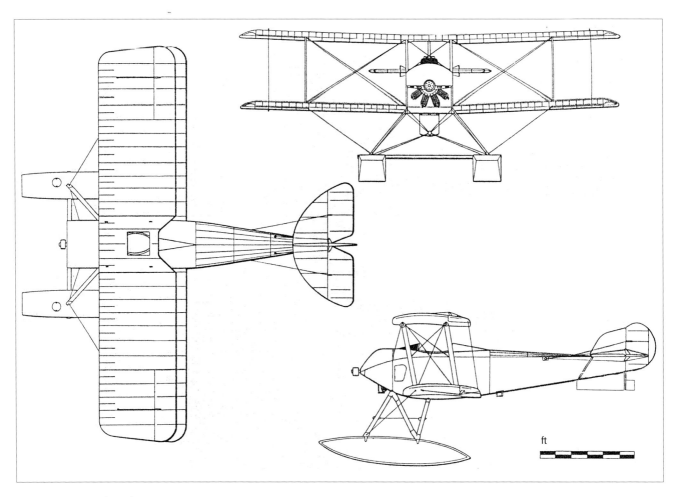

Sopwith Tabloid (1914): Wing Span: 25 ft 8 in (7.82 m). Length Overall: 22 ft 10 in (6.96 m). Wing Area: 241 sq. ft (22.38 m²).
Weight Empty: 1,220 lb (553 kg). T-O Weight: 1,700 lb (771 kg). Max Wing Loading: 7.05 lb/sq. ft (34.42 kg/m²). Gnome Monosoupape rotary of 100 hp

of the early pioneers, British or otherwise. A Manchester lad, coming from a good but not wealthy family, he had trained with A.V. Roe, another northerner at Brooklands, depositing £30 as security against breakages and working for nothing in return for flying instruction. Sad-faced, immaculate in his dress and with a neat, waxed moustache, he was a born pilot and easily gained his licence, certificate no. 50, in January 1911 in an Avro, a few months after Tom Sopwith, who gained certificate no. 31 on 22 November 1910. Sir George White of Bristol fame had recognised Pixton's ability and tempted him away from Avro to do naval demonstration flying in the Boxkites. When Harry Hawker went off to Australia with the Tabloid demonstrator, Sopwith, who knew Pixton well, engaged him as test and demonstration pilot for his biplanes. Pixton's main activity before the Schneider event had been the testing and delivery of Sopwith three-seat biplanes to the War Office and test-flying Churchill's Tweeny. The Schneider race was just another job of work. He survived to the ripe old age of more than eighty, dying in 1972 in retirement in the Isle of Man.

Sopwith's main problem was to design water gear for the Tabloid. During the preceding year, he had done a great deal of work on seaplanes, producing his Bat Boats

alongside with twin-float and single-float seaplanes. Hawker had won the Circuit of Britain Race in a twin-float machine. Despite this and no doubt influenced by the success of the Bat Boats, Sopwith and Sid Burgoyne conceived a single main-float configuration with wingtip floats and a rear float, on struts, to support the tail. The main float was a simple punt-shaped affair with a plain, stepless bottom constructed from ash and plywood. It

Monaco 1914: Sopwith Schneider Tabloid (100 hp Gnome Monosoupape).
(*Musée de l'Air*)

Monaco 1914: Howard Pixton, the 1914 winner (in helmet), next to Jacques Schneider, wearing a light Trilby, and Sopwith's chief mechanic, Victor Mahl, with his trousers rolled up. (*Flight*)

was mounted on a plain four-leg wire-braced water chassis utilising the mounting points of the wheel and skid land chassis.

Just as soon as it was completed, the machine was shipped to the Hamble river and assembled by Victor Mahl's team of fitters on a slipway which still exists alongside the Bugle public house. At high tide the handling crew carried it into the water, Howard Pixton got aboard and the machine drifted gently into the stream with the engine ticking over. But as soon as Pixton – 'Picky', they called him – opened the throttle it became catastrophically plain that the main float was mounted too far aft. Here Hawker's hand might have saved the day; the design team had obviously not taken full account of the extra power and weight of the engine. The machine turned gently on its nose and sank, tipping Howard Pixton, already in the grip of a cold, into the

cold and muddy Solent. At that state of the tide the machine could not be recovered and there it had to stay until low tide when it could be hauled up on the beach and unrigged for transport back to Kingston. The party meanwhile disconsolately returned to their hotel to revive their spirits with champagne, generously provided by Sopwith.

It was already early on 1 April, with less than sixteen days to go before the race proper. Desperate measures were called for. After a quick conference Sopwith and Burgoyne decided to play safe and go back to the double-pontoon float configuration they had used on the Hawker and Kemp's 1913 Circuit of Britain biplane. It had been the only entry to start and had put up a fine performance before retiring at three-quarters distance. With no time to build new floats, Burgoyne simply sawed the original wide central float down the middle and skinned-in the inner sides. A couple of interfloat struts completed the job and the whole outfit was mounted on the standard Tabloid land chassis. Naturally care was taken to get the centre of buoyancy further forward than before. The new arrangement also did away with the weight and drag of wingtip floats. Meanwhile, Victor Mahl quickly stripped and rebuilt the engine to get rid of the Hamble river mud.

Because of this mishap there was precious little time to spare, certainly not enough to return with the machine to the Hamble. The only course was to go with it to the nearby Thames. So at the crack of dawn on 7 April, the small party erected the machine on the bank by Kingston Bridge with the object of making a short test flight. Unfortunately some bailiffs from the Thames Conservancy Board, being about their business equally early, thought otherwise and forbade anything but flotation tests.

It didn't take long for Victor Mahl, with a Londoner's contempt for all forms of authority, to work out that the Thames Conservancy Board's authority ended at Teddington Lock. So at an equally early hour the following morning, the aircraft was taken down to the reach opposite Glover's Island, downstream of the lock, and this time Pixton managed to get airborne, flying downstream towards Eel Pie Island before authority could step in. The flight was a short one but long enough to prove that the aircraft unstuck cleanly and handled well with the new floats.

It is open to conjecture at what stage a Deperdussin was offered to William Thaw, the American entry, when it became obvious that his sagging Curtiss boat was uncompetitive. It is unlikely to have been the second works machine allocated to Janoir and subsequently flown by Carbery. More likely it was an odd, larger two-seat machine which was used in 1913 practice powered by an uncowled nine-cylinder 124×150 mm 100 hp, two-valve Gnome of the type announced at the same time as the Monosoupape. Wherever it came from there is no record of Thaw flying it in the race or at any other time. The other American reserve entries were those of Lawrence Sperry, son of the Sperry of gyroscope fame, and Lincoln Beachey, the American aerobatic pilot. Just what aircraft they were meant to fly is difficult to ascertain. Could it be that this was also Thaw's entry? Sperry's machine could have been the auto-pilot demonstrator, for some of his pioneering auto-pilot trials were currently taking place in France, at Bezons, the headquarters of Franco-British Aviation.

Burri, the Swiss pilot of FBA, was a great favourite with the French crowd. Although born in Switzerland he had spent most of his flying life in France, having trained at the Sommer school, gaining his brevet in 1912. His great claim to fame, and the main reason for his popularity in France, was his flying exploits in the Bulgarian war against Mustapha Pasha and the Turkish armies. He was almost certainly the first pilot to attract anti-aircraft fire, having been shot at by super-elevated 75 mm Krupp artillery weapons while observing the Turkish positions at Adrianople in 1913. After his exploits in the Balkans, Burri had joined FBA as chief

Monaco 1914: Garros taxying his Morane-Saulnier. (*Musée de l'Air*)

test pilot. It was his job to demonstrate aircraft and in this role he was flying in the Schneider Trophy race. It is a measure of his skill and the ability of the aircraft that later, in the week after the race, during a spell of particularly bad weather, he was the only pilot to land in the open sea and taxi back into the harbour.

Ernst Stoeffler, the one German entry, was mainly interested in the Monaco Air Rally, with the Schneider race to finish off the week and provide a German entry. It was also a long-distance test for the Mercédès 90 hp four-cylinder, water-cooled engine which propelled his machine. On 9 April he had left the German starting point of the rally, at the Gotha Wagenfabrik airfield – an aerodrome famous later as the home of the Gotha V bomber. After a fairly uneventful flight via Frankfurt and Dijon he finally had to force-land in a vineyard on the banks of the Rhône at Villeneuve-lès-Avignon with engine trouble. The aircraft was badly damaged but not beyond repair. Stoeffler managed to have it taken by road to Marseilles where he and his mechanic Decamp repaired it and fitted the floats in readiness for the Marseilles–Tamaris–Monaco leg of the rally.

The Race

In April, Monaco and the whole surrounding area was agog with the celebrations of the twenty-fifth anniversary of Prince Albert's reign. All society was there including President Poincaré who had arrived in early April and was safely ensconced in L'Hermitage. A little way down the coast, in Beaulieu-sur-Mer, Gordon Bennett held court, in his yacht, the *Lysistrata*. Meanwhile the Earl of Mar was duly required to deliver a speech of congratulation on behalf of the British colony.

All the best people were present that spring, and the season, which normally finished at the end of March, had been brought forward, so that the exact date of

Monaco 1914: Ernest Burri, the pilot of the Swiss FBA flying-boat. (*Musée de l'Air*)

Albert's anniversary could be celebrated.

More important for the purposes of this chronicle, the Schneider Trophy aircraft were dribbling in. Garros's and Brindejonc de Moulinais's machines were there, having already covered the rally route. They would be held at Monaco for the French trials, now moved forward to 8 April, prior to being taken back to Buc for a further run over the rally *parcours* with the chance of better times. The Monaco Rallye Aerien was scheduled to finish on the 15th in the middle of the motorboat events and Garros was destined to be the winner. Espanet's and Weymann's Nieuports were also already present, both tried and tested machines although a little *passé* compared with the offerings from Deperdussin. The Deperdussin Schneider was on its way south from Paris by railcar, as was the little Sopwith, hurriedly packed into a large case and having to face the hazards of both the British and the French railways.

William Thaw had turned up with his Curtiss flying-boat which transpired not to be the auto-pilot demonstration machine but a standard Curtiss; the type with the empennage supported on struts from the main hull. Power was supplied by a Curtiss V-8 engine. With baggy covering, piano-wire bracing and shabby black dope, it was not a worthy representative of the pioneering aviation nation. This fact did not elude its pilot, who weighed up the opposition and made arrangements to use the Deperdussin, already mentioned, in the race.

Burri's FBA was also present on the quayside at Fontvieille, jealously guarded against prying eyes by its ground crew. It was rumoured not to have flown before its arrival.

The other foreign entry, Stoeffler's Aviatik was still being rebuilt at Marseilles after its forced landing among the vines of Villeneuve.

Because of the arrival of the French navy's one and only seaplane carrier, FS *Foudre*, present to mark the visit of President Poincaré, and the need to moor her alongside in La Condamine, the fastest machines had been moved over to Fontvieille on the west side of the Palace promontory. There a rough harbour had been created by tipping rubble to form a breakwater. The machines were housed in a row of eleven Hervieu tent hangars. The procedure was to launch them at Fontvieille and taxi them round to the main harbour where they used the slips for maintenance.

French National Eliminating Trials

The day appointed for French trials was 8 April, the day before the opening of the Monaco Motorboat and Hydroaeroplane Meeting and some time before the international machines arrived. The weather was none too good, a moderate breeze raising a sea which was bad enough to cause the committee to invoke the 'no

Monaco 1914: a Caudron biplane being hoisted aboard the French warship *Foudre*. (*Musée de l'Air*)

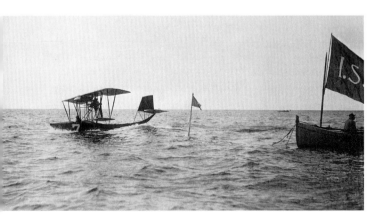

Burri taxying his FBA across the start line for the 1914 race. (*Musée de l'Air*)

alighting' clause in their regulations. The turnout was a good one, practically all the entries being available with the exception of Stoeffler, Moineau and Bertin who were otherwise engaged with the Monaco Air Rally. Prévost (Deperdussin), Brindejonc de Moulinais (Morane-Saulnier), Roland Garros (Morane-Saulnier),

Janoir (Deperdussin), Espanet (Nieuport), Levasseur (Nieuport) were all present.

Both Deperdussins were ready to go, with engines and airframes in a full state of tune. But whether a sudden magic spell had been put on the engines, or whether the pilots did not like the looks of the weather, it was a fact that neither Prévost's Gnome nor Janoir's Le Rhône could be persuaded to start. There should have been no problem; the engines were perfect, and both pilots swore that switches were on and engine controls were properly set. But despite heavy doping through the intakes there was not a sign of life. Finally A.C. Burgoyne of *The Aeroplane*, suggested that the tail of Prévost's machine, which drooped heavily in the water at rest, should be raised to improve the fuel level in the carburettor. A boat was duly obtained and the tail of the machine was raised. This time the engine started and Prévost taxied round the harbour for a few yards before the motor stopped and resisted all attempts to restart it. The machines were put back in their tent hangars and there they stayed.

Conditions suited the well-tried Nieuports better. At

Monaco 1914: Garros in his Morane-Saulnier (80 hp Gnome Monosoupape) arriving at the end of the Monaco Air Rally in time to compete in the Schneider Trophy event. (*Musée de l'Air*)

Monaco 1914: Espanet's Nieuport. This illustrates the difficulties of handling and servicing floatplanes from small rowing boats. (*Musée de l'Air*)

twenty minutes after midday Espanet brought out his 160 hp machine and, taking advantage of smooth water in the lee of the old town, took off and completed his four qualifying laps in 23 min 54 sec. Levasseur followed his example but after two laps in the buffeting wind, returned to harbour after recording a time of 12 min 25 sec for half of the test, 20 km.

Of the Moranes, Garros taxied his machine out into the sea, taking off in rough water and completing one lap in 7 min 3 sec before returning to harbour. De Moulinais also got his engine running and taxied out of the harbour. He took one look at the sea and went back in again.

As a result of these trials Espanet, Levasseur and Garros were nominated for the race with Prévost, having been the winner in 1913, as first reserve and Janoir second reserve. In many ways the results of the trials were sad because they eliminated the fastest French machines at one fell swoop before the race had even started. However, in fairness it should be said that if these fast Deperdussins had been tested and airworthy they would have been worthy of representing their country.

There was sporadic flying during the week. The Caudron biplane from FS *Foudre* and the old Voisin–Fabre floatplane which was on its original inventory, made short flights round the bay. Brindejonc de Moulinais was also out with a new machine bearing number 3, his Monaco Rally number (this was the Sopwith number in the Schneider race) endeavouring to do an extra stage (Monaco–Genoa) of the rally. His original rally machine had been wrecked in alighting at the end of the Marseilles–Monaco leg and the machine he had at Monaco was a replacement. He very nearly wrote this one off too when, in worsening weather, the engine cut on take-off outside the harbour and he pancaked nine feet into the water.

The case containing the little Sopwith Tabloid was not released to Sopwith until the 15th, only three days before the date allocated to the race. The little biplane was hurriedly erected and the engine, which had

misfired badly on the illicit test flight and had acquired a coat of rust on its steel cylinders during the long rail and sea journey, was hurriedly overhauled by Victor Mahl. When Saturday 18 April, the day of the race, dawned the Sopwith was barely ready to fly and quite untested.

Fortunately the weather was not *au point* either; cold air in the Alps and a low in the Bay of Genoa had brought the mistral funnelling down the Rhône valley and into the Mediterranean, making flying hazardous for the frail machines of the era. In the event the committee decided to postpone the race until the following day. Those aeroplanes which did attempt to fly in the conditions prevailing on the 18th were all damaged. Among these was Lord Carbery's Morane, which was so badly wrecked that repairs were impossible in time for the race. Carbery's answer was to arrange to borrow Janoir's Deperdussin, which had been designated as French reserve but was unlikely to be used.

By Sunday the 19th the mistral had blown itself out and the weather pattern had settled to the usual spring diurnal pattern of early morning calms and easterly breezes freshening to 30 knots or so by midday. Taking local advice the aviators were out early, being anxious not only to take advantage of the weather but also to avoid a clash of spectator interest with the final motorboat race for the Prince of Monaco's Cup.

This was the first opportunity for the Sopwith Tabloid to make an air test off the sea. Pixton had the aircraft out of its hangar by 5 am. With a full fuel load the little machine was quickly and cleanly airborne after a notably short run compared with the French machines. After a brief flight, eight minutes has been mentioned, hardly long enough to make an accurate fuel consumption check, Pixton skimmed the machine back into Fontvieille. Although of short duration this was the longest flight thus far by the aircraft, long enough for French observers to note its behaviour on the water, its speed and the ease with which its pilot handled it.

Apart from noting that the tail float had not nearly

Monaco 1914: Janoir's Deperdussin. (*Musée de l'Air*)

enough buoyancy to keep the tail out of the water when the machine was under tow – the pilot had to get out of the cockpit and stand on the floats to redress the balance – Pixton reported that the large-diameter fine-pitch propeller with which the machine was fitted was pushing the engine revs too high, 1,350 rpm, to achieve the air speed they reckoned they needed to win the race. This was too much for continuous operation and after consultation with the Gnome service crew, who were present in force, it was decided to fit a coarse-pitch, Integrale propeller of smaller diameter. This had the double advantage of reducing engine speed to the 1,100 rpm which suited the Monosoupape best for continuous operation. At the same time it reduced the diameter of the propeller disc to keep it clear of spray which had damaged the larger propeller.

The Gnome Monosoupape developed its maximum power of 104 bhp at 1,200 rpm when fuel consumption was 10 gallons of petrol and at least three gallons of castor oil per hour. The air speed attained by the Tabloid during its short test suggested to Sopwith that a duration of three hours should be aimed at, especially as he had private ideas about going for a distance record while the FAI timekeepers were there, if his machine should finish the race. This endurance would have been too much for the 24-gallon tank, which had been retained from the landplane version. Accordingly extra tankage was obtained by lashing a 6-gallon tank, probably a spare oil tank and no small object, alongside the

pilot in the tiny cockpit. Fortunately, deteriorating weather as the day wore on forced yet another 24-hour race postponement and provided time for the changes to be made. An extra set of float-bracing wires was also fitted, there being signs of stretch in the existing ones.

Meanwhile at Marseilles, Ernst Stoeffler, aided by his engineer, Decamp, had finally got the Flèche airworthy. By 4.55 pm on the Sunday they were ready for take-off to Monaco. Stoeffler opened the throttle, the machine gathered speed and was almost airborne when a wingtip dipped, touched the water and the machine cartwheeled and sank. Poor Stoeffler and Decamp were thrown out and dragged ashore by life guards. They were definitely non-starters.

Race Day

On Monday morning, 20 April the committee, prompted by local weather experts, decided that the race could be held that day. It was indeed a perfect morning with scarcely a ripple disturbing the water. The air had that clear, liquid quality which lures so many Francophiles to the Côte d'Azure in the spring. In those days people were about their business in the very early hours and it was nothing out of the ordinary for the aircraft and their attendants to be out and about by 5 am. Engines were warmed up and short test flights were made by a number of the competitors, including Espanet and Pixton, before the official starting time of eight o'clock.

In keeping with the noisy Monaco custom of starting races for motorised devices early, the start was signalled at exactly 8 am by a couple of maroons bursting with a loud report and a puff of smoke above the Tir aux Pigeons. The contest was on. Almost immediately, at 4½ minutes past the hour Espanet, who knew only too well that the wind would get up as the morning drew on, was seen to taxi across the mouth of the main harbour and commence a rather leisurely, long take-off run into the light south-easterly breeze. A minute and a half later he was followed by Levasseur, who skimmed across the line and whirred off in the direction of Cap Martin.

The two compulsory *amerrissages* called for in the regulations were indicated by marker boats. To test the skill of the pilots these were located on the downwind leg, leaving the airmen with a nice decision to make. The rules called for an *amerrissage très net,* in other words a quite positive landing, after which the machines were meant to take off immediately and to be airborne before the second marker boat. To do the job according to the rules, pilots should have turned into wind for a proper alighting, which would have cost them valuable time. The alternative was to approach downwind, touch the water alongside the markers and immediately open up and hope to gain sufficient air speed to get off the water before the second marker. Levasseur achieved this by barely touching the water and hardly losing flying speed. It was not really a positive landing but it seemed to satisfy the officials. Espanet was not so lucky – or more conscientious – and overshot the second boat, having to go back. As a result his first lap time was 9 min 17 sec compared with 8 min 55.6 sec for Levasseur.

Meanwhile Burri in the FBA had completed the formalities and bounded into the air with a porpoising take-off which reminded observers only too vividly of Gaudart's lamentable accident in the Artois the previous year. After making his formal alightings, two splash-downs, he gave the Gnome full throttle into the 'corner' leading into the short straight opposite the Tir aux Pigeons; the elapsed time for this first round was 6 min 17.4 sec. He soon settled down to a lap speed of a fraction under six minutes – his time for the first five laps was 29 min 17 sec – which put him just one minute and four seconds behind Espanet (28 min 13 sec) and ahead of Levasseur who took 30 min 5 sec to cover the 50 km.

Shortly after 8 am the engine of the Tabloid was fired up in the makeshift Fontvieille harbour and Pixton taxied round the promontory of Old Monaco to the line. With 30 gallons of fuel and 7 gallons of oil on board, and the coarse-pitch Integrale to pull him along, he knew that his take-off would be longer than the electric departures he had been able to achieve with the fine-pitch Lang propeller he had used before. So with first-class airmanship he started his take-off run early and was airborne at 8.16 am only fifty feet or so after crossing the line.

Taking a tip from the French, Pixton's *amerrissages nets* were in the true spirit of the Trophy itself, a dragonfly kissing the waves, and in 4 min 27.3 sec he was

Monaco 1914: Burri's FBA sesquiplane. (*Musée de l'Air*)

back across the line, banking more steeply round the marks than the crowd had seen a seaplane bank before and heading in the direction of Cap Martin, tail up, like a homing pigeon. His next lap was 19 seconds faster and from then on he gave a display of consistent speed-flying with laps of 4 min 4 sec (third), 4 min 6 sec and 4 min 9 sec. After ten of the twenty-eight laps, which occupied only 41 min 33 sec, he was only 40 seconds behind Espanet, the fastest Frenchman, on absolute time and nearly 10 minutes ahead of him in the race, the Nieuport having taken 51 min 43 sec. Moreover, he had gained more than 13 minutes on Levasseur, who had taken 54 min 46 sec to cover the same distance. Burri was a worthy fourth, using up 57 min 54 sec for this initial 100 km and lapping with clockwork regularity.

The speed of the British contender must have been painfully obvious to the pilots of the two Nieuports in the race, for the Sopwith must have passed them twice in the first ten laps. It was equally evident to the pilots sitting in the harbour waiting to see the outcome before they committed themselves. The situation wasn't encouraging for Espanet and Levasseur because the Sopwith was gaining an average of 37 seconds a lap on the one and 50 seconds a lap on the other.

At eighteen and a half minutes past nine Pixton had started on his sixteenth lap, more than half distance. Espanet and Levasseur, who had started eleven minutes earlier had completed fourteen and thirteen laps respectively. Back in the harbour Weymann and Garros bided their time. They knew that it was fruitless to try to match the times of the Sopwith. And they preferred not to waste their precious engines in trying to do it. Better to see if the little biplane would complete the course. If it failed they could then go out and see what they themselves could do in terms of time and distance.

Lord Carbery had, in Janoir's Deperdussin, the only aircraft qualified to start and able to equal or better the Sopwith in speed. It was carried out of its hangar and this time the Le Rhône did not hesitate to start.

Monaco 1914: Janoir's Deperdussin under tow off the famous waterfront. (*Musée de l'Air*)

Although unaccustomed to the machine his Lordship – he disliked the title and later relinquished it by taking American citizenship, respelling himself Carberry in the process – had no difficulty in getting the Dep. across the line and off the water. But after only one lap he was down again, complaining of misfiring. At first it was thought that the engine was tightening up but investigation revealed that two of the plug leads were crossed. The cowlings had to be removed to put this right and it was some time before the engine could be restarted. Sportingly Carbery taxied out to continue the race but was back after only one more lap with the same engine symptoms. Whether this was more crossed leads one cannot ascertain from this distance in time but the problem was obviously insoluble because the machine stayed in port.

The more informed onlookers knew better than to think that at this stage the race was in the British bag. Aircraft engines had not yet reached that degree of reliability. Their cynicism, if any, might have seemed to be justified when, as the Sopwith came round on the fifteenth lap the smooth whirr of the Monosoupape had taken on a rough edge. A plug had cut and the engine was down to eight cylinders. With less than eight-ninths of the original power to fly on – the dead cylinder caused pumping losses – Pixton's lap time dropped immediately, his sixteenth lap taking 4 min 22 sec. This was still better than the Nieuports could do, but it was dangerously near to their level.

But the little engine continued to run without any increase in vibration although the lap times became erratic as Pixton nursed the machine along. His times, varying between 4 min 22 sec and 4 min 31 sec with an abysmal one of 4 min 44 sec, reflect the work he was putting in. It was proof of the inherent rightness of the single-row Monosoupape that nothing untoward happened, save a loss of power, and the machine was able to

keep flying on. Not so with the two-row engines in the two Nieuports. Only a few minutes after stop-watches showed that the Sopwith was in some kind of trouble, Espanet's Nieuport – on its sixteenth lap – was seen to alight on the water opposite the Tir aux Pigeons and taxi back into the harbour, followed a lap later by Levasseur's machine. Both had retired with partially seized engines.

Meanwhile Pixton realised that his engine was not going to stop and his flying became more precise although lap times were well down, averaging a very consistent 4 min 26 sec for fifteen laps compared with 4 min 10 sec for the first half of the race.

So it was that, with a huge ovation from the crowd, the little Tabloid crossed the line 2 hours and 13.4 seconds after taxying across the start line. Before the start Tom Sopwith had arranged with Pixton to do a further two laps to bring the total distance flown to 300 km. This arrangement served the dual purpose of preventing a reoccurrence of the Prévost incident the previous year and gave a safety margin in case of an error in lap-counting – Pixton's sole means of assessing progress was by throwing overboard one of twenty-seven drawing pins stuck in the instrument panel each time he passed the line – and with the FAI timekeepers present it gave the opportunity to establish a new world record over 300 km on a closed circuit. It was typical of the thorough way Sopwith conducted his affairs.

The morning was yet young and Burri was stolidly soldiering along in the FBA flying-boat. At the end of twenty laps he made a prearranged landing in the open sea, taxied into the main harbour for replenishment of fuel and oil and rejoined the contest. Without further incident he completed his twenty-eight laps in a total time of 3 hr 24 min 12 sec, again made a faultless alighting on the open sea and entered the harbour under his own power. Pixton could well have done the same. But after putting down on the surface he relaxed for a moment and the sea damaged the elevator, which drooped in the water in the best of conditions. He had to wait for Victor Mahl in the tender to come and tow him into harbour.

Although Pixton's performance appeared unbeatable, the race, or time trial to be correct, was not officially over until sunset. Prévost, as a first reserve in the French team, was eligible to compete in the absence of Garros, who had signified his intention not to try to beat the British performance. Accordingly the big engine of the Deperdussin was swung – it fired this time – and Prévost headed out of Fontvieille for the starting line. It was not his day. As he rounded the point of Old Monaco, the spray raised as he buffeted into the chop, caught his broad-bladed propeller and split it. This was really the end of the French effort. At about 11 am Levasseur came out of harbour, did a lap, returned for further adjustments and then took off once again to complete nine laps before returning finally to the harbour. He was classified third in the final results although no times were published for his subsequent laps.

The French were, inevitably, shattered by the experience of being beaten by a technically superior flying

Monaco 1914: Ernest Burri. (*Musée de l'Air*)

Howard Pixton, the winner of the 1914 Schneider Trophy at Monaco. His oil-soaked trousers testify to the amount of engine oil lost during each flight. (*Flight*)

machine although they had the satisfaction of having provided the power unit and the know-how for the propeller, which was a French-designed Integrale made under licence in the UK. Pixton's victory was hailed by the French technical press as a striking victory for Sopwith, reflecting the stimulus being given to British aviation by the military. They admired particularly the sturdy design and impeccable workmanship of the Baby.

As a matter of course Pixton was fêted by the French and British press. He was a naturally modest type who simply remarked that the British excelled in all other sports, why not in this one? Harald Penrose repeats a story Sopwith told about Pixton at a banquet by the Royal Aero Club to honour the victory. At the prize giving on the Tuesday at the Sporting Club, with champagne flowing like water, Jacques Schneider offered Pixton a celebratory drink. 'Mine's a small Bass, thank you very much,' said the hero of the hour.

Of the other pilots Charles Weymann took part in only one more aviation event before abandoning his flying to concentrate on his automobile business in Paris where, besides high-quality cars, he marketed a wide range of automotive parts. The Nivex petrol gauge bore his name in small print, as did the radiator thermometers fitted to Bugatti racing cars. His name came to be universally known among motorists for the method of coachbuilding he devised, using a leathercloth-covered flexible framework.

Weymann, as an American citizen, would not be called upon to fight for France but both Dr Gabriel Espanet and Roland Garros were flying immediately war started. Garros pioneered the modern style of airfighting with a fixed gun mounted on the aircraft and firing through the propeller. He was captured early in the conflict, eventually escaped and was killed in a dogfight in 1916.

Conclusions

As a sporting competition, the 1914 Monaco Hydroaeroplane Meeting was probably less of a success than that of the preceding year. Only half a dozen aircraft finished the Great Monaco Rally, which was billed as the most spectacular aviation meeting up to that

Monaco 1914: Howard Pixton, the winner, in front of the Sopwith Schneider Tabloid. On the left is Tom Sopwith with his chief mechanic Victor Mahl (in rolled-up trousers). (*Musée de l'Air*)

time. On top of that there was a great dearth of flying during the fortnight because of the weather. Only the Schneider event proved of real aviation interest. On the other hand the technical impact of the event, and the Sopwith victory, was immense.

The effect of the Sopwith win on the French aviation industry was shattering. It was proof indeed that one can never rest on one's laurels. Progress in aviation never stands still. At that time it was moving like wildfire. The French had eased off, lulled into a sense of false security by their successes in every kind of aviation contest, especially those for speed, which were dominated in the landplane classes by Deperdussin. So far as they were concerned, racers had to be monoplanes, and biplanes were slow, cumbersome, general-purpose machines suitable for low-flying reconnaissance.

In Great Britain things were different. Accidents to monoplanes had caused the War Department, rightly or wrongly, to place a ban on that type of aeroplane for military use. Thus the design of fast biplanes was heavily promoted. The Tabloid was at that time the ultimate development of the fast, small biplane. Sopwith had shown that, by using the right wing section, he could design an aeroplane with sufficient wing surface to carry two people with the minimum of drag. Reduction of wing area in aeroplanes pays dividends with compound

interest because smaller wings need less bracing, which in turn means less weight and parasitic drag. Sopwith saw that the biplane configuration was ideal for a simple wire-braced structure. These thoughts took tangible form in the single-bay format typified by the Tabloid and never improved upon right until the end of the biplane era. Efficient wire-braced monoplanes had to await further development, better understanding of the stresses in wing structures and the acceptance of very much higher wing loadings than could be countenanced in 1914. The Prévost Deperdussin was on the right lines but far too little time was devoted to its development.

Even while the Schneider Trophy race was being contested and won, Sopwith Scouts, which were virtually replicas of the Tabloid fitted with aileron control instead of wing-warping, were coming off the production line at Kingston-upon-Thames for delivery to the newly formed Royal Flying Corps. For the first, and not the last time it was being demonstrated that the Schneider Trophy was a key development area for fighter aeroplanes. Even though at that time armed aircraft were only being seriously considered by the French, the little Tabloid was the forerunner of a long line of famous biplane fighters, which were all directly derived from it. Of the French entries only the little Morane could be regarded as a fighter prototype. Nieuport learned the lesson and developed the famous Nieuport biplane fighter. The great Louis Béchereau was already designing the first SPAD biplane using the Deperdussin fuselage construction for the newly formed company headed by Papa Blériot.

If the French had been shattered by the result at Monaco the Americans must have been even more so. The country which had led the world in aviation had lost its initiative, mainly through the Wright brothers' secretiveness and their attempts to 'do a Selsden' and gain a stranglehold on aviation through their parents. There seems to have been even more complacency on their side of the Atlantic than there was in France, with the result that there was no competitive aeroplane available to the American flyers at Monaco and they had to rely on a rented Deperdussin.

As ever the Schneider Trophy race was acting as a sure indicator of a country's progress in fighter design. Throughout World War One the Americans did not have a fighter of their own because of this lack of progress, and had to rely on the products of the French and British aircraft industries to equip their squadrons when they eventually joined the conflict.

In one area there was desperate need for progress. All the aeroplanes in the 1914 race had been powered by rotary engines, all except one of them coming from the Seguin factory. The Deperdussin experience proved how temperamental they could be in the higher powers even when maintained by a crew from the works. Their only virtue was the high power-to-weight ratio for the period. Against this had to be set inordinately high oil consumption and an overhaul life of only a few hours. Added to this was their effect on aircraft handling due to gyroscopic precession. This was fine and dandy while people were only too eager to get into the air at any cost; but the need for a lightweight economical power unit had still to be fulfilled.

The Aircraft

The Sopwith SS seaplane

There was certainly nothing complex about the little Sopwith that the enthusiasts drew out in chalk on the floor of the skating rink at Kingston-upon-Thames. By the standards of the day it really was tiny, being a single-bay biplane with equal-span wings of only 25 ft 6 in with swept-back tips and a total wing area of 241.3 sq ft. Lateral control was by wing-warping with 4-deg movement either side of the datum. The fuselage was a simple box-section lattice girder structure built up from $1\frac{1}{8}$ sq in ash longerons and uprights braced with 12 SWG piano wire, surmounted by a Vee-turtle back. The longerons were extended forward to support an ash cross-bar for the propeller shaft steady-bearing of the Gnome engine after the style of the Nieuport.

The H-section wing main spars were machined from the solid. The front spar was in spruce, only the upper mainplane rear spar, because of its small depth, being machined from ash to gain advantage of the greater modulus of that material. The curved leading edges were

beautifully spindled sections in yew. Three-piece wing ribs were fabricated from poplar with ash flanges attached by myriads of tiny brass screws.

Simplicity was also the keynote of the large semi-circular empennage, which was of conventional construction with an ash main spar and leading edge and poplar wood ribs. On the definitive landplane version – the prototype did not have a fin – total rudder and fin area was 6.125 sq ft, of which the fin accounted for only 1.875 sq ft. On the seaplane adaptation, to equalise the areas of lateral resistance when floats were added, the rudder and fin area were increased. To this had to be added a further fin area of approximately 4 sq ft for a deep, fin-shaped tail float faired into the rear fuselage and a water rudder formed as a lower extension of the fin and rudder. The original seaplane conversion featured a separate rear float supported on three struts. The conversion to the combined rear float and fin was made during the rebuild after the Hamble débâcle.

Physically the 100 hp Monosoupape, announced the previous year and used experimentally in the Borel and Deperdussin monoplanes at the 1913 Monaco meeting – this probably accounts for the conflicting accounts of the power unit fitted to the latter – was very little larger than the 80 hp fitted to the prototype and production Tabloid: the stroke was 150 mm compared with 140 mm for the seven cylinder 80 hp, allowing it to fit neatly between the fuselage longerons and calling for only minor changes to the existing cowling. However, the cowling was cut away underneath to increase exposure of the cylinders to the airstream in view of the fact that the aircraft would possibly be a little slower than the landplane version despite the extra horsepower.

A main installation problem could have been the extra weight of the engine. It weighed almost 60 lb more than the seven cylinder 80 hp unit fitted to the landplane version. On the definitive seaplane version this would be offset to some extent by the extra weight of the rear float on the end of the long lever arm of the fuselage. Modifications to the fuselage were minimal, being restricted to changing the cockpit and controls to single-seat configuration.

As recounted elsewhere the original floatplane design called for a single main float with stabilising floats on the wingtips and a tail float mounted on short struts, and was set so far aft that the machine nosed over as soon as the throttle was opened. This single float had its own wire-braced, four-strut chassis. After the accident on the Hamble river, the big single float was sawn down the middle, the open sides filled in and a new, diagonally braced, four-strut chassis was built with the floats widely spaced by spreaders bolted to the tops of the floats. This modification was entirely successful and the Sopwith Baby went on to win the 1914 Schneider Trophy race in this form.

During World War One a number of Sopwith Baby floatplanes were built for the Admiralty for operation off cross-channel steamers converted to seaplane carriers with hangars on the after deck. Fitted out as single-seaters with a single Lewis gun mounted on the upper wing, they could also carry a light bomb or Ranken anti-personnel darts. When required for operations the procedure was to wheel the aircraft out of the deck hangar, rig them on deck and crane them over the side with the engine running ready for take-off. In 1916 they were briefly, and unsuccessfully, used on anti-Zeppelin operations in the Heligoland Bight.

Sopwith Baby seaplane dimensions

Wing span	(upper)	25 ft 6 in	7.77 m
	(lower)	25 ft 6 in	7.77 m
Chord		4 ft 9 in	1.49 m
Wing area		241.3 sq ft	22.4 sq m
Overall length	(Airframe)	19 ft 4 in	5.89 m
	(with floats)	20 ft 15 in	6.47 m
Tailplane	span	8 ft 3 in	2.5 m
	chord (max)	3 ft 8 in	1.12 m
	area	23.6 sq ft	2.19 sq m
Fin and rudder	height	3 ft 6in	1.09 m
	area	7.7 sq ft	0.72 sq m
Floats	length	8 ft 3 in	2.5 m
	beam	1 ft 8.5 in	52.1 cm
	depth	1 ft 7.7 in	50.0 cm
Weight		1,120 lb	509 kg
Wing loading		4.64 lb/sq ft	22.72 kg/m^2
Fuel capacity			
(with extra tank)		30 gal	136.38 ltr
Engine		Gnome Monosoupape	
Number of cylinders		9	
Configuration		Rotary	
Power		100 bhp	
rpm		1,200	
Bore		110 mm	
Stroke		150 mm	
Capacity		12,829 cc	
Weight		270 lb	122.7 kg

Nieuport II

The least modified French aircraft were the Nieuports of Espanet, Levasseur and Weymann. Undoubtedly the company lacked the inspired drive of Charles and Édouard Nieuport. The main changes were in the power units adopted. Espanet had fitted a 160 hp 14-cylinder Gnome in place of the 100 hp 14-cylinder unit he had used the year previously. Levasseur's Nieuport also sported a 160 hp twin-row Gnome.

Weymann, probably in search of reliability, had moved over to the Le Rhône company for power. This 18-cylinder, 160 hp Le Rhône engine was considerably heavier than the 14-cylinder Gnome of equivalent horsepower; 464 lb as against 396 lb. No doubt Weymann felt that the weight penalty was worth putting up with if piston seizure could be avoided. Le Rhône was attractive in this respect, having cast iron cylinder sleeves instead of the all-steel cylinders favoured by the Seguin brothers. Moreover, lubrication was more positive since the mixture and the lubricating oil were not mixed inside the crankcase, the mixture being transferred from the carburettor through radial pipes to the inlet valve.

From the pilots' point of view the most fundamental airframe change must have been that Nieuport had changed round the controls of their 1914 machines. Prior to 1914 the 'rudder' bars had been connected to the wing-warping while the rudder was operated either by swinging the control column from side to side or turning a wheel mounted on the control column. Nieuport now came into line with everyone else with a rudder bar to steer with in the normal manner while lateral and pitch control were by means of a control column operating the wing-warping and elevators.

The Nieuport float gear was identical to that of the 1913 machine with Tellier three-step keel floats, each having small anti-nose-over hydrofoil mounted on its nose, rather like a cavalry moustache. This float configuration and the bomb-shaped metal rear-float were perpetrated on Nieuports well into the 1920s whenever the *flotteur derrière*, tail-float, configuration was employed.

Nieuport II seaplane dimensions

Wing	span	39 ft 4 in	1.2 m
	chord	8 ft 0 in	2.9 m
Wing area		255 sq ft	23.7 sq m
Overall length		28 ft 8 in	8.75 m
Tailplane	span	10 ft 3 in	3.2 m
	area	43 sq ft	3.99 sq m
Fin and rudder	area	7 sq ft	0.65 sq m
Weight		1,607 lb	730 kg
Wing loading		6.3 lb/sq ft	30.8 kg/m^2
Engine		Gnome	Le Rhône
Number of cyls.		14	18
Configuration		radial	rotary
Power		160	160
rpm		1,200	1,150
Bore		124 mm	105 mm
Stroke		140 mm	140 mm
Capacity		23,669 cc	21,820 cc
Weight		397 lb (180.4 kg)	464 lb (210.9 kg)

Deperdussin Schneider Special

Float design apart, the airframe of the 1914 racer exemplified Béchereau at his best. Just as his 1913 Schneider winner was an aerodynamic disaster, so this 1914 racer was a triumph of streamlining; it was years ahead of its time.

Unlike the abortive 1913 Deperdussin Schneider Special, which was monocoque to the rear centre-section bulkhead and lattice-framed thereafter, the 1914 Special was pure monocoque, diagonally planked with three skins of tulip-wood covered inside and outside with linen. This construction and the hand-rubbed finish – the final coats were milk-chocolate-coloured with the flying surfaces decorated with a white coachlined check pattern – caused observers, as in 1913, to mistake it for a converted Gordon Bennett racer. This was not so. The disposition of the cockpit relative to the cabane, and the quadripod, pyramid cabane structure disproves this supposition. The 1914 Deperdussin Schneider was, in any case, a bigger aeroplane than the Gordon Bennett machines, it being the French custom to build their seaplanes with a wing area about one third bigger than the equivalent landplane. This Schneider machine is calculated to have a span of 8.6 metres and an overall length of 6.2 metres.

The quadripod wing pylon seems to be a first and a last for Béchereau. His 1912 Gordon Bennett aircraft and the 1913 Schneider Special had five-strut pylons with two inverted Vs per side and a transverse ridge pole. The 1914 Special's four-strut cabane configuration is taken by some to indicate that the machine was fitted with a two-bank Le Rhône but this supposition is unlikely to be correct because Le Rhône did not have a 200 hp engine at the time; moreover, the pylon design would be the same for either engine.

In the Deperdussin Schneider machine, refinement of aerodynamic detail was the keynote. Prévost had a thing about windscreens, believing that they caused more drag than people's heads, so the cockpit was a plain elliptical hole without a screen or even a headrest. Presumably Béchereau felt that the aeroplane was not going to be fast enough to need one. He had pioneered this essential aerodynamic device in the 1913 Gordon Bennett race on Prévost's machine, when it was just what it was called, a rest for the driver's head to steady it against wind pressure.

Power was provided by a potential package of trouble in the shape of the new 200 hp 18-cylinder Gnome, driving a broad-bladed Integrale propeller. The motor was mounted in the usual Béchereau manner, the main rear mounting being on a reinforced bulkhead, while the front end was supported by a floating bearing on the propeller shaft braced by radial wires to the forward edge of the stressed cowling. The snag with this arrangement would appear to be the difficulty of removing the cowling for engine maintenance, although with a rotary it is possible to traverse all the cylinder heads past a single inspection opening by turning the propeller.

In contrast to the Gordon Bennett racers, the wing planform was strictly rectangular instead of being a reversed taper. All the records indicate that the span was 8.6 m and the chord can be estimated at 2 m, giving a total lifting surface of about 16 sq m. Wing construction featured the usual composite hickory and ash spars with pine ribs. The wing bracing was the same as that of the Gordon Bennett machines, consisting of two lift and two landing wires per side, picking up with the front spar and a similar number of warping wires attached to the rear spar. All of the upper wires led to the apex of the quadripod cabanes, while the lower wires were attached respectively to the lower roots of the front and rear float struts.

Compared with that of the 1913 seaplanes, the dart-shaped Deperdussin empennage was considerably increased in area by at least 50 per cent. And the side area was further increased by a streamlined pylon supporting the rear float. Details of its construction are

interesting. The streamlined sectioned tailplane had a formed ash and ply leading edge, poplar inner ribs and ash stringers to support the fabric. The fixed fin was framed throughout in Columbian pine, while the rudder itself was ash-framed except for the spar webs.

Judging by a surviving photograph Tellier and Béchereau appear to have produced a novel float arrangement, possibly incorporating a hydrofoil between the floats about one third of the float length back from the bows. In the photograph one of the service crew appears to be standing on this. The floats themselves were of the normal, swim-bowed type attached to the aircraft by wide-chord, streamlined, wooden struts in N-configuration. The rear struts and diagonal braces were in one piece, beautifully faired where they joined the rear float attachment at the inner edges of the pontoon. Spreaders bracing the top edges of the float hulls were equally well streamlined. They passed right through the floats and acted as desk beams. What appear to be small quarter-elliptic springs acted as extra stays between the float spreaders and the inner sides of the pontoons.

The rear float is best described as being shaped like half of a tear-drop, or apple pip. It was mounted on a short, wide-chord streamlined pylon, which was an extension of the rear fuselage. The only extra staying was a pair of tiny jury struts, bracing the edges of the float to the rudder kingpost.

The second Deperdussin, race no. 4, allocated to Emile Janoir and flown by Lord Carbery in the race, seems to have been a revamped version of the 1913 Special which did not start in the race, with wider, more deeply cambered wings braced with four wires instead of six. From photographs the new wings appear to have been attached to the short stubs of the old wings. Although the punt-shaped floats were the same, the water chassis was much simplified with the object of reducing drag. Whereas the 1913 machine had wire-braced side float struts, the 1914 version had Warren or N-configuration strut bracing, set the reverse way to that of the Prévost aircraft, that is, with the diagonal picking up with the front lower float brackets. Also, the warping control levers previously mounted on the rear spreader had been replaced by the simple arrangement of pull-wires like that used on Prévost's aircraft.

In this system the warping wires were taken from a pulley on the control wheel, down the sides of the horse-shoe-shaped control column and directly round pulleys let into the faired junction of the rear float struts. The rear float was the same shape as that of the no. 1 aircraft but in this case was supported on tubular steel struts. To improve handling, the balance of the side area had been redressed by enlarging the fin area by about 50 per cent and doubling the rudder area compared with the 1913 machine. Further, to reduce drag the cockpit opening was reduced to the same size as Prévost's machine by extending the coamings upwards.

Power was provided by a 160 hp Le Rhône engine, not by a Gnome as mentioned in some reports.

Monaco 1914: the FBA being towed into the harbour with pilot Burri holding the tow rope. (*Musée de l'Air*)

The FBA flying-boat

The biplane FBA (Franco-British Aviation Company) flying-boat was the work of André Beaumont, a French naval officer and, as already mentioned, was constructed at the FBA works at Bezons. Despite the British content in the name, it was very much a French firm with mainly French capital. The general configuration was Donnet-Leveque, that is with the tailplane and rudder mounted on an extension of the fuselage. In this case it was not mounted directly on the boat hull but was supported by a minuscule strut structure. Construction of the elegant scorpion-tail hull was in laminated wood after the style of the Deperdussin, with thin planks laid diagonally in layers with oiled silk between them, to render the hull watertight. Beaumont had cast convention aside when he conceived the wing construction of the FBA, basing both the upper and lower mainplanes on steel tubular spars, the front spars forming the leading edges of the wings. Wooden ribs were attached to these spars by thin steel strips.

Effectively, the lifting surfaces were arranged in two-bay, unequal-span biplane, almost sesquiplane, configuration, the upper wing forming the main lifting surface and being provided with ailerons for lateral control. The high aspect ratio, smaller-span lower mainplane, although it would provide some lift, appears to have been mainly of structural importance as a main member of the wing truss and as a support for the wingtip floats. The upper wingspan was 10.5 m and that of the lower wing 8.5 m, giving a total area of 22 sq m. Wooden tapered but unstreamlined interplane struts were utilised with piano-wire bracing.

The whole wing structure was virtually autonomous and was mounted on short steel tubes above the hull of the boat and just proud of it. The 100 hp Gnome Monosoupape engine was carried on a separate steel tubular structure inside the middle bay of the wing, the

motor mount legs picking up with lugs brazed to the tubular spars. Fuel was carried in a torpedo-shaped tank mounted under the wing and above the engine with feed by gravity. Mounted high above the waves on a scorpion-like extension of the boat hull, the tailplane was of normal wooden and fabric construction with a total area of 2.9 sq m. The wire-braced fin and rudder were of approximately half this area.

In two respects FBA made Schneider history. Theirs was not only the first flying-boat to fly in the series, it was also the first aircraft of any type to fly in the races with lateral control by ailerons. Stoeffler's Aviatik was the only other entry with aileron control but, as recorded elsewhere, it was damaged beyond repair before the race.

Reports on the FBA's handling vary. It had a reputation for porpoising, which seems to be borne out by its display when starting in the race. Burri, its pilot, certainly had difficulty in controlling it then. On the other hand all reports point to its handling on the surface in a bad sea as being excellent. The first FBA with an 80 hp Gnome was an eminently practical aircraft and held a number of records. It may be that the extra power and weight of the Gnome Monosoupape engine exacerbated the take-off behaviour of Burri's machine in the race. After its Schneider performance the FBA went from strength to strength, with rather similar designs for naval use and in developed form as the FBA-Schreck, which went into production after World War One, belying any suggestions that it was not a practical type.

The Morane-Saulnier

The Morane monoplanes were little-changed in design from the previous year. The main difference was in the power units and the method of mounting them. However the two aircraft which flew in the rally and were entered for the Coupe Maritime were somewhat bigger. Garros's and Lord Carbery's machines had a wing area of 16 sq m to go with the 160 hp fourteen-cylinder, two-bank Gnome engine with which they were powered. In essence they were all landplanes fitted with floats. Raymond Saulnier did build a proper seaplane but it was a huge biplane with a mere 80 hp engine to drive it, and was quite unsuitable for racing. Incidentally, Gilbert made the first flight with this latter machine on the Seine, near Jette island, in 1913.

The main design difference in the race aircraft fitted with two-row engines was that the fuselage longerons were extended, à la Nieuport, forward of the engine to support a cross member carrying a steady-bearing for the propeller shaft. Since, with rotary engines, the crankshaft is fixed and attached to the front fuselage bulkhead while the propeller is, in effect, mounted on an extension of the crankcase, prudent constructors always provided a propeller-shaft steady-bearing although they were not absolutely essential for the smaller-horsepower, single-row rotaries. However, the extra weight and overall length of the two-row rotaries demanded this support bearing so that the engine was slung between two points rather than overhung.

Another change was that the aircraft had full circumference cowlings – Deperdussin-style – but without the large bulbous Deperdussin spinner. Instead Garros's aircraft sported a slightly dished disc mounted behind the propeller to reduce the annular intake area. Air was exhausted through the segment of a circle formed by the rear of the cowling and the flat bottom of the fuselage. A useful addition, to improve water handling, was a small elliptical water rudder under the rear float operated by an extension of the rudder post.

Brindejonc de Moulinais's machine differed from the Carbery and Garros seaplanes in being smaller and was basically the little 1913 monoplane with a cleaned-up float chassis. The jury struts to the edges of the floats were dispensed with and the side struts had been splayed to pick up with the outer edges of the floats. It was one of the earliest Moranes to be fitted with the new 9-cylinder 100 hp Gnome Monosoupape and was fitted with a large-diameter, all-enveloping cowling.

The Aviatik Flêche

Ernst Stoeffler's entry was basically a military machine built for endurance rather than racing. It was derived from the standard German Army Aviatik Flêche type which was an unequal-span, swept-wing biplane with an upper wingspan of 14 m and a lower one of 10.8 m. The wing area was some 45 sq m and the all-up weight was 1.130 kg. The wings were braced by a four-bay arrangement of struts and wire bracing with extra diagonal struts running from the lower ends of outer vertical struts. In this form, with its standard 100 hp four-in-line Benz engine, the Flêche would have been scarcely a match for anything present except the FBA amphibian. In fact the type's main claim to fame was a flight of 2,160 km in 24 hours on 14 October the previous year.

From photographs it appears that Stoeffler's machine was much modified with the upper mainplane reduced to the same span as the lower one. The records also indicate that one of the new 130 × 180 mm, 120 hp, 6-cylinder, in-line Benz engines had been substituted for the 4-cylinder model. It was an ideal machine for the Monaco Air Rally, being amphibious to the extent that it had a quickly detachable float chassis consisting of a wide single main float fitting directly to the legs of the undercarriage after the wheels had been detached. A tail float and small wingtip floats were added in the interests of stability.

Structurally the Aviatik Flêche embodied stressed-skin techniques which were taken up by light aircraft designers after the War and persist until today. This was the use of a ply skin glued and pinned to the fuselage lattice in place of the usual wire bracing. The fuselage vertical and horizontal panels were based on framed-up ply bulkheads. A certain amount of double curvature was given to the fuselage by ash stringers mounted beneath the fabric covering the sides of the fuselage.

The Benz engine was mounted directly on top of the upper longerons on metal brackets and was partly enclosed within the forward end of a streamlined metal turtle back which extended right back behind the cockpits. The cockpit openings were cut in the top of this turtle back, which also incorporated the instrument panel.

The Gnome Rotary Engine

There is little doubt that without the Gnome rotary engine aviation progress in the first five or six years of the art would have been lamentably slow. In no area of engine design is power-to-weight ratio of such paramount importance as in power units for aircraft. The engine which sustained the Wright brothers in the air and enabled them to experiment with controlled flight produced one horsepower for every eleven pounds of weight. It was not powerful enough to get the machine off the ground, and take-off had to be by means of a catapult variation of the Roman ballista. It is usually accepted that the French, who led in internal combustion engine design at this critical period, had the distinction of providing the motive power for the first unassisted take-offs with engines producing of the order of one horsepower for every five pounds of weight.

One of the main problems, once unassisted take-off had been achieved, was to stay up there. Early lightweight engines overheated badly and the lightweight construction made them mechanically unreliable. This was all changed when the Seguin brothers, notably Laurent the designer, produced the first Gnome engine whose main novelty was that the cylinders rotated round

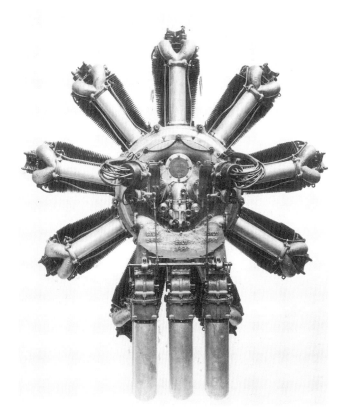

Gnome twin-valve 9-cylinder rotary engine. This and the Monosoupape version were the most favoured engines in the early years of the Schneider Trophy. (*Derek N. James*)

a fixed crankshaft. By so doing it cooled itself by self-induced airflow, while the radial configuration of the cylinders enabled it to achieve a high power-to-weight ratio. Rotary engines had been made before but the one known attempt was obscure and unsuccessful. The Gnome was the complete opposite; by dint of first-class workmanship and sound design the nominally 50 hp Gnome engine would produce between 45 and 47 bhp at 1,000 rpm on the brake for a weight of 167 lb (76 kg) with great reliability so long as it was fed with suitably large quantities of petrol and castor oil. This was equivalent to 3.55 lb per horsepower, which was a major advance in itself. Admittedly figures of about 5 lb per horsepower were being bandied about at the time, but the designers of these units usually forgot to add in the weight of radiators, magnetos and induction systems.

An additional attraction of the Gnome for the do-it-yourself pioneers was the ease of installation. The Gnome was an autonomous unit and the only mounting it required was a strong, flat bulkhead to which the crankshaft flange could be bolted, and a cross-bar to support the propeller shaft. Moreover, because of its lack of vibration it gave the frail airframes of the period a very easy time compared with some of the in-line engines then extant.

During the relatively short period during which this engine dominated aviation, two main types were built, both of them four-strokes but working on different principles. The first type, which came on the market in approximately 50 hp form with seven cylinders and was eventually built with as many as eighteen cylinders, operated on the Otto principle with the usual induction, compression, firing and exhaust strokes. Mixture was fed from a carburettor mounted on the inboard end of the crankshaft into the crankcase and thence into the cylinder via an 'atmospheric' inlet valve in the top of the piston. Spent gas was exhausted through a push-rod operated valve in the top of each cylinder.

The second type, the Monosoupape, introduced in 1913, worked differently. As its name suggests it had only one valve, the one in the cylinder head which acted as the exhaust valve in the first engine. The valve in the piston, which had always been troublesome because it had to be carefully counterbalanced and required meticulous setting of the closing spring, was abolished and the single valve was called on to do all the work.

The *modus operandi* of the Monosoupape merits a short description. Supposing we start from the point where the charge in a cylinder has been ignited and the piston is on the way down with one valve closed to contain the pressure of the burning charge. Instead of staying closed until the piston has reached bottom dead-centre the valve was opened when it is about two thirds of the way down, relieving the pressure in the cylinder by allowing some of the exhaust gas to escape to atmosphere. As it travelled further down the cylinder the piston uncovered a row of vertical slots cut in the cylinder wall and communicating with the crankcase, which is filled with a petrol/air mixture which is so over-saturated that it will not be ignited by the remaining

exhaust gases. At this point in the cycle there appears to be no flow through the slots in either direction, the residual pressure in the cylinder balancing the crankcase pressure, resulting in equilibrium. Meanwhile the piston has moved back up the cylinder to expel the remaining exhaust gas.

Normally the exhaust valve would close at this point and the inlet valve would open to admit a fresh charge. There being no inlet valve, the exhaust valve is caused to stay open until the piston is about one third of the way down the cylinder, thereby admitting a quantity of pure air into the cylinder. As soon as the valve snaps shut a depression is created which draws rich mixture out of the crankcase as the piston uncovers the inlet slots. This rich mix combines with the air in the cylinder to form a combustible mixture which is compressed on the next upward stroke of the piston and fired in the normal way.

The notable difference between the two-valve and single-valve versions, apart from the construction of the engine at the base of the cylinder, was the method of creating the mixture. The two-valve type drew it from a conventional carburettor while in the 'Mono' fuel was sprayed through a nozzle into the crankcase at a pressure of about 5 psi and combined with air admitted through the hollow rear journal of the crankshaft.

Despite their virtues these engines had a number of major drawbacks. Lubrication was a major problem, as ordinary mineral oil would have been diluted by the mixture, resulting in bearing failure. The answer was to use castor oil which, being vegetable based, did not combine with the mixture. It was used on the total loss principle, being pumped from a tank in the aircraft and allowed to find its way to atmosphere via the exhaust ports. Consumption was claimed by the makers to be in the proportion of one part of oil to seven parts of petrol. In practice the ratio was more like three to one with the result that engine cowlings were essential to prevent the pilot being blinded by used oil. Even with these guards the pilot and the airframe would get a liberal coating of oil and it was not unknown for the former to suffer the usual results of a dose of this lubricant, while the build-up of oil on the tail surfaces of his machine could drastically upset the trim. Furthermore, Gnome engines were thermodynamically very inefficient – the nine-cylinder Mono had a swept volume of 12.9 litres and produced only 100 bhp – consuming petrol at the rate of about 1 pint per bhp/hour, so the weight of fuel and oil precluded their use on long-distance machines.

The Gnome's mechanical construction was of the highest order. Despite its lightness it was built entirely from nickel-steel, weight being saved by using very thin sections. The cylinder walls, for example, were only a few millimetres thick with finely machined fins. Each cylinder was machined from a solid billet of steel weighing some 98 lb, calling for the removal of more than 90 lb of metal to end up with a cylinder weighing 5 lb. The crankcase was also machined from the solid. This was one of the earliest engines to use master and slave rods. They were machined all over and were fitted with delicate steel pistons with gunmetal rings. The only light alloy casting in the engine was the oil pump body. Exhaust operation was by pull rods in early engines but later models used push rods with counterbalanced rockers.

Many notable flights were made with Gnome engines. They powered the first aeroplane to exceed 100 mph, the first to cross the Mediterranean and the first seaplane to rise, unassisted, off the surface of the water. Both pre-1914 winners of the Coupe d'Aviation Maritime were Gnome-powered. Many countries built Gnomes under licence. In America it was built by the General Vehicle Company, in England by Daimler Limited and in Germany by Bayerische Motoren Gesellschaft, who built the early type but with two valves in the piston.

One little-recognised but enduring result of the widespread use of Gnome and other rotary engines during World War One came about because of the huge fortune it made for Mr Charles Cheers Wakefield, later Lord Wakefield, one of the main suppliers of castor oil to the RFC and RNAS under the trade name Castrol. Lesser men would have pocketed their fortunes and retired discreetly to some tax haven. Not so Charles Cheers, who was a great patriot, and devoted a great deal of this money to financing British record-breaking attempts during the interwar years. Thanks mainly to him, Britain, for many years, held the land speed record and at one time the maxima for land, sea and air as well as innumerable class records. It was he who bought and paid for the development of alcohol versions of the Rolls-Royce R engine for his powerboats. It was one of these alcohol engines, installed in a Supermarine S.6B Schneider machine, which gave Britain the honour of being the first country to exceed 400 mph in the air and later, on land.

Bournemouth 1919

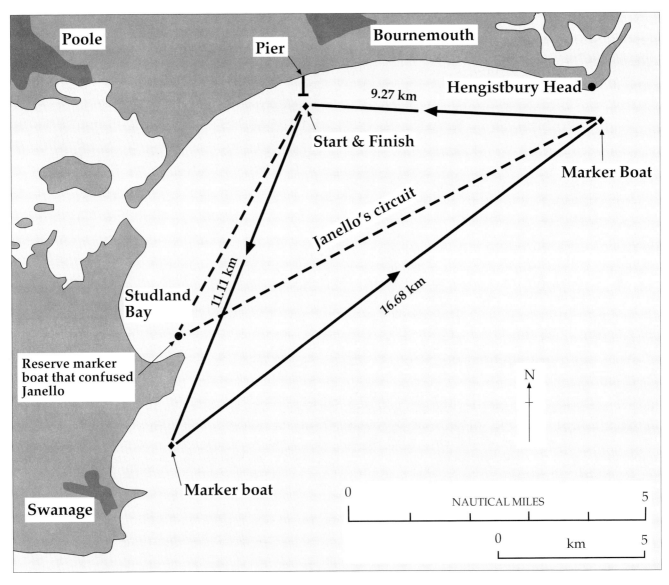

Schneider Trophy Contest Course: Bournemouth 1919.

Run-up

On 1 May 1919, less than six months after the signing of the armistice and before the Treaty of Versailles was ratified, the British skies were reopened to civil flying. In Britain it was a different world from that of 1914 although the British people, overjoyed at the thought of peace and with the survivors of their menfolk streaming home, were slow to see it. The cost of victory had been tremendous in terms of money and political influence. In 1914 Britain had been by far the greatest of the world powers. She came out of the War to End Wars a debtor nation, with massive debts to her allies virtually spelling the end of the British

Empire. The British people would have to wait through a long armistice and another war for that truth to be driven home.

Meanwhile there was a booming interest in flying. Whereas before the War the number of pilots in any European country could be counted in the low hundreds, they now numbered tens of thousands. And a great industry had sprung up to manufacture and maintain the machines they flew.

In Britain the big aviation news was the contest for the first non-stop crossing of the North Atlantic. The reward would be the rich £10,000 prize put up by the *Daily Mail* proprietors six years previously. Engines and machines had been developed during the War which now made the feat possible and a minor air force of rival competitors had foregathered in Newfoundland to make the attempt on the easier west–east crossing. On 14 June the Rolls-Royce Eagle-powered Vickers R.27 Vimy bearing Alcock and Brown lumbered into the air from Lester's Field, Newfoundland and, 16 hr 27 min later, put down in a bog near Clifton, County Galway. It was the third machine away. Harry Hawker and Mackenzie Grieve in the Sopwith Atlantic had come down and been picked up. The Martinsyde A with Raynham and Morgan aboard had crashed on take-off.

While this, and air racing practically every weekend of the summer, was holding the attention of the air-minded British public, the Royal Aero Club, as holders of the Schneider Trophy after Howard Pixton's win at Monaco, were making their preparations to host the 1919 event.

With improvements to aircraft it was decided to lengthen the race, which was set to be run on 10 September 1919. The triangular circuit laid out over the sea off Bournemouth. This was a traditional seaside resort and provided a natural amphitheatre for the event. The course measured 20 nautical miles for each of the ten laps called for. For this special occasion the Royal Aero Club had obtained the loan of the steam yacht *Ombra*, of 350 tons, to accommodate their members. The plan was that the yacht should act as a committee boat and would act as outer marker of the official starting and finishing point of the race which was Bournemouth Pier.

Prior to the race, on Wednesday 3 September, there were to be eliminating trials for the British entrants to sort out the three machines which would represent Britain and there would be seaworthiness trials for all machines as part of the contest proper.

The course is shown in the map. It will be seen that the aircraft took off from Bournemouth, flew to a marker boat anchored in Swanage Bay, leaving Studland Bay to starboard and turned north-east to round a marker boat anchored off Hengistbury Head, near Christchurch, before turning back to Bournemouth. The circuit, as already mentioned, measured 20 nm, the first leg being 6 nm, the second leg from Swanage Bay to Christchurch 9 nm, and the final leg along the coast from Hengistbury Head to Bournemouth, 5 nm.

As at Monaco the machines were required to make two 'landings' and take-offs at set points. This alighting and take-off area was originally meant to have been between Boscombe and Bournemouth piers but it was later decided that the distance between them was too short and two marker boats were provided instead. Both touchdowns were to be on the first lap.

The Entries

As defender of the Coupe Schneider, it was logical that Tom Sopwith should go to some lengths to prepare a suitable and special seaplane for the event. The Sopwith Schneider was an entirely new design powered by the sensational new, Fedden-designed, Cosmos Jupiter radial engine of 450 hp. Being a Sopwith of the period,

The Sopwith Schneider of 1919: fuselage and Cosmos Jupiter 450 hp engine. The fuel (upper) and oil (lower) tanks are between the engine and the cockpit. (*Flight*)

it was naturally a single-bay biplane, descendant of a line of wartime Sopwith fighters, which in their turn stemmed from the little Tabloid of 1914. The Sopwith scaled 2,200 lb ready to fly, a horsepower-to-weight ratio of 0.51, which was so impressive at the time that the correspondent of one of the most respected British aviation journals was of the opinion that the Sopwith Schneider was so powerful that it could not help climbing if full power were used! In fact, there were equally powerful machines in the entry, but none with such a good power-to-weight ratio. The legendary Harry Hawker, Sopwith's great friend and chief test pilot, was a natural choice as pilot for the machine. Earlier that year he had been involved in a transatlantic adventure when his Sunbeam-engined Sopwith Atlantic had come down in the middle of that ocean. He had been picked up by the coaster *Mary* which was not equipped with radio. His reappearance, after being missing for two weeks, had made him and his companion front page news and national heroes. Naturally he had a say in the design of the Sopwith Schneider, just as he had in the Tabloid. Undoubtedly the goodwill and support of the whole British public and the whole weight of the national press would be behind this particular pilot and machine.

A less newsworthy entry but none the less significant was that from Supermarine of Woolston, Southampton. Founded by that great aviation character, yacht-broker, Noel Pemberton-Billing in 1913 and financed by Gerald Delves-Broughton, Pemberton-Billing Ltd had been mainly sub-contractors during the War despite a number of offerings from their own design office. However, towards the end of the conflict they had been responsible for some outstanding high-speed, single-seat, flying-boat fighters which had not been taken up because of the proximity of peace.

Pemberton-Billing became a Member of Parliament in 1916 and ceased to have any connection with the company he had founded, control passing into the hands of Delves-Broughton, C. Cecil Dominy and Scott-Paine. At this juncture the name was changed to Supermarine, which was the telegraphic address coined by Pemberton-Billing. The company was destined to become one of the most important British constructors of flying-boats between the wars before moving on to build fighter aircraft.

Pemberton-Billing had hired red-headed Hubert Scott-Paine – later to become nicknamed 'Red Hot' because of his hair colour – as his manager and general factotum. Scott-Paine was destined to run the company after Pemberton-Billing took to politics. Incidentally, lest it be thought that he was a draft-dodging politician it should be recorded that as a Lieutenant in the RNAS he had organised the first successful bombing raid of the War in November 1914 when he led a flight of four Avro 504s to attack the Zeppelin hangars at Friedrichshafen.

re-engined with one of the sensational new Lion engines designed by A.F. Rowledge for Napier. It was christened the Sea Lion in honour of the occasion. It was to be flown by Squadron Commander Basil D. Hobbs, Supermarine's chief test pilot, a superb airman with an impressive war record.

Fairey Aviation's contribution to the Schneider proceedings was a modified version of their heavy-weather Fairey III reconnaissance machine cut down for racing. Charles Richard Fairey, founder of the company bearing his name, had started in aviation as a successful model aircraft builder, later going on to manage the Blair Atholl syndicate set up to build John William Dunne's inherently stable monoplane. He joined Short Bros as works manager in 1913 and founded the Fairey Aviation Co. Ltd in 1916, making use of the experience gained at Short's to build floatplanes, of which the very successful Fairey III was one of the first.

Fairey had used as the basis for their entry the actual prototype Fairey III floatplane, N.10, which had seen service with the Royal Naval Air Service and had been bought back from a disposal sale after the cessation of

The Supermarine Sea Lion, with a 450 hp Napier Lion engine driving a pusher propeller, is towed away from the slipway at Woolston by the launch *Tiddleywinks*. (*Flight*)

Aircraft and their pilots and mechanics had to share the beach with the enthusiastic crowd of spectators. (*Ralph Barker*)

A wartime acquisition at Woolston was one Reginald Joseph Mitchell, a 22-year-old printer's son from Stoke-on-Trent who joined the company as a draughtsman in 1917. In 1919 he had replaced James Hargreaves, designer of the Sea Baby fighter flying-boat, from which the Sea Lion entered for the Coupe Maritime was derived. Mitchell's new appointment was coincident with a general post-war reorganisation at Supermarine, in the course of which additional finance was provided by Squadron Commander James Bird, who joined the company as a director at the same time.

Supermarine's entry was a developed version of one of their wartime Sea Baby flying-boat fighter prototypes

hostilities. Normally powered by a Rolls-Royce Eagle of 375 bhp, it was yet another British entry to be re-engined with one of Napier's new broad-arrow, twelve-cylinder Lions. The machine was prepared in Fairey's works at Hamble, practically on the spot from which the maiden flight of Pixton's little Sopwith Tabloid floatplane had been made and would be flown by the firm's test pilot, an old friend of Fairey's, ex-Cambridge graduate Colonel Vincent Nicholl, DSO.

Finally there was a first, and last, entry from Avro. Alliott Verdon Roe was one of the great British pioneers and undoubtedly the first Englishman to take off and fly a powered aircraft in the UK, as distinct from Samuel

The Avro 539A during assembly. This was selected as the reserve aircraft for the British team. (*Flight*)

Franklin Cody, who was an American citizen. A quiet man of enormous determination, A.V. Roe built a number of prototypes leading up to the immortal 504 of 1913, which was in service throughout World War One as first a bomber/reconnaissance machine and from 1915 as a trainer, in which role it persisted with the RAF until 1924. After that it gained a second lease of life as a joyriding mount, a role in which it served until World War Two.

The Avro entry for the Bournemouth event was the little Avro 539, the company's first racer, hurriedly designed and built as a seaplane expressly for this event. It was the smallest aeroplane of conventional construction that could be designed round the six-cylinder 240 hp Siddeley Puma engine. H.A. Hamersley had been nominated as pilot.

Naturally France was anxious to regain the Cup. To this end two Nieuport-Delage 29 biplanes, powered by the new 300 hp Hispano-Suiza Modèle 42 engines had been prepared. One of these was based on the Type 29-C-1 racer but with slightly larger-span wings and mounted on long floats to avoid the need for a tail float, this was allocated to Jean Casale. The second machine was similar to the 29G used in the post-war seaplane

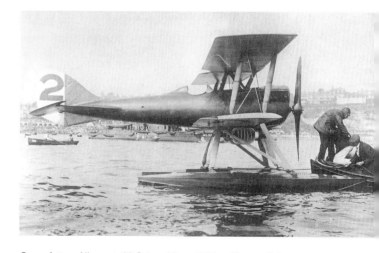

One of two Nieuport 29-C-1s with a 300 hp Hispano-Suiza engine. Unfortunately one crashed during an attempt to alight on the Medina River off Cowes at the end of the positioning flight from France for the 1919 event. (*Musée de l'Air*)

contests at Monaco and was altogether heavier and slower. It was most likely to shine if the weather on race day turned foul. The pilot was to be Lieutenant Malard.

Sadi Lecointe's SPAD-Herbemont with a 340 hp Hispano-Suiza engine. Following damage during the 1919 preliminaries it was eliminated. (*Flight*)

Sergeant Guido Janello's Savoia S.13 with a 250 hp Isotta-Fraschini engine. Although it flew the 1919 course most successfully for eleven laps it was disqualified because Janello had failed to round the Swanage course marker boat correctly. (*SIAI-Marchetti*)

The Nieuports were backed up by a SPAD-Herbemont. This descendant of the Deperdussins – so called because Herbemont, the successor to Béchereau, was the designer – was in much the same idiom as the Nieuport, but with the essential difference that it was designed as a two-seater but with the rear cockpit faired in for this race. It featured the same wooden monocoque fuselage construction and the same 300 hp V-8 Hispano-Suiza Modèle 42 engine which were the hallmarks of high-performance French machines of the era. It was also a single-bay biplane sitting with its tail out of the water and supported on two floats. Other differences were that the radiator, instead of being slung beneath the wings like the Lamblin design of the Nieuport, was of conventional construction, mounted ahead of the engine behind the propeller, like that of the Avro, but was elliptical to match the fuselage cross-section and of more elegant appearance than the boxy, British radiator. It was to be flown by the great French racing pilot Sadi Lecointe.

For the first time there came a challenge from Italy. Spurred on by the French, Italy had developed a considerable aviation industry during the War. Their single entry was a Savoia S.13 biplane flying-boat with clipped wings and a six-cylinder, 250 hp Isotta-Fraschini engine. The company's test pilot, Sergeant Guido Janello, a very experienced racing pilot, was nominated to fly it in the race. This lone, but most welcome, Italian entry came from a company whose name was destined to be one of the most illustrious in the annals of Italian aviation.

Societa Idrovolanti Alta Italia (SIAI) and its twin organisation, Savoia, headed by Umberto Savoia, had been set up in the Varese area of Italy by an international aviation entrepreneur, D. Lorenzo Santoni, who was involved in a number of projects in France and the UK. The object at that time was to build wartime fighters under licence. In England Santoni used the British Christian name of Lawrence when he started the British Deperdussin Syndicate in London before World War

One. Macchi had been formed at the same time as SIAI and Savoia with much the same aims. It had not taken the intensely creative Italians long to start initiating and building their own designs with the emphasis on flying-boats for use on the Italian lakes. Savoia's designer was the gifted Rafael Conflienti, whose trademark was the hollow-bottomed hull which was such a notable feature of the Savoia 'boats.

Preliminaries

For the British race organisers, the proceedings, as distinct from the preparation work carried out by firms entering aircraft, began on 3 September with the usual national eliminating trials to decide which of the four British entrants should represent their country. Cowes, in the Isle of Wight was the venue but on the appointed day fate took a hand and the trials did not take place. The Sopwith Schneider damaged a float just prior to the trials and could not take part. The Avro suffered a similar mishap, hitting floating debris and damaging one float very badly, so that she had to be towed back into Cowes. The trials were therefore cancelled although the Supermarine Sea Lion and the Fairey III were ready to show their performance.

So far as the race committee was concerned the choice really lay between the Supermarine Sea Lion and the Avro Puma. They were content that the Fairey III and the Sopwith Schneider should go ahead without eliminating trials to represent Britain. A further trial was therefore arranged for Monday 8 September between the Sea Lion and a much modified Avro 539 Puma. These tests showed that the Avro was marginally faster than the Sea Lion, even though the latter had been fitted with a more suitable propeller. However, the Sea Lion was the better seaboat, showing up well on take-offs and alightings. On this score it was decided that it should represent Britain and be the third member of the team. The Avro was nominated reserve aircraft and as a sop, and to give the Avro Company a bit of publicity on race day, Hamersley was given the job of high-speed course marshal.

Meanwhile, the French had been having their problems. The first two Nieuports prepared for the race had been lost in alighting accidents on the Seine – this waterway was obviously as full of rubbish as the Solent – and two replacement machines had been prepared for Casale and Malard.

On Sunday 7 September, Casale set off to fly his machine from Paris to Cowes. On arriving at Cowes, he decided that the seas in the Solent were running too high for his machine and elected to set it down in the mouth of the Medina River, opposite Cowes. Unfortunately, the tide carried him onto one of the fairway buoys, damaging both the floats and causing the machine to tip on its nose. Casale was picked up by launch, none the worse for wear except for a ducking. His machine was salvaged and moved smartly into Saunders' yard for emergency repairs.

With barely 48 hours to go before the race this was an emergency effort and while Saunders' men worked through the night to build new wings, the French mechanics stripped the aircraft and fitted a new engine and floats sent post-haste from the factory in France.

Malard had left Paris early on Monday the 8th with the intention of following in Casale's footsteps to Cowes via Dieppe. But when the evening came he had still not appeared at Cowes. It was thought that he might have put in at Le Havre with engine trouble, but enquiries revealed that he was not there. The race committee approached the Admiralty to set up a sea search but while the inevitable attempts to cut red tape went on a report came through that Malard had been picked up in mid-Channel after clinging to his machine for almost 24 hours. It was lucky for him that weather conditions were good enough for him to stay afloat for so long.

The SPAD company, on the other hand, played safe and bought their machine by steamer under the watchful eye of Herbemont and erected and rigged it in Sammy Saunders' shop in Cowes. After preliminary trials and having seen the Sopwith flying, Herbemont decided that the speed of the SPAD might be improved a little by reducing the span of the very adaptable upper mainplane of this machine. This decision was made the day before race day and involved mechanics in all-night work in Saunders' hospital yard.

The Race

Wednesday 10 September at Bournemouth dawned with one of those sea mists which is such a characteristic of British coastal waters. Visibility was so bad that the end of the pier was invisible from the shore. The only activity was a few boatmen scrubbing their boats on an otherwise deserted beach. Local experts reckoned that the fog would burn off by eleven o'clock. They were right, but not for long. Urged on by a slight breeze, the mist dispersed and briefly there was visibility of several miles along the coast to Hengistbury Head, nominally

the Christchurch turn, the eastern turning point along the coast.

There was little to see apart from some nautical activity where the warships HMS *Barham* and HMS *Malaya*, moored in the Solent, were generating ship-to-shore traffic and various Royal Navy torpedo boats were cruising around preparatory to policing the course. However, shortly after eleven o'clock the sky became alive with the sound of an aircraft engine. This first arrival was Hubert Scott-Paine and his pilot in one of the big Supermarine Channel boats which were already familiar to the populace through their pleasure-flying off Bournemouth beach, an activity intended to boost the ailing post-war finances of Supermarine. It alighted, made fast to a mooring buoy near Squadron Commander Bird's launch, *Tiddleywinks*, and disgorged Scott-Paine, R.J. Mitchell and a Supermarine engineer.

Next to arrive was the yacht *Ombra*, which had picked her way across the Solent from Cowes and anchored off the pier, ready to act as committee boat and as a restaurant for 170 members of the Royal Aero Club who had paid £2 per head to take lunch and tea on board. They were to join her later from a special Royal Aero Club enclosure on the pier.

As the weather cleared, bathers appeared in the shallow water of the beach, and rowing boats, manned by holidaymakers, started to meander into the seaplane alighting area. It was past twelve o'clock before another aircraft engine was heard. This time it was the smooth roar of the Napier Lion in Lieutenant-Colonel Vincent Nicholl's Fairey III. Even in racing trim, with its short wings it seemed to stagger past the pier, looking so slow that *Flight* magazine commented that Richard Fairey must have been praying for a gale so that the machine could take advantage of its seaworthiness. Nicholl, who was Fairey's test pilot and a director of the company, turned round the marker buoy and flew over to Hengistbury to look at the weather before returning to alight and run up into a roped-off enclosure set up by Fairey's handling party on the beach.

At 12.20 pm the sound of two engines was heard and Lecointe in the SPAD and Janello in the Savoia flying-boat came racing by in loose formation, disappearing in the direction of Swanage before returning to alight among the bathers and rowing boats. Janello had a near miss with a rowing boat, swerving wildly to avoid an accident with one of the British holidaymakers. Like many of their ilk that day they seemed completely oblivious to the danger in which they were putting themselves and the airmen; not to mention the damage they could do to the precious racers.

The Savoia was taken in tow by launch and moved across to *Ombra* for a few words with the committee – no doubt checking the starting procedure – before being beached without any protection from the over-inquisitive crowd. Meanwhile the SPAD arrived from Cowes, alighted between the two piers and moored to one of the seaplane buoys normally used by the Supermarine Channel flying-boats.

The next to arrive was Hobbs in the Supermarine Sea

Squadron Leader B.D. Hobbs relaxes on the bow of his Supermarine Sea Lion, G-EALP. (*Flight*)

Lion from its base at Woolston. It was obviously very fast and, after overflying the pier, made off in the direction of Swanage to check the course. This left only two of the race machines to come; the Sopwith Schneider and Casale's Nieuport. However, the next machine to appear was Hamersley's Avro 539, which, in addition to its job as course marshal, had been nominated as reserve machine in case one of the other British entrants was unable to start or suffered a mishap. He alighted alongside *Ombra*, porpoising badly before coming to rest. At the time two-float seaplanes were still something of a rarity and comment was made on the fact that, while the machine handled quite well on the water, the tailfloat machines with water rudders, like the Fairey III could manoeuvre more surely and at a lower speed.

Meanwhile, Hobbs in the Supermarine had returned, put his machine down without fuss and moored off the pier. By this time the Savoia had been pulled away from the beach and the poking fingers of inquisitive spectators, and moored to a buoy along with the SPAD, the Avro and the Sea Lion. It was noticed that the SPAD was developing a list to port, obviously due to a leaking float. This was a bad sign with only an hour and a half to go before the race started. On the other hand the two missing British competitors were treating the whole

The SPAD-Herbemont moored off the beach at Bournemouth. For its time a very smooth profile and surface finish was achieved by the SPAD craftsmen. (*Musée de l'Air*)

affair with a *laissez-faire* more worthy of the Latin countries than phlegmatic Britain.

It was two o'clock, only half an hour before the start, before Hawker, in the Sopwith, arrived abreast the pier travelling at a great rate of knots; 165 mph was the estimate. He put down perfectly on the smooth surface and taxied onto the beach west of the pier. There remained only the Nieuport to come from Cowes, where Sammy Saunders' men and her French ground crew had been working non-stop to get her ready for the race.

Just before 2.30 pm Vincent Nicholl in the Fairey III, who had won the draw for first to start, was pushed off from the beach and taxied over to the starting line, ready for the starting procedure. However, a signal went out that the race was postponed temporarily. There was good reason for this. The weather had clamped down again off Swanage and Hengistbury and the committee had decided to hold up the start in the hope of improved visibility later in the afternoon. This decision was just as well for the French because it was not until 2.50 pm that Casale arrived overhead in the short-wing machine, put down and moored to one of the buoys near the pier. Casale, in his leather helmet and goggles, wearing a short leather flying-coat over his shore clothes, was taken off by launch to report to *Ombra*.

Meanwhile Hobbs sat in his shirt sleeves, dangling his legs over the bows of the Supermarine, wearing a most unnautical trilby hat. In common with the other pilots he took a very cynical view of the whole proceedings, simply waiting to see which way the race committee would turn next. Aboard *Ombra*, this august body seemed to be losing its grip on the conduct of the race and was in a flurry of indecision as to whether or not to cancel and try again another day. To be fair to them a postponement would bring in its wake the difficulty of rearranging all the major and minor details of a race taking place over hundreds of square miles of sea. The sadness was that no contingency plans seemed to exist.

Meanwhile, as the weather deteriorated, so did the watertightness of the SPAD and Nieuport floats. The leak in the SPAD floats reported earlier had now become so acute that the machine had been towed over to the beach for hurried repairs by the SPAD fitters, accompanied by a fit of Gallic temperament from Herbemont. The Nieuport was in similar trouble and had also been beached for hurried repairs. Both crews were grateful when a rumour from the *Ombra* suggested that the start had been postponed until six o'clock. They reckoned to be able to make a decent repair by then and planned their work accordingly. They had not reckoned with the race committee, whose decisions were geared tightly to the weather. So, when, about four o'clock, the fog quite unexpectedly started to drift away and blue sky could be seen overhead, a hasty signal was sent round by launch that the race would start in fifteen minutes' time; hardly enough time to start engines, let alone warm them up carefully. This decision was despite the fact that there had been no report on conditions in Swanage Bay and was made in the face of knowledgeable local opinion from yachtsmen that the shift in the weather was not only temporary but local to Bournemouth.

Someone on the committee must have realised the technical impossibility of starting at such very short notice. In a few minutes another launch was sent round to increase the fifteen minutes to half an hour.

Meanwhile, in this atmosphere of uncertainty the Napier Lion in the Fairey III was fired up and the aircraft taxied over to *Ombra*, ready to start.

At this point let us take a look at the race-starting procedure, which was not only unusual but seems not to have been properly explained to the competitors! The drill was that a red flag would be raised five minutes before each aircraft was due to start. When four minutes and forty-five seconds of this time had elapsed the flag would be dipped preparatory to being raised again, fifteen seconds later, as a starting signal. Vincent Nicholl, who had been hurriedly poured into his aeroplane, was obviously uncertain just how long the red flag had been raised. In any case, being accustomed to more orthodox starting signals, he opened his throttle as soon as he saw the flag dip, accelerated the Fairey across the line and swung off low above the sea in the direction of Swanage.

Casale's Nieuport was number two in starting order but, to the despair of the ground crew and Sammy Saunders, who had worked themselves into the ground over the past thirty-six hours, replacing the engine and floats and rebuilding the wings, the aircraft was not ready. André Herbemont, in tears of frustration, also withdrew his SPAD. Sadly they had to declare themselves non-starters. Hawker's Sopwith was meant to be the first away but Hawker was still sitting on the beach and his engine had not even been started. Rumour had it that he refused to start until the very last moment because his plugs would foul up if he had to taxi around with the engine running slowly. Another body of opinion reckoned that he had a leak in one of the floats and they would fill up if the Sopwith had to float on the water for any length of time.

In this whole atmosphere of uncertainty and tension, with no communication between the committee boats and the beach executive launch (it was before the days of walkie-talkie or short-wave radio), Hobbs, in the Supermarine, cruised up to the starting line and took off without any signal at all, having to jink round some rowing boats in the process. By this time the Sopwith mechanics had fired up the Cosmos Jupiter engine of Hawker's machine and he also set off in the direction of the start line.

Once again there was indecision in the starting launch, the flag being hesitatingly raised and then lowered again. Hawker, never patient with officialdom, could stand it no longer, opened the throttle and took off in the direction of Swanage. While all this was going on the Isotta-Fraschini engine of the Savoia had been started up and Janello had quietly got it into position east of the starting line ready for take-off. This time the starting procedure was carried out correctly, Santoni and Janello having gone to the trouble to find out what it was. Fifteen seconds before the appointed starting time the flag was dipped, raised, timekeepers Ebblewhite and Reynolds clicked their watches and Janello opened the throttle to make the only correct start of the lot.

It now remained to wait for the aircraft to come round on their first lap. Quite suddenly and almost on

Janello's Savoia S.13 races along the Bournemouth foreshore. (*Musée de l'Air*)

The Supermarine Sea Lion being towed off Woolston by the launch *Tiddleywinks*. (*Flight*)

time the Fairey appeared but instead of coming from the direction of Hengistbury, it appeared from inland, set down on the water and taxied to the beach. Nicholl had decided to 'chuck it in', convinced that the other competitors would do likewise when they saw the conditions in Swanage Bay. There the fog was dense and more than 100 feet above the surface, filling the bay like a bowl of milk. In searching blindly for the marker boat, he had had a near miss with another aircraft. This obviously decided him that if he was going to be an old airman he must forthwith cease to be a bold one.

The airmanship displayed by these pilots should not be deprecated. They had no gyroscopic instruments with which to let down into the fog. All they had were their airspeed indicators, read in conjunction with primitive cross levels backed up by information from the seats of their pants. Hobbs, searching for the marker boat, twice let down into Swanage Bay, taking his bearings from the topography of the cliffs which stood just proud of the seamist. In his first venture into the mist, where he found visibility only a few yards, he narrowly avoided collision with the Fairey, which was on the same errand. Surfacing above the mist for a few moments, he got his bearings again and descended as near to the sea as he dared, hoping that the fog might be less dense close to the sea. The only result was that he became thoroughly disorientated. Realising that Swanage Bay is a very finite area when you are dashing around it at 120 knots with a spinning compass, and that the boundaries of that area were very solid cliffs, he decided to put down and work out his position when his compass settled.

Once on the surface of the sea, there was, of course, no visibility and therefore no landmarks to get a bearing on. However, he was able to take off on a compass-heading for Bournemouth. It was not his day. On take-off there was a terrific thump as the machine hit a large piece of flotsam. The trandling of the machine told him that the damage done in no way impaired the flying qualities of the boat but he was left in great doubt about its seaworthiness.

However, once above the fog he was able to satisfy

himself that he had rounded the mark, using the Purbeck Hills as a reference. Flying back to Hengistbury Head on a compass bearing, he rounded the marker boat there, which was well in the clear, and proceeded to make the first of his compulsory 'landings' alongside the motor launch marking the compulsory alighting area east of Boscombe pier.

It was fortunate for Hobbs that the motor launch was there. The accident in Swanage Bay had torn a great hole in both the outer and inner skins of the bottom of the hull. The moment he put down the machine filled up and began to sink nose first, throwing the pilot into the water. He was picked up almost immediately by the marker boat. A few minutes later Scott-Paine and the handling crew, who had rushed up in the launch *Tiddleywinks*, were able to secure the Sea Lion before it sank completely. They towed it into shallow water alongside Boscombe pier and, with the aid of tackle rigged from the pier, managed to get it onto an even keel and recover it when the tide went out.

While this drama was being enacted, Hawker, in the Sopwith, after trying one lap, had come to the same conclusion as Vincent Nicholl and retired. Thus the only competitor still going was Janello in the Savoia. He was lapping with annoying regularity after some excusable confusion in the first lap when, after making his two compulsory landings quite correctly, he saw all the other machines pulled up on the beach and was undecided whether or not the race had been abandoned. He decided that he might just as well finish the course and carried on, lapping with regularity in about 10 minutes, which surprised everyone, indicating as it did, an average speed of 120 knots, which Tom Sopwith and other informed observers reckoned to be far beyond the capabilities of the Savoia.

It was well into evening and the sun was beginning to set below the Dorset skyline when, an hour and three-quarters after take-off, Janello crossed the line, put down and taxied back to *Ombra*. Lorenzo Santoni immediately went over to the flying-boat in his launch and instructed the pilot to make one more lap just to be

The TSY *Ombra* anchored off Bournemouth pier to mark the start/finish line of the 1919 course. Janello's Savoia S.13 passed overhead on one of its eleven laps of the course. (*Flight*)

sure. No doubt he had in mind the débâcle of Prévost in the 1913 race and Pixton's extra lap in 1914. Unhappily, Janello was almost out of fuel and doubted whether he would be able to make another lap. Nor was there fuel on board the launch for him to take on. Despite protestations he disappeared from view and was not seen for some time until a search party discovered him sitting in the middle of the bay with a dry tank.

While this little drama was taking place the race committee had been able to talk to the crew of the marker boat from Swanage Bay. They reported that they had not seen the Savoia once during the race. It became fairly obvious that Janello, in good faith, had been rounding the wrong marker boat. For reasons best known to themselves, the organisers of this peculiarly British fiasco had stationed the reserve marker boat in Studland Bay instead of placing it at Bournemouth, where it would have been equally well located to replace the Hengistbury Head or Swanage boats. Maybe the occupants simply wanted a better viewpoint for the race.

Whatever the reason, Janello's mistake is readily understood by any pilot. Topographically, both Studland Bay and Swanage look almost alike to an airman. Both are billhook-shaped with sandy beaches and both have high cliffs on the south side with what were then small villages nestling in a bight of the bay with roads running

east and west leading to them. In fact, judging by 1919 maps, they would have looked identical from the air, the only difference being that Swanage Bay is about three-quarters the area of Studland Bay. Janello's error in turning round the reserve marker boat instead of the official one was far more excusable than the committee's decision, if they were capable of making one that sad day, to place it where it was.

However well Janello had flown, the committee had no alternative but to declare the race void. In this decision they were later backed up by the FAI. But there was no doubt about the general feeling that the race should have been awarded to the Savoia. However, this was patently impossible under the regulations, despite the fact, strongly expressed in a series of letters from Santoni to the Royal Aero Club that Janello had rounded three properly identified markers on each lap. It was entirely the club's fault that one of these was not the correct one. To make up for this omission, to placate their wartime allies and to mark their admiration for the way Janello flew the race in bad conditions, it was eventually decided that the honour of staging the next event should go to Italy. It was the end of a sad incident which reflected no glory at all on the ability of the British to organise a major seaplane event. With hindsight the attractions of Bournemouth bay as a natural amphitheatre – it had crowded beaches and high cliffs to accommodate tens of thousands of spectators – were offset by the frequency of summer sea mists in this area. Provision should have been made to carry the organisation over to another day if the weather had clamped down, as it did. It was quite wrong to attempt to start the race in the prevailing conditions but one feels that the race committee was literally forced to do so because of the elaborate organisation, their commitment to the yacht *Ombra* and the elaborate luncheon arrangements for Royal Aero Club members. It was an error that they were not likely to make again.

Nor were the British entrants pleased about the outcome. If they could have flown the race fair-and-square against the Savoia, either the Sopwith or the Supermarine would have been more than a match for it, the race would have stayed in Britain and we would have been spared the situation in which the next two races became purely Italian national events.

One has to spare a lot of sympathy for the French competitors. The original intention seems to have been that the aircraft should spend some time on the beach to allow the public to have a close look at them and then move them out to moorings immediately prior to the race. Beaching them caused the floats to leak and precluded lying at moorings. So they had to stay on dry land until the last moment. One would have expected their hosts to provide some kind of back-up organisation, even if it was only to hold the public back and provide marine transportation to *Ombra* and Cowes. A postponement of the race would have given the French competitors an opportunity to get their machines sea and airworthy and made for a better contest. As it was, the French were eliminated by what amounted to an impromptu seaworthiness test.

The Aircraft

The Avro 539

This tiny machine, the smallest seaplane which could be built round a Siddeley-Deasy Puma engine, was rushed through the Avro works at Hamble and, in common with the Supermarine Sea Lion, was barely ready in time for the British preliminary trials on 3 September.

Designed by Roy Chadwick, the 539's construction followed the Avro practice of the time, the fuselage being based on a wire-braced, wooden lattice framework. A plywood turtle back over the rear fuselage followed the lines of the front cockpit cowling and engine cover which, in turn, took their form from the rounded top of the cowling, surrounding a gill-type radiator located, car-style, between the engine and propeller. The uncompromising profile of this radiator was reminiscent of that fitted to the immortal Avro Baby. The fuselage was metal-skinned right back to the aft cabane struts, the sides being well louvred to extract hot air from the engine compartment.

The unswept, wooden, fabric-covered wings, based on spindled wooden spars, were rigged without stagger and were relieved by elegant elliptical tips. Only the lower wings, which were separate structures, carried dihedral. The upper span was a mere 25 ft 6 in, with the lower wing measuring one foot less. Bracing was single-bay with inclined, wooden interplane struts and streamlined wire bracing. The short fuselage moment arm called for a relatively large tailplane with swept leading edge; it was complemented by a pretty, ovoid, wire-braced, fin and rudder. In profile this was not a pretty aeroplane, mainly due to the lumpy power plant, but in plan view it was not unattractive.

Adoption of the inefficient and not entirely reliable Siddeley Puma engine was probably conditioned by cost as much as by any other factor, there being plenty of these engines on the war-surplus market. Although of light alloy construction it was surprisingly bulky and heavy for its output of 250 bhp, to the extent that it had to be installed with the valve cover protruding through the top of the engine cover. The fact that its power-to-weight ratio, at 2.5 lb per horsepower, was the worst of any of the engines in the race was made up for by Chadwick, whose compact, lightweight airframe offset this handicap to the extent that the 539's power loading was about the same as that of the Nieuport.

The long, twin pontoons were quite conventional box-section affairs, with punt bows and a single step, two-thirds of the length from the bow. Set at a track of 7¼ ft, they were supported on a wire-braced chassis with streamlined steel-tube struts.

Bearing civil registration G-EALG, the 539 first flew, piloted by Captain H. A. Hamersley, on 29 August 1919, four days before the eliminating trials at Cowes on 3 September. Hamersley reported severe yawing during the short flight. Further flights were made before the little Avro – it is said to have been called the Falcon by the works – was flown over to Cowes for the team selection trial. However, during the first take-off a float struck one of the myriad of floating objects which abounded in the Solent and the trials had to be postponed until the 8th. This provided a heaven-sent opportunity to do something about the handling, so while repairs to the floats were under way the very pretty parabolic fin and rudder on the original version were enlarged to improve directional control. This consisted of adding a horn-balance to the rudder and building-on a huge dorsal fin extending almost to the cockpit. This fin was enormous, large enough to have the word Avro emblazoned on it in large letters. The original fin and rudder area were quoted by the factory as 4 sq ft and 5¼ sq ft respectively. With this modification, the fin area was at least trebled and the rudder area increased by 25 per cent.

As mentioned elsewhere, although the 539 proved fractionally faster than the Sea Lion in the match the committee decided that, as the better seaboat, the Sea Lion should become the third member of the team.

The Fairey III Schneider 1919

The Fairey Aviation Company's contribution to the proceedings was a version of the heavy-weather Fairey III carrier-borne reconnaissance machine, cut down for racing. In keeping with the mood of the times a new machine was not contemplated. Instead Fairey bought back from the Admiralty a prototype, usually referred to, affectionately and somewhat confusingly, as N.10 although it had been built to Admiralty specification N.2(a) and bore the constructor's number F.128. Delivered to the Admiralty in late 1917, it was the subject of considerable experimental use on floats and wheels at the Isle of Grain test establishment before being returned to its makers when war finished.

Charles Richard Fairey, founder of the company, had started in aviation as a model-maker, later going on to manage the Blair Atholl syndicate, before joining Short Bros as works manager in 1913. He founded the Fairey Aviation Co. Ltd in 1915, making use of the experienced gained at Short's to start a line of seaplane designs, of which the Fairey III was one of the earliest. It had quickly come to be recognised as one of the best service seaplanes of its day. One of its most significant features was its full-span, trailing edge flaps, referred to in those days as a variable-camber wing.

There was little that was revolutionary about the IIIF except for its homely but sound aerodynamics. The structural materials were the usual spruce and ash, the fuselage being the lattice girder type with wire bracing and steel fittings, while the 46 ft span two-spar mainplanes of the service type were strut-and-wire-braced in two-bay configuration. Generous ailerons were fitted to the upper mainplane while full-span flaps, hinged on the rear spars, occupied the trailing edges of the lower wings. At the time this was billed as the Fairey variable-camber wing. N.10's original power unit had been a twelve-cylinder Sunbeam Maori giving 260 bhp and driving a tractor propeller.

For the Schneider race the old girl was given a thorough rebuild and the airframe modified to take one of the newly announced Napier Lion engines. This would provide more power and speed while the experience gained would stand Fairey's in good stead for the future. In addition, again with speed in mind, two sets of wings were built and tried, one pair being the full-span, 46 ft, standard wing and the other a pair with a span of 28 ft, which reduced the area from 460 sq ft to 270 sq ft. This small-span set was rigged with a single pair of struts per side.

The water gear was the standard Service type with square-section, single-step plywood floats mounted on a six-leg chassis with streamline section struts. The large tail float, faired into the fuselage, provided extra fin area aft and incorporated a water rudder connected to the air rudder by a torque tube. Beauty of line was not the outstanding characteristic of the Fairey III, especially the empennage, which suffered from an extraordinarily ugly fin-and-rudder arrangement – the latter could have been taken for a barn door – with a tail-float faired into the fuselage, complete with water rudder. An uninformed bystander might have been forgiven the impression that the rear end of the aeroplane was built from the leftovers in some hangar. The Fairey III was in fact the result of much experience of heavy weather conditions when serving with the Royal Air Force seaplane units and its choice as a foul-weather standby was a wise one.

Work on the machine was carried out at Fairey's works at Hamble, where their moulded wooden dinghies were made after World War Two, and was practically on the spot from which the disastrous first flight of Pixton's little Sopwith Tabloid floatplane had been made. Lieutenant-Colonel Vincent Nicholl DSO, Fairey's test pilot and a director of the company, who had flown the old girl on her delivery flight to the Navy two years earlier, made the maiden flight of N.10.

The Sopwith Schneider

Designed by Herbert Smith, whose chief draughtsman was Wilfred George Carter, the Sopwith entry for the Coupe Maritime was an entirely new machine, and, being a Sopwith of the period, it was naturally a single-bay biplane, descendant of an illustrious line of wartime Sopwith fighters, which in their turn emanated from the little Tabloid of 1914.

The layout of the fuselage was conditioned by Sopwith's decision to use Roy Fedden's brilliant new Cosmos Jupiter 450 hp radial engine. To be visually and aerodynamically satisfactory this demanded a circular-section structure which was achieved by superimposing ply formers and stringers on the traditional, Sopwith rectangular, lattice girder frame. The engine was mounted on a metal-faced ply bulkhead with specially shaped fuel and oil tanks located forward of the cockpit on top of and on the port side of the main structure inside the circular fairing. The engine cowling followed the circular fuselage form, leaving only the cylinder heads protruding, and was finished off by a large-diameter propeller spinner. Typical of the attention to detail were the long fairings behind each cylinder head. The tanks and ancillaries were covered by formed metal panels which extended back to the forward cockpit bulkhead.

Wide-chord wooden struts separated the uncompromisingly rectangular, 24 ft mainplanes which were rigged with 2.5 inches of stagger. Ailerons were provided on both wings and coupled with the RAF section wire which was used throughout the rigging. Small-section cabane struts supported the upper wing centre section. Having a relatively heavy engine to deal with, Smith and Carter gave the fuselage a very short forward moment arm – the cylinders of the engine were virtually in line with the wing leading edges – and a long rear fuselage to balance it. This would seem to account for the remarkably small fin and rudder, having a total area of only 9 sq ft. In contrast the tailplane and elevator area totalled 23 sq ft of which 9.75 sq ft was accounted for by the control surfaces.

The Sopwith Schneider's flotation gear consisted of 13 ft, box-section, stepless wooden floats and watertight bulkheads. They were mounted on streamlined wooden legs braced with streamlined wire and wooden interfloat struts. The general shape of the floats was similar to those conceived by Burgoyne for the 1914 machine, but they were longer, 13 ft overall, each with a beam of 2 ft, and had vee-bottoms to improve directional stability when taking off and alighting.

The Sea Lion I 1919 G-EALP

During the War, Supermarine, apart from building other people's floatplane designs, had built a number of prototype flying-boats to Air Department specifications. The resident designer was F.J. Hargreaves, assisted latterly by R.J. Mitchell. One of these projects, to Air Department specification N.1B, was the Sea Baby, one of the very few single-seater fighter flying-boats to be ordered by the British government. Before peace intervened, causing all military contracts to be cancelled, one prototype, N.59, had been flown and N.60, with a number of modifications, had been started on out of an order for three. These little aquatic fighters attracted a great deal of attention by reason of the fact that their performance and manoeuvrability was almost equivalent to that of a landplane fighter of equivalent power.

The Sea Baby was an unequal-span, single-bay, pusher biplane with monocoque hull, high-mounted tailplane and deep, narrow, wingtip floats faired into the lower mainplane. N.59 was powered by a 200 hp Hispano-Suiza engine while N.60 was intended to have a Sunbeam Arab. There were useful identifying differences in the hydrodynamic design; N.59 featured an experimental, prognathous, anti-spray bow to its planing surfaces and had wingtip floats with the chines brought up to the tops of the curved stem posts. The planing surfaces on the projected N.60, on the other hand, were smoothly faired into a cigar-shaped nose, while the wingtip floats had flatter bottoms with chines originating low down on vertical stem posts.

With the advent of peace all wartime contracts ceased. On the principle of beating swords into ploughshares Scott-Paine, looking round for a market for the Baby design, conceived the idea that it might be saleable as a civilian sporting machine, and for this purpose, bought back N.59 from the Air Ministry and had it converted into a lower-powered sporting aircraft designated the Sea King. To make this conversion Hargreaves increased the Baby's wing area by extending the span by 5 ft to 35 ft 6 in, the lower mainplane being extended in proportion. The new, lower wings had the ailerons removed and larger, unbalanced control surface ailerons were fitted to the upper mainplane, which had a small cut-out in the trailing edge to clear the pusher propeller. The wooden, fabric-covered, two-spar wings were constructed as four panels attached to a wide centre section. Total mainplane area was quoted as 339 sq ft for an all-up weight of 2,500 lb. It was rigged as a single-bay biplane with splayed, wooden interplane struts faired into the wings with plain cuff fairings. A notable feature of the completed machine which was carried over to subsequent Sea Kings and Lions was the use of an engine mounting independent of the wing structure but based on the lower strong points of the centre-section struts.

The tailplane of the Baby (carried over to the Sea King I) was set above the fin and rudder with an air gap in between and, supported on an untidy arrangement of three struts per side, had nicely radiused tips. To offset thrust from the high-mounted engine it was given a pronounced reverse camber. A small, rectangular extension of the inadequate-looking rudder protruded downwards to act as a water rudder. An unusual feature of the Baby and the Sea King I was a tiny supplementary fin mounted in the middle of the upper surface of the tailplane; it just had to be an afterthought.

The circular-section, monocoque hull of the Baby was a typical Linton Hope-type, 26.3 ft overall, built up from wide, thin (about $1/16$ in), Honduras mahogany planks superimposed on closely spaced, $1\frac{1}{8}$ in square-section elm ribs. The edges of the planks were butted, carvel-fashion and attached to $1\frac{1}{2} \times 1\frac{1}{2}$ in stringers running the full length of the hull by thousands of tiny brass woodscrews. The end result was a beautifully strong but flexible cigar-shaped structure to which the planked planing surfaces were attached to give a double-bottomed construction. This second bottom was so carefully faired into the main monocoque that the method of construction was not at all apparent. When complete the structure was covered with madapolam, doped in place, dope-finished and then treated with a special varnish. It was an enormously labour-intensive way of building a hull, which relied on the huge reserve of cheap, skilled yacht-building labour then available in the Solent area.

The engine fitted to the Sea King was the less powerful 160 hp Beardmore, which, in combination with the increased wing area, suggests, to the writer at least, that Scott-Paine had civilian aspirations for this machine. However, a Sunbeam Arab was tried as an alternative power plant. 'Red Hot' liked to keep his options open.

Although he was destined to leave Supermarine in 1919, Hargreaves was still responsible for design although Mitchell was becoming increasingly influential and would replace him within a few months. Their modifications to the Sea King I airframe to convert it into the

Sea Lion consisted mainly of redesigning the upper mainplane with reduced span, increasing the chord by 8 in to 6 ft and giving it enlarged, reverse-tapered, horn-balanced ailerons. At the same time the rudder was enlarged by extending it above the tailplane in the form of a horn-balance to match the ailerons. The fin was also enlarged and faired into the tailplane to abolish the air gap. A minor modification was to the cockpit coamings, which were extended inboard to reduce the opening.

The Napier Lion engine was mounted tight up against the upper wing, to permit the use of the largest possible two-bladed propeller and was supported on a new, N-strut pylon to transmit the increased thrust of the Lion. Cooling was provided by a handsome, oval radiator faired into the front of the slipper cowling. A characteristic Supermarine feature was the canvas-covered vertical spray deflectors, about 2 ft high, stretched between the lower ends of the midships interplane struts.

Flight tests were delayed by non-delivery of the propeller due to a strike and the machine was only just ready the evening before the British trials scheduled for 3 September. Torrential rain and unserviceability of the Avro contestant caused these to be put off until 9 September. Basil Hobbs made the first flight on 5 September, when the propeller was found to be unsuitable. This was changed in time for the official trials, when the Sea Lion was chosen as the third member of the British team in preference to the Avro 539. After the race the damaged but repaired hull of the Sea Lion I was donated to the Imperial College in Kensington.

The SPAD-Herbemont XX Schneider

The SPAD-Herbemont – so called because André Herbemont, Béchereau's protégé and successor was the designer – was in much the same idiom as the Nieuport, being derived from a World War One fighter design, Herbemont's brilliant SPAD SXX two-seat combat machine of 1919. It had quickly established itself in air-racing by winning the 1919 French Prix Deutsch de la Meurthe race flown by Sadi Lecointe. The original design featured a swept-back, single-piece upper mainplane slightly longer than the straight, lower mainplane in which the ailerons were mounted.

For the Prix Meurthe the upper wing was shortened, qualifying the machine for the SXXbis designation. However the rear cockpit was left open and was occupied by Sadi Lecointe's ground engineer during the race. For the 1919 Schneider race the rear cockpit was faired in and the machine mounted on a pair of plywood floats borrowed from an earlier seaplane racer. A distinguishing feature of the float chassis was the cruciform forward float legs, supplemented, on the Bournemouth machine, by an extra set of four jury struts picking up with the outer edges of the floats.

The float chassis apart, this was an extremely clean design, employing the wooden monocoque fuselage construction and the 300 hp V-8 Modèle 42 Hispano-Suiza engine which were the two hallmarks of high-performance French machines of the era. The upper wing was supported on a rakish N-strut cabane while the single I-profile interplane struts were to provide inspiration for biplane designers for years to come. Another difference from the Nieuport was the radiator: instead of being slung beneath the wings like the Lamblin design of the Nieuport, it was of conventional construction, mounted ahead of the engine behind the propeller, like that of the Avro, but was of more elegant design than that boxy device. As well as being apparently cleaner, aerodynamically, than the Nieuport – or any of the British machines – it was lighter, scaling 1,130 kg against 1,220 for the Nieuport.

In common with the latter machine the SPAD SXXbis – the 'bis' seems to signify that the lower main-plane was shorter than that of the SXX and lacked the balanced ailerons – was utilised as a general-purpose record-breaker. To this end the upper wing was built in a variety of spans, a large-span wing for load carrying and when used as a two-seater for altitude tests – it set a number of height records – and a shorter-span wing for high-speed work, either on or off the floats. Moreover, Herbemont did not hesitate to tailor the upper wing to suit the occasion, as he demonstrated at Bournemouth when he amputated about two feet from each wingtip in an effort to gain enough speed to beat the Sopwith. In this role, with interchangeable wing, the SXXbis was intended for the annual seaplane competitions at Monaco, which continued to be held after the War. The rules of these contests called for a general purpose machine, and included a height competition, short take-off, and seaworthiness tests.

The Nieuport Schneider

In common with the SPAD SXX the Nieuports for the 1919 Schneider Race were adaptations of fighter designs, in this case Delage's latest single-seater 29-C-1. One of them was a short-span racer fitted with single-step floats long enough to support the aircraft without the need for a tail float; the other was more of a weightlifter with wide-span, two-bay wings mounted on short floats supplemented by the traditional, Nieuport, aluminium, torpedo-shaped tail-float. On the long-float machine a lower fin made up for loss of the side area of the rear float. Also in common with the lone SPAD, the Nieuports were powered by the latest French-built Hispano-Suiza Modèle 42, 300 hp engines, the best the French had available at that time to pitch against the British 450 hp Napier Lion.

Nieuport had their own way of building the then-popular, diagonally planked, monocoque fuselage. It wasn't a true monocoque in that the skin was superimposed on a framework of four circular, plywood bulkheads and sixteen spruce longerons. The two skins of tulip-wood planking were laid diagonally on top of this and tapered in thickness from 4 mm to 2 mm, making the skin 8 mm forward, tapering to 4 mm aft. On both machines the control surfaces were on the lower wings, those on the wide-span machine being extended at the tips to form aerodynamic balances.

The only part of the design reminiscent of the 1914 machines was the float chassis, which had wooden fore and aft bracing struts to the main legs and an M-strut configuration for transverse bracing, the point of the 'M' picking up with the float spreaders. The V-bottomed, single-step floats were beautifully made from mahogany planks with curved decks and sides and polished brass chine strips.

Great pains had been taken with streamlining the airframe. All the tail surfaces were carefully faired into the fuselage, as were the pilot's wind-deflector – it was opaque – and headrest.

The V-8 Modèle 42 Hispano engine was close-cowled with stub exhausts and drove a laminated wooden propeller. Cooling was by a pair of Lamblin lobster-pot type radiators, slung between the float struts.

The Nieuport and SPAD between them could truthfully be seen as the prototypes of the Schneider racing seaplane for the next six years. With their wooden monocoque fuselages, low frontal area V-engines and *'sans flotteur arrière'* configuration – not forgetting the I-profile interplane struts pioneered by Folland in 1914 – they were the forebears of the Curtiss seaplanes which dominated the Schneider Cup scene between 1923 and 1925. Indeed, the Curtiss engineers for whom the 1920 James Gordon Bennett race which was such a débâcle, cannot have failed to be impressed by the sleek Nieuport and SPAD racers. The only poor feature of the design of the 1919 Nieuport Schneider was the untidy float chassis, which was descended directly from that of the 1913 Nieuport seaplane, even to the fore and aft tie-rod between the spreaders, which united the inverted Warren girder transverse struts.

The Savoia S.13bis Corsa

In common with Macchi, Savoia made their own creations, specialising in flying-boats. Their designer was young Rafael Conflienti, whose trademark was the hollow-bottomed hull which was a notable feature of the Savoia 'boats.

The basis of their entry for the 1919 Schneider Trophy Race was their standard S.13 two-seater fighter reconnaissance machine. Of all-wood construction powered by an Isotta-Fraschini, six-in-line (not V-6 as the type name suggests), Asso tipo V-6 of 250 hp, it was a single-bay, unequal-span, biplane – tubular stays supporting the intersections of the wing-bracing wires made it look like a two-bay machine – with an upper wingspan of 11.08 m and a lower one of 8.10 m. The control surfaces were on the upper wing; the lower wing, of slightly smaller chord than the upper, supporting the wingtip floats.

The single-step wooden fuselage was the usual two-skin, diagonally planked type using boatbuilding techniques but, unlike the Linton Hope construction used by Supermarine, the hollow-section bottom was single-skinned and planked with plywood. The wing and empennage were of conventional wood-and-fabric construction, the tailplane being braced by a pair of lift-struts.

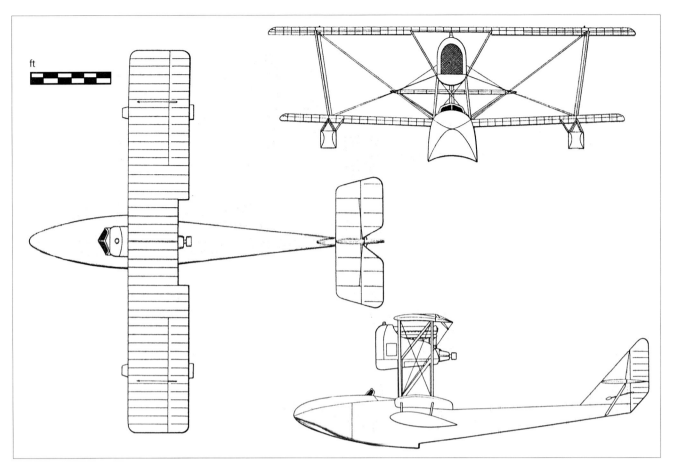

SIAI Savoia 13 Flying Boat (1919): Wing Span: 26ft 6 in (8.10 m). Length Overall: 27 ft 2 in (8.28 m). Wing Area: 211 sq. ft (19.60 m²). Weight Empty: 1,610 lb (730 kg). T-O Weight: 2,075 lb (941 kg). Max Wing Loading: 9.83 lb/sq. ft (47.99/m²). Isotta-Fraschini engine, liquid, of 250 hp.

Wide-chord struts in N-configurations supported the engine and provided a base for the cabane struts. The engine, driving a pusher propeller, was half-cowled and cooled by a car-type radiator mounted in the nose of the cowling.

Conversion to a racer consisted of shortening the hull by roughly five inches, shortening the front fuselage by removing a fuselage bay amidships – and drastically reducing the span of the upper and lower mainplanes by about 12 per cent. The consequent shortening of the bracing wires permitted the jury stays to be thrown away. This, in combination with the shorter wings and a smaller, single-seat cockpit opening, considerably reduced drag.

The same machine, again in the hands of Janello, and with a highly tuned engine, had its wings cropped even further and appeared at the 1920 Monaco seaplane meeting.

The Savoia S.13bis. (*SIAI-Marchetti*)

Venice 1920

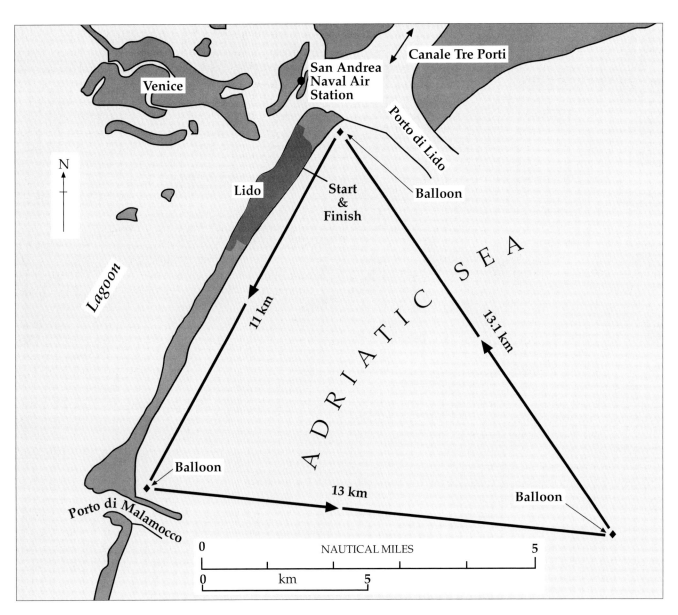

Schneider Trophy Contest Course: Venice 1920.

Run-up

Having decided between themselves, in recognition of Janello's display of airmanship in the 1919 race, that Italy should be given the honour of organising the 1920 event, the FAI and the British Royal Aero Club unwittingly almost set the scene for Jacques Schneider's Trophy becoming Italian property in perpetuity.

In accordance with the deed of gift the Aero Club d'Italia had the privilege of choosing the venue for the race. Their choice of Venice was tempered by many considerations, some political, some sentimental, for Italy was a new nation and this part of the Adriatic was the focus of a great deal of national fervour as a result of the dispute over Trieste.

Sadly, significant and beautiful as the setting for the race was, it was a far cry, even from France, let alone Britain, who were the main challengers. The railways of the warring nations, only two years after the greatest conflict of all time, were run down and in near-chaos. The alternative, by ship, was equally tedious, involving a voyage through the Mediterranean, round the 'toe' of Italy and up the whole length of the Adriatic. Nor was it feasible for machines to fly there. It was out of the question for the British, and the French would have had to fly from Monaco in stages, using the Italian lakes as alighting places for refuelling. Temperamental racing engines do not take kindly to this kind of touring activity. Shipping delicate machines to a far corner of Italy would take many weeks and cost much money. The latter was of special consequence to the frugal British, who had just entered the first of their post-war recessions.

What is more, the whole economy of Europe was moving towards a depression, and the industries of the competing countries were engaged in a fight for survival. Only the USA, which had been the banker of the Allies, was booming. France was economically sick and would not recognise the fact, but could always find money to spend on armaments, which included aircraft.

In Britain, inflation was on the rampage, with prices more than twice what they had been in 1914. The artificially inflated aircraft industry was starved of orders because of the huge stocks of airframes and engines left over from the war, and was being dramatically slimmed down. Sopwith was in voluntary liquidation and typically paid 100 per cent of its debts. Folland, of the Nieuport and General Aircraft Company, had announced that he would have to give up aircraft manufacture temporarily. However the Receiver had allowed him to send the Goshawk to the Gordon Bennett races in Paris. On the bright side, Short had just completed the first ever metal monocoque fuselage, and the de Havilland Company was in the process of being formed.

Supermarine, in the capable hands of Hubert Scott-Paine and Bird were solvent, but were unlikely to have the resources to send a machine to Venice, although they expressed an intention to do so. In common with other British constructors, they were preoccupied with an important Air Ministry competition for civil aircraft with big money prizes and the prospect of orders to follow. They were destined to win an enhanced second prize of £8,000 in the amphibian section with their big 'Commercial' flying-boat. An expensive trip to Italy would have occupied funds that they could ill afford in more ways than one, for the effort with the 'Commercial' was the beginning of their specialisation in large military flying-boats.

So far as France was concerned there was certainly no doubt in the mind of the editor of the French *Echo des Sports*. On 15 September, a fortnight before the race, he wrote '*La France – et selon tout probabilité L'Angleterre – ont renoncé a la Coupe parce que les appareils Italiens sont superieurs et que ni l'un ni l'autre de ces deux nations ne veut risquer la defaite.*' (France, and in all probability Britain, have renounced the Coupe because the Italian aircraft are superior and neither of these two nations wishes to risk defeat.) One wonders whether he really spoke for his nation's aviation industry. In fact the one foreign entry did come from France.

Italy had its problems too. It was a time of great political change. Benito Mussolini, the son of a blacksmith of Forli and an ex-member of the Second International, was in the throes of forming the first National Socialist party, the *Fascisti*. Although it was soon to ban strikes and lockouts, it was because of these that it gained power. So far as the Italian constructors were concerned this politicking would hamper the construction of special aircraft.

It must have pleased the Italian industry when the Royal Aero Club put up, and the FAI accepted, the proposal that the race machines for 1920 should be capable of carrying a commercial load of 300 kg. Theirs was a country to which the flying-boat was admirably adapted. With a long coastline in relation to its land area and huge lakes in the north, the country was ideal for operating large waterplanes. Moreover the regulations would encourage their constructors to build and race flying-boats rather than floatplanes, of which they had little experience. And the load rule would develop a commercially useful type of aircraft rather than lightweight high-speed machines of little commercial use except to accumulate data for military applications.

There was similar thinking behind the British proposal, for they saw load-carrying flying-boats as ideal for spanning their still-vast empire. But when it came to the crunch none of the British constructors could afford to send seaplanes all the way to Venice, nor had the Royal Aero Club the funds to encourage them.

It was unfortunate for the challengers that the Italian club contrived to choose 28–29 August as the date for the race. It was just a month before the great Gordon Bennett races near Paris. Any possibility that the French would send machines seemed to be ruled out by the fact that their two main racing constructors, Nieuport and SPAD, were totally occupied with producing a winning machine for the Gordon Bennett. The only thing in doubt was which one of them would have the honour of building it.

Nevertheless, all the countries invited expressed the intention to race although they ultimately withdrew. The most positive entries were from France, a SPAD-Herbemont S.20, which would be flown by Jean Casale, and a Nieuport 29, for which no pilot had been nominated, although it could have been the great Sadi Lecointe. There was also – shades of 1914 – a Borel flying-boat. There was even rumour of an entry from neutral Switzerland.

When the cards were down, it was left to the Italians to supply the whole field. Their entries were five in number, two from the Savoia concern and three from Macchi, or, to give the company its full name, the Società Anonima Nieuport-Macchi. In common with Savoia, in a nearby town Macchi had been set up during the 1914–18 war to manufacture French designs under licence, in their case the Nieuport Bebé, in Varese. This was a traditional furniture and carriage manufacturing area of Italy – Macchi were coachbuilders – and it was natural that the powers that be should turn to these trades as they did in World War Two, to build aeroplanes.

The Savoia entries were an S.12bis with Luigi Bologna as pilot. Guido Janello, their ace test pilot and race 'driver' was to fly a one-off racer, the S.19, built 'without consideration for commercial gain', as the company put it, especially for the event.

Bologna's S.12bis was one of Savoia's standard bomber-reconnaissance, two-bay, pusher flying-boats with the wings cut down and the tailplane drastically reduced in area to reduce drag. However, Janello's machine, the S.19, was an out-and-out racer designed specifically for the event. Something of a mystery ship, it appears to have been an enlarged derivative of the S.13 via the S.17 built for the Monaco contest. It was a pusher biplane with equal-span, equal-chord wings and single-bay rigging. And in common with its stablemate it was powered by a 550 hp Ansaldo San Giorgio engine.

The main entry from Macchi was Ing. Alessandro Tonini's new M.19, powered by the mighty wartime 57-litre Fiat A.14 V-12 bomber engine. The M.19 had been specially designed and built to meet and exceed the 300 kg load requirement.

The second Macchi entry was the M.17, a half-scale prototype of the M.19, which in its turn drew inspiration from Macchi's first flying-boat fighter, the M.5, designed for them by Buzio and Calzara. The M.17 was powered by a single Isotta-Fraschini Asso V-6 250 hp

engine and sporting strange trifurcated interplane struts as part of its single-bay configuration. It was hardly likely to meet the payload requirement and appeared to have been entered either as a makeweight or because someone at Macchi had not read the rules.

Finally, there was the Macchi M.12 to be flown by 'Nino' de Briganti, Giovanni, to give him his full first name. The M.12 was an old but attractive design, having first appeared in 1918 as a twin-boom high-speed day bomber with sufficient performance to operate without a fighter escort. How many times in the future was aviation to hear this story? Nevertheless, the M.12 seemed a good foul-weather standby machine for the event, in the absence of anything better.

Macchi soon realised that the M.17 was not really a practical machine for the race and withdrew the entry. It had been designed with the Grand Prix de Monaco half in mind and was quite incapable of meeting the Schneider payload requirement since its useful load was a mere 200 kg which had to include the pilot, fuel and oil.

As a point of interest two M.17s were scheduled to be built, and the first of these appeared at the Monaco

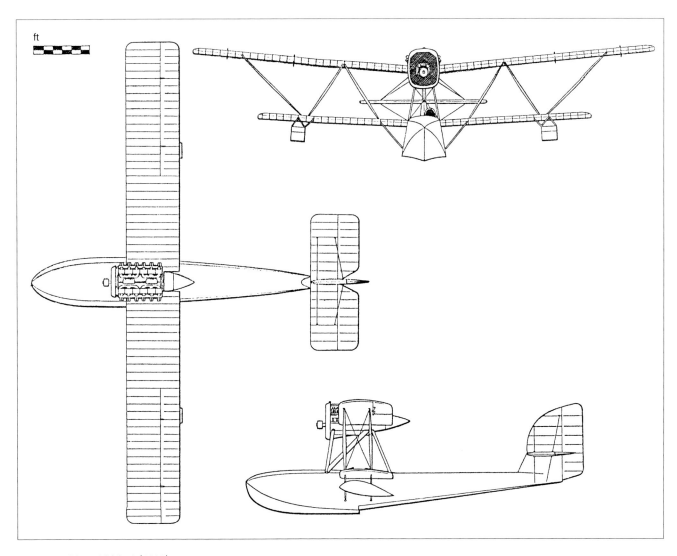

Nieuport-Macchi M.19 (1920): Fiat Engine of 650 hp.

seaplane meeting at the end of April and beginning of May with Arturo Zanetti at the controls. In company with Riccardo Morselli flying another Macchi, Zanetti took part in the Grand Prix, challenging Count Bernard de Romanet, flying a SPAD-Herbemont floatplane. Zanetti demonstrated the very high performance of the machine when he won the speed event handsomely with an overall speed of 153.4 mph (247 km/h) but cartwheeled on landing, destroying the machine and giving himself a bloody nose. No more M.17s were built that year; the works was fully occupied with the military M.18 bomber, and in getting the big M.19 ready for the Schneider race.

Macchi had no more success with the M.19. It was completed in good time but on its first flight test pilot Zanetti landed complaining bitterly about the massive rudder forces he had to use to keep the machine in the air. Tonini had miscalculated the fuselage moment arm, the length of the fuselage, and it would have to be extended, an impossible job to complete in time for the race.

Logic and the pitfalls of aeronautical design thus left the race organisers with the two Savoias, one, the S.12bis, suitable for the event, the other one marginally so. Both were ready and waiting for the planned date, but in the absence of foreign entries and in the hope that Macchi might produce the M.19 in time the Italian club progressively put back the date until it was finally fixed for the four days beginning 18 September.

It was not a good date for a number of reasons. One was that it conflicted directly with the Gordon Bennett races in France, which went on for weeks. This precluded any possibility of French, British or even American entries. It will be remembered that the Americans were making their first foray into Europe since the Wright brothers with the innovative Dayton-Wright RB monoplane and the flamboyant S.E.J. Cox's Curtiss-powered and Curtiss-built racers, the Texas Wildcat and Texas Kitten. Their effort to take the Gordon Bennett Trophy back to America was a glorious failure but the derivatives of the engines that powered the Curtiss racers were destined to transform the nature of the Schneider race only three years later.

The other factor that crept in was the Adriatic weather pattern. The new date took the race out of the period of warm, gentle summer weather that characterises the northern end of the Adriatic, into the winter system. A feature of this system is the bora, a cold, turbulent wind which blows down from the Alps to the sea. It reaches speeds up to 100 mph, and 70 mph is commonplace. In many ways it is like the mistral, which blows down the Rhône valley into the Mediterranean.

The Race

By the morning of 18 September the bora was making the first of its annual appearances, raising white horses and a short chop in the Laguna Venezia. It was even worse outside in the Adriatic where the triangular, twenty nautical mile course had been set out with striped balloons, moored to lighters, marking the turning points along the shore. Now these balloons strained at their cables as they swung wildly in the gale force winds. Even *Il Mas*, a steamer chartered by the organisers to act as an observation post and to mark the outer point of the triangle, was unable to put to sea because of the weather.

Journalists, gathered on the roof of the Excelsior Palace Hotel on the Lido island, watched as Bologna took the Savoia S.12 through the navigability test, the spray breaking right over his machine as he taxied between the buoys marking the test course. It was a measure of the pilot's airmanship and seamanship, as much as the quality of the Savoia, that allowed him to complete the test successfully. Janello, in the heavily laden, relatively lightweight S.19, rightly judged that the weather was too much for his machine. It was withdrawn from the event, leaving Bologna the sole contestant.

The weather on race day, Saturday 20 September, was hardly better, with the bora blowing as hard as ever. Nevertheless, Bologna, game to the last, managed to get the S.12 airborne in the sheltered waters off the San Andrea Naval Air Station, situated on an island just inside the mouth of the lagoon, crossed the line and set off on his fly-over. But the wind, gusting to 70 mph, was clearly too much for the machine, and after five laps, completed in 1 hr 15 min 24 sec, the gallant Bologna had to return to his base. It was a bitter disappointment for him and the few spectators, but there was another day.

The following day started almost as badly, with the sea so high that once again *Il Mas* was unable to get on station. At 2.30 in the afternoon, the wind gauge at San Andrea was recording 28 metres per second (69 mph). Nevertheless the organisers decided that the wind might drop as the sun declined, and in the absence of *Il Mas*, sent out a torpedo boat to mark the outer turning point. It was also there to act as a rescue boat in case of disaster to the one and only contender.

At 4.30 pm the wind started to drop as predicted and the watchers suddenly saw Bologna's S.12 appear over the houses of the Lido, and set out to fly the course. This time he was successful, covering the entire distance in 2 hr 10 min 35 sec, an average speed of 105.75 mph (170.19 km/h). This is based on a nominal distance of 371.17 km. The word 'nominal' is used advisedly because of the difficulty of keeping the outer marker boat on station in the prevailing conditions. Race distances of 371.17 km and 375.56 km have been mentioned in records. The former is the most likely and would be due either to the difficulty of positioning the offshore marker boat or the Savoia being blown off course by the high winds.

Looking back at the 1920 race, it was won by a machine designed for a different purpose two years previously. As a consequence the lessons learned can hardly contribute a great deal to aeronautical progress. The lack of foreign competitors, due mainly to European economic problems, exacerbated by frequent changes of race date and aggravated by the geographical situation of Venice, enabled the Italians to retain the Coupe

Schneider with a walkover. The local papers barely bothered to report the race. Everyone looked forward to a more competitive event the following year.

The Aircraft

The Savoia S.12bis

In standard form the Savoia S.12 was a sturdy service biplane flying-boat with equal-span, 15-metre wings, an all-up weight of 2,600 kg and a useful load including pilot and fuel of 1,000 kg. It was the ideal size of machine for the event and probably as near as any to the type of machine Jacques Schneider had in mind when he framed the deed of gift of the Coupe Schneider.

Structurally it was strictly in accordance with the wartime Savoia pattern, the hull being of all-wood construction using a mix of plywood and diagonal planking, depending on the amount of double curvature required. The two-spar, fabric-covered wings were also of wood and were braced like those of the S.13bis of 1919 with hinged, small-section steel tube interplane struts between the main struts. Savoia used very long, wide-chord streamlined bracing wires in single-bay configuration, that is four wires per side, and these articulated struts supported torpedo-shaped junction fairings where the bracing wires crossed to reduce interference effect and control flutter.

Strictly speaking, the S.12bis was a single-bay biplane with appendages. The wings of S.13bis racer of 1919, being smaller, could do without the appendages when they were cut down. All these early Savoias had the same N-configuration engine-mounting with the lower ends of the centre-section struts picking up with the engine-mounting points.

To improve its performance and to trim it exactly to race requirements, a specially cut-down version of the S.12, designated the S.12bis by various writers, was prepared to bring its payload down to exactly 300 kg and to increase its speed with a slight sacrifice of alighting speed. To this end the upper mainplane was reduced in span from 15 metres to 11.4 metres, and the lower mainplane from 14 metres to 10.6 metres. The tailplane area was almost halved to match. The standard Ansaldo 4-E-28 San Giorgio engine of 550 hp was retained to provide motive power. It was unchanged apart from some tuning. These modifications raised the maximum speed from a standard 222 km/h to about 250 km/h.

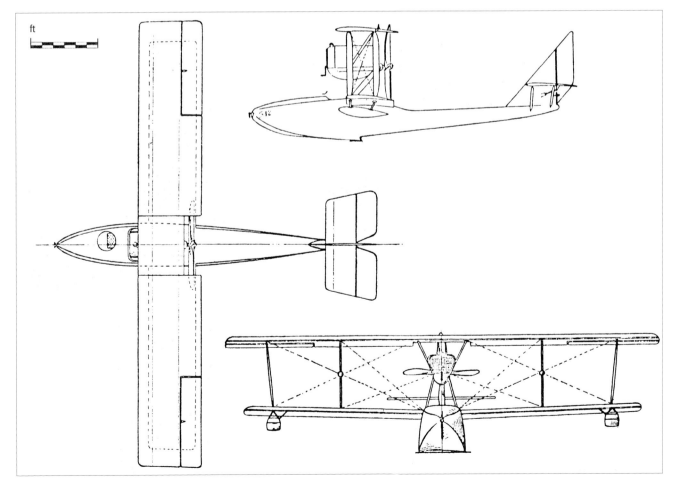

Savoia S.12 bis, the 1920 Trophy winner. This was a specially modified version of the S.12 to meet the race requirements. Wing span: upper 37 ft 4 in (11.4 m), lower 34 ft 8 in (10.6 m). Length overall: 29 ft 6¼ in (9.01 m).

The SIAI Savoia S.12 powered by a 550 hp Ansaldo with pusher propeller was piloted by Luigi Bologna at an average speed of 107 mph to win at Venice in 1920. It was the ideal size and probably as near as any to the type of aircraft Schneider had in mind. (*SIAI-Marchetti*)

Venice 1921

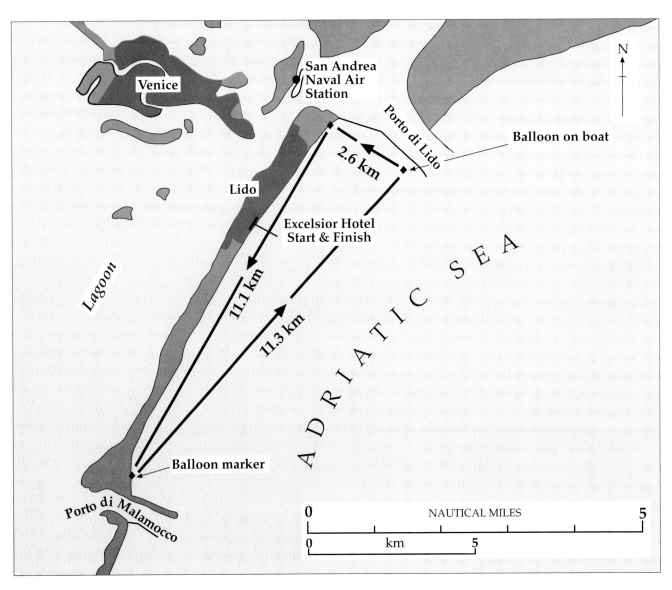

Schneider Trophy Contest Course: Venice 1921.

Run-up

As indisputed victors in 1920, Italy was once again the host nation to the competitors for the Coupe Maritime Jacques Schneider. But this time they had a more direct influence on the regulations, unlike the previous year when they were accorded the honour of running the race but the Royal Aero Club of Great Britain had a say in framing the race rules. There was no doubt that, worthy as the idea was, the 300 kg Commercial weight rule proposed by the Royal Aero Club and welcomed by the Italians not only reduced the potential entry but also spoilt the race as a spectacle. After all, who wanted to see a collection of transports lumbering round a race circuit?

It took no time at all, with the agreement of the Fédération Aéronautique Internationale at their annual end-of-season meeting, to throw away the 300 kg load requirement and substitute a seaworthiness test, which was destined to feature in all future contests, calling for machines to be moored, unattended for six hours. An amendment from the Royal Aero Club that the machines should be made to race with any water shipped during the flotation test was turned down on the score of safety. Another first-time requirement was a deposit of 5,000 francs with every entry. The money was to be refunded when the machine crossed the starting line. It was not a vast amount of money but enough to put off ill-considered entries like that of the M.17 the previous year. The money that was retained would be distributed as prizes for the placed men. The second pilot home would receive half the entry fees plus 3,000 lire, third home would have one third plus 1,500 lire and fourth would get the rest. The winner, of course, received the trophy and the sum of 10,000 lire, which was donated by the organising club.

The date fixed for the race was 7 August and was to some extent conditioned by other happenings in Venice on that date. This placed the event three weeks after the British Aerial Derby and almost two months ahead of the Coupe Deutsch de la Meurthe, which had taken the place of the Gordon Bennett in the European calendar now that the latter had been won in perpetuity by Sadi Lecointe and Nieuport for France. It was well clear of the American Pulitzer race which was not scheduled until 3 November, late in the autumn.

So far as the Americans were concerned this was one race which did not interest them. Another year had to pass before the classic Curtiss CR series racers made their debut, and yet another before they were put on floats. The British constructors were still concerned with their domestic problems. Financial stringency was the order of the day. Despite the Royal Aero Club's offer of cash prizes for British machines which finished in the first three carried over from the previous year, £250 for a first place, £150 and £100 for second and third, British constructors remained uninterested. Their only seaplane specialists, Supermarine and Short Brothers saw their future in bigger, long-distance passenger machines.

Short's lacked either the time or inclination to build a racer and ship it to Italy. Supermarine were busy operating a successful passenger service across the English Channel from Southampton to Guernsey with the pale, fey but very experienced Henri Biard as chief pilot. Variations of the 'boats developed for this service were being sold to a variety of foreign customers as far-flung as New Zealand, Japan, Chile and Norway. The Supermarine Commercial – one feels that it lent its name to the 1920 Commercial weight rule – was being tested by the Air Ministry, the single-engined Seal was being busily developed and there was a batch of Siddeley Puma-engined Channel II boats to be built, with the possibility of a further batch for the Japanese navy.

After the 1919 farce Scott-Paine had donated the remains of the Sea Lion I hull to the Imperial College, while he retained N.60, now the Sea King II; the man-hours it would have taken to convert it into a racer could be more usefully employed elsewhere. Moreover, the distance of Venice was a very real drawback. It had been easy to make an entry when the race was ten minutes' flying time from the factory. It was another thing entirely when it meant sending many of his best craftsmen and engineers on a long sea voyage which would take them away from the factory for weeks.

Other British companies had their sights set on races for landplanes with orders for fighters for the RAF in view. The newly formed Gloucestershire Company, who had recently acquired the services of the brilliant H.P. Folland, were then preoccupied with a landplane racer in

the shape of the Bamel development of the Nieuport Nighthawk with Napier Lion power plant. Their sights were set on the Aerial Derby and the Coupe Deutsch later in the year. Direct developments of this machine would distinguish themselves late in the history of the Coupe Schneider, but not in 1921.

Bristol had the 170 mph Bullet, which would have made a good floatplane racer, but seaplanes were not their scene, while Avro had taken the floats off the 539A and were developing it as a landplane racer. So far as all these firms were concerned, Venice was a long way away and they had better things to do than build seaplanes for a race which was unlikely to bring in orders. Moreover, tragedy had struck British aviation. One of its greatest pioneers, Harry Hawker, had died in the air while testing his Nieuport Nighthawk powered by the disastrous, Bradshaw-designed Dragonfly engine – his name was to be perpetuated by Tom Sopwith, who named the Hawker Company after him. An even bigger tragedy had occurred when the airship R.38 had broken up and crashed in flames over the Humber estuary, killing the two crews, one British, the other American. This disaster was one of the writer's earliest aviation memories. As a four-year-old he was dragged from his bed by his parents to see this great machine float over his home on the Humber bank. Minutes later it was a tangled wreck.

It was indicative of the hard times the British were facing that the whole industry only managed to send just two machines to the Paris Air Show at the Grand Palais that November. However, massive undercurrents in favour of maritime aviation were in train. Later that year the Washington Naval Conference proposed that the USA, Britain and Japan should scrap most of their existing warships and refrain from further construction until 1931. New aircraft carriers, though, would be allowed, with a limit of 80,000 tons for the USA and Britain and 48,000 tons for Japan. It was an agreement which laid the foundations of a swing to seaplane construction, whose influence would be strongly felt in forthcoming Schneider contests.

So far as American participation was concerned, the country which had seen the first fledgling flights of heavier-than-air machines now sat back while Europe developed the idea. Progress had been so slow that the US services had no suitable aircraft when the time came to fight in World War One. Their airmen had to go into battle in French and British machines. The ignominy of it was deeply felt and since that time a new technology was being forged in the white heat of competitive flying. Service participation in the classic Gordon Bennett and Pulitzer races had produced engines and airframes of great technical merit and real performance. The Dayton-Wright RB, with retractable undercart and variable-camber wing, which had competed in the 1920 Gordon Bennett and would have won if the designer had given the pilot a view ahead, was twenty years ahead of any other aircraft present while the Verville VCP-R showed that the Yanks had caught up with conventional fighter types. And the Curtiss Wildcat and Cactus Kitten taken over by the brash and flamboyant Cox were powered by engines which were to influence liquid-cooled engine design for the next decade. Even as the 1921 race was being run a biplane racer was being erected in the Curtiss shops at Garden City, Long Island which would change the face of the Schneider Cup races.

Nor was France dragging its heels. The French knew more about the design of high-speed airframes than most of their competitors at the time. Their industry was at the peak of its interwar ability with sleek designs like the SPAD-Herbemont, designed by Louis Béchereau's protégé André Herbemont, and the Gordon Bennett-winning Nieuport-Delages so beautifully demonstrated by pilots of the calibre of Sadi Lecointe and Georges Kirssch. These Nieuport machines, designed by Gustave Delage, dominated the world speed record scene in 1920, 1921 and 1922 until the advent of the Curtiss R-6.

Unhappily, only one of these countries so rich in speed machines, was forthcoming with a firm entry. France in the person of Nieuport proclaimed the intention to send the great Sadi Lecointe with a Nieuport floatplane to wave the tricolor of France. It was left to Italy to produce the rest of the field.

The Italians, on their part, were all set to make a great aviation spectacle as part of the celebrations of a visit by the Italian Crown Prince to Venice and the unredeemed Italy of Trentino and the Istrian peninsular. The head of the Adriatic was truly in the news at the time, d'Annunzio was deep in the throes of his Fiume adventure, the Austrian fleet was due to be handed over at Trieste and the Treaty of Rapallo was in the making. Venice was right at the centre of things and an aviation week had been organised which included, apart from the Coppa Schneider, another 400 kilometre race for the Coppa Amcilotto e Gran Premio Venezia Velocità, an international navigability test, and the Coppa di S.M. il Re del Gran Premio Venezia Trasporto. Freely translated the last-named race seems to have been a King's Cup for transport machines. There was also a 410 kilometre rally for flying-boats from Milan to Venice using rivers and lakes as alighting places.

A new circuit was adopted for 1921 to make the whole affair a spectacle and give everyone a better view of the goings-on. The previous year's circuit, although correct in being an almost equilateral triangle, had taken the one competitor out of sight of the shore for most of the race. The new circuit was arranged with a long base leg of about 11.1 km running parallel with the beach and marked by shore-mounted pylons at Porto di Lido and Alberoni. The aircraft would then turn back and fly almost parallel with the beach for approximately 11.3 km before turning round a tethered balloon flown from a lighter moored about 2.6 km offshore but inside the shelter of the Porto di Lido breakwater. The start and finish were opposite the Excelsior Hotel, from which the Crown Prince would have an excellent view of the aircraft twice on every lap; spectators along the beach would be equally well placed to view the race.

The Italian eliminating trials were fixed for 3 August and proved to be more of a spectacle than the race itself.

The navigability trials were arranged to take place on 6 August over a shortened triangular course with the take-off and alighting area in front of the Excelsior Hotel. After taking off, machines were required to fly round a marker moored in the lagoon behind the Excelsior, just off the San Andrea naval aviation base.

The original intention of the Italian club had been to double the 200 nm distance approved by the FAI in their regulations to 400 nautical miles. This would have been beyond the endurance of some of the machines entered and it is probably for this reason that the Italians adhered to the original, 200 nm, distance. The regulations called for sixteen laps of a 25 km (13.50 nm) course which made the distance up to 400 km for international record breaking purposes and at 216 nm gave a little in hand so far as the FAI were concerned. Unfortunately the club's survey turned out to be a little adrift and the final course measured 24.632 km (13.30 nm). Thus the actual distance flown was 394.1 km, or 212.8 nm.

The quality of the Italian entry for the Schneider race can best be judged by the pilots allocated to the machines. Guido Janello, because of his performances at Monaco and in Britain at the Bournemouth Schneider débâcle was probably the most experienced and best-known high-speed exponent. His mount was yet another offering from Savoia in the shape of the diminutive S.21, an inverted sesquiplane flying-boat, that is one with the lower wing much larger than the upper one. In this case the lower measured 7.69 m and the upper 5.1 m, and the machine was powered by a 550 hp Ansaldo San Giorgio 4-E-28 engine driving a four-bladed pusher propeller. It had a typical Conflienti hollow-bottom, single-step hull with a cruciform empennage. The high aspect ratio mainplanes were braced by Warren-girder struts devoid of wire bracing. It was a clever design because the wide lower wing provided a wide base for the wingtip floats to counteract the torque from the necessarily high-mounted propeller. Its fragile appearance belied its maker's claims of aerobatic and military potential.

Janello's SIAI Savoia S.21 for the 1921 event.

The Macchi M.19 flown by Arturo Zanetti at Venice in 1921 which retired after catching fire.

The Macchi M.7 flown by Giovanni de Briganti at an average speed of 117.9 mph to win at Venice in 1921.

The next most important entry from Savoia was their big, twin-engine, push-pull S.22. Powered by a pair of Isotta-Fraschini Asso sixes and designed with racing in mind, it was nevertheless claimed to have accommodation for eight passengers. Assigned to Savoia's pin-up pilot, Umberto Maddalena, it took part in the Monaco meeting in April that year but was destroyed in flight trials shortly afterwards. Next favourite after the S.21 was the mighty Macchi M.19 powered by a massive Fiat 57.2-litre, 700 hp, direct-drive A.14 engine. Arturo Zanetti was the pilot and, with load to spare, for the first and last time in the Schneider series a mechanic, Pedretti, was to be carried as a second crew member. Since its disappointing first flight, prior to the 1920 race the fuselage had been lengthened to improve directional control but it is not certain whether the problem had been completely solved. Perhaps the mechanic was there to supply extra muscle power if required, or to monitor the engine; in racing one does not carry extra weight unless it is essential, even in a machine as large as the M.19.

Third in order of importance was a pair of M.7bis machines from Macchi for Giovanni de Briganti and Piero Corgnolino. The M.7bis was a stripped and lightened version of the Macchi M.7 fighter flying-boat. With span reduced from 9.90 m to 7.7 m and an empty weight of 725.7 kg instead of 775 kg, it had a top speed close on 200 km/h with the Isotta-Fraschini 250 hp in-line six engine.

Just for good measure Macchi had entered a brace of M.18s with Alessandro Passaleva and Guzelloni as pilots. The M.18 was designed in 1920 as three-passenger transport and later modified to a military configuration with folding wings and a Vickers gun on a ring in the nose cockpit. With an all-up weight of 2,805 lb (1,275 kg) and a span of 51 ft 10 in (15.80 m), it could hardly be considered competitive, even when stripped and cleaned up, bearing in mind that the propulsive unit was the inevitable Isotta-Fraschini V-6 of 250 hp, the same as that of the lighter and smaller M.7.

The Macchi M.18 flown by Alessandro Passaleva at Venice in 1921.

A further entry from Macchi was a flurry of three standard Regia Aeronautica M.7s piloted by Marescialli (Warrant Officers) Falaschi, Buonosembiante and Desio.

These extra, makeweight M.7s were undoubtedly a flag-waving operation on the part of the Macchi factory to counter six military Savoia S.13s to be flown by Majors Giartosio, Bologna, Arcidiacano, and Warrant Officers Minciotti, Riccobello and Conforti.

An Italian entry which did not materialise was proposed by the ingenious Giovanni Pegna, editor of an Italian aviation magazine, who was responsible for a number of way-out designs in the twenties and thirties. One is never quite sure whether to regard Pegna as a brilliant innovator or an ill-informed aviation editor; he had to be one or the other. The majority of his ideas were not entirely original. The configuration he proposed for the 1921 race, namely a shoulder-wing monoplane flying-boat with the engine and tractor screw mounted in a pivoting frame to enable the propeller to revolve clear of the waves during take-off and then be lowered when airborne, had already been proposed elsewhere.

But Pegna's interpretation of this layout, which was unfortunately not built, was an elegant one using an unbraced, cantilever monoplane wing when such devices were in their infancy. To his credit he had already done a great deal of practical work on hydrofoils and he had tangible aviation interests, with engineers Rossi and Bastianelli, in the huge PRB flying-boat.

Against this Italian armada of the air was arraigned the sole tangible French entry, the Nieuport-Delage of Sadi Lecointe, and the only pontoon machine, which was billed as having been specially built for the contest with the financial aid of the French government. Just which type of Nieuport this machine was based on has been the subject of much conjecture by Schneider historians. We still await the answer and a photograph of the machine. In view of the six-hour flotation test it would have been logical for the factory to have sent a *flotteur a queue* type to Venice. However, one has to take into account the effect on the French constructors of claims by SIAI that the Savoia S.21 was the fastest seaplane in the world. They would want to match this with a speed machine and one feels that the mystery machine could have been one of their out-and-out racers mounted on floats. It is extremely unlikely, but not quite outside the bounds of possibility, that it was one of the Coupe Deutsch sesquiplanes – they were really monoplanes – which were booked to appear at the Coupe Deutsch meeting the following month. One other French entry, from Breguet, was talked about but did not materialise.

In all, 5,000 francs in deposits had been paid on some seventeen Italian entries although their presence in the race was still subject to an eliminating race, quite apart from the seaworthiness test proper. Only three would be able to qualify to cross the start line on 7 August and reclaim the entry fee. One has to surmise that the eliminating trials were regarded by the Italian constructors as a separate spectacle in which they could demonstrate their wares. This seems to be confirmed by the trouble taken to identify the different machines for the benefit of the spectators because, although they all bore numbers, signs in the form of coloured rectangles, triangles or stars were painted on the sides of the fuselages. Race numbers and identification marks were allocated by the Italian team organiser Colalti. For example de Briganti's M.7bis was distinguished by a red rectangle, Passaleva's M.18 had a yellow circle and Janello's S.21 a white rectangle with red vertical bands.

When the great day came for the Italian trials the most notable absentee was Janello's S.21, officially because Janello was indisposed. The pilot was indeed seriously ill but his reserve pilot Guarnieri could have taken the machine had it been serviceable. Engine trouble was rumoured but the most likely reason for its non-appearance is that Janello was the only man who could handle this machine, which had an extremely high wing-loading for that day and age. In the event its place was taken by an M.7 with Guarnieri at the helm.

In these trials, held over six laps of the nominally 150 km Schneider course Zanetti, in the big, Fiat-engined M.19, proved an easy winner with a speed of 215.12 km/h (132.05 mph) from Piero Corgnolino in one of the M.7bis at 194.945 km/h (121.1 mph) and de Briganti in the other M.7bis with a speed of 193.007 km/h (119.9 mph). Maresciallo Minciotti brought one of the S.13s into fourth position with an elapsed time of 48 min 11.2 sec for the nominally 150 km course. The distance was in fact 147.792 km, 24.632 km per lap, due to inaccurate location of the marker boats. The speeds given above take into account this discrepancy. Minciotti's speed was 184.02 km/h by the same reckoning and is a measure of the relative performance of the M.7bis, which was Macchi's latest fighter 'boat, and Savoia's S.13 with the same pretensions. Comparing the speeds of the two M.7s, both in the trials and later in the race, it would seem that Corgnolino had the slightly hotter engine. Eventually it was not to his advantage.

The Italian team for the Schneider was thus whittled down to the Macchis, the M.19 and the two M.7bis of de Briganti and Corgnolino. Their only international opposition was Sadi Lecointe's Nieuport, which quickly eliminated itself three days later on 6 August, the day of the seaworthiness tests, by buckling a float strut on landing. Repairs were not allowed under the regulations, which called for the machines to be sealed before the test. Thus the sole foreign competitor had to be withdrawn.

The Race

To describe the race itself as an anticlimax would be praise indeed. It was clear from the lap times that Zanetti's M.19 had the edge on the two M.7s despite its size, and it droned round, taking an average of 30 seconds a lap from Corgnolino and 40 seconds from de Briganti. But just as victory seemed a foregone conclusion the voice of the M.19's mighty Fiat engine was abruptly stilled and smoke was seen pouring from it, as Zanetti hurriedly plonked the M.19 down on the water. The crew abandoned ship and were picked up by a rescue boat. A connecting rod had broken, punching a hole in the crankcase and starting an oil fire. It was quickly extinguished by the crew of a launch but the machine was out of the race.

It was now a contest between Corgnolino and de Briganti. After a slow start de Briganti had piled on the power, and from the ninth lap onwards he was equalling, and at times bettering Corgnolino's times. Maybe, as becomes a pilot who was destined to become one of Italy's and indeed Europe's outstanding airmen, he had been assessing his fuel consumption in the conditions before pushing the throttle up to the stop. If this were so it was good airmanship because, on the final lap and having rounded the Porto di Lido marker for the last time, poor Corgnolino's motor faltered and then stopped. He alighted quite safely to watch de Briganti swoop low over his head and cross the line, victor of one of the least auspicious of all the Schneider contests. One can only hope that the Crown Prince was duly impressed. Certainly de Briganti was; he received the trophy, 10,000 lire and all the remaining entry fees.

The 1921 winner at Venice. The Macchi M.7, powered by a 250 hp Isotta-Fraschini engine, flown by Giovanni de Briganti at an average speed of 117.9 mph.

The Aircraft

Macchi M.7bis

Conceived, like the Supermarine Sea Baby, as a single-seat flying-boat fighter, the M.7 was introduced in 1917 to operate off the Italian lakes and intercept the marauding Phoenix D.II and D.III fighters of the Imperial Austrian Air Force. At the time it was claimed to be the world's fastest flying-boat fighter. Only eleven examples were built, three of them after cessation of hostilities. Most of these were acquired by the Aviazione di Marina (Naval Aviation).

Powdered by a single Isotta-Fraschini 250 bhp V-6 driving a pusher propeller and armed with twin Vickers-Terni machine guns, the M.7 was claimed to have a maximum speed of 130 mph, although this is unlikely because the lightened racing version was not much faster than this. Alighting speed was 56 mph. The M.7ter was

introduced in 1927 and was initially powered by a 200 hp Asso V.4, more powerful engines up to 480 bhp being fitted later. It went out of service in 1928 after eleven years.

Construction was the usual Italian style with wooden hull and fabric-covered wings, the round-section steel interplane struts being streamlined with wide-chord wooden fairing. Configuration was wire-braced two-bay with unequal-span wings and large, undamped ailerons located in the upper mainplane. For the 1921 Schneider race the upper span was reduced from 9.90 m to 7.7 m – some sources say 7.75 m – and the lower wing cut down proportionally. The length of the hull was also reduced by shortening the bow and tail sections. Both de Briganti's and Corgnolino's machines had tuned engines, the latter apparently producing a little more than the former.

Macchi M.19

Designed by Alessandro Tonini, one of Italy's great aviation pioneers, who had joined Macchi during World War One and had overseen most of their early flying-boat designs, the M.19 was designed specifically around the 1920 300 kg load-carrying rule. It will be recalled that initially it was almost uncontrollable due to too short a fuselage moment arm. Labour problems prevented it being revamped with a new fuselage in time for the 1920 event but when 1921 came along, its reserve of power from the big 700 hp Fiat A.14 engine gave it a considerable advantage over the other Macchi entries despite its size. It was developed directly from Tonini's M.17 and owed a great deal to experience garnered with the ubiquitous M.7. However, the sesquiplane M.17 broke new ground for Macchi by having its Isotta-Fraschini Asso engine mounted above the upper wing, which was given pronounced dihedral to lower the power unit relative to the hull. This feature and the skeletal interplane I-struts with 'sparrow foot' extremities are the distinguishing features of the M.17, which proved to be an able and fast competition machine, excelling itself at Monaco.

When the M.19 came along the engine was seen to be driving a four-bladed tractor screw – all previous Macchi 'boats had been pushers – and was buried in the wing. Moreover, the wing bracing had been changed to the bridge-builder's Warren-girder configuration with three pairs of struts per side, each pair being wire-braced. A departure for Macchi was additional bracing struts, two per side between the lower mainplanes and the chines of the hull; they were, in effect, extensions of the inner interplane struts. The pronounced upper mainplane dihedral remained a feature and the hull was given a very pronounced vee-bottom. Four sturdy, streamlined steel legs supported the Fiat A.14 engine and provided attachment points for the inner ends of the wing spars.

Structurally the machine followed the usual Italian lakeside pattern, with a plywood and planked hull surmounted by wooden, two-spar, fabric-covered wings. The interplane struts were circular-section steel tubes with wooden fairings.

The direct-drive 700 hp V-12 Fiat A.14 engine – sometimes referred to as the 650 hp Fiat – first appeared in 1917 and was originally developed for heavy bomber and airship propulsion. Structurally it followed European practice at the time, having individual forged steel cylinders with welded-on sheet steel water jackets, mounted on a two-piece light alloy crankcase. The narrow-angle, overhead valves worked in pent-roof combustion chambers and were operated by a single, shaft-driven, overhead camshaft for each cylinder bank. Forked connecting rods were used, running on a seven main-bearing crank. Mixture was drawn from a pair of duplex carburettors mounted in the vee of the engine and was fired by four Dixie 120 magnetos, two at each end of the engine.

With cylinder dimensions of 170 × 210 mm the swept volume amounted to no less than 57,199 cc (3,490 cu in). Normal rated output was 600 bhp at 1,500 rpm with 720 bhp at 1,700 rpm available for short periods. Naturally it was no lightweight, scaling 1,739 lb dry without the cooling system, so it needed a big aeroplane to carry it. The Achilles' heel of all V engines of the period, because of the properties of the very primitive bearing materials then available, was that main-bearing design envelope was always marginal. Designers had to make a hairline choice between specifying large-diameter journals and risking high rubbing speeds or calling for long, smaller-diameter bearings and ending up with a whippy crankshaft and a long engine. Whichever path they trod, the great danger was overspeeding the engine, which brought rapid and catastrophic failure. In this respect, even by the standards of the day, this particular Fiat engine looks very short of bearing area for the power and weight of its reciprocating parts. Zanetti was to discover all this to his cost.

Savoia S.21

It is fairly safe to assume that the S.21 came off the same drawing board as the S.51, namely that of Ing. Alessandro Marchetti. One reason would be that Conflienti had already departed from Sesto Calende with Lorenzo Santoni to found Chantiers Aéro Maritime de la Seine (CAMS); the other indication would be the Warren-truss arrangement of the interplane struts which became Marchetti's trademark. In common with other single-seat Italian 'boats, it originated as a fighter flying-boat prototype. At least that was the excuse and one *could* look upon it as a logical successor to the elderly S.13. It had a considerably higher wing-loading, 18 lb/sq ft against the older designs, 11 lb in racing trim and was claimed to be fully aerobatic with a service ceiling of 19,000 ft.

The configuration was certainly novel but quite logical with a large-span lower wing to give a good base for the wingtip floats and a small upper plane which not only brought the wing area up to the design requirement but acted as the upper flange of a Warren-girder configuration of which the trusses were the interplane struts.

The feature of this high aspect ratio, biplane flying-boat, which represented a complete turnaround from previous Savoia practice was to use the 7.68 m (25.2 ft) lower wing as the main lifting surface with the control surfaces mounted on it. The upper mainplane, set above the fully cowled engine, had a smaller lifting surface, 5.1 m (16.73 ft) span, and one would be forgiven for assuming that it was 'adjustable', like the upper mainframe of the SPAD-Herbemont, by replacing it with a larger wing for load-carrying. The wing shown in photographs would appear to be the smallest possible.

The four pairs of wooden struts supporting the upper wing had wire bracing between each pair of struts. It was further supported by a pair of N-struts from the engine mounting. Looking at the layout one can imagine the designer saying to himself, 'I'll fit a big wing to lift the fuselage and pilot and I'll give the engine a little wing all to itself.'

Photographs indicate that considerable development work was done on the machine because there is an early version with uncowled radiator and two-blade propeller, and a later modification with a streamlined nose-cowling and larger, four-bladed screw, which seems to indicate more power.

Details of the construction are lacking but it almost certainly had an all-wooden fuselage of mixed ply and planked construction. The Conflienti influence persisted in the hull form with a modest vee at the bow running into a concave section at the step.

The fabric-covered wings were of two-spar, wooden construction with wood-faired, steel-tube, interplane struts. Ailerons were fitted to the lower mainplane only

and there was a large, braced, cruciform tailplane with full-depth rudder to counter the torque of the 475 hp Ansaldo San Giorgio V-12, water-cooled engine. This was mounted in the usual Savoia fashion on N-struts. In the aircraft's final form the engine was completely enclosed in a beautifully formed nacelle with a cowled radiator. It drove a four-bladed wooden pusher propeller.

Flying the machine was the exclusive preserve of Guido Janello, which implies that it was something of a 'hot ship' as the wing-loading suggests. In flight tests Guido Janello flew the S.21 at speeds in excess of 160 mph and, given good health and a reliable engine, could easily have outpaced the M.19 in the race.

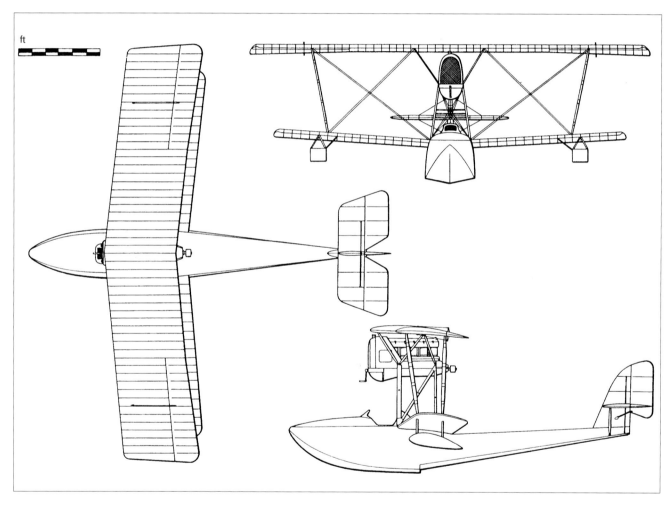

Macchi M.7bis (1921): Wing Span: 32 ft 7 in (9.90 m). Length Overall: 26 ft 6 in (8.10 m). Wing Area: 286.3 sq. ft (26.07 m²). Weight Empty: 1,710 lb (776 kg). T-O Weight: 2,381 lb (1,080 kg). Max Wing Loading: 8.32 lb/sq. ft (40.62 kg/m²). Isotta-Fraschini 6-cylinder, liquid-cooled, engine of 250 hp.

Naples 1922

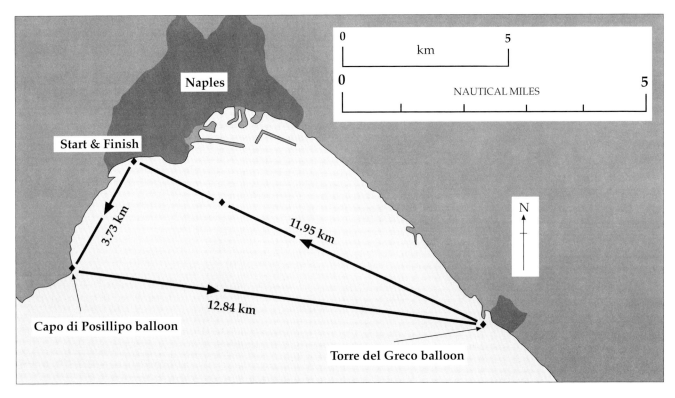

Schneider Trophy Contest Course: Naples 1922.

Run-up

The Italian-organised contests for the Coupe d'Aviation Maritime Schneider in 1920 and 1921 at Venice can only be regarded as the nadir of the contest. This was not the fault of the organising club. They produced their own share of entries. Only the French attempted to make the contest international when they entered a SPAD-Herbemont in 1920 and fielded Sadi Lecointe in a Nieuport 29 floatplane in 1921. Other countries had not been interested or had disliked the 1920 weight-lifting rule.

Let us now consider the public attitude to long-distance travel. People at that time were used to a more relaxed rate of progress. In most minds Paris was a place one went to once in a lifetime for a month's holiday. One visited Venice in the course of a six months' Grand Tour. London to Milan by air had not even been thought of. Even the London to Paris route was only just being opened up to a few intrepid travellers. Aircraft constructors in Britain and France, well versed in building prototypes in a few weeks, did not take too kindly to having their creations take weeks or months to get to some out-of-the-way place with the prospects of

delays by Customs and the possibility of losing the machines *en route*.

For these reasons the decision of the Italian club to hold the 1922 event in the Bay of Naples was a welcome one. Rail communications with Naples were not good but the port was easily accessible by sea from France and Britain. Moreover, the club's decision the previous year to abandon their payload rule had opened up the possibility of building pure racing machines for the race rather than the modified military types which had been the general rule in 1920 and 1921. The date had been fixed for 26 August with the navigability trials and flotation test, very little changed from the preceding year, taking place on the 24th and 25th. The ordained circuit was a triangular one of 15.4 nm (28.521 km), to be flown thirteen times, with the start and finish line off the seaplane base at what is now Villa Communale. Turning points, marked by balloons flown from lighters, were at Capo di Posillipo and Torre del Greco, outside Naples harbour. As in 1921 a massive entry fee was imposed to discourage irresponsible entries, the monies so obtained being disbursed as prizes.

Big political changes had taken place in the host country. After a period of intense political indecision it had espoused a new doctrine, Fascism, under Benito Mussolini – he became Premier in 1922 – and Italy was at least heading in a single direction – right or wrong – rather than several all at once. The new regime, urged on by that air-minded poet, Gabriel d'Annunzio, was dedicated to the extension of Italian air power.

France did have political stability at that time. Patriotism was not dead and its aircraft industry was busy with military orders aimed at building up an air arm of 200 squadrons. Sporting aviation in that country was actively encouraged but was preoccupied with racing and record-breaking landplanes. However there were a few seaplane meetings, like the annual one at Monaco, which attracted some attention from the major constructors. All of these contests, whether for landplanes or seaplanes, were aimed at producing better military aircraft through competition.

In Great Britain the immediate post-war slump was beginning to give way to a halting return to prosperity. The demob gratuities had been spent and the nation was beginning to come to its senses and at last realise the vastness of its war debts. The effect on the aircraft industry was predictable since it relied mainly on government contracts. In that year the reduction in the Air Estimates from £15 million to £10 million was a hard blow because it meant a proportional reduction in the income of the aircraft industry. As a consequence the British industry had to look hard at the export field and sell exports to live. There was very little money to be made out of maintaining the 32-squadron Royal Air Force and its diminutive Fleet Air Arm.

As a measure of the puny orders forthcoming from the government, the Air Estimates that year called for 92 new aircraft with a further 65 to be converted and 361 to be rebuilt from existing machines. The one bright spot was that civil aviation was at last getting under way, although it was far from being in its stride, and sporting aviation was gaining adherents, but despite the government of the day, not because of it.

Even with the change in the rules, international entries for the Coupe Maritime did not exactly pour in, but those that were made were mainly viable. After Sadi Lecointe's bad luck with his floatplane the previous year the French had obviously decided that there was more logic in the Italian preoccupation with flying-boats. Accordingly two new CAMS 36 machines from the Chantiers Aéro Maritime de la Seine were entered, designed by our old friend Conflienti using the Savoia hull form built under licence from his old firm. Following in the footsteps of his managing director, Lorenzo Santoni, Conflienti had moved from Savoia the previous year to start a French company on the Seine at St Denis, away from the political unrest in Italy. Conflienti's place at Savoia had been taken by Alessandro Marchetti who had left Vickers-Terni to take the post. It is reasonable to assume that the CAMS machine represented the type of aircraft that Savoia would have been building if Conflienti had not left them.

Although the one British entry, Hubert Scott-Paine's Supermarine Sea Lion II, has been hailed as a great sporting gesture, it was in fact a calculated attempt to gain kudos and orders for Supermarine. Of the British manufacturers, Sopwith-Hawker, Fairey, Avro, Blackburn and Handley Page, companies which had produced satisfactory designs of their own during the War, were getting most of the government's orders at that time.

As erstwhile subcontractors, Supermarine were being left out in the cold. There was work to be done on military and civil flying-boats – the cross-Channel flying-boat service was proving a success – but not enough to keep the workforce busy. Above all, Scott-Paine, as a flying-boat specialist, needed somewhere to prove his wares.

The Schneider Trophy race was the ideal place to do it. There was no equivalent event in Great Britain, nor in France. And Scott-Paine had not been oblivious to the way things were going with the race, nor to the mediocrity of the winning aircraft. The decision to build a special machine had been made in 1921 and the Sea King II prototype/demonstrator had been quietly modified in a hangar at the back of the main works in Woolston. Indeed, so secretly had this been done, that Henri Biard, the firm's test pilot, by his own account, did not even know of the existence of the modified machine, although, when he was confronted with it he must have been hard-pushed to distinguish it from the aircraft he had been demonstrating and flight testing earlier.

Scott-Paine cleverly found backers for his project. It was not too difficult because there was a general realisation in British aviation circles that under the three-win rule the Trophy would be lost forever if the Italians won it for a third time. It was really too important a property to languish in Italy and something had to be done about it. It helped politically that he proposed, as before, to power his machine with the outstanding Napier Lion engine. This unit, at the time, was far and away the best of the European aero engines on the basis of power-to-weight and reliability. It made it possible to put at least 450 hp into a relatively light machine.

It is interesting to note that the design of the Supermarine SS Racing Amphibian, which was the drawing office title of the Sea Lion II, was initiated late in the first half of 1921 by young Reginald Mitchell under the instructions of Commander Bird. This was just a month before de Briganti scored his victory by default at Venice in the veteran Macchi 7B. It causes one to wonder if the machine was really intended for the 1922 Aerial Derby – hence Amphibian – for which it was entered as the Sea King II, and diverted to the Schneider race at the last moment after the 1921 result. Bird's partner, Scott-Paine, probably considered that it could be a walk-over if the opposition was of the calibre of the M.7bis.

For their part the Italians, having won the event twice, were determined to keep the Trophy in their country. This is reflected in the strength of their entry. Altogether six machines were proposed, two from the

The winner at Naples in 1922. Henri Biard's Supermarine Sea Lion powered by a 450 hp Napier Lion engine driving a four-blade pusher propeller.

Savoia company, two from Macchi and an interesting but rather ephemeral one from the Pegna-Bonmartini-Cerroni concern. It has been suggested that the Italian entry was government sponsored. Evidence does not support this but there is little doubt that success would be rewarded with military orders and there was the added attraction that the race would be an excellent showcase for the one new design.

This, the most competitive entry, was the S.51 from Savoia. Coming from the drawing board of Alessandro Marchetti, it was an interesting and very fast, Itala-Hispano-powered, sesquiplane flying-boat whose pilot was to be Alessandro Passaleva. Macchi were fielding the ageing M.7bis which had won the previous year in the hands of de Briganti and was to be flown by Corgnolino, and the relatively fast M.18 to be piloted by Arturo Zanetti.

Savoia's second World War One entry type, designated the S.50, was not really a Savoia at all. It was in effect an ageing World War One fighter design from the Vickers subsidiary at Terni, mounted on floats. It is usually referred to as the MVT, Marchetti-Vickers-Terni, to include the name of designer Marchetti, who no doubt took it with him in his baggage out of sentiment when

The 1922 Savoia S.51 powered by a 300 hp Hispano-Suiza engine. (*Musée de l'Air*)

he moved to Sesto Calende in 1921. It was eliminated very early in the proceedings when it crashed during tests on Lake Garda, reputedly killing the Savoia test pilot Guarnieri, who had been back-up pilot to Janello in the S.21 the previous year. In any case the whole conception of this biplane machine with its bird-platform wings, wing-warping and wire trailing edges was pre-1914 and even when propelled by a 280 hp SPA motor, it could hardly have been competitive.

Unfortunately the PBC Pegna Pc.2 floatplane, in common with his entry in 1921, was destined not to be completed in time. This was a pity because, like the big PRB flying-boat with which Pegna was also associated, it showed great promise. The Pc.2 was a beautifully streamlined, cantilever monoplane, powered by an Italian-built Modèle 42 Hispano-Suiza engine. It was derived from a design which was to materialise a year later as the Piaggio P.2 fighter. Pegna was in the throes of selling PBC to the Genoese shipbuilders Piaggio during this period – the deal was clinched in August 1923 – and the alternative designation of the Schneider floatplane is Piaggio P.4 (or P.4 Pc.2 for the pedantic).

As already stated the race had been scheduled to take place on 26 August and had been allocated that date in the aviation calendar. Without reference to anyone but themselves the Aero Club d'Italia, possibly under political pressure (administration problems were the excuse), made the shock announcement in mid-July that the date would be brought forward to 12 August. It would be unkind to suggest that there was anything but *force majeure* in this. It was just coincidental that the Italian machines could be got ready in time for this date while the opposition, hundreds of miles away, might conceivably be less fortunate.

This change of date was too much for Chantiers Aéro Maritime de la Seine. The machines were completed, we are told, but too late to 'catch the train'. This was unfortunate because the CAMS 36 fleet fighter prototype which Conflienti had created was an interesting and advanced machine, although posing problems for the pilot because, it being a tractor design, he was located behind the lower mainplane, where he could see little except wings and fresh air. The engine was the inevitable Hispano-Suiza 200 hp Modèle 42.

At Woolston, on Southampton Water, the Supermarine contender was complete, having been constructed during the preceding winter. However, it had not been air-tested when the revised race date was announced. Biard's biographer describes how he took off for the first test flight and had the engine cut out above a mass of moored shipping. Pilots of that era always had a funk hole in sight out of the corner of their eyes and Biard successfully put the machine down on Southampton Water. It was towed back to the works and the fuel system modified to eliminate the air lock which had stopped the engine. The following day marked the beginning of a series of test flights to explore speed and handling, which resulted in a number of modifications. When it was seen that speeds of the order of 160 mph could be expected and that there had been no loss of flying qualities as a result of increasing the wing loading, the machine was crated for transit.

In view of the reduced time schedule and impending strikes on the continental railways, Scott-Paine was fortunate in having among his friends the management of the General Steam Navigation Company, who had an interest in his passenger-carrying activities with flyingboats. They generously came to his rescue and not only offered to divert their SS *Philomel* to Naples, but as a bonus offered him and his crew-members free passage to Naples as sole charterer. This was typical of the practical help which everyone gave to what was generally, and rightly, looked upon as a patriotic gesture. Shell contributed the petrol, H.T. Vane of Napier, as recorded elsewhere, lent the special Lion engine. Charles Cheers Wakefield of Castrol, a great patriot who was ever mindful of the potential publicity of a win like this, donated the oil and financial help as well. One of the British insurance companies even unbent so far as to give cover at half rate.

Thanks to the General Steam Navigation Company and their Captain Field, the Supermarine team was able to dock at Naples in good time for a decent practice period. This gave the Supermarine crew the time to get the airframe rigged to perfection, and the Napier mechanics were able to set the carburation right for the hot conditions of southern Italy. Naturally the natives were keen to weigh up the performance of the challenger. To help them along, 'Red Hot' Paine gave full notice to the organisers whenever he intended to practise the machine. Biard would then proceed to do a 'slow' act (lapping at about 140 mph and taking turns wide to give the impression that the Sea Lion was a bit of a handful for the benefit of the Italian engineers who occupied every vantage point to assess the Sea Lion's performance. Meanwhile there were less-public flat out tests outside the bay to confirm carburettor settings. Biard even had time to take a look inside the Vesuvius crater and experience the massive thermal created by the hot lava.

Navigability and Seaworthiness Tests

In Naples a number of reasons were given for the absence of the CAMS entries at the seaworthiness and navigability tests which commenced on 10 August. One was that the railway strikes, which caused the Sea Lion to be taken to Naples by sea, had delayed the French machines. Another report even went so far as to say that they appeared at Naples but were not ready in time to take part in the tests. The bare facts of the matter were that the machines were not complete in time to carry out full flying trials and did not leave France. The machines were not, in fact, *au point* until after the race had been run. However, they were finished off and flown with 200 hp Hispano engines before being put into storage ready for the 1923 race, for which they were extensively modified, re-engined and redesignated the CAMS 36bis. For the record the pilots nominated for 1922 were Lieutenants Teste and Poire although the latter was intended to be replaced by Lieutenant de Vroman.

Of the aircraft which were actually present at Naples,

all except the Savoia S.51 satisfactorily completed the flotation tests on 10 August, which, as at Venice, consisted of lying at anchor for six hours and remaining afloat without being bailed out. The tiny, flat-section stabilising floats of the Savoia S.51 positioned at a high angle of incidence to the water, were effective in stabilising the machine when it was under way, but had little to offer in the way of buoyancy when the machine was at rest, to resist overturning forces. These could be considerable because of the high centre of gravity and the windage of the high, effectively monoplane, upper wing, exacerbated by the fact that Marchetti was addicted to making heavy wings, with hardwood spars and saving weight on the main structure. The theory was proved when a puff of wind struck the S.51 during the flotation test and overturned it. Only prompt action by its own crew and that of a nearby launch prevented it from sinking. There was a lesson to be learnt here because the more conventional equal-span biplane machines, with their large-volume wingtip floats and longer lower wingspan had a much bigger reserve of seaworthiness. The Sea Lion II was a good example of this because the wingtip floats were of very large volume, due to their deep section being extended right up to the wing. When an overturning force was applied to the machine, the floats gained buoyancy as they sank deeper into water.

There was the additional aerodynamic advantage in that, being faired into the wing, they created the minimum interference compared with strut-mounted floats. It was scarcely surprising that the Savoia overturned. Be that as it may, according to the rules, the S.51 should have been eliminated from the contest and the entry withdrawn by the Italian club. However Hubert Scott-Paine, in the sporting spirit of the times – in Britain it was considered 'not done' to protest in a major international sporting event – refused to protest and the Savoia was allowed to stay in the race. One could be cynical and say that 'Red Hot' judged the machine not to be competitive with the Sea Lion. Had he known its actual performance he might not have been so easy in his mind, but it is highly unlikely that he would have done other than he did.

The navigation test on 11 August was staged in the Bay of Naples on a 10 nm closed circuit. Machines were required to cross the line on the water, take off and complete five laps, in the course of which they had to alight, taxi for half a nautical mile, take off again and alight ahead of the finishing line, which they crossed on the water. For this purpose the Naples–Torre del Greco leg of the main course was used, the Naples turning point being treated as the start line with a series of buoys to mark the take-off and alighting points.

All machines successfully completed this last test,

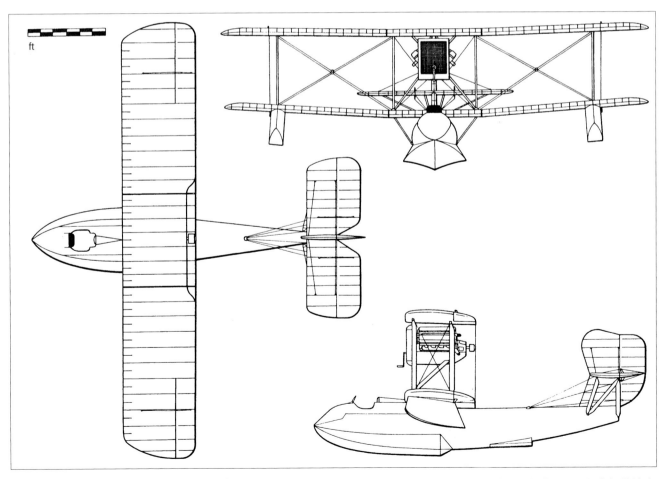

Supermarine Sea Lion II Flying Boat (1922): Wing Span: 31 ft 10 in (9.6 m). Length Overall: 27 ft 6 in (7.5 m). Weight Empty: 2,381 lb (1,080 kg). T-O Weight: 3,163 lb (1,435 kg). Napier Lion, liquid-cooled, 12-cylinder 'W' configuration engine 450 hp.

which was held in perfect conditions. Only Passaleva was unhappy, the S.51, apart from other defects, suffering from vibration caused by the propeller, which was beginning to delaminate after its wetting the day before. According to the rules this was one part of the machine's equipment which could not be changed.

Despite the intensely cordial atmosphere which reigned between the Italians and the British, the contest was still very much a needle match. Both sides dearly wanted to assess the performance of the competition so that they could plan their race accordingly. The Sea Lion II, as a lone entry, was particularly vulnerable against three Italian machines. For this reason, Henri Biard was especially careful not to reveal the performance of his machine in the navigability trials. Being a very experienced flying-boat pilot he naturally handled the machine beautifully on the take-off and put it down precisely between the alighting buoys. But during the air tests he was careful not to use the full performance of the Lion engine and again he took his turns wide to give the impression that the machine was awkward to handle.

With the exception of the S.51 the Italian machines performed equally well on their water and air tests. Naturally the Italian pilots had less reason to hide their performance during the air tests, quite apart from the national tendency to 'have a go'. Consequently

the performance of the Savoia especially, and even the Macchi M.17, appeared to be better than that of the British machine, and the betting of the highly partisan crowd which had gathered in Naples to watch the contest swung heavily in favour of an Italian victory.

The Race

Following the pattern set in previous years, the 15.4 nm course was laid out in the Bay of Naples with marker boats flying balloons on short cables to mark the turning points. It was in the shape of a short-based triangle with its base between the port of Naples and Capo di Posillipo and its apex off Torre del Greco. Present-day travellers would recognise this as the terminal for the Naples–Palermo car ferries. The start and finish line was laid out off the seaplane base opposite what is now Villa Communale, on the outskirts of Naples. The course was taken anticlockwise, the machines flying south-south-west from the start for about three nautical miles before turning off the Capo di Posillipo and heading east to the sharp turn at Torre del Greco. Because of the intense midday heat during the Italian summer, most sporting events are timed to start in the late afternoon, when the temperature is falling, and continues to fall during the event. The Schneider race was no exception. A start

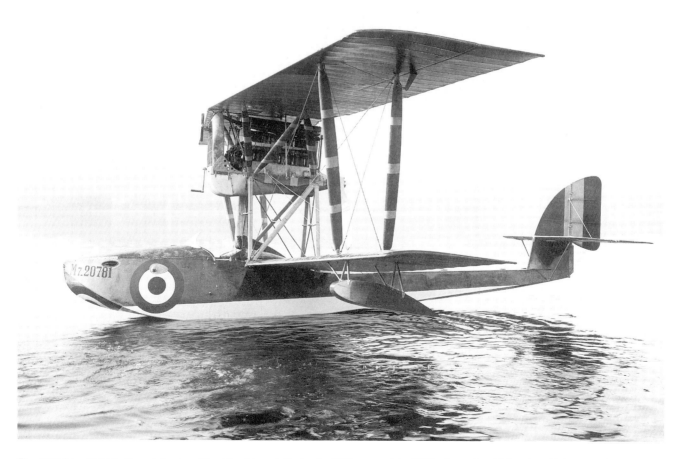

The 1922 Macchi M.7. One of the two Macchi entries at Naples in 1922 powered by 260 hp Isotta-Fraschini engine driving a pusher propeller. (*Aeronautica Macchi*)

was arranged for four o'clock in the afternoon, giving time for the dignitaries and the local population to finish off their leisurely Italian lunches before moving out to watch the fun. It also gave the teams good time to get their machines ready after the navigability tests of the preceding day.

Lots had been drawn for starting order and Biard was lucky to be first to go. At least this meant that he could make his first lap, unimpeded.

Even at that time in the afternoon, the sun was beating down, creating a heat haze round the shimmering cone of Vesuvius, which dominated the whole proceedings. The sea was like a millpond when, a minute after 4 pm, to be exact, Biard, attired casually in an open-necked shirt and flannel trousers, gently opened up the throttle of the big Napier engine until it was giving its all, hauled the Sea Lion off the limpid, 'sticky' water and headed across the line in the direction of the first marker balloon at Capo di Posillipo.

His plan was to go flat out from the start and hopefully to demoralise the Italians sitting in their cockpits behind the starting line. His first lap, in 7 min 10 sec – the fastest of the race – must have had the desired effect, representing as it did a speed of 129 knots (149 mph), about 10 knots faster than the Italians had credited the machine with. The Italian engineers, from their timekeeping activities during practice and by eyeball estimation, had credited the Sea Lion with a maximum speed of about 122 knots (140 mph), which would give a lap time of a little less than 8 minutes.

On this basis their tactics must have been to send Corgnolino off in their slowest machine, the Macchi M.7bis, to pace Biard, because as the Sea Lion came down from Torre del Greco on its second lap, Corgnolino took off and crossed the line as the Sea Lion went past. Unfortunately the Sea Lion was too fast for him. By the time he had got the Macchi airborne, Biard was banking hard for the Capo di Posillipo turn.

Before either machine had come round again, Arturo Zanetti was airborne and, at 11 minutes 6 seconds after the hour, roared across the line in the Macchi 18 just ahead of Biard, now completing his first lap. Passaleva remained sitting in the fastest Italian machine, waiting with his engine running.

Biard had crossed the line and was well into his second lap before Passaleva, by now aware of the speed of the opposition, joined the fray and set off to try to equal the Britisher's times, knowing full well that his machine, though a match for the Supermarine in normal trim, was now scarcely airworthy. With sagging fabric after its soaking, and a delaminating propeller, it needed a brave and determined man to fly it at all. Alessandro Passaleva must have been just that kind of man because, as an experienced pilot, he knew well that the unbalanced forces created by the propeller could very well shake the engine out of its mountings, when the whole wing structure would collapse and hurl the machine into the sea. Probably for this reason the S.51's first round in 7 min 31.7 sec, was almost its slowest. Passaleva seems to have been tentatively nursing the machine along, feeling its

strength. However, his time must have cheered the British contingent, although they had no means of telling Biard that he could have eased off a little. Meanwhile Zanetti and Corgnolino were lapping in more than 8 minutes, their first lap times being 8 min 2.6 sec and 8 min 39.2 sec respectively. Their only hope was that one or both of the two fastest machines would retire. It was more likely to happen to the Savoia than to the Supermarine.

Biard had no way of knowing this and was flying wonderfully consistently, taking the turns tight in vertical banks, turning in times of 7 min 10 sec, 7 min 10.4 sec, 7 min 10.4 sec, 7 min 10.6 sec for his first four laps.

Passaleva's take-off time had been at 17 minutes, 1 second after four o'clock, just 3 minutes, 19 seconds before Biard crossed the line for the second time. Zanetti's Macchi had just completed its first lap, just 30 seconds ahead of him, while the M.17 was still on the final leg of its first round.

Biard's first encounter with the opposition would have been on his fourth lap when he found himself rocking in the slipstream of the M.18 at the end of the Posillipo–Torre del Greco leg. Sneaking a little height he dived past the Italian as they rounded the marker balloon and had hauled out a 31-second lead from him by the time he passed the timekeepers for the fourth time.

This, if anything, gave the Italians visual evidence of the superior speed of the Sea Lion. It was also an indication to Biard that he easily had the legs of the second fastest Italian machine. Moreover, he would be able to see the unmistakeable silhouette of the S.51 ahead of him. It was well into the Posillipo–del Greco leg as he crossed the start line in the early stages of the race and he could see himself closing on it lap by lap. Possibly for this reason he eased off a little, his lap time dropping gradually from 7 min 11.60 sec at the end of the fifth lap to 7 min 19.4 sec by the eighth lap.

Despite his reduced speed Biard could see that he was gaining on the S.51 to the extent that on his seventh lap he had reduced the gap between the two machines to little more than the shortest leg of the circuit, 112 seconds, and was approaching the starting line turn as Passaleva was rounding the Posillipo marker balloon. On the next lap this margin was down to 1 minute 10 seconds and they were both well in sight of each other. No doubt Passaleva could see the British machine closing on him but he dare not push his rattling, vibrating aircraft any harder. On his part Biard could see that he had the race in the bag, and eased off as if to keep station, his times on the last four laps roughly matching those of Passaleva. During these last laps of the race Passaleva was flying in fairly close company with Zanetti and Corgnolino, the former having overtaken his team-mate on the circuit on the eighth lap. Passaleva did not move ahead of these two until the penultimate lap. At least it gave the spectators value for money. All of this time, to the uninitiated, the Italians appeared to be two miles ahead of Biard. However, he was the best part of three laps in front of them owing to his early starting time. His thirteenth and final lap was the slowest of all, 7 min 29.3

sec but the machine was by no means spent and after completing the course he put in two extra laps, as Scott-Paine said, 'just to make sure'. No doubt he wanted to see if Passaleva would speed up because, until the Italian had completed his full quota of laps, there was no certainty that Biard had won the race, although he must have been sure in his own mind after his very fast first seven laps. But the main purpose was to raise the distance flown to 400 km by prior arrangement with the FAI timekeepers. This enabled the Sea Lion to annexe world closed-circuit records for the 100 km, 200 km and 400 km distances. It might also explain Biard's higher speed over the first seven laps, which represented the 200 km distance.

Biard need not have worried. Although Passaleva did speed up during his last two laps, there was no chance of him making up the time that Biard had saved at the beginning. Biard's elapsed time was 1 hr 24 min 51.6 sec, more than 2 minutes quicker than the Italians, 1 hr, 26 min 54.2 sec. He had in fact, clinched the race by his brilliant flying in the first seven laps of the race.

So the Schneider Trophy returned to Britain again, to the scene of much rejoicing when the victorious team steamed up the Solent in the little SS *Philomel*, bearing the cup with them, to be greeted by the Lord Mayor of Southampton.

Note: Accounts of the race state that the machines crossed the start line on the water. If the race times are to be believed this is patently not so because the first laps would all be the slowest. In point of fact Biard's first lap was his fastest; this could not have happened if he had to take off across the line.

In his 'ghosted' autobiography *Wings*, Biard describes how the three Italian machines, flying together, 'closed the door' on him in the turns so that his only tactic was to gain height and overtake the whole

formation in a dive. One has, regretfully, to assume that this incident was recalled long after the race and embellished by the writer to establish one of the myths with which Schneider folklore is so liberally sprinkled. A computer analysis of the race, adding the cumulative times to the starting time and back-calculating the time taken by each aircraft on each leg – possible because the race was flown in virtually still air – shows that, unless the published times are catastrophically wrong, at no time in the race did Biard get closer than within a couple of miles of Passaleva. Zanetti and Corgnolino did fly in company for a considerable time in mid-race and eventually the faster M.18 drew ahead, but at this phase of the contest Biard was on the other side of the course. The only time he passed Zanetti was on the Posillipo–del Greco leg of his fourth lap, while Corgnolino was overtaken on the first leg of his sixth lap.

Conclusions

When Henri Biard crossed the finish line at Naples and went on to make two extra laps and establish a seaplane speed record, little did he realise that he was seeing the end of an era in the history of the Schneider race. Mussolini's Fascist government had given moral support to Savoia and Macchi but they were hardly in a position to commission special machines that would come later. The following year the US government were to step in and henceforward the race would increasingly become a government concern.

The machine Biard flew, although the most powerful in the race, was not the fastest. Passaleva's S.51, which despite its inferior power loading, 7.921 lb against 5.51 lb per hp, was aerodynamically so much cleaner that it was able to challenge the Supermarine, despite a delaminated propeller, and average 229 km/h (141 mph). Just how fast it was, materialised later when, in December 1922 it was flown both ways over the measured kilometre to set a new world seaplane record at 280.15 km/h (174.07 mph). It could be said that Britain won the contest on the strength of a delaminating propeller. On the other hand it could also be said that the Italians lost it because the designer of their entry made a gross error when calculating the volume of the stabilising floats which resulted in his creation being capsized by a puff of wind. The S.51 was not a seaworthy design and was scarcely within the spirit of the regulations. For this it paid the price of defeat.

As a final note it was to be regretted that the French machines were not ready. It was a story that was to be repeated again and again in the history of the race, even though CAMS did manage to field two machines the following year.

The Aircraft

Macchi M.18 I-BAHG Race No. 9

It is not certain whether the little Macchi M.18 flown by Arturo Zanetti at Naples was the second of two aircraft built, or whether it was the one which was crashed at

This emphasises the low level at which competitors rounded the marker balloons at Naples in 1922. (*Stato Maggiore Aeronautica*)

Monaco in 1921 and was subsequently rebuilt. Its main purpose is said to have been to act as a half scale proto-type for the big M.19.

Although some Italian authorities refer to the M.17, which was Alessandro Tonini's first try at a racing seaplane, as being developed from the M.7, it is difficult to see the logic of this. Although it is similar in being a biplane pusher flying-boat, both the hull and the wing arrangement differ. The difference in the hull was that it was proportionally deeper than that of the M.7, and the vee of the planing bottom was more acute, with the pilot sitting well-down behind a tiny vee-screen. The large, strut-mounted, Fabre-type wingtip floats, set at a high angle of incidence, seemed to reflect the designer's concern about the rather top-heavy form of his creation.

The wing arrangement was unusual in that the inner ends of the upper wings were attached to the upper ends of the engine pylon struts which were in the usual double N-strut configuration with very wide-chord front legs. As a result the 260 hp Isotta-Fraschini Asso engine, in a slipper cowling with a large honeycomb radiator, in effect sat on top of the wing, looking huge in relation to what was really a very small aeroplane with a wingspan less than that of a Tiger Moth. This arrangement also gave the upper mainplane a rather acute dihedral.

Both the upper and lower wings were of high aspect ratio, about 8.7 for a span of 8.8 m. The wing loading was high for the period at about 8 lb per sq ft. Probably because of the small chord, Tonini chose to use single interplane struts set between the front main spars with curious jury struts to the rear spars and wing leading edges. Ailerons were unbalanced and on the upper wing only.

It was only aft of the wing that the M.17 showed any real similarity to the M.7, the typically Macchi cruciform, strut-braced tail surfaces and abbreviated rudder appearing to be identical in design but somewhat smaller.

Its speeds in the race from a 250 hp engine are very creditable.

Savoia S.51 I-BAIU Race No. 7

In his second racing flying-boat design for Savoia, Alessandro Marchetti reversed the configuration he had adopted for the S.21, making the upper mainplane of his new creation the main lifting surface and using a vestigial lower wing as an outrigger for tiny streamlined floats and as a lower flange for his favourite 'W' for Warren-truss strut arrangement. Apart from its aesthetic appeal it had the apparent advantage of keeping the main wing away from 'ground' effect and above the waves which must have tended to wash over and swamp the S.21 mainplane. The stabilising floats were set on N-struts angled outwards to increase the stabilising effect and, in common with the hull, had Conflienti's patented planing surface, which started as a vee-section at the bow, merging into a concave section in the run of the planing bottom.

Construction was mainly of wood in the Italian lakes tradition, the hull being beautifully planked to give a streamlined, rounded form. There was a tiny opening for the pilot's cockpit with a long, streamlined headrest. The typically Marchetti wing was of very thin section, probably with double hardwood spars. In all likelihood it would be made in two panels attached to the upper portion of the engine cradle. This arrangement would have the added advantage of making rail transport easier. The engine nacelle was neatly faired into the wing with the exhaust stacks, which discharged through the top of it rather than, more logically, out of the sides. The reason for this is difficult to understand because the pipes would have to be routed round the cylinder blocks, making for a wider nacelle. It is fairly safe to assume certainly that the wing struts were wood-faired steel tubes. Apart from their stress-bearing activities – aside from keeping the wings apart they bore all the lift and alighting loads – they must have contributed a certain amount of lift.

Looking at the aerodynamics of the S.51 and comparing them with those of the S.21 it would appear that Marchetti felt that he had gone too far with the previous design and reduced the wing loading, mainly by increasing the chord and giving the S.51 a lower aspect ratio. The design was extremely pleasing aesthetically, the only untidy area being around the tips of the lower sponson wing where there was a general coming-together of struts of varying sizes which must have created aerodynamic interference.

The main shortcoming of the S.51 was that Marchetti seems to have miscalculated the volume of the stabilising floats in relation to the righting lever arm. In other words, being set close to the hull, the floats should have been bigger than if they had been set at the tips of an ordinary wing; as it was they were smaller with the inevitable result.

Cowes 1923

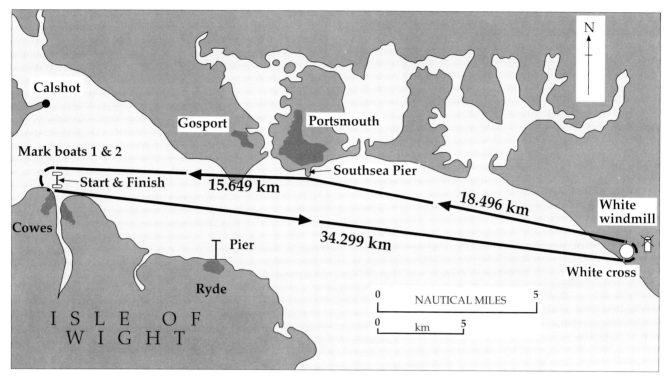

Schneider Trophy Contest Course: Cowes 1923.

Run-up

Henri Biard's lone victory at Naples in the Sea Lion II brought the Schneider Cup race proudly back to a Britain which was in the grips of roaring depression, with one and a quarter million unemployed out of a population only half of what it is today. This spelled hard times for the British aircraft industry. In 1921 its total labour force had fallen back to 2,500 souls against 9,250 in France. Only two hundred aircraft had been built in Britain in that year, most of them military prototypes for the Royal Air Force, which was working on the precept that any threat of another European war would show up ten years in advance. Their policy was to foster new designs but not to give production contracts for large quantities of aircraft which would be obsolescent if the threat of war did loom. It had estimates of only £12 million to keep itself and the British aircraft industry in existence. However, there were signs of expansion and in 1923 the Royal Air Force had been given the job of forming a home defence force which meant the creation of thirty-two new squadrons.

In private flying there was a preoccupation with low-powered, low-cost aircraft, powered by motorcycle engines, with the object of providing cheap flying for the masses and as an economical way of building up a reserve of pilots in case of war. To promote this movement the Duke of Sutherland, the then Under-Secretary of State for Air, had offered a prize of £500 for a competition. The theme was taken up by the *Daily Mail* newspaper, who offered their own prize of £1,000 with the result that the competition became known as the *Daily Mail Motor-glider Competition*. Technically, progress was slow. The proponents of metal construction were fighting a hard battle against a conservative element brought up in the wood-and-fabric tradition. Professor Junkers had sent his chief engineer to the Royal Aeronautical Society in January 1923 to read a paper on metal construction using Duralumin. His prophetic pronouncements on metal fuselage construction and the fundamentals of thick airfoil sections fell on the stony ground of prejudice and, in many cases, ignorance. His ideas were so far ahead of their time they were not to be utilised in Schneider racers until the end of the series.

Against this background of austerity, traditional competitions like the Aerial Derby and the King's Cup Race continued to be organised, the former acting as a proving ground for prototype landplane fighters. In common with the Pulitzer race in the USA it had as a side product the development of suitable airframes for floatplane use in the Schneider race.

Meanwhile France was building up a massive air force. In contrast with the total British production of 200 aircraft the French labour force of 9,250 had produced 300 civil machines and no less than 3,000 military aircraft. French manufacturers were in honour bound to support air racing and were European leaders with the Nieuport sesquiplane which dominated classic air races such as the Coupe Deutsch de la Meurthe. French military pilots flew the aircraft and there was close collaboration between the French Armée de l'Air and the aircraft industry. Any entry for the Schneider Trophy Race was likely to be state subsidised.

Italy was in much the same straits as Great Britain, only worse. Untypically, the new Fascist regime, despite a dedication to air power, had imposed a very tight military aircraft development budget until it got its house in order. There was little or no hope of government support for an entry and even had it been forthcoming there were no suitable engines. Consequently, the decision to send aircraft was delayed until almost the day of the race. In any case there was only one suitable aircraft, the Savoia S.51. Italy at that time did not have an engine with a suitable power-to-weight ratio to give it a chance. Sardonically, C.G. Gray quipped in *The Aeroplane*, 'there is no Italian entry due to the volcanic state of the Italian people'.

In America the situation was different, more potent forces were at work. This erstwhile European colony, which in 1914 had been a debtor nation, stood revealed by the conflict as the world's mightiest industrial power, a creditor with the whole of Europe its debtors. Despite protestations of isolationism and cries of 'peace in our time', just a very few wise men there could see that this situation brought with it enormous responsibilities. Moreover, they could see a threat on their Pacific seaboard from the burgeoning military potential of Japan, who had already fought a successful modern war against the Russians and had clear ambitions of an Eastern empire.

Despite its industrial potential America had gone into the 1914–18 War in the inglorious position of having to buy combat aircraft and engines from the Allies because they did not have anything suitable themselves. Determined never to let this happen again, they were now intent on building up their strength, including Army and Navy air forces armed with machines of entirely American design and construction. So there was money to spend; not a lot was allocated, but enough to build up squadrons and to buy prototypes. One aspect of this general movement was that the Army and Navy, urged on by the indomitable Brigadier-General Billy Mitchell and craggy Rear Admiral William Adger Moffett, were actively involving themselves in air racing with the emphasis on the National Air Races and the Pulitzer Aviation Trophy, which in 1920 had been transformed from a long-distance race to a round-the-pylons, closed-circuit event.

The object was to promote indigenous, advanced designs for pursuit aircraft and at the same time extend the skills of their pilots for later use in the flying-schools.

It was also meant to make the nation air-minded. Their method was to commission special machines for this purpose, and to allow service pilots to fly them in competition. With the added incentive of inter-service rivalry this policy had been remarkably effective. One of its major manifestations was the line of Curtiss Racers and the revolutionary series of Curtiss V-12, water-cooled engines that propelled them.

One facet of Mitchell's policy was to prove American designs against those of Europe, especially the French, who were generally regarded as the leaders in high-speed aircraft design. His first move in this direction had been to promote the Army entry of the Verville-Packard VCP-R racer in the 1920 Gordon Bennett Cup race at Étampes in France. This had developed into an American invasion with the Texas Aero Club, financed by brash and showy oil millionaire Seymour E.I. Cox, making its own entry and sending two purpose-built Curtiss racers, the Texas Kitten and the Texas Wildcat, powered by Curtiss C-12 geared engines. Yet another important American entry had been the innovative Dayton-Wright RB monoplane with its spruce and balsa cantilever wing and retractable gear.

For the Americans, the Gordon Bennett race was a hard lesson. Of the Texas Aero Club entry only the Texas Wildcat biplane was assembled. It flew briefly but crashed on its second flight despite a new pair of wings built, overnight, by Morane-Saulnier. The Texas Kitten monoplane was not even taken out of its crate. The hastily installed Packard 1A-2025 engine in the Verville VCP-R.1 was found to be undercooled. Moreover, it had badly designed engine air intakes and only completed one lap before retiring in a state of near-combustion. The Dayton-Wright also landed after its first lap with control problems; a rudder cable was found to be severed but there was the further difficulty of restricted forward visibility. The race result was a win for France by Sadi Lecointe at 168.5 mph in a Nieuport-Delage 29 Vitesse powered by a Modèle 42 Hispano-Suiza engine. This was the third French win in succession and the Gordon Bennett Trophy passed to France in perpetuity.

The Entries

In mid-July the Royal Aero Club committee finally approved the Solent as the venue for the 1923 race. In view of the excellent aeronautical services available in the Solent area at the various establishments of the flying-boat manufacturers, and especially since Sammy Saunders had again offered his East Cowes yard for maintenance and hangarage of visiting aircraft, it would have been difficult to go elsewhere in the British Isles and find the same facilities. However, alternatives were considered including a cross-Channel circuit with turning points on the French and British coasts. The date of the race was fixed for late September as the final event of the air racing season.

The very lively and likeable director of Civil Aviation, Sir Sefton Brancker, had already flown over the course and given it his blessing prior to the approval of the

The Supermarine Sea Lion III of 1923 with an early example of 'nose art'. (*Flight*)

Royal Aero Club. It was carefully chosen to avoid the area in Studland Bay which had caused so much anguish four years earlier because of its susceptibility to sea mists and fog. To this end it was laid out as a shallow, broad-based triangle, with the starting line set between two marker boats anchored 300 yards off Victoria pier, at Cowes. From Cowes the machines were to head for Selsey Bill and make an acute turn around a white cross set out on the ground in front of the old windmill on the Bill. From here they flew across the mouth of Southampton Water back to the start line in almost a straight line, only making a slight diversion to round a marker boat anchored off the South Parade pier at Southsea.

With memories of the *Ombra* débâcle of 1919 still very much alive in their minds, the Royal Aero Club committee had located their headquarters in the building at the end of Victoria pier, Cowes, where they would be in full contact with the competitors at all times. The members who had repleted themselves aboard *Ombra* in 1919 were this time allowed to man the ramparts of the exclusive Royal Yacht Squadron

building and enjoy Squadron hospitality. There was a truly military flavour about the Race Committee. Lieutenant-Colonel M.O. Darby was given the job of Clerk of the course. His marshals were Lieutenant-Colonel A. Ogilvie, acting on behalf of the Americans, Captain R.J. Goodman Crouch, looking after the French and D.C. McLaughlan in charge of the Italian entry. Captain L.T.G. Minsell was responsible for the British entrants. There is no doubt that the whole committee had learned by its mistakes at Bournemouth and the members were out to show that they had realised the error of their ways.

Not unexpectedly one of the first countries to announce its participation was France, as early as March, whose Aéro Club submitted six entries from three companies, Société Industrielle de Caudebec-en-Caux (SICC), Société Aéronautique Blanchard and Chantiers Aéro Maritime de la Seine. At the same time it was revealed that the United States Navy would be entering three machines and that there was the possibility of three Italian machines.

The US entry was particularly interesting to the

Europeans because this was only the second time any government body had actively participated in a European sporting event. The only other instance had been the US Army entry of the Verville-Packard in the 1920 Gordon Bennett. The opinion was that if this was the best the US armed forces could do, their Navy was not in with much of a chance, especially when it was announced that they would be bringing floatplanes, a type of machine which the Europeans considered unsuitable for serious sea work.

In contrast to the American attitude, the head of the Royal Air Force, Air Marshal Sir Hugh Trenchard, was actively opposed to the idea of military machines and pilots taking part in air races. The Air Ministry showed very little interest in the Schneider Trophy race, which, one would have thought, would have been an ideal experimental platform. Entreaties from all sides, including questions in the House of Commons, fell on deaf ears. It was pointed out that if the Trophy went to America it would cost a great deal of money to get it back. But, assuring themselves that private enterprise had brought the Trophy back from Naples the previous year, the best they would offer was to buy the airframe of the winning aircraft for £3,000 so long as it was of British design and manufacture and had not won before.

Predictably, there were members of the British aircraft industry who were sufficiently public-spirited to offer to defend the trophy against a large foreign entry. Initially only two British entries were received by the Royal Aero Club, the most promising being the Sopwith-Hawker Rainbow biplane racer, powered by a 400 hp Jupiter engine, which was destined to take second place in the Aerial Derby early in August. It had started life as the Sopwith Schneider and the manufacturer proposed to put it back on floats especially for the event. Blackburn Aircraft of Brough in Yorkshire, for the first and last time, also put in an entry. Although the company was busy with new designs and construction, Robert Blackburn felt that he would not only be supporting his country but also proving its validity as a constructor of naval aircraft if he made an entry. Like the others this was a purely private venture. Company profits were low at the time and the shareholders were pressing for dividends. It was a case of dividends or a Schneider entry. The Schneider entry won.

In the early stages there was no entry from Supermarine. This came after the Sopwith Engineering Company went into liquidation, to be replaced by the H.G. Hawker Engineering Co. Ltd, and it was seen that the main preoccupation of the new company was with winning the Aerial Derby, and there would be difficulties in putting the Rainbow on floats in time for the Schneider race. Cynical about the prospects of Blackburn producing a competitive flying-boat, Hubert Scott-Paine hastily borrowed the old Sea Lion II back from the Air Ministry, to whom it had been sold after the Naples win, and hurriedly converted it into the Sea Lion III, with shorter wings and a more powerful Napier Lion IIA engine. Just how last-minute this entry was is shown in the pages of the British aviation press, who

depicted the old Sea Lion II as the British entry only the week before the race.

Confirmation of the American entry came in early July. There had been American entries before. Charles Weymann was the first in the very first Schneider race, but in a French machine, while the American Curtiss entry in 1913 had been a serious underestimation of the situation. But this latest entry was different because the US Navy decided to use floatplanes. To the British, anybody's navy is the senior service and therefore the challenge would be well considered and efficiently carried out. Moreover, the four aircraft entered included two of the latest Curtiss racing machines piloted by a team of America's most experienced service pilots with a great record of test-flying and racing behind them. It was an entry which was to change the nature of the race from one between patriotic private firms to a contest between governments.

Many reasons have been given for the American decision to enter. Some of them have been mentioned. It would not be unreasonable to think that one of them was that they wanted to show the Europeans just how far they had advanced in the aeronautical sciences. If this might seem a poor reason in this era of easy international communication, it should be remembered that in the early twenties, the British and Europeans were far more ignorant of what went on in the USA than they are now. The only means of personal communication was by sea and this was for the rich. The only cheap trips were one-way affairs for immigrants. Radio broadcasting was at the headphone-and-crystal-set stage. There were no talking films to accustom us to the Yankee accent. The only way countries had of judging each other was through the media of news films and newspaper reports which were, to say the least, biased to suit the political or financial ambitions of their proprietors. The European man in the street tended to regard the Yankees as brash and boastful, whose products' claims rarely came up to expectations. On the aviation side, in particular, reports of the performance of the American racers were regarded with scepticism. It was universally believed that if speed runs were made in America it was seldom under controlled conditions and that only the tail-wind speed was reported. They were judged as a nation by the Tin Lizzie Ford rather than the Pierce-Arrow and Duesenberg. Above all there was uninformed resentment among the masses about their late entry into the 1914 War when, in fact, they needn't have entered it at all.

In this ambiance, reports by serious aviation magazines about anything that happened in the Union were coloured with shades of disbelief and irony. Undoubtedly the people who mattered and who had personal knowledge of America, welcomed the naval entry. They saw it as an international gesture of goodwill. Certainly it was a great compliment to Jacques Schneider's idea that the US government should mount a million-dollar expedition to uplift a simple European trophy.

The machines entered by the US Navy were two

Curtiss CR-3 floatplane racers powered by the then-new direct-drive Curtiss D-12 engines. As related elsewhere they were originally ordered by the Navy as landplane racers and officially designated CR-1 and CR-2 for the 1921 Pulitzer Trophy race. A last-minute rule change made this a civilians-only race and it was won by Curtiss test-pilot Bert Acosta flying a CR-2, borrowed for the occasion. Much modified and officially designated CR-2s by the Navy, they were beaten by new Army Curtiss R-6 machines in the 1922 Pulitzer. Smarting under this defeat, the US Navy had no doubt decided that they ought to put up a maritime showing: after all, soldiers could not be expected to fly seaplanes. Moreover, if they managed to beat the Europeans on their own ground it would go some way to avenging the American failure in the 1920 Gordon Bennett and at the same time rub the Army's nose delicately in the dust. To this end the CR-2s had been taken out of storage, redesigned in considerable detail, and fitted with floats especially for the 1923 Schneider Race. In this new guise they took the CR-3 designation.

The third American machine was the equally interesting Navy-Wright NW-2 floatplane. Originally designed by Jerome C. Hunsaker as the Navy-Wright NW-1 to provide a race vehicle for the new Wright T-2 and T-3 Tornado V-12 engine, America's most powerful aero engine, it had started life as a sesquiplane directly inspired by the Nieuport-Delage racer of the same configuration. Two had been built; the second of these was converted by the Navy to pure biplane form – just how much Hunsaker influenced this modification is not clear – and mounted on floats.

Back-up was provided by a more or less run-of-the-mill TR3-A, a product of the Naval Aircraft factory. It was a cleaned-up Service type which had already successfully raced in the Curtiss Marine Trophy. For the 1923 Schneider race it was fitted with wing radiators, the wing configuration modified and its Wright Model J1 engine replaced by a more powerful 285 hp Wright-Hispano E4 Tempest engine.

Among practical aviators doubt was cast on whether the American floatplanes could cope with conditions in the Solent. No doubt they were thinking of the float trouble experienced in 1919, which had eliminated all the floatplanes and led Europeans to turn to the flying-boat even for the high-speed Schneider event. There were also fears, nay hopes, that they would porpoise badly on their long floats in the choppy Solent seas and be unable to get airborne. Even serious magazines like *The Aeroplane* did not mince words and referred to the American racers as 'racing freaks' stuck on a pair of floats, and cast doubt on their ability to weather anything more tempestuous than a flat calm.

As the Europeans were to find to their cost, there had been no lack of preparation on the American side. Although the race was not until the end of September the pilots had been selected early in the year. The team leader was Lieutenant Frank W. 'Spig' Wead, an experienced racing pilot. His team were Lieutenants David Rittenhouse, the aforementioned A.W. 'Jake' Gorton

and Rutledge Irvine. All of them had a fund of test-flying experience to draw on. Gorton had won the 1922 Curtiss Marine Trophy race in the Curtiss TR3-A seaplane which was included in the entry. Rittenhouse had been the pilot nominated for the Loening BR2 in the 1922 Pulitzer race while Irvine had been one of the pilots originally nominated for the Navy-Wright NW-1 Mystery sesquiplane for the 1922 Pulitzer Trophy. Both he and Rittenhouse had their introduction to seaplane racing in the 1922 Curtiss Marine Trophy race.

Gorton, as the most successful seaplane pilot – he in fact only won the Marine Trophy because the leading machine ran out of fuel on the last lap – had the choice of machines and opted to fly the NW-2 with its 700 hp Hispano-inspired, Wright Tornado engine. Rittenhouse and Irvine were allocated the Curtisses and after a rough-water seaplane handling course at the US Naval Air Station at Anacostia, went off to Port Washington to learn to fly them. Gorton was posted to Philadelphia to the US Naval Aircraft Factory, where the NW-2 was waiting for him, and his first flight was on 23 July.

There is an apocryphal but attractive story that, during their sojourn with Curtiss at Port Washington, Rittenhouse and Irvine were not only able to shake down on the CR-3 aircraft but are said to have indulged in a little profitable gamesmanship. Curtiss had a very convenient speed course of 4.26 nautical miles between Execution Rock and Stepping Stones lighthouse in the Long Island Sound, a distance which could be accurately measured on the Navy charts, and the two Navy pilots, who made their first flights in the CR-3 on 23 July, were quickly able to assess the speed of their mounts by hand-timing. It was very obvious that these were the fastest seaplanes in the world. A timing session was laid on and witnessed by Navy and Curtiss executives, during which the aircraft made four speed runs between the two points and recorded an average speed which was put out as 175.3 mph. This speed bettered by 29.3 mph the existing seaplane world speed record of 146 mph set by Captain Henri Biard at Naples the preceding year and the Curtiss publicity men were not slow to tell the world. The story goes that, to fool their opposition at the Wright Aeronautical Corporation, it was not revealed until the team got to England that this speed was in knots and not statute miles per hour and that the true speed was in fact 201.7 mph.

With respect to the historians, one wonders if it was in fact their legs which were being pulled. There was indeed a record-breaking session on 30 July, reported to be made under FAI rules, and witnessed by Commanders M.A. Mitscher and W.G. Child of the US Navy, and F.H. Russell and W.L. Gilmore, respectively vice-president and chief engineer of Curtiss. Admiral Moffett inspected the machines before the attempt prior to an engagement at the Naval War College, but did not see the flying. The average speed over a number of runs was 175.3 mph. However, it is open to doubt whether the CR-3's speed was anything other than just that. It would be difficult to prove that it was ever a 200 mph seaplane. A year later, at the Baltimore seaplane meeting which substituted for the cancelled Schneider Trophy race, flying A.6081 with a more highly developed engine and airframe improvements. Lieutenant George T. Cuddihy recorded 188 mph to set a new world speed record for seaplanes. This would be a logical improvement on the 175.3 mph recorded a year earlier with the same machine; but is a long way short of 201.7 mph in an activity where the square law prevails.

Even as a landplane without the drag of floats the CR-3 in CR-2 guise had difficulty in topping 200 mph. We know that a speed of 196.7 mph was credited to A.6081 prior to the 1924 Baltimore record session but, as the record book shows, this was obviously one of those downwind, flash speeds in uncontrolled conditions about which the Europeans were so derisory.

Certainly if there was gamesmanship, and the Wright camp was persuaded to believe that the CR-3 was a 200 mph machine when it wasn't, it was detrimental to the American challenge and cost a valuable aeroplane and almost the life of an even more valuable pilot.

Meanwhile, Gorton had flown the NW-2 and, having recorded 180 mph, firmly believed he had the fastest machine, which was logical because although it was not so aerodynamically clean as the Curtisses it had 250 hp more to pull it along.

In early August the American pilots, the handling crews, a small team from Curtiss and various friends embarked on the liner *Leviathan* for England, taking with them enough gear to fill a fifth of the hold capacity of the liner. The machines were shipped separately aboard the cruiser *Pittsburgh*. The destination was Cowes, where the machines were to be quartered at Sammy Saunders' yard on the Medina River. By 25 August *Pittsburgh* was dwarfing the yachts in the Solent, the machines were ensconced in Sammy Saunders' sheds and the whole team was ready for a full month of practice before the event. And the Sea Lion III was not even finished.

As already recorded, two of the French entries came from the Société Industrielle de Caudebec-en-Caux, manufacturers of the Latham flying-boats, two from Société Aéronautique Blanchard and two from Chantiers Aéro Maritime de la Seine. To the English the Blanchard was particularly interesting, because of its British-designed Jupiter engine made under licence by Gnome et Rhône. The machines were in fact built by Blériot to the designs of Blanchard. Sadly they were destined not to materialise in the event. The Lathams were regarded by everyone, including the French, as a heavy-weather standby, being twin-engined naval flying-boats with an all-up weight of 2,700 kg powered by pairs of Lorraine V-8 engines arranged in tandem.

This left the CAMS machines as the main French challenge. The company was run by Lorenzo Santoni – or D. Lawrence Santoni – who must have been the only constructor on record to be established as a manufacturer in Britain, Italy and France. The designs were the work of Ing. Rafael Conflienti, designer of the beautiful Savoias, who had moved over to join Santoni in 1921. Santoni had sold out his interest in SIAI the previous

year, reckoning that the Italian economic situation was unsuitable for any kind of comprehensive aviation activity. He established Chantiers Aéro Maritime de la Seine at St Denis in the same year. By 1922 he had four main types in production, ranging from the type 30E, a two-seater training and touring flying-boat, to the big 33E with two Modèle 42, 260 hp Hispano-Suiza engines in tandem. This machine differed from other Conflienti designs in having a vee-bottom instead of the usual hollow bottom.

Conflienti had, as already reported, prepared a biplane flying-boat for the 1922 Schneider Trophy race but it was completed too late to race. It was a light-weight, 28 ft 3 in span tractor machine with the pilot sitting aft of the lower mainplane, where his viewpoint was less than good. After the machine had flown, Conflienti had second thoughts and decided the pusher configuration was preferable. The outcome was the CAMS 38, with the same span but higher aspect ratio wings, giving a higher wing loading than the 36B. The pusher configuration allowed the pilot's cockpit to be located forward of the mainplane where he had a much better view of what was going on around him. The CAMS 38 was meant to be the spearhead of the French challenge for the trophy. As a reserve the old type 36 was taken out of storage and modified to 36B standards by the installation of a 380 hp Hispano-Suiza engine of the same type that powered the type 38. Lieutenant Pelletier d'Oisy had been chosen to fly the latter machine while Lieutenant Maurice Hurel took the 38.

Late in the day came the news that the Blanchard-Blériot had been withdrawn. This was a disappointment. The machine looked good and purposeful in photographs published in the technical press. Sadly, as so often happens in aviation, the prototype failed to live up to expectations when it was flown, and was too slow. A second machine, fitted with a boosted Jupiter engine, was faster but it was fated to crash after a mid-air collision. It was yet another frustration of Capitaine de corvette Teste who had also failed to make the race at Naples.

The original plan was that the French machines should be transported by sea from France to Cowes in naval vessels. Unfortunately, the frigate which was to have transported Santoni's machines had an engine breakdown. Since the CAMS were virtually out-and-out racers and to have flown them over would have been fraught with disaster, they were transferred to the corvette *Verdun*, which had been scheduled to transport the Lathams. These, being ostensibly heavy-weather devices, were instead flown over by the two pilots, Alphonse Duhamel and Lieutenant Benoist, leaving late on the afternoon of 25 September to be in time for the navigability trials, programmed for 27 September. Unfortunately the weather that day deteriorated into a full gale which tested to the full both pilots and machines. Despite all his efforts to hold a heading for Cowes, Benoist's machine was driven eastward by the gale. In desperation the pilot had to make a precautionary landing in shoal water off the entrance to Littlehampton harbour, where wind and tide were

The *Verdun* of the French navy at Cowes in 1923. The large sloping-sided 'boxes' on deck were available for transporting the French entries. (*Flight*)

raising a heavy surf. The combination of wind, sea and the enthusiastic efforts of the local populace to salvage the machine damaged it beyond immediate repair.

Duhamel, however, reached Cowes successfully, and heading high up the River Medina to find sheltered water, pulled off a beautiful landing after a very rough ride.

The British defenders, shorn of the government backing enjoyed by the Americans and French, responded as best they could. As already said the initial response was from Sopwith, with his 1919 machine, and Blackburn with a new single-seat biplane flying-boat. The Sopwith Schneider, designated the Rainbow in landplane guise, had already gained a second place in the Aerial Derby, flown by Walter Longton. Modifications to convert the aircraft to a seaplane had already begun with the fitting of a spinner and cylinder-head fairing, when during a test flight, still fitted with a land chassis, the propeller spinner came adrift and lodged in the flying wires. Longton, who was flying the machine, put it down successfully on Burgh Hill Golf Course, slipping it neatly between a pair of poplars. Unfortunately it turned over on the landing run and was too badly damaged to be repaired in time for the race. Thus the main British

defender was eliminated before it was even mounted on floats.

The other British entry came from the Blackburn Aircraft and Motor Company at Brough on the Humber bank in Yorkshire. This pioneer company had become involved in naval construction during the recent conflict and their new chief designer, Major Bumpus, was busy updating and modifying their successful Dart torpedo-bomber and designing the Cubaroo, a large, Napier-engined coastal defence biplane powered by a single Napier Cub engine, to Air Ministry specification 16/22. Nevertheless Robert Blackburn decided to enter a small flying-boat in the Schneider Trophy Race as a purely private venture. He said, after the race, that as a patriotic gesture he chose to complete this machine rather than pay dividends, which his shareholders were pressing for and which were at something of a premium at the time. This was probably said with his tongue in his cheek. The fuselage for the machine was already in existence, having been built to the same Air Department specification as the Supermarine Sea Baby. The Napier power unit proposed for it was a racing version of the Lion loaned by their friends at Napier.

Reg Kenworthy, Blackburn's chief test pilot. (*Flight*)

Christened 'the Pellet' – it would soon be nicknamed 'the Plummet' – and bearing the civil registration G-EHBF, the Blackburn entry was duly completed in early September, three weeks before the race. Unfortunately, on its first outing it was caught by wind and tide immediately after launching and, due to insufficient buoyancy in the downward wingtip float, capsized and sank, obligingly giving Reg Kenworthy, the Blackburn test pilot, time to scramble out of the cockpit and be picked up before it did so. With time at a premium the machine was hastily repaired and re-bagged, larger wingtip floats fitted and the engine stripped and rebuilt before being shipped by rail, without a preliminary test flight, for assembly at Fairey's Hamble factory.

This second time the Pellet was launched successfully, Reg Kenworthy donned his leopard-skin helmet, got aboard, the engine was fired up, and after wallowing badly and shipping a great deal of water, the pilot managed to ease the machine into the air and headed towards Cowes. Two faults were immediately apparent. The first was that the machine flew extremely nose-heavy, despite the fact that the engine thrust line was angled almost three degrees above the horizontal. Secondly it was obvious from the soaring water temperature that the radiator surface area was madly inadequate. By the time Kenworthy was abeam of Calshot the engine was boiling merrily. Prudently, he put down off the Calshot buoy and waited almost an hour before a motorboat could come over from Saunders' and tow him across to Cowes.

With the eliminating trials due to take place on the following morning, 27 September, something had to be done quickly to correct the Pellet's main faults. Mr Newman, Saunders' yard manager, had the boat stripped as soon as it got into Cowes and set a team of fitters to work to revise the cooling system, supervised by Bumpus, Bob Blackburn and the deaf, card-playing Kenworthy. Obviously the surface radiator, of the same type as that fitted to the Curtisses, did not have nearly enough surface area for the heat output of the engine. In fact, from photographs, it was barely a quarter of that used on the American machines, notwithstanding the fact that the engine was more powerful and the aircraft slower. The only possibility was to fit a completely new, conventional radiator of greater surface areas.

Someone found a Lamblin 'lobster-pot' radiator – they were being used on a number of British racing aircraft at the time and were so fashionable that no manufacturer of repute could afford to be without one – and it was jury-rigged on stays below the engine nacelle. New pipes had to be made up but this was no problem for airframe fitters of that era. The nose-heavy trim problem was not so easily solved. It is fairly certain that the Blackburn riggers would have altered the tailplane incidence as much as they could to give some extra nose-up trim. One assumes too that the engine thrust line had been angled with the object of giving a certain amount of lift when the aircraft was in flight. The real problem was that the Pellet's hull had been designed for a much lighter engine than the Napier. Photographs show the engine almost pressing the hull down into the water. These thoughts aside, the aircraft was ready and airworthy, or at least as airworthy as it ever would be, on the morning of the 27th ready for the navigability tests.

Although the Supermarine entry was a late one, the machine was ready in time. And even while the Sea Lion II was being modified at Woolston, Mitchell was already at work on a floatplane which would be one step ahead of the Curtisses; the S.4 monoplane. Scott-Paine and Commander Bird were nobody's fools. They didn't have to be visionaries to see that so long as they held together, and given reasonable weather, the Curtiss floatplanes were not only going to win the 1923 race, but as floatplanes they were pointing the way high-speed seaplane design had to go. Scott-Paine and Bird had ample opportunity to assess the performance of the American racers quite accurately by timing them in the Solent. It must have also have become clear to them that the Schneider race would inevitably become an out-and-out speed event and that, if the Schneider Trophy were to go to America, a monoplane floatplane would be the best configuration to bring it back.

As already related, the Italian entry of two Savoias did not materialise owing to difficulties in obtaining engines, although the machines were expected up to the last moment. Their problems were very real. Santoni had assessed the Italian economic situation pretty accurately when he decided to leave the country and form CAMS. The country was in political and economic turmoil as Mussolini took over the reins of power. Out of this was to come the Fascist dictatorship and ultimately the Italian Schneider programme, which was destined to push the development of racing seaplanes right to the forefront of all high-speed aviation development. But in the meantime there was no help for Savoia from the Italian Air Ministry and therefore no entry. Lack of suitable engines was a valid excuse.

Whilst all the turmoil, political manoeuvring and rush development were going on amongst the Europeans, the Americans, with their well-tried Curtisses, were getting on with the job of learning the course and getting snags out of the aircraft. The one unhappy member of the team was Gorton. His confidence that he had the fastest machine in the team, as a result of achieving 185 mph with the Navy-Wright, had been rudely shattered when he was told that the Curtisses were not doing 175 mph as had been announced, but an alleged 200 mph.

Gorton and Wead decided that if this were true the only way to boost the speed of the NW-2 was the old air-racing trick of fining the propeller pitch – they could to this with their adjustable three-bladed prop – to allow the engine to run up to 2,300 rpm and so develop more power. It was an old dodge made easy because the machine was fitted with an experimental three-bladed 'fan' with adjustable blades. The real question was whether the twelve-cylinder Tornado engine would sustain the speed increase without falling apart.

The T-2 power unit fitted to the NW-2 was the first production engine, so a cable was sent to the Wright Aeronautical Corporation, asking for a full-power test at 2,300 rpm on the prototype unit, which was still in their hands, to assess the likely consequences of pushing up the speed. It was the third week in September before word came back that the engine had stood up to a full-power test at 2,300 rpm for five hours. With this assurance Wead was happy to give the go-ahead to change the propeller pitch and make the necessary air tests. The change certainly did the trick and Gorton was able to see 201 mph on a tentative flight along the Hampshire coast. However, on a full-scale test flight on 24 September, the last day before the navigability trials, a big end let go and the engine blew up in dramatic fashion at around the 200 mph mark, bursting the engine, puncturing the floats and throwing the NW-2 out of control.

In his retirement Gorton gave Tom Foxworth a graphic description of how he was flying along normally one moment and the next moment pieces of engine started to fly past his head, followed by an almighty splash as the machine hit the water. He was a lucky man to be thrown out of the cockpit and escape with nothing

worse than a ducking and a severe shaking. The latter ailment seems to have been cured by a strong dose of the kind of medicine produced north of Hadrian's Wall. To cover up the engine failure, the story was put out that a blade had come off the propeller and pierced a float, causing the machine to sink on alighting. The fact that the engine would have shaken itself out of the frame if this had happened seems to have escaped comment.

The loss of the NW-3 left the American team short of a machine. It was therefore arranged that Spig Wead should fly the TR3-A practice machine in the race, and race no. 5 was transferred from the NW-3. This was good tactics because it not only made the team up to three but, had the CR-3s fallen by the wayside, the TR3-A stood a reasonable chance against the Supermarine Sea Lion III.

Navigability Trials

With the lessons of 1919 firmly in mind, the Royal Aero Club was this time determined to make a proper job of the navigation trials arranged to take place off Cowes. Aircraft were called upon to taxi across the race start line opposite the Victoria pier, take off and alight ahead of a pair of buoys anchored half a mile apart, then taxi, at a speed of not less than 12 knots, between the two buoys before taking off again and repeating the operation between a second set of buoys. Following that, they had to take off yet again, fly round the full course, alight ahead of the finishing line and taxi across it before being moored for a minimum period of six hours. No work, other than washing down and changing propellers – shades of Naples – was allowed between termination of the flotation test and the race.

After the storm of the previous day, when Duhamel had arrived with such a fine display of airmanship, it seemed unlikely that the weather would settle sufficiently for the supposedly fragile Curtisses to put up a good performance. The American team made no secret of the fact that they did not relish the idea of having to cope with bad conditions, although looking back it was obvious that their machines were far more capable than the chauvinistic British press gave them credit for. Certainly, rough weather would have favoured the flying-boat entrants. However, fortune was on the side of the Americans. On 27 September day dawned with almost a flat calm, and a clear sky. What wind there was came from the west and was just enough to ruffle the water.

Proceedings were scheduled to start at the early hour of 7 am and officials got themselves out of their warm beds to be there ready for the first machine. Unfortunately for them, this did not happen until 10 am when the Sea Lion III came out from Saunders' yard, taxied across the starting line, opened up and took off in a cloud of spray to fly down the Solent to the half-mile navigation courses.

The Supermarine had hardly disappeared before the Curtisses taxied out to give many spectators their first view of the American machines in action. It had been expected that they would need to reach a high take-off speed because of the difficulty of getting the tails of their long floats down in the water. When the engines were opened up, the machines disappeared in a cloud of spray as the propellers stalled before they got under way. Then, contrary to expectations, observers saw the CR-3s lift sweetly on the steps of the floats before the pilots pulled back the sticks, when they literally stood on the heels of the floats before lifting clear at a speed reckoned to be as little as 70 knots. It was noticed that there was a tendency for the floats to porpoise a little halfway through the take-off before the aircraft had gained flying speed. Alighting on the water was simply a reverse of the take-off procedure. The pilots held the machines off until the tails of the floats touched, then maintained this attitude until they gently flopped level on the water.

Unfortunately Rittenhouse had not fully understood the rules and taxied to the two half-mile navigation courses instead of flying to them. He was intercepted just before he finally made fast to his moorings and was sent out to repeat the trials. It was possibly because of the time lost in repeating the test that the Curtisses were late mooring for the flotation tests and missed the tide, with the result that the machines had to stay out for twelve hours instead of six hours because Saunders' slipway was unapproachable when the tide was out. Another setback, a more serious one, for the Americans was that when it came time to fire up the TR3-A, a shaft in the inertia starting gear snapped and no amount of old-fashioned prop swinging would get it going. So poor Wead was left standing on the slipway and the American team was reduced to two machines.

After the Americans, out came the French with their CAMS 38, its elder brother the 36B and the Latham twin-engined machine. The CAMS machines took kindly to the smooth water, after all, their hull form was developed on the placid lakes of northern Italy, and they ploughed through the sea pushing a great 'bone in their teeth' with water heaped up over the nose and swilling over the upper fuselage before getting up on the step and gaining enough speed for elevator control, leaving a very clean wake once they were on the step before getting airborne. On the water the machines handled immaculately but Pelletier d'Oisy had problems with his take-off in the 36bis. When the pilot pulled the stick back this tractor machine leapt 15 feet in the air and fell back with a terrific belly flop. A second attempt resulted in three leaps and no aviation, so he went back and started again. Otherwise the performance of the machines was quite satisfactory.

After Santoni's machines had done their acrobatic act, the Latham came out and completed its tests, hiding itself behind a cloud of spray while it was on the water, and creating a great din at all times due to the interference effect between the front and rear propellers. It was then moored for the statutory six hours, and afterwards was hauled up on the mud in front of Saunders' yard for the night.

The Blackburn Pellet's performance was another thing altogether. Saunders had finished the machine by 11.45 am and Kenworthy, possibly because of the time,

seemed to be in a great hurry to get the test over and done with. Maybe, sensitive pilot that he was, he had learned to heartily dislike the Pellet. He came out when the wind was at its strongest for the day, about six knots, and a motorboat and a couple of rowing boats had strayed onto the starting line. In avoiding these, Kenworthy tried to take off at right angles to the wind and untypically pushed the throttle open violently instead of allowing the machine to gain speed gradually before applying full power. As the machine quickly gathered way, engine torque, aided by the side wind, submerged the starboard wingtip float just as the machine was getting onto the step. At this it started to porpoise and roll violently and simultaneously with Kenworthy working hard at the controls to correct it. One moment it was completely airborne, then it would fall back into the water. Before it could gain proper flying speed the pilot finally managed to haul it off, but all was in vain. The port wing dropped and there was insufficient aileron control to pick it up. The big wingtip floats touched the water, and in a cloud of spray it cartwheeled and overturned. Kenworthy was trapped upside down in the cockpit, but, holding his nose, managed to free himself and to the relief of the observers, bobbed up in the water like a cork almost a minute after the machine had gone down. Hauled aboard Lord Montagu's launch, he passed out and had to be artificially resuscitated by his wife. The Pellet was finally recovered at low water, far too badly damaged to be repaired in time for the race, even if it had been permitted. Kenworthy was pumped dry and appeared none the worse for his experience.

The Race

In contrast to the last time the Schneider race had been held in England, the day of the race dawned bright and clear. It was a repeat of the conditions which prevailed on the previous day, when the navigability tests had been a minor triumph for the Americans and a major disaster for Blackburn. It was a measure of the seaworthiness and structural integrity of the American machines that they had ridden at their moorings in the Medina River, not for six hours, but for twelve hours, due to missing the tide which would have allowed them to be pulled up to Saunders' slip. Despite this, and despite the fact that they had taken off and 'landed' three times before the flotation test, they had taken on no water and were ready to race the next morning after an overnight clean and polish. The Latham was also ready to race after being hauled off the mud when the tide went out and cleaned up on Saunders' slipway.

All the marker boats were in position in good time before the official start of racing at eleven o'clock and any reserves were well out of the way. The big white cross at Selsey, in front of the white windmill, was duly laid out with a post in the middle of it to act as a bull's-eye. The marker boat off the Southsea pier, just by the Spit Fort, was in position, as were the two start-line marker boats directly off west Cowes, neatly in line with

On the slipway at Cowes in 1923. From left: the Curtiss CR-3, the Supermarine Sea Lion III and the CAMS 38. (*Flight*)

each other, round which the aircraft were to turn on each lap. The machines would pass between them on the water to start the race and fly between them to finish it. Each lap measured 37.2 nautical miles, equivalent to 42.86 land miles or 68.98 km, and the aircraft would do five laps, making a total distance flown of 186 nautical miles. The course was taken anticlockwise.

As on the previous day, what wind there was was blowing from the west. Later in the morning it was due to freshen slightly but not to the extent of making life difficult. Being where it was, the only problem it posed was that competitors had to take off into wind in the reverse direction of the circuit, crossing the starting line from east to west and then making a 180-degree turn round either of the marker boats, to get onto the first leg of the course. For this reason all the first-lap times are longer than they would have been.

While the aircraft were being readied, crowds had gathered everywhere round the course. Naturally the promenade at Cowes was thick with spectators. There were more at Selsey, although they were kept clear of the turning point by marshals. Selsey beach and front had its

The US Navy Curtiss CR-3 on the slipway at Cowes. (*Flight*)

own crowds and there were spectators at Gosport to view the contest. Dominating the anchorage at Cowes was the US cruiser *Pittsburgh*, backed up by the French vessel, *Verdun*, and, making a tardy and diminutive appearance, a P class patrol boat of the Royal Navy. The RAF was also busy with seaplane tenders, keeping the take-off and alighting area free of the small craft which had fouled up proceedings at Bournemouth four years earlier and were a contributory cause of the Pellet crash. To complete the scene there was a full attendance of well-ordered, well-heeled, nautical sightseers aboard the flotilla of yachts anchored in the Roads, while, high above Cowes, in the liquid sunlight, an old DH 9A circled lazily, keeping well out of the way and enjoying a wonderful bird's eye view of the proceedings.

It had been agreed that the Americans should take off first. They had the lowest numbers anyway. About ten minutes before 11.00 am, race starting time, the spotless grey machines with their yellow fins and white rudders bearing the numbers 3 and 4 outlined in white on their fuselages, were launched from Saunders' slip, fired-up, and taxied out to a point about a mile or so east of the starting line, and started to taxi towards the line. As the one-minute cone went up on Victoria pier, they accelerated, judging their pace so nicely that when the cone dropped for the start, they were a bare 100 yards from the line. This was the signal for them to open up the D-12s and, holding the machines down on the water, they crossed the line with Irvine's A.6080 just ahead of his team-mate. They made the typical Curtiss take-off, sitting up and begging on the heels of the floats, before getting off at what seemed a remarkably low speed. By prearrangement, to avoid interference with each other, they turned right and left round the outer and inner marker boats, and headed for Selsey Bill.

While they were still out on their first lap, the Supermarine taxied out, attended by Bird in *Tiddleywinks*, the motorboat he had made for himself out of an old wartime flying-boat hull. Biard started his take-off run as the cone was dropped, well aware that he would be timed when he crossed the line and not from the time of the starting signal. In the short quarter of an hour since the Americans had taken off, the wind against the tide was creating a little bit of a chop, and as she crossed the line, the Sea Lion III made one of the uncontrollable leaps which were ultimately to be her downfall, bounding over the line in a cloud of spray. Biard was not aware that he was actually in the middle of this bounce as he crossed the line. As he took off and turned towards Selsey, the race committee, anxious not to appear partisan, announced that he would be disqualified for crossing the line in the air. There was panic in the Supermarine camp as James Bird argued with the committee, trying to get the decision reversed. Eventually reason, in the person of Sir Sefton Brancker, prevailed and the one British defender was allowed to stay in the race.

Even as Biard was crossing the line, the two Curtisses hove into sight, travelling fast, almost two minutes ahead of schedule. The public still believed that they were capable of only 150-mph laps, but the times they were making showed their speed must be well above 170 mph, completely off the speed charts published in contemporary aviation magazines. Even then, this first lap's speed was a slow one because of the time lost in the east-west take-off. They also appeared to lose time in the wide, sweeping turns they made rounding the Selsey, but practice had shown that less speed was lost this way.

Irvine's time was 15 min 27.6 sec for this first round, while Rittenhouse, who was already pulling ahead, had turned in 5 min 6.4 sec, an average of 170.1 mph. As the two Navy racers disappeared in the direction of Horse Sand Fort and Selsey Bill, they were pursued at a more-than-sedate pace by the Sea Lion, which, despite its apparent aerodynamic untidiness, was travelling at close on 170 mph in an endeavour to keep up with the floatplanes. On this second lap the Curtisses made tight turns round Selsey, though not as tight as Biard, who pulled so much G that his engine was cutting out as the petrol in the carburettor float chambers flowed away from the jets. Biard's time for this first lap was 17 min 11.2 sec (149.5 mph), slow compared with Rittenhouse, who covered the second round in 14 min 22.2 sec (178.8 mph) and Irvine, who clocked 14 min 43 sec, a speed of 174.6 mph. In comparison, Biard's next lap time was more typical of the Sea Lion II's performance, the 16 min 13.8 sec recorded being equivalent to 158.3 mph, just 20 mph less than Rittenhouse's speed.

The Americans were flying precisely, holding their height and flying a pencil-straight line between the markers. Rittenhouse's third lap occupied 14 min 24.8 sec and his fourth lap 14 min 22.2 sec. Irvine was approximately 20 seconds a lap slower due to A.6080's larger-section float struts and inborn headwind. On the fifth and final lap, both American machines opened up slightly to put in their best times for the race, Rittenhouse turning in 14 min 11 sec (181.1 mph) and Irvine 14 min 29.6 sec, equivalent to 177.3 mph. Biard also opened up slightly and managed a lap at 160.8 mph (15 min 59 sec).

Meanwhile the CAMS machines had come out at about 11.30 am. Hurel, in the faster type 38, was in fact a little early and, to fill in time, took off and warmed up the machine thoroughly before alighting and presenting himself for the start. His team-mate Pelletier d'Oisy in the type 36B, the one with the tractor propeller and the cockpit behind the wing, was not so fortunate. On his way to the starting area, taxying on the surface, his extremely poor field of vision prevented him from seeing one of the official yachts, which he proceeded to ram with little effect on the yacht, but to some detriment to his machine, putting it out of the race. It was withdrawn hurriedly to Saunders' yard for repairs, where it joined the Latham, which was standing there with one engine dead owing to a sheared magneto drive. Thus at two strokes the French team of three was reduced to one. That one, Hurel in the type 38 pusher CAMS, made what appeared to be a copybook start. But, unnoticed by the spectators as he rotated the machine to take off, a wave struck the starboard elevator, wrecking the

A CAMS 38 being assembled with the help of French naval personnel. (*Flight*)

outboard hinge and leaving the tip of the panel flying in the wind. Hurel carried on, probably unaware of the damage, flying low and banking steeply round the marker points, and put in a first lap in 19 min 42.6 sec, an average speed of 130.4 mph. Then, to pile on the anguish, on his second lap the aircraft started to vibrate, the Hispano began to lose power and he had to put down off Selsey and await a tow home. It was a sad end to a gallant effort. Little did the spectators know that it was to be the last appearance of a French aircraft in the French-conceived Schneider Trophy race.

Poor Santoni's effort, despite all his careful preparation, had been in vain. His hopes were dashed by the failure of a part of the machine which was not of his manufacture. His disappointment and that of Conflienti must have been deep indeed. While they stood on the pier at Cowes wondering what had happened to their machine, and listening to false rumours that it had dived into the sea, the Americans had swept across the finishing line, turned unobtrusively over Cowes and slid into beautiful, well-judged landings. The great American aviation tradition had been restored in Europe.

Twenty minutes later Biard, in the Sea Lion, dived across the line and zoomed up to 3,000 feet on full power before dropping down and putting the little 'boat onto the water and taxying in. By the time he arrived the hullabaloo over his start had been settled by a ruling that the machine was not truly airborne when it crossed the line. His race speed of 157.17 mph was a good one, even though it was more than 20 mph slower than Rittenhouse's 177.38 mph winning speed.

Comment on the 1923 Schneider Trophy Race

Above all, the 1923 Schneider Trophy race proved that in the five years since the War the Americans had caught up and passed Europe in their technical ability to produce racing aeroplanes. The engine work originated by Walter Kirkham of the Curtiss Aeroplane and Motor Company in 1915, and brought to a brilliant conclusion by Arthur Nutt, had given them an engine which, in terms of frontal area and weight related to horsepower, was the best in the world. Even more remarkable was that the company who built the engine also produced an airframe of equal quality to go with it. William Gilmore of Curtiss must be credited with leading the design team which produced the Curtiss CR-1 series of racers. Using Walter Loening's thesis that low frontal area was the essential quality for any high-speed aircraft, they had produced the fastest biplanes in the world as vehicles for their engines. Nor should the contribution of Albert Sylvanus Reed be forgotten. His revolutionary propeller made it possible to run the D-12s at reduction gear speeds without a reduction gear and was fundamental to the American success. Without it they would not have achieved the speeds they did, although they could still have been faster than the Sea Lion.

At that time, because of the success of the Cosmos Jupiter and the Wright series of radial engines, the military air arms of most nations were looking towards the air-cooled radial as a power unit for fighters. In Europe at least, the success of the CR racers changed all this. Military engine designers almost immediately started thinking in terms of in-line engines and water-cooling. Much power was given to the elbows of those companies, like Rolls-Royce and Napier, who were committed to liquid-cooled in-line engines. Even to them the light-alloy, monobloc-cylinder construction of the Curtiss D-12 was confirmation of the lead set by Marc Birkigt's Hispano and consequently was such a profound influence that they were soon making this type, and fifteen years later, when the next war came to be fought, with few exceptions all the most effective fighters were powered by engines of this type.

In the short term the impact of the American design and team organisation was electric. The self confidence of the British particularly was badly shaken. They saw that the aircraft designs of which they were so proud were suddenly out of date. The aviation press saw to it that the Americans' attention to detail and their meticulous preparation was drummed in. Suggestions that the professional approach of the American navy was unsporting met with a sharp rebuke.

One feels that the French were not so impressed. They had their own racing aeroplanes which regularly beat the British and were at least as fast as the best American machines; in fact, in 1923 they were on their way to taking the outright speed record from the Americans. However, their almost congenital lack of preparation showed up badly against that of the American team.

A result of the American victory was that it opened up the contest. Theoretically the Italians, who were delighted at the result, could still win the Coupe Schneider outright under the three-wins-in-five-years rule; but they would have to go a long way to do it. And there was always the possibility of an *America*'s Cup syndrome when the trophy, once in American hands would be doubly difficult to retrieve.

What had become painfully obvious to the parsimonious British government was that the Schneider Trophy had crystallised into a high-speed contest between nations. The 1923 US invasion – should it be intervention – set it on its way to becoming an international inter-service contest with the best machines from each aircraft industry being pitted against each other, with governments footing the bill. Little did they know how valuable the lessons about to be forced on them would

be sixteen years later, or that the American experience would be mainly wasted.

Latham No. 1 which failed to complete the course in 1923. (*Musée de l'Air*)

The Aircraft

Latham L.1 F-ATAM and F-ESEJ 1923

When planning their challenge for the 1923 race the French government had the lessons of 1919 firmly in mind. They were well aware that a flying-boat had won and that French floatplanes had proved too fragile. Nor had they forgotten Malard's experience in the Channel. They were well aware that the weather on the British side of La Manche, in combination with the complex tidal system in the Solent, could produce sea conditions inimical to seaplane operation. It was therefore decided to include a heavy-weather machine in the team inventory, the order going to SICC-Latham et Cie, the Société Industrielle de Caudebec-en-Caux, a relatively new company set up by a young cousin of Hubert Latham, the pioneer aviator. The machine they produced, the first prototype as early as 1922, was a large single-seat, biplane, single-step, flying-boat powered by a pair of Lorraine-Dietrich engines mounted back-to-back in pull-push configuration. Judging by its 1922 registration it is possible that the first machine, F-ATAM, had been ordered for the 1922 race and was not ready in time.

Structurally, the Latham appears to have followed the contemporary pattern, having a vee-bottom, plywood hull with curved decks and the empennage mounted on a rather elegant hull extension culminating in a T-configuration, strutted fin and tail. The comma-shaped, aerodynamically balanced rudder was reminiscent of that of the Avro 504. The equal-span, square-tipped wings were of the usual two-spar construction, fabric-covered and with ailerons on both wings synchronised with streamlined, tubular steel connecting rods.

Latham's 1923 entry with two Lorraine-Dietrich V-8 engines: one 'pushing', one 'pulling'. (*Flight*)

Wing configuration was single-bay with single, interplane I-struts. These latter, in common with the aileron rods, appear to have been made from specially formed steel tube with cuff-fairings, the same material being used for the engine mounting and cabane which varied between the two machines. F-ATAM, which was placarded Latham no. 1, had the engine mounted on a pair of elongated N-struts with the cabane formed from four inverted V-struts. Lamblin cuff-radiators were mounted on the front engine legs. On this machine the engine nacelle was of rectangular section which formed a dead area ahead of the rear propeller. On the other hand, F-ESEJ had a more teardrop-shaped, round-section nacelle with the engine cylinder heads exposed to the elements and the engines supported on two pairs of V-struts. Oil radiators were located on the underside of the nacelle.

The pilot's cockpit was located directly beneath the front engine with access between the maze of struts and rigging wires. These latter, incidentally, were a Latham patent consisting of multiple strands of varying-diameter, round section wire arranged one behind the other to form a streamline pattern.

Lorraine-Dietrich of Lunéville, who provided the engines, was part of the Alsace-based De Dietrich empire, one of the bigger French industrial complexes, with interests ranging from railway engineering and automobiles to domestic equipment and ceramics. Their cars were made under licence from Tourcat-Mery, the Tourcat of this duo being the grandfather of the illustrious Concorde test pilot. During the 1914 War they had the distinction of building engines for the Germans in their Niederbronn factory and for the French at Lunéville only 100 km away. The Lorraine prefix was added after the War to assuage French anti-Teutonic sentiments.

The Latham Lorraine-Dietrich Modèle 13 V-8 engines came from a range of aeronautical power units that emanated from the De Dietrich design office just as the War ended, and which comprised engines with up to twenty-four cylinders, arranged in W-configuration. The cylinders of all these units were fabricated in pairs from steel forgings with welded-on water jackets and had four valves per cylinder with push-rod operation. To fulfil a French government requirement both the carburettors and exhausts were on the outside of the engine. The cylinder dimensions of the Modèle 13 were 120 × 170 mm, giving a swept volume of 23.07 litres.

Maximum power was quoted as 410 bhp at 1,730 rpm from a dry weight of 862 lb (383 kg). An advantage of the back-to-back, tandem installation used by Latham and others was that the propellers rotated in opposite directions and cancelled out torque reaction. It was British practice to use propellers of different pitch for the front and rear engines of similar installations but apparently this idea did not appeal to the SICC designer.

For the race the older machine was allocated to Alphonse Duhamel, the works test pilot, and although delivered safely to Cowes by dint of fine airmanship, was put out of the race immediately before the start by a sheared magneto drive. The second L.1 was allocated to Lieutenant Benoist and was the machine damaged by unskilled handling in the surf at Littlehampton.

1923 Blanchard-Blériot C.1 F-ESEH

Designed specifically for the race as the reserve entry in the French government-backed challenge, contemporary reports refer to the C.1 having been designed by a French naval officer named Blanchard and built by Blériot Aéronautique. Others suggest that the designer is unknown and that it was built by the Société Aéronautique Blanchard (SAB) at Les Coteaux de St Cloud. The writer's hunch is that SAB was one of the manifestations of the tortuous Blériot empire and that the designer was indeed Blanchard. It was a monoplane tractor flying-boat powered by a Jupiter engine built by Gnome-Rhône under their newly acquired Bristol licence.

Construction was predominantly of wood, the single-step hull being ply-covered of mainly box-section, with an unusual square-cut, swim bow. The wooden, two-spar wing with ply-covered leading edge was braced with parallel lift struts and supported by a double N-strutted steel pylon/cabane which doubled up as the mounting for the bulky, cowled Jupiter engine. Stability on the water was provided by a pair of box-section stabilising floats mounted on wire-braced outriggers from the hull. The pilot sat in a cockpit well aft of the engine but with a reasonable view, thanks to the absence of a lower wing. The unusual cruciform, strut-braced empennage was mounted directly to the fuselage and featured a fin extension above the tailplane which had all the makings of an afterthought.

Two machines were built, with Lieutenant-Commander Teste as test pilot. The first C.1, registered F-ESEH, failed to come up to expectations, a maximum speed of 168 mph being reported. A second machine, presumably with improved aerodynamics and fitted with a Jupiter boosted to 550 bhp was built, but met with a destructive accident before its potential could be assessed. It would be interesting to know whether the first or second machine was the subject of what appears to be the sole surviving record of the type.

Sea Lion III

In view of the limited time available to build a contender for the 1923 race, Scott-Paine used his connections with the Air Ministry to borrow back N.157, the Sea Lion II,

and gave Mitchell the unsavoury job of adding another 10 knots to its already high speed. It was achieved by a joint effort by the designer and the engine builders Napier.

Napier's contribution was the 525 hp Lion III engine, an extra 50 hp over the 1922 Schneider engine. Mitchell's job was a little more difficult. To reduce drag he cut the wing-span from 32 ft to 28 ft, moving the outer struts inboard, designed new, streamlined, strut-mounted stabilising floats and worked on the hull. Engine installation on previous Sea Lions had always been untidy. He put this right on the Sea Lion III by enclosing the Lion in a compact, ovoid cowling, leaving only the cylinder heads protruding. Cooling air was admitted to the radiator, mounted in front of the engine, through a circular opening in the nose of the cowling.

Some work is said to have been done on the nose section of the hull to reduce drag, although the scope for this would be limited and does not show up on contemporary photographs. Any gain would have been more than offset by the extra struts its designer added to the empennage.

One unfortunate result of the modifications was that the gentlemanly take-off characteristics of its predecessors were banished. Maybe because the reduced lifting surfaces and the consequent higher take-off speed caused the planing bottom to come into its own as a lifting surface, or maybe because of 'ground effect', the Sea Lion III had the vicious habit of leaping off the water before it had gained flying speed. This manifested itself during the start of the race and almost caused the machine to be disqualified.

After the race the Air Ministry asked for their property back. The return must have been delayed, and perhaps Scott-Paine had hopes of keeping the Sea Lion, because the writer has a print of a Supermarine works arrangement drawing, drawn by Frank Holroyd, traced by S. McG and dated 20 Dec. 1923. It depicts the SS Amphibian Racing Flying-Boat, which is none other than our old friend the Sea Lion III, as raced at Cowes, with a retractable undercarriage. The original date of this historic document is 7 July 1921, so it spans the whole history of the Sea Kings and Sea Lions. One only wishes they were all shown on it.

Biard eventually flew the Sea Lion to the Isle of Grain experimental station, probably in 1924. It is on record that on 5 July 1924, despite being warned of the vicious take-off characteristics, which required full engine power to combat them, one of the test pilots, Flying Officer Paull-Smith, opted for a part-throttle take-off. The Sea Lion bounced once, shot forty feet into the air and plunged straight in, destroying the machine and killing the pilot. It was a sad end to an illustrious period in Supermarine history.

The CAMS 36bis F-ESFC and 38 F-ESFD 1923

As already recorded Lorenzo Santoni despaired for the aircraft industry in strike-ridden Italy immediately after

CAMS 36 biplane with 4-bladed tractor propeller powered by a 300 bhp Hispano-Suiza Modèle 42 engine. (*Flight*)

flying-boat and the big 33T with capacity for eight passengers in addition to the pilot and a mechanic. This latter machine was the first Conflienti machine with a vee-bottom throughout, it having been finally realised that the hollow step hulls were not all they might be in a seaway.

It was a measure of French government confidence in Santoni and his designer that they allocated the contract for two CAMS 26 racers in 1922 and persisted with it into 1923 after setbacks with the 1922 machines. Tests of the Type 36 at Le Pecq, fitted with its original 300 bhp Hispano-Suiza Modèle 42 engine, showed that it was capable of 155 mph, enough to have won the Naples race, given sufficient reliability. This was a typical Conflienti, single-bay biplane flying-boat with the difference that, for the first time, it was a tractor machine with the pilot sitting in the rear fuselage with his view forward restricted by the lower mainplane. The Type 36 also marked the first Conflienti venture into I-strutted wings, a departure he abandoned when he came to redesign the surviving Type 36 – the prototype had been lost in a crash in 1922 – to take a 360 bhp Hispano engine.

the Kaiser-War, and in 1920 moved over to St Denis on the outskirts of Paris. His designer Ing. Rafael Conflienti joined him a year later, once manufacturing facilities were established. By 1922 Chantiers Aéro Maritime de la Seine were well ensconced and at the 1922 Salon showed the little Type 31E (for École), side-by-side, two-seater school machine, the T.31 single-seat fighter

With twin interplane struts and revised bracing to suit, and powered by the more powerful engine, the Type 36 for the 1923 Schneider attracted the 36bis designation. Concurrently, Conflienti laid down designs for the Type 38 pusher machine using virtually the same

The French navy moves a wingless CAMS 38 through the streets of Cowes in 1923. (*Flight*)

hull and wings and powered by a similar engine to the Type 36bis.

Following the pattern laid down with the Savoia designs, construction of the hull was mainly plywood with the more complex shapes, such as the concave planing bottom, double-diagonally planked. The swept, strut-braced cruciform tail with its vertical hinge line was Conflienti's trademark, and graces both types. Equally typical was the straight, one-piece upper mainplane devoid of control surfaces, dihedral was built into the lower wing, which also carried large ailerons and supported strutted stabilising floats. Wing construction was straightforward using spruce mainspars, plywood ribs and a wire trailing edge. To accommodate the pusher propeller of the Type 38 a large cut-out in the upper wing was called for, substantially reducing the surface area.

The engines of both types were mounted on N-strut pylons and encased in elegant, polished aluminium nacelles neatly faired into the wing and with big propeller spinners of the same material. Cooling was by vertical, cylindrical, Lamblin radiators mounted independently and ahead of the front engine legs. Interestingly the tractor machine was fitted with a four-bladed propeller and the pusher with a two-bladed, paddle type.

In interviews Santoni commented that the 38 was by far the faster machine because of its pusher configuration. In tests it was credited with 167 mph compared with 160 mph for the 36bis.

The Curtiss racers

The great American expedition to the last of the Gordon Bennett races taught the overseas visitors a number of lessons. To the Curtiss engineers who accompanied the Wildcat and the Texas Kitten, one of these lessons was that Curtiss had potentially the best racing engine in the world in the 425 hp, geared C-12 in terms of power-to-weight ratio and frontal area. Its only competitors were the 300 hp Hispano-Suiza, which had the same frontal area but less horsepower, or the British Napier Lion, which had as much power but was heavier and had a greater frontal area. The other lesson was that a well-designed conventional biplane, as clean as the Nieuports and SPADs, fitted with the C-12 would be a more practical device – and would be more attractive to military customers – for winning air races than the way-out Texas Wildcat and Kitten they had designed for Seymour E.J. Cox.

Although the C-12 was a good racing engine with a limited life, it had reliability problems for military use (which was one of its main purposes in life), in the

US Navy CR-3 at Cowes attended by the required boats, mechanics and handlers wearing waders. (*Flight*)

reduction gearing and in crankshaft bearing life. Around the end of 1920 the Curtiss chief engine designer, Finlay Robertson Porter, who had created the C-12 out of Charles Kirkham's original Curtiss K-12 power unit, decided to return to the automobile industry and his assistant, 26-year-old Arthur Nutt took over.

Apart from his excellent professional qualifications Nutt was a practical engineer and a born 'engine man'. He could see that the C-12 engine was being pushed too hard for its architecture and part of that architecture, the reduction gear, needed a lot of development. He reckoned that throwing the reduction gear away would remove one lot of headaches and that running the engine at a lower speed, necessary to match it to the efficiency of the wooden propellers of the period, would do away with a lot more. On the credit side he would gain the power lost in the reduction gears. This would have been of the order of 40 bhp at least, so the engine was having to give off 465 bhp at 2,250 rpm to deliver 425 bhp at the propeller. When asked to give 330 bhp at 1,800 rpm without the reduction gears most of the C-12's reliability problems were solved. Fortunately the management agreed, the US Navy amended a contract to purchase an engine, and the Curtiss CD-12 was born.

The Navy was happy with the CD-12; it gave as much power as the Liberty engine for three-quarters of the installed weight and was much smaller. Their response was to order two more examples as replacements for the 300 hp Wright-Hispano in existing service aircraft and then to quickly change their minds and order two racing biplanes for the 1921 Pulitzer Trophy as vehicles for their two CD-12s. A main requirement was that the landing speed should not exceed 75 mph.

There is always confusion about early Curtiss racer designations. It would appear that the two machines were originally designated CR-1 and CR-2 because of slight differences in their specifications, and allocated Navy serial numbers A.6080 and A.6081. It is even possible that CR-2, which one authority tells us was finished first, was given the lower serial number. The design team was Harry T. Booth and Mike Thurston (a Harry Routh had also been mentioned) assisted by William Wait under the overall supervision of William L. Gilmore, Curtiss's chief engineer. French influence was very evident in the classic single-bay biplane configuration this team produced, only the Curtiss designers had gone one better when it came to looks. With their smooth fuselage lines, close-cowled engines, parabolic wingtips and N-interplane struts these two machines were debatably the most handsome, and aerodynamically clean, machines of this type yet to be seen. They were only marred by the French Lamblin lobster-pot radiators mounted between each pair of undercarriage legs. Their influence on biplane fighter design was destined to last right through to the monoplane era.

The appearance of these racers was undoubtedly helped by the German-inspired, all-wood, semi-moulded construction which Curtiss had first used on their Model 18 triplane. This method called for the fuselage to be built as two halves of a monocoque on left- and right-handed hardwood formers using 2-in wide strips of Curtiss-ply – said to be $^3/_{32}$-in thick two-ply – in two layers laid diagonally in opposite directions and bonded with casein glue. The strips were held in place with brass pins driven through to the former. When the glue had set the skin was peeled off and the tips of the pins clenched over. Stringers and bulkheads were then glued and pinned into place in a female jig, after which the two halves of the fuselage were glued together along the centreline. Engine bearers were also made of wood and glued in place during the construction of the monocoque.

The multi-spar wings were built the same way, using formers to maintain the section, the ribs and five solid spars being glued to the top skin in a jig, with the lower skin going on last. The wire-braced fin and tailplane surfaces were built the same way. Final finish was by sanding down to a smooth surface and finishing with either varnish or paint. Even the N-interplane struts were built up from laminations of wood, and looked for all the world as if they were cut from a sheet of plywood. The ailerons, fitted to the lower wings only, and the other control surfaces were steel-framed using fabricated sheet-metal ribs attached to torque tubes with sheet-metal trailing edges and covered with doped fabric.

An interesting feature of the wing structure was the 'razor-blade' thin pylon which replaced the usual cabane structure and necessitated two pairs of steady-wires running from points midway between the interplane struts to the engine bearers. The main rigging wires were duplicated and were of streamlined section similar to RAF section wire and, as a further aid to drag-reduction, the size of the cockpit aperture was reduced by a detachable 'horse-collar' fitted after the pilot was installed.

The first machine to be completed, A.6081, was first flown by Bert Acosta, the Curtiss test pilot, on 1 August 1921 at Roosevelt Field. On landing, a hollow in the ground caused the Curtiss to nose over and subsequent inspection revealed that the fuselage seam had split at the cockpit opening. It was duly reinforced and there was no more trouble.

At the last moment government economy measures caused Army and Navy support for the 1921 Pulitzer to be withdrawn and the race became a purely civil contest and was run as part of the programme of a flyers' reunion at Omaha. However the Navy were quite willing to lend A.6081 to Curtiss for the event. Flown by Bert Acosta and somewhat slowed by a couple of broken flying wires – possibly the cabane steadies – CR-2 won the race at a cracking 176.75 mph from the Cactus Kitten triplane, which returned a creditable 170.34 mph. Later, on 22 November, with the machine all in one piece, Acosta went out over an officially measured kilometre at Curtiss field and made an FAI-timed and observed attempt on the World Air Speed record with A.6081. His best was 197.8 mph (318.33 km/h) and the average 184.8 mph, not enough to break the 205 mph set by Sadi Lecointe in the Nieuport-Delage sesquiplane two months earlier. The Nieuport represented the first move towards the monoplane record-breaker and before long all outright speed records would be held by single-wing machines. But Curtiss would not be denied their moments of glory.

Spurred on by William Mitchell, there was government support for air racing in 1922. As a consequence the two Navy CRs were dusted off, given the common, and official, designation CR-2 and extensively cleaned up and modified in readiness for the Pulitzer Trophy race. Modifications included fitting wing radiators in place of the Lamblins, enlarging the empennage and fitting streamlined wheels. The wing pylon was also extended rearwards and a small vertical oil cooler fitted ahead of it. An indication of the importance of the cabane bracing was the replacement of the rear ones on A.6081 and the front ones of A.6080 with streamline struts, presumably to take landing loads. The former machine was also fitted with Nutt's new D-12 engine, a developed version of the CD-12. Incidentally this latter engine was by that time returning 405 bhp at 2,000 rpm as a result of a rise in compression ratio to 6.1:1 and the use of 50/50 petrol/benzole fuel.

Meanwhile inter-service rivalry had caused the Army to buy developed versions of the CR-2 which Curtiss had built as a private venture. Given the Army designation R-6, they incorporated all the experience gained with the CR. They were smaller and lighter versions of this machine with reduced wing area, down from 168 to 136 sq ft, single interplane struts, a wing pylon of increased chord and the new surface radiators.

Power was provided by the D-12 engines. Flying the second R-6 to be built, Lieutenant Russell Maugham of the Army broke all records in the 1922 Pulitzer with a 205.8 mph win. His comrade in arms Lieutenant Lester Maitland was second in the companion machine. The older and larger CR-2s, in the hands of Navy Lieutenants Hap Brow and Alford Williams, had to be content with third and fourth places.

In 1923 there was yet another major development at Curtiss which was to be fundamental to the ongoing success of the direct-drive D-12. This was a revolutionary new propeller devised by aerodynamicist Dr Sylvanus Albertus Reed. In the course of his researches, he had found that it was possible for a propeller blade to work efficiently at supersonic speeds if the tip sections were thinned down and given knife-edges. Working on this precept he had developed a new, forged Duralumin propeller, twisted from a flat blank, with razor-sharp edges and a thin section, like that of a modern jet wing, which allowed the propeller to work efficiently at up to 2,300 rpm, instead of the 2,000 rpm limit imposed by the wooden propellers. This increased efficiency allowed the D-12 to be speeded up and develop 475 bhp at 2,300 rpm, a rate of rotation which had previously called for the C-12's reduction gear.

When the US Navy made its decision to go for the Schneider Trophy, its two CR-2s were the obvious hardware to do it with, if only because their larger wing area fitted them to carry the extra weight of floats without

Curtiss CR-3 for the 1923 event. A metal Reed propeller contributed to its performance and winning speeds.

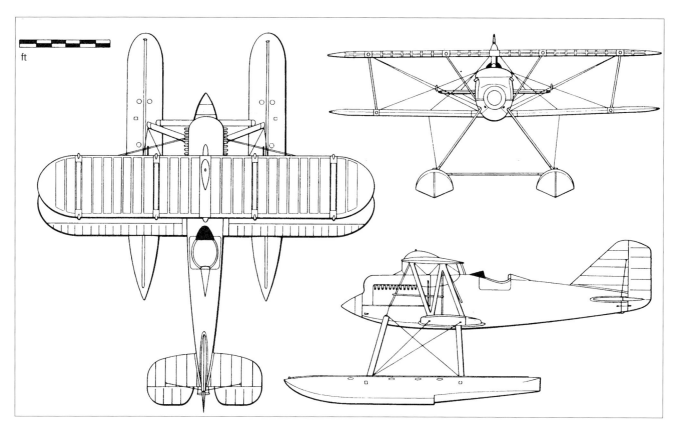

Curtiss CR-3 (1923): Wing Span: 22 ft 8 in (6.91m). Length Overall: 25 ft (7.62m). Wing Area: 168 sq. ft (15.61 m²). T-O Weight: 2,747 lb (1,246 kg) Max Wing Loading: 16.35 lb/sq. ft (79.83 kg/m²). Curtiss D-12 V-12 engine, liquid-cooled, engine 465 hp.

being enlarged. However, the modifications to convert them to seaplanes almost amounted to a complete rebuild. The D-12 was by this time developing 480 bhp with the high-speed Reed propeller, and for this reason and because the engines would have to work harder during take-off, the wing radiators were extended to provide additional cooling capacity. A larger, fin-type oil cooler was also fitted in front of the wing pylon and extending above the wing. The pylon itself was shortened and increased in section – presumably it acted as an oil tank – and the remaining steady-wires (inner lift wires) were replaced by struts. There was the greatest attention to detail; just one example was the care taken to recess the control surfaces into the wings and empennage to eliminate leaks between the upper and lower wing surfaces. Originally the CR-2 had rubber seals in this area and they had been known to blow off, with alarming effects on the controls. The fin and rudder were also enlarged to correct the out-of-balance aerodynamic forces created by the forward area of the floats.

The 17 ft 11-in wooden floats were almost as long as the aircraft and were the standard form developed by the US Navy, having vee-bottoms, a single step and rounded tops extending right down to the chines. Construction was the same as that of the fuselage and each one housed an eighty gallon petrol tank with a hand-operated wobble-pump provided in the cockpit to transfer fuel to the main tank. The floats were mounted on a simple wire-braced, four-leg chassis with wide-chord streamlined wooden legs and spreaders of the same section.

Delivery of the CR-3s, still bearing their original Navy serial numbers, was in mid-July, giving good time for Lieutenants David Rittenhouse and Rutledge Irvine to familiarise themselves with floatplane handling.

The Navy-Wright NW-2

The story of the Navy-Wright NW racers is really the story of an engine; the V-12 Wright T-2, a large, water-cooled unit whose role was to act as a more powerful alternative to the Liberty engine within the same

Navy-Wright NW-2, the 1923 challenger from the USA. (*Flight*)

external dimensions. Based on a US Navy requirement, it was called on to give at least 500 bhp on straight petrol. In practice the T-2, in service guise, gave 525 bhp at 1,800 rpm with a compression ratio of 5.25:1 running on this fuel, compared with the Liberty's 400 bhp at 1,700 rpm. A high-compression version (6.5:1) gave 600 bhp at 2,000 rpm. When developed into the T-3 with the same cylinder dimensions of 146 × 159 mm (31 litres) it produced 600 bhp in low-compression form and 675 bhp with high-compression pistons. A maximum output of 780 bhp at 2,200 rpm is quoted.

Structurally it was a more modern engine than the Liberty, having light alloy blocks in four units of three cylinders mounted on a light alloy crankcase. The one-piece cylinders had open top, inserted steel liners and a single overhead camshaft for each cylinder bank, operating four valves per cylinder by means of forked rockers. Seven main bearings supported the crankshaft in the upper half of the crankcase and the whole of the rotating and reciprocating parts were the subject of an exacting jigging and gauging programme to ensure complete interchangeability of parts without hand-fitting. Moreover, the number of connections on installation was kept to a minimum of seven: two oil, three water, one petrol and one oil pressure. The carburettors and induction system were designed as a single unit located in the cleavage of the cylinders. At 1,155 lb dry in direct-drive form, with propeller and all fittings, the T-2 scaled approximately 250 lb more than the Liberty but was five inches shorter, although fitting the same engine mountings. They were arguably the most powerful engines then available and were destined to earn an enviable reputation for reliability before being overtaken by the US services' decision to go for the air-cooled radial.

Stemming from a Navy specification it was predictable that the Navy should want to subject the Wright T to a racing programme to force development. In the absence of a suitable airframe it was decided to produce one, and Commander Jerome Hunsaker, head of the Navy Bureau of Aeronautics design office, was assigned the task. Logically, rather than trying to break new ground, he cast around for the fastest known design from which to draw inspiration. This was the Nieuport Sesquiplane with which Sadi Lecointe had recently established a new World Speed Record.

Although the NW-1 'Mystery ship' – so christened by the Press because of the cloak of secrecy surrounding its construction – followed the Nieuport configuration it was much bigger, mid-wing rather than shoulder-wing and sported a larger-span lower mainplane set between spatted wheels with leading link wheel suspension.

Built by Wright in premises rented from Chance M. Vought, the two machines ordered, NW-1 and NW-2, were structurally quite different from the Nieuport. Instead of a wooden structure Hunsaker opted for a welded-steel, wire-braced, lattice-girder fuselage built out with formers and multiple stringers to give a rounded section. The two spar mid-wing was set exactly on the thrust line and was plywood-covered back to the aft false spar. The ailerons and empennage had fabricated steel frames and were fabric-covered. There was a minimum of flying wires, the wing being braced to the undercarriage and vestigial lower wing with lift struts giving a head-on configuration reminiscent of the Savoia Warren-girder theme.

NW-2, the US Navy's 1923 entry, with a 780 bhp Wright T-2 V-12 liquid-cooled engine. (*Flight*)

Flown in the 1922 Pulitzer race, NW-1, although no match for the Army Curtisses, gave a creditable performance until overheating set in and pilot Sandy Sanderson had to put it down in a lake, wrecking the machine and almost drowning himself.

NW-2 was completed, test-flown and assessed by the Navy under near-arctic conditions before it was decided that any further aquatic tendencies should be properly exploited by converting it to seaplane form as the third team machine for the 1923 US Navy expedition to capture the Schneider Trophy.

This conversion was made back at the Chance Vought premises but Wright were at this time responsible for the design work and it is not unreasonable to suppose that ex-Curtiss engineers Harry T. Booth and Mike Thurston, who had joined Wright early in 1923 to design the F2W racer, had some influence on the layout. The modification amounted to almost a complete redesign with proper biplane, I-strutted wings, a larger empennage, wing radiators in place of the NW-1's Lamblins and a new Hamilton three-bladed metal, ground-adjustable propeller. The 780 bhp engine called for larger wing radiators, which now encroached on both wings. Consequently the NW-2 seaplane was given small-span ailerons on upper and lower mainplanes,

connected by streamlined tubular rods, while the interplane struts had to be splayed outwards to make room for the lower wing radiators, which were located outboard to avoid the interplane float struts. The wooden floats were standard Navy pattern constructed from diagonally wrapped and glued Curtiss-ply.

Blackburn Pellet G-EBHF 1923

The fuselage of the 'Pellet', as it was originally christened (it came to be known as 'the Plummet') was in fact that of a small flying-boat fighter N.1B, designed to the same N.1B Air Department requirement as the Supermarine Sea Baby but never completed. As originally laid down by designer Harris Booth it was intended to be a single-bay, unequal-span biplane with biplane tail and twin interplane rudders propelled by the wartime 200 hp Hispano-Suiza engine. Built in the Blackburn works in Leeds, only the fuselage had been completed by the time peace and the successful deck-landing trials of the Sopwith Pup caused the flying-boat concept to be abandoned and the contracts to be terminated. Since then it had gathered dust in store.

To create the racer, Bumpus, using the N.1B hull as a basis, added closely spaced, high aspect ratio biplane wings, the lower one being of sufficiently small chord for

No white-coated assemblers in 1923. The Blackburn Pellet, which crashed out of the pre-event trials. (*Flight*)

wing spacing to be reduced to a minimum without interference effect. The object was to allow a Napier Lion engine to be mounted tractor-fashion on top of the upper mainplane without setting the thrust line too high. To cool it Bumpus created what appears to be the first ever British surface radiator mounted on the upper wing. The sesquiplane wing structure was braced by the V-type interplane struts and by a pair of N-struts forming the engine pylon. An unusual feature was secondary outboard struts bracing the sterns of the wingtip floats to the upper mainplane, giving the impression, at a glance, that the machine had N-type interplane struts. The pilot sat ahead of the propeller with his head perilously close to the arc. He was merged with the slipstream by a headrest. The result was a very neat and purposeful-looking machine, aerodynamically clean except for the boxy vee-bottom wingtip floats.

The Napier Lion III engine fitted to the Pellet was reputed to have come from the Gloster Bamel. It was housed in a neat, close-fitting streamlined nacelle devoid of excrescences and cooled by one of the very earliest British surface radiators. Fuel was drawn from a small header tank topped up by a Rotherhams wind-drive pump from a tank in the hull. After its second test-flight at Cowes, when Reg Kenworthy had to alight because of engine overheating, the surface radiator was removed and replaced by a lobster-pot Lamblin procured by Saunders at Cowes. At the same time a Curtiss-Reed propeller was fitted.

Despite protestations that Blackburn were patriotically building a Schneider defender rather than declaring a dividend, the Pellet was built on a shoestring using the minimum of new techniques. The two-step hull – the aftermost step was little more than a skeg – was a Linton Hope-type, fabric-covered over carvel planking and with plant-on planing surfaces to give a double-bottom structure. The wings were the contemporary wooden, two-spar type with fabricated wooden ribs, the same technique being used for the cruciform empennage.

Despite a request from Kenworthy to have the machine ready for early August to give adequate time for test-flying, the absence of the engine while flying in the Aerial Derby – which was won by Larry Carter's Gloster I, in which it was installed – coupled with Bumpus's and the works' preoccupation with Air Ministry designs, caused the machine not to be ready until early September. When at last it was launched from Blackburn's slipway at Brough it was promptly caught by wind and tide and turned over. Despite the fact that by this time Supermarine had declared their entry of the Sea Lion III, Blackburn was determined to get the machine to the trials. It was returned to the shop for re-rigging and the fitting of enlarged wingtip floats. Meanwhile Napier stripped and cleaned the engine of mud and sea-water. This work occupied almost three weeks. It was 23 September before the machine could be shipped by train to Southampton, where the Blackburn team took three days to assemble it at Fairey's Hamble factory.

Baltimore 1925

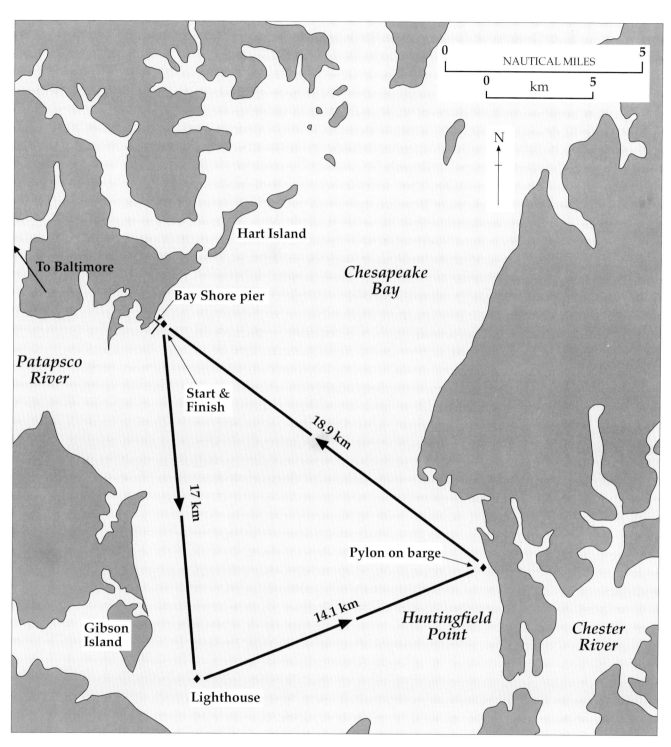

Schneider Trophy Contest Course: Baltimore 1925.

Run-up

Having deprived the Marylanders of the privilege of seeing the world's fastest seaplanes competing against each other in 1924 it was only fair that the American National Aeronautic Association

(NAA) should once again choose Bay Shore Park as the setting for the 1925 event. Bay Shore Park was a pleasure beach owned by a Baltimore tramway operator, the United Railways and Electric Company, who had their own railway line running down to the beach and amusement park. Apart from being located in the sheltered water of Chesapeake Bay its main asset from the point of view of the race organisers was its long causeway capable of providing standing room for up to 10,000 spectators. Its biggest drawback was the lack of hangarage for visiting aircraft, or for any aircraft at all, and the gently shelving shore, which was so attractive to bathers, called for dredgers to cut a channel for the seaplanes and their tenders to get them away from the slipway. Nevertheless the setting in Chesapeake Bay – it is really more of a sound – was ideal and not too far from large centres of population on the eastern seaboard.

Although the original Coupe Maritime regulations called for the course to be measured in nautical miles the NAA had already decided, in preparation for the 1924 race, with the approval of the FAI, that the circuit should be measured in kilometres. They accordingly laid out a course in the Bay measuring exactly 50 km, the first time in Schneider history that the lap measurement had no decimal points in it. The advantage foreseen in this arrangement was that speeds set up during the race would automatically qualify for consideration as World Closed-Circuit records if they were fast enough. Seven laps added up to 350 km (188.86 nm) which accorded with the minimum distance laid down in the original deed of gift of the Coupe Maritime. This facility was used to good effect in 1924 when, in the absence of the race, the US Navy Curtiss CR-3s set a number of international records. The course, with minor relocations of turning points but distance unchanged, remained unaltered for 1925.

Turning points of the almost-equilateral triangular 1925 course were to be located at Bay Shore, marked by a pylon on a lighter located to give a good view from the causeway; a lighthouse 17 km south of Bay Shore off the tip of Gibson Island, and another barge and pylon east-north-east of the lighthouse, moored just off the opposite shore and to the south of Huntingfield Point. To allow the machines to take off into the wind, two alternative starting lines were provided for. In the case of southerly winds the line would be located immediately after the Bay Shore marker; if the wind was in the north the timers and judges would be located on a lighthouse conveniently located alongside the course about 3 km before the Bay Shore marker on the Huntingfield–Bay Shore leg.

The navigability tests were arranged to take place over a small triangular course of about 6 km laid out close into Bay Shore. Just for good measure a 3 km FAI-homologated speed course was carefully measured along Bay Shore should the decision be made to go for world records after the race.

Elaborate safety precautions were laid on, with police boats patrolling all legs of the course – two on the cross-bay leg – and marker boats were anchored at intervals on the line of flight of every leg. In addition two rescue boats would circle the middle of the circuit to pick up any pilots who were forced to alight. And, determined not to have a repeat of the incidents at Bournemouth and Cowes when spectator boats had put machines and pilots at great risk, the mouth of the Patapsco River leading from populous Baltimore would be sealed off by a row of seven police boats to hold back any intruders.

The Entries

For the first time the French, with their own Coupe Beaumont on the same date and struggling with underlying political problems, did not propose an entry although they had done so in 1924. It was therefore left to Italy and Britain to make the European challenge.

In both countries the political situation had changed little since the previous year. Italy, a mere 54 years old as a nation, having embraced National Socialism, was on the verge of becoming a Fascist dictatorship under Benito Mussolini and was destined to stay that way for another twenty years. Great Britain still had its first Socialist government, acquired the previous year under the leadership of Ramsay MacDonald. Although it was a government dedicated to peace it was wise enough to see that this could not be achieved through military weakness. Thus the rehabilitation of the RAF initiated by Baldwin's Conservative government was continued and given added impetus by the new administration, which was now prepared to order experimental racing aircraft and loan them to the constructors for the race. In this respect the British were better off than the Italian constructors who, although called upon to produce designs to uphold the glory of their country, were expected to pay for them out of their own pockets. This was, in fact, nothing new to them, for it was the European continental custom at that time for firms to vie for military orders through success in international speed contests. However, some help was forthcoming in the form of free use of the facilities of the Commissariato d'Aeronautica, the Italian government aviation research and development department. This gave interested manufacturers access to wind tunnels, and the possible loan of engines.

As builder of some of the best of the Italian flying-boat fighters for the newly formed Regia Aeronautica it was logical that Aeronautica Macchi should once again come forward with two separate designs for high-speed machines. Their aspirations were no doubt encouraged by the acquisition, in 1922, of a gifted new technical manager. Mario Castoldi, in common with many other brilliant designers, is said to have found a formal engineering education less than easy going although it did not prevent him gaining a Laureate in Engineering at the Milan Polytechnic in 1913. At the beginning of the War he had joined the Air Directorate in Turin and had his first taste of the industry when he was seconded to the Società Polmisilio in 1916. After hostilities he had moved to the military aviation experimental establishment at Montecelio, where he had carried out important work at a time when aviation in Italy was becoming a neglected science. He had joined Macchi from this assignment and his first complete design for them seems to have been a handsome single-seater biplane 'boat, the M.26, strongly reminiscent of the Sea Lion III, powered by a Hispano-Suiza H.S.42 engine of 300 hp.

One of Macchi's entries was designated M.27 and could have been a development of the M.26. It was abandoned in the design stage in favour of the more impressive M.33 project. This was for the first cantilever monoplane to be build by Macchi and the one and only cantilever wing flying-boat ever to fly in the Schneider races. Of all-wooden construction with a span of 32 ft 10 in (10 m) and an all-up weight of 2,777 lb (1,255 kg), it was powered by one of the Curtiss D-12 engines imported on the instructions of General Guidoni for appraisal by the Italian aero-engine industry. It was a shoulder-wing machine with the engine housed in a nacelle mounted on a steel tube pylon ahead of the pilot. In common with all of Castoldi's designs it not only looked right, with a graceful hull terminating in a braced cruciform empennage, but in trials proved very fast and quickly established itself as a potential aspirant for the World Speed record for flying-boats.

It was typical of its designer that the underwater shape of the hull was developed empirically by Castoldi using models pushed through Lake Garda by a high-speed motorboat fitted with a forward-facing derrick and spring balances.

Two M.33s were built and entered, one for Macchi's test pilot, Giovanni de Briganti, the winner of the 1921 race, and the other for Riccardo Morselli.

As ever, there was a paper project from the fruitful board of Giovanni Pegna, now working with Piaggio. Designated the P4 by its makers and Pc.3 by its designer, it was a cantilever monoplane on floats, powered by a Curtiss D-12 engine. It is said that construction was started and then abandoned, possibly when the news came through that practically the whole Italian stock of D-12 engines had been allocated to Macchi.

Another interesting Italian entry, very similar to that of 1924 from the same source, came from Dornier's Pisa establishment. It was probably a carry-over from the project put forward in 1924 and may have been a foil to give Dornier access to wind-tunnel facilities.

It was a great pity that France and Germany who, a mere eight years ago, had been leaders in aeronautical design were not represented. Germany's absence was understandable because Treaty obligations forbade her to build machines of more than a certain power, but in typical fashion her observers were present at all the important aviation meetings, busy taking note of everything that went on around them. However, so far as the French were concerned, that country was more advanced than the Americans with pure speed machines and currently held the World Air Speed Record at 278.48 mph (448.17 kph) with the very significant Bernard V-2 monoplane flown by Sous-Lieutenant Florentin Bonnet.

The Trophy defenders in America were not unobservant of what was going on abroad. They would be fully aware of the imminence of a 700 hp Napier Lion VII, with a power-to-weight ratio of 1.161 lb/hp. They would also know that Supermarine were going ahead with a monoplane design despite the veil of secrecy which the makers endeavoured to draw over details of their project. In the same way the Americans could deduce, even if they did not know definitely, that Gloster would be mounting the new Napier Lions in their racing biplanes.

So far as the British themselves were concerned they were grateful that the Air Ministry had at last given them the backing they had been asking for. Despite Air Chief Marshal Trenchard's misgivings about letting Air Force personnel fly in the races, the Technical branch were now convinced that in air-racing they had an unrivalled proving ground in which development would be forced along in the white heat of competition. The Air Ministry felt that allocations from their experimental funds were more than justified by this development and by the experience service personnel would obtain in flying and servicing high-speed machines. However, in deference to Trenchard, they would be loaned to the makers, flown by the makers' pilots and maintained by their crews when actually racing.

American fears were not unfounded. Mitchell of Supermarine had laid down a mid-wing, cantilever float-plane which had much in common with the Bernard V-2 world record machine but was even cleaner aerodynamically, and aesthetically more pleasing. Had surface radiators been available to Mitchell – they were under development but were not ready in time – the S.4, as it was designated, would have enjoyed a lower drag coefficient than the American Curtiss biplane racers. Mitchell could see that Curtiss had brought the biplane close to the peak of its development as a racing machine and the next logical step was a monoplane. He had the advantage that he was free to choose the configuration of his design while they were restricted by military contracts with service departments dedicated to the biplane. To be fair this reflected American experience with monoplane racers which had not been happy and Curtiss would have been loth to abandon their beloved biplane configuration.

The Supermarine floatplane contender was in fact a joint venture by Supermarine and Napier, the decision to go ahead with construction being made on 18 March 1925. Whereas the Gloster Aircraft Company were given a contract by the Air Ministry for their biplane racers, the government, apprehensive as ever of monoplanes, agreed with Supermarine and Napier that they would buy their machine if it was successful. The machine, designated S.4 by Mitchell, was completed in five months and made its first flight on 24 August at Calshot with Henri Biard at the controls.

All the flight trials of the S.4 were made at Calshot because of the long take-off run required compared with the earlier Sea Lions, and were so successful that, to emphasise the state of readiness of the British effort and maybe to cock a snook at Gloster, the decision was made to go for the World Seaplane record before the machine was crated for America. The attempt was successfully made at Calshot on 13 September with FAI timekeepers, under conditions of near-secrecy. The speed attained, 226.742 mph, fully justified Mitchell's design and the maker's aspirations and created a sensation when it was announced to the Press in early October immediately after homologation.

The British Air Ministry's reluctance to put money down on the S.4 while giving Gloster a contract, underlines the fact that their real preoccupation was with the well-tried biplane. Their request from the biplane-orientated Gloster Aircraft Company was for a brace of new machines on the lines of the Gloster II of the previous year. Accordingly, for 1925, Folland of Gloster's had drawn out a developed version of the Gloster II, a single-bay, all-wooden biplane, wire-braced and featuring the first Gloster wooden monocoque rear fuselage. The thin-section, fabric-covered wings were designed to take surface radiators although, in common with those for the S.4, they were destined not to be ready in time. Designed to meet Air Ministry specification 2/25, two machines were built for a total cost, to the government, of £16,000. One of these was to be the other British entry for the Schneider race.

For some reason unbeknown to all except the die-hards at the Royal Aero Club, the second Gloster machine was designated as a reserve although it could have been made a firm entry, since every country was allowed three machines by the contest rules. Unfortunately for the British effort this did not appear to have been fully understood by the Royal Aero Club. The official line when this became public knowledge was that, when the entries were made the club was not aware that more than two machines would be available! Finally there were the offerings of the host nation. The Curtiss machines were going to be difficult to beat. Since Cowes in 1923 the power output of the Curtiss D-12A race engines had been increased from 470 bhp at 2,350 rpm to 565 bhp at 2,400 rpm in the V-1400. Moreover, they were installed in cleaner airframes which Curtiss had evolved from the Pulitzer-winning Navy shoulder-wing, R2C-1 biplane built for the 1924 National Air Races. The R2C-2 floatplane adaptation of the R2C-1 had been made ready the year before. It would now act as reserve to three of the new R3C-2 floatplanes; conversions of the R3C-1 landplane racer commissioned from Curtiss as a US Army and Navy combined exercise for the 1925 Pulitzer. In view of the close proximity of the Pulitzer and Schneider contests in the aviation calendar the R3C was designed for quick conversion from landplane to floatplane configuration.

Preliminaries

Taxi trials of the first Gloster III, allocated service serial N.194, began at the RAF seaplane base at Felixstowe on 16 August and, despite high winds and rough water, the machine was ready to fly on the 29th. Hubert Broad made the first short flight and came back with the bad news that directional stability was poor, the machine yawing out on turns. His suggestion was to put dihedral into the straight upper wing but, with passages for the team and their machines booked for 26 September, a major modification of this magnitude was out of the question and a compromise was struck. The Royal

Aircraft Establishment (RAE) at Farnborough suggested that a solution would be to enlarge greatly the upper and lower tail fins to improve straight-line stability. This was done on both machines, bringing them to what has become known as IIIA configuration.

But time was so short prior to crating the two racers for America that Broad had only flown N.194 four times with a total of five minutes' full throttle time. Bert Hinkler, his back-up pilot, had made only one short flight in N.195 although he had acquired a little experience of high-speed floatplanes in the Bamel. This old warrior was being used as a test hack for the Short metal floats which had replaced the short May, Harden and May type fitted to the Gloster II. Hubert Broad, too, had managed to put in time on the Bamel to extend his floatplane experience. Hinkler later expressed regret that he had not flown the Gloster III for long enough to get the bugs out of it. One wonders whether he would have discovered that the yawing phenomenon was in reality a mechanical and not an aerodynamic problem caused by over-sensitive rudder controls. The good thing was that the trials were free from the kind of disaster which had struck Hubert Broad in the Gloster II the previous year.

While examining the Gloster IIIs at Felixstowe before their departure for America, the more informed members of the Press may have been reminded of the Macchi M.33 which was recently revealed to the Press by our old friend General Guidoni (now Italian Air Attaché in London), by the twin Lion-engined cantilever wing, Rohrbach flying-boat standing on the apron. It was one of two purchased by the RAF for appraisal and its configuration was not only very much like that of the M.33 but was typical of the way European designers were thinking. The same could be said of its all-metal construction.

Over in Italy the graceful, wooden Macchis had flown their trials over a simulated circuit laid out by the thoroughgoing Castoldi on Lake Garda. They had been passed-off as satisfactory although their pilots had misgivings about flying them at maximum speed because of incipient wing and aileron flutter. Possibly unaware of the dramas experienced with the Verville cantilever monoplane racers in the USA until their canvas wing-covering had been replaced with plywood, Castoldi had specified fabric-covered wings – some authorities say plywood but photos don't bear it out – for the M.33. As a result the same phenomenon that had beset the first Verville R.3 was creating alarm and despondency in the hearts of de Briganti and Morselli. Possibly the M.33's wingtip floats mitigated the situation by acting as mass dampers but what was at that time a new aerodynamic problem could not have been encouraging when encountered in an unfamiliar aeroplane at speed.

Before they left Genoa on the liner *Conte Verdi*, on the same day that the British team left Southampton, the Macchis had demonstrated that they were able to maintain 199 mph. Bearing in mind that they were reputedly getting only a doubtful 400 bhp from their engines and that they were dragging plate-type radiators through the air this was a commendable performance and a measure of the aerodynamic cleanliness of the design, which must have been almost as good as that of the S.4. Unfortunately it was not fast enough to be in the running, as Castoldi well knew. However, he did have the satisfaction of having produced the world's fastest flying-boat to date.

It was indicative of the financial strategy of the American defence that they had to chance their arm by racing their new R3Cs in the Pulitzer and then having to quickly mount them on floats for the Schneider. Should the Curtisses crack up in the landplane race, all the defenders had to fall back on was the single R2C-2 from 1924. However, Curtiss were not to disappoint them, although they must have had their moments of doubt.

The first RC3 had been handed over in landplane form on 11 September and was immediately flown by the Navy's Alford Williams and the Army's Jimmy Doolittle in that order. Both pilots experienced structural defects, Williams having one of the aluminium wheel covers blow off and the other crack, while Doolittle had the traumatic experience of seeing the port upper wingtip start to fail at close on 300 mph. He quickly throttled back and landed for repairs! Before the week was out the wing had been repaired and strengthened and he had flown the Pulitzer course at 254 mph (404.8 km/h). In straight-line dashes from a dive, both he and Williams had clocked ground speeds close on 300 mph. In fact Williams had recorded 302 mph from a steep dive, maybe with a little help from the wind.

At the age of twenty-nine, Doolittle was the Army's outstanding test pilot. Born in California in 1896, he had spent three years at mining school before moving on to the School of Military Aeronautics at Berkeley in 1917. His flying training had been at Rockwell Field and early in 1918 he qualified as an instructor and was commissioned. His qualities as a pilot emerged when he flew an old DH.4 across the continent, from Pablo Beach, Florida to Rockwell Field in 22 hr 35 min flying time. This feat helped him to the Massachussetts Institute of Technology where he gained a Doctorate of Science in Aeronautics in an incredible two years. With academic and flying qualifications he had all the trappings of a modern test pilot. Quiet and unassuming, he combined consummate skill with great physical and mental courage. Because of his small size he was resistant to G and he must be given the credit for investigating the phenomenon of blackout using himself as a guinea pig. Even at that time he was showing the makings of the great man that he was to become.

There was the hint of Doolittle's epic combined operation with the Navy, when he led a force of Army B-25 Mitchells off the carrier *Hornet* to raid Tokyo, in the Army R3C-2 which they entered for the Schneider. They were certainly breaking protocol in trespassing on the preserves of their sea-going compatriots. However, it was a premeditated and agreed trespass, for their R3C – it never acquired an Army designation although R-9 has been mentioned – had been designed for quick conversion to floats and within a week of winning the Pulitzer the black and gold Army machine had been

fitted with sea-going configuration and despatched to Baltimore.

Doolittle had been nominated as pilot for the Schneider, his team-mate First Lieutenant Cyrus K. Bettis having been given the privilege of flying the Pulitzer, which he duly won from the Navy. Bettis, a retiring bachelor, was capable of wringing the last ounce of speed out of an aeroplane in the air while yet keeping it in one piece. For the Schneider Trophy race he would be Doolittle's reserve pilot in case of illness or accident; the Army did not have a reserve aircraft. They were to fly the Pulitzer-winning machine which had been quickly converted to floats after the race.

Navy pilots for the Schneider were Lieutenant Ralph Ofstie and Lieutenant George Cuddihy. Both were born in the same year as Doolittle and both had served their regulation three years as sailors before taking to the air. George Cuddihy gained attention for his skill at air gunnery and Oftsie for his general flying skill, which brought them together as test pilots on the Naval Test Board. These were the two pilots who had made record flights at Bay Shore Park after the 1924 Schneider was cancelled and held world speed records in the CR-3. Cuddihy was due to fly A.6979 which Lieutenant Alford Williams would pilot in the Pulitzer prior to conversion to seaplane guise while Ofstie was given A.6978. This, the first R3C to be built, had been test-flown as a landplane and then converted to floats and reserved for the Schneider. Powered by a 'freak' V-1400 engine which had shown an impressive 619 bhp on test, it was the Navy's hope for a second win.

The first arrivals at Baltimore were the Britishers, transported there in the SS *Minnewaska* free of charge by the patriotic owners of the line in fulfilment of their offer of the previous year. They arrived well in advance of any of the promised facilities at Bay Shore, bringing with them the S.4, the Gloster IIIs and the Bamel as practice hack. Led by Captain C.B. Wilson, who acted as non-flying captain, the party included Reg Mitchell and H.P. Folland, the designers, Commander Bird, managing director of Supermarine, the three pilots Biard, Broad and Hinkler, airframe fitters and riggers. A.V. Roe joined the contingent at the last moment and naturally H.T. Vane of Napier was in the party with his contingent of engineers and fitters to see to the well-being of the Lion engines. Thanks to the steamship owners, never before had the frugal British done anything in such style.

The crossing had been extremely pleasant and restful in between the numerous parties held on board, but not without incident. Biard – Broad described him as fey, crazy – had slipped when playing deck tennis and broken his wrist. Fortunately he was able to nurse it while the team hung around in Baltimore's Southern Hotel waiting for hangars to be erected at the race site. The machines stayed in their crates at the open beach. The Pulitzer race was on in Detroit at the time and most of the team went over to look at it, entertained to sandwiches and drinks by Dick Fairey, who was heavily involved negotiating a licence with Curtiss to build

D-12 engines. Hubert Broad was not one of the racegoers. He waited patiently, anxious for the opportunity to get his machine assembled and in action. It was a bad time for the visitors because they were losing valuable flying time which could be spent building up much needed familiarisation time on their aircraft.

They had to wait until 13 October, only ten days before the preliminary trials and seaworthiness tests, while the machines languished in their packing cases. In commendably quick time the Baltimore club had dredged the channel, built a long slipway and made a concrete apron. But the best that was available in the way of covered accommodation was a series of leaky wartime canvas Tee-hangars and the packing cases that the machines had arrived in. To cap the general air of misery the weather was cold, wet and windy, as befitted the time of the year in Maryland. It was all a far cry from the shirt-sleeve weather of the Solent and the spacious hospitality of the Saunders hangars, and Mitchell and Folland were appalled at the conditions their ground crews had to work in compared with the facilities that had been available back on the Solent in 1923.

Castoldi and his men from Varese in their turn must have been missing the more benevolent climate and the good wines of their native Lombardy. Nevertheless in this strange land of continuous high winds, rough seas and prohibition they did not let conditions get the better of them.

One consolation was that they were able to take a really close look at the American and the British floatplanes at first hand. They could not fail to be impressed. Castoldi, especially, was made to realise as much as anyone present that the floatplane configuration had most to offer in terms of reduced frontal area and structural integrity. Since the rules allowed floatplanes he could see that the Schneider machine of the future would have to be of this configuration despite the attractions of the more seaworthy, but slower, flying-boat. The Schneider Trophy races had become a shop window for the fastest seaplanes a country could produce. It was a polite way for nations to show their teeth. The nation that could produce the fastest floatplanes was obviously in a position to build the fastest fighters. In this atmosphere nobody was interested in flying-boats. The Italian engineers therefore took it upon themselves to learn as much about floats as they could.

On 13 October, the day of the Pulitzer race, Broad's Gloster IIIA – the alpha signified the addition of increased rudder fin area – was rigged and ready to fly although the reserve machine and the Bamel were still in their crates. Hubert abstained from joining the British party at the races and made a short flight to check engine and control function and put the machine away in readiness for the preliminaries on the 23rd. Commander Bird was concerned about Biard's wrist and delayed the S.4's first flight until the last moment.

On the 16th the weather and the physical state of the one and only S.4 pilot seemed to be propitious. Biard made a couple of short flights and then retired to his bed with influenza. He chose the right time to do it, for the weather deteriorated from that point into gales and even more rain, blowing the flimsy hangars down and damaging the machines, including the S.4, whose empennage was badly damaged, calling for a concerted effort by the Supermarine 'chippy' and riggers to repair the damage. The conditions were clearly more appropriate to a badly organised Boy Scout camp than a vital aeronautical contest between nations. The hosts missed the worst of it, arriving with their Curtisses just as the storms were abating.

The navigation trials, billed for 23 October, the day before race day, came soon enough. All that was required of the machines was to take off across the start line and fly two laps of the course during which they had to alight twice and taxi at not less than 12 knots in both directions of a ½-nm course marked out by two buoys off Bay Shore. After that they would be towed away untouched by their ground crews to complete a six-hour mooring test. Engines were sealed before the test and the seals could not be broken until after the race. In the same way no repairs to the aircraft were permitted unless damage was the result of causes beyond the responsibility of the pilot and constructor.

As the result of a draw the first away at nine o'clock was Ralph Oftstie in the original, unraced R3C-2 with the 'freak' engine. He was followed by George Cuddihy, who had a flying wire break on his first attempt; it was quickly replaced, he completed his test without further mishap and the machine was towed away for the mooring test.

Third machine in the draw was de Briganti's Macchi. It took time to start his engine, which called for much priming before it would fire. The Italian pilot made a few circuits to warm things up and then alighted to start the test. This was the signal for the engine to die on him. The Macchi was towed back to the slipway, restarted and this time completed the test without trouble. De Briganti put in a competent display of flying but the performance of the engine did not augur well for the race.

While this was going on Hubert Broad was launched in the Gloster IIIA, made an impeccable take-off and proceeded to fly his two laps. He was on the second of these when Biard squeezed himself into the cockpit of the S.4, the engine was fired up by the Bristol two-stroke starter they had brought with them from England, and the machine was pushed down the slipway into the chilly waters of Chesapeake Bay. Biard was still suffering from the after-effects of his influenza but seemed fit enough to fly.

Biard took off across the line well enough and all eyes were on the beautiful S.4 as it eased off the water. Observers record that he made a wide turn over the aircraft camp (this would be necessary because of the very tight turn at the end of the navigability circuit), aimed for the start line in full view of the judges and then put the machine into a steep, high-speed bank to line it up for the first mark. Suddenly the machine changed from a steep right-hand bank into an equally steep left-hand one. The aircraft then went on to stall and yaw repeatedly until it entered what we would today call a deep stall and fell flat into the sea from what one observer estimated to be 100 feet.

Biard had fought for his life to get out of what seems to have been a combination of control reversal and wing-flutter as the aircraft approached the high-speed stall condition in the turn. High-speed stall normally occurs in steep turns when G-forces multiply the weight of the aircraft to many times its design weight.

According to one report Biard found himself trapped in the cockpit with his head in the muddy bottom. *The Aeroplane* correspondent described the machine as hitting the water flat the right way up and the float chassis breaking up as it hit the water. Other accounts say that it turned over and that Biard was trapped upside down in the cockpit until he managed to extricate himself. The one available photograph taken after the accident shows the S.4 inverted in the middle of a pile of debris with a tow rope round the tail.

Mitchell, who had been sitting in a rescue launch, clad in a swimming costume ready to rescue his man in the event of disaster, went nearly frantic when the launch's engine stalled hundreds of yards from the disaster. Meanwhile, Hubert Broad had alighted at the end of his second qualifying lap and taxied over to the wreckage to see if he could help. Leaping out on the float he spotted what appeared to be a pair of goggles floating on the surface. A closer look revealed that they were fastened to a vocal and very much alive Biard. As Broad hung onto him the launch arrived and Biard was hauled aboard, bruised and shaken, with his wrist broken yet again but otherwise intact. 'Is the water warm?' asked Mitchell as he wrapped a blanket round poor Henri.

Opinions vary about the cause of the accident. The Italians were convinced that the accident began with a high-speed stall in the turn. Biard was convinced that it was wing-flutter. Hubert Broad, who saw it all happen as he taxied back, felt the same. Certainly the quick left bank immediately after initiating right bank points to control reversal, which is associated with flutter. An official inquiry came to the same conclusion as the Italians.

This left the British team with only one aircraft. The obvious move was to get the reserve Gloster IIIA out of its packing case and rig it for Hinkler. It was remarkable that this had not already been done. Maybe Gloster felt that it was safer where it was after seeing the accident to the S.4, and wanted to keep it intact. The Gloster crew set to with a will to get N.195 rigged and ready to fly.

In the midst of all this excitement Morselli's Macchi was launched ready for the test. The M.33s were a better type for this part of the contest than the floatplanes and both de Briganti and Morselli had more hours on the type, accumulated during their simulated circuit tests on Lake Garda, than their British counterparts had on theirs. Their only worries were about the tendency of the fabric-covered cantilever wings to flutter and the reluctance to start of their well-used Curtiss D-12-A engines. There was dramatic confirmation of this when Morselli's engine refused to fire-up for the test despite, or maybe because of, all the tricks of the trade. The engine was sealed and to break the seals would have

entailed disqualification. Sadly the Macchi had to be returned to its hangar and withdrawn, leaving de Briganti the sole Italian challenger.

It was an unhappy time for the Italians. The cold, Atlantic weather was in sad contrast to their warm, placid Lake Varese, and the so-called hangarage for their machines and workshops was deplorable. Worst of all, the pilots did not like the machines and were reluctant to fly them to maximum performance because of the fear of wing-flutter, a problem new to them but inherent in early cantilever wings.

The Gloster mechanics were equal to the occasion and by four o'clock the machine was ready, and by five, Hinkler was in the machine and on the water. The little Australian made a perfect take-off, and set off on his qualifying laps but before he could complete them a flying wire carried away and, since they were not duplicated he flew gently back to the slip for repairs. A spare was quickly fitted but by this time the sun had dipped below the horizon and night was falling. Hinkler wanted to take the test despite the conditions and no doubt he could have done it. But the team captain thought otherwise and according to the rules Hinkler was out of the race.

These rules stated that the preliminary trial should be completed on the allocated day. Bearing in mind that the race was on the next day it seemed out of the question to fit in a flying trial and the flotation test even if a waiver of the rules could be obtained. But the race was not until 2.30 pm and Clement Keyes, the President of Curtiss, realised there was just time to fit the full navigability test into the morning if, and it was a big 'if', the other competitors would sign a waiver. The very sporting race committee went into session and agreed that the rules could be bent to allow this; typically only the British had to be persuaded. Eventually the vital document was signed by all the other team captains and the officials and pilots girded their loins for a dawn start the next morning.

In the event the weather on race day was so bad that when the Gloster IIIA was launched at daybreak bad water conditions forced Hinkler to turn back from his taxi run without getting airborne. In fact the weather was so rough that the race had to be postponed for two days, until Monday 26 October, to allow the storm to blow itself out. This it did, but not before it had wrecked the race camp once again and destroyed seventeen machines out of six squadrons of Martin floatplanes which were moored out in preparation for a pre-race display.

First thing on Monday morning Hinkler was once again ready to take the test. Very sportingly the painstaking race officials were out of their beds and in the observation and marker boats by 3 am to give the British entrant the chance of racing. The delay due to the weather had given the Italian team time to reconsider their decision about the waiver and, fearful of creating a precedent, tried to withdraw it at the last moment. They got little sympathy from the committee who, by that time, had sent out the marker boats and had no quick way of recalling them. At 7 am the Gloster IIIA was launched in the smooth water in the lee of the shore and Hinkler taxied it on the surface towards the first of the marker boats.

As he approached the start line, which was in calm water in the shelter of the shore, Bert Hinkler could see white horses out in the bay as the last of the gale spent itself. Undaunted, he opened up the Lion and made a perfect take-off. But when he came to make his first landing the sea was against him. The heavy water loads as the Gloster touched down were too much for the Gloster type float chassis; a fitting gave way causing the companion strut to buckle and allowing the propeller to bite into the float. Hinkler cut the engine and waited for a launch to tow him back to the shore. He scarcely got his feet wet but nevertheless the British were back to a single entry.

The Race

While the Gloster ground crew worked to repair their damaged IIIA the wind and sea gradually dropped and by ten o'clock the race committee was able to decide that the race was on, with the first machine to be away at 2.30 pm. With the wind in the north, the alternative line by the lighthouse had been chosen and the judges and timekeepers were duly ferried over. Meanwhile the organisers amused the Monday morning crowd with parachute drops while F.H. Conant II, who was destined to join the team the following year, provided a polished display of aerobatics.

Biard, in the S.4, had drawn to be first away. In his absence the honour went to Doolittle in the black and gold Army R3C-2, which taxied over to the start in a cloud of spray and crossed the line at 2.38 pm, getting off the water with the minimum fuss, making a low turn round the Bay Shore marker and heading like a dart for the lighthouse off Gibson Island. Broad, as ever, mindful of his machine, had had the Gloster towed across and, three minutes after Doolittle's take-off, Britain's one and only hope was gunning his engine across the line just as the Curtiss was streaking across to Huntingfield Point on the second leg. There was still quite a sea running and to avoid getting his Curtiss soaked in spray Cuddihy took off and flew over to the start line. He was the third to go and was rounding the lighthouse as Doolittle swept past the Bay Shore causeway at the end of a scintillating 8 min 21.2 sec lap, equal to a speed of 223.16 mph (359.138 km/h), a lap speed which no other machine in the race would equal despite his 'standing start'.

Broad was the next man to appear. His time of 9 min 35.71 sec for the first lap was equal to 194.28 mph (312.657 km/h). Almost as accomplished a pilot as Doolittle, he was having to fight the Gloster round the turns as it yawed out owing to insufficient keel area. It was clearly no match for the Curtiss racers as Cuddihy demonstrated by sweeping past the British machine as he came round after his first lap, recording a time and speed of 8 min 48.6 sec and 211.59 mph (340.522 km/h). As

Broad crossed the line for the first time Ofstie, in the second Navy R3C-2, was making his take-off. His mount, A.6978, was the machine which had been built from the outset as a floatplane and had never before raced, and was powered by the oddball engine supposedly giving above-average horsepower. Potentially he was the Navy's challenge to Doolittle although his first round, in 8 min 57.83 sec, belied the claimed potential of the engine.

De Briganti's M.33 was the last away at 2.55 pm and as he started his take-off run Doolittle shot overhead to begin his third lap, having taken only 16 min 20.05 sec to cover 100 km from take-off, corresponding to a speed of 228.14 mph (367.16 km/h) for the last two laps. A couple of minutes later two dots coming from the Huntingfield marker grew into Broad in the Gloster and Ofstie in the Navy's A.6978. The Curtiss raised a cheer as it shot past the British machine. As Ofstie made his turn, wider and not so neat as Doolittle's, the watches said 8 min 57.83 sec (211.59 mph). Hubert Broad in the Gloster, holding the Lion III back a little to allow it to warm through, had made 198.64 mph (319.68 km/h) on this, his second round. But it was obvious that only a disaster to the American machines would put him into the running.

Next to appear was Cuddihy in the Navy's second R3C-2, on his second lap averaging 216.25 mph (348.027 km/h) from take-off. His second lap at a speed of 221.128 mph (355.872 km/h), was no match for Doolittle, who was lapping consistently at better than 233 mph (375 km/h). In common with Ofstie he was taking his turns wide with the throttle up against the stop. Doolittle, on the other hand, was rounding the pylons in a steep bank inducing high G-forces in the process. De Briganti, in the M.33, adopted a different style which was later to become a tradition when the Regia Aeronautica formed its own high-speed flight. His method was to lose speed at the markers by making a climbing turn and then use the height so gained to take the next leg in a very shallow dive at increased speed. Doolittle's technique meant that he flew the shortest distance and his skill in handling the Curtiss ensured that he dropped off very little speed as he changed direction. In effect what he was doing was roughly the same as pulling out of a high-speed dive laid on its side. Physically he was better adapted than the others to the high G-forces that this style induced because of his day-to-day work which, among other things involved stressing airframes to the maximum by pulling them hard out of terminal velocity dives.

Hubert Broad, in the British Gloster IIIA, had his cornering technique forced on him by the tendency of the machine to yaw out on the turns – he called it skidding – but despite this his machine was the leading European and lying fourth in the race behind Ofstie's Curtiss. Enigmatically this last machine, though reserved for the Schneider and fitted with the 'freak' 619 bhp engine with the intention of winning the race for the Navy, was the slowest of all the US entries. Nevertheless it was lapping 16 or 17 mph faster than the lone British entry. On the other hand the Napier Lion in Broad's Gloster was running faultlessly; it was the least of his worries, whereas the failure of Ofstie's V-1400 to deliver the extra power that legend credited it with seemed to indicate that all was not well within it.

De Briganti, last away, was another pilot unhappy with his D-12 Curtiss engine. A standard D-12, giving only 450 bhp, compared with the 550 bhp or so of the highly tuned American V-1400's entrants, it was further handicapped by having to drive a wooden propeller which did not allow it to be run at maximum speed and power. However, there was some solace in this because, had the engine been able to give its rated power de Briganti would have been reluctant to use it because of the flutter which had dogged the M.33 wing since its inception. To add to his sorrows he had mistaken the markers on the second lap and flown an extra seven kilometres, which had dropped his average for the first two laps to 161.114 mph (259.288 km/h). After this he seemed to pick up and his third lap was his best in 10 min 43.32 sec, equivalent to 173.86 mph (279.799 km/h). But as he watched Doolittle streak past him as he started on his first lap – the American was on his third at the time – and pass him again before he had started on the third leg of the same lap, he must have realised that the Macchi was completely outclassed and that his only course was to fly to finish and hope that at least some of the other machines would drop out.

He was not to be disappointed. As he ploughed round on his fourth lap he saw Ofstie's Curtiss, which had passed him minutes before, down on the water between Gibson Island and Huntingfield with a broken magneto drive. At the same time Cuddihy in the other Navy Curtiss was living a drama. As the lap had rolled by he had watched the oil temperature gauge mounting steadily. With six laps gone the engine was still delivering power, as his lap times show. But his engine was steadily losing oil; the records don't tell us how much but it could have been a leaking radiator. He had passed the Bay Shore marker and the finishing line on his final lap when the engine gave out – it is highly likely that a connecting rod broke, punctured the crankcase and started an oil fire – seized and erupted into flame. The pilot acted promptly, operated the engine fire extinguisher to douse the flames, and put the Curtiss smartly down on the water to finish off his fire-fighting job. The fire was out before the rescue launch could reach the scene.

Doolittle had completed his final lap minutes before the Navy dramas had started. As he crossed the line he pulled the stick hard back to knock off speed and put the black and gold Curtiss into a triumphant climb before coming in to one of those feather-light touchdowns which so annoyed the Navy pilots.

This time the Navy had very little reason to be satisfied as it watched its two machines coming in towards the shore on the ends of tow ropes. Doolittle's speed for the race was 232.573 mph, 55 mph faster than David Rittenhouse's when he won the previous race at Cowes, and 33 mph faster than Hubert Broad in the Gloster,

who had crossed the line as the Navy launch was rushing out to help Cuddihy. De Briganti had two more laps to go as the faster machines were being hauled up the slipway. He droned round to finish half an hour after Broad to take third and last place.

Hindsight

Looking back at the race the main factor which had brought victory to the Americans was better preparation of machines and men. This came naturally from the joint experience of the services and Curtiss's expertise in building machines for the National Air Races. Moreover, the Curtiss airframes were undoubtedly the best in the race and, allied to the Curtiss V-1400 engine with its low frontal area, were unbeatable while they were flying.

But there must have been the nagging feeling at Garden City that their Curtiss engine was on the ragged edge of its potential. Of the five Curtiss engines which faced the starter, one had failed to fire up, one had broken an ancillary drive and the other had caught fire. It was not a good record and the following year the lesson learnt would give other engine manufacturers a chance.

However, the writing was on the wall. Had the S.4 seen more development and, with respect to Henri Biard, been flown by a pilot with more experience of high-speed machines, it could well have pressed the Curtiss machines despite the built-in headwind represented by its clumsy Lamblin radiators. The rest of the machine was cleaner than the American biplanes, beautiful as they were, and the extra power of the Napier Lion engine would have made up for the greater frontal area. Moreover, the Napier was reliable in spite of the extra horsepower that its makers had squeezed out of it. And there was more to come. On the other hand the V-1400 had obviously been developed to its limit in the form in which it was raced. It is probably significant that no military orders were placed for it apart from the development contract.

But of the designers present at Baltimore, the man who learnt most of all was Ing. Mario Castoldi. In return for enduring the wet, cold blasts of autumn on the US Atlantic seaboard, he and his engineering team had been able to see, touch and physically feel just what the Americans and British were up to. He was able to perceive at first hand that the Coppa Schneider was developing into a straightforward speed contest between nations with much prestige at stake. He may, or may not have foreseen that the landplane fighters for the next war would be derived from the Schneider race. But what he was able to see was that the all-conquering Curtiss machines were fighter prototypes on floats and that this would be the trend.

It must also have been clear to the Italian designer that the only way forward with high-speed seaplanes was to reduce drag by adopting the monoplane configuration in line with Mitchell. In common with the great British designer – and no doubt lured on by the success of the French Bernard – he had been attracted to the unbraced cantilever wing with its freedom from the unwanted drag of bracing wires. What both had learnt on the chilly shores of the Patapsco River was that while the cantilever wing was fine for lumbering old Fokker and Junkers transports, the know-how to stress it for high-speed flight would have to be learnt step by step.

The Americans, Loening and Verville, were finding out the same thing at the same time, paving the way for the monoplane fights of the late thirties. Castoldi also had recognised the aerodynamic qualities of the thin wing for racing and high-speed flight generally, a fact which is proved by modern knowledge. The engineer in him must also have seen how the floatplane configuration lent itself to lightweight braced monoplane structures, whereas it is almost impossible to design a monoplane flying-boat with advantageous bracing-wire angles. In any case, having been forced to forsake the seaworthiness thesis in favour of speed at all costs, it was more logical in the interests of reducing frontal area to put the two bulkiest components, the engine and the pilot, one behind the other instead of one above the other as he had done with the M.33. That his mind was set in this direction before he left Bay Shore Park was indicated by the amount of interest shown by the Italian contingent in the detail design of the floatplanes, and their particular interest in the Short-built floats on the Gloster.

The Aircraft

Gloster III

Despite the two disasters with the Gloster IIs the British Air Ministry was sufficiently impressed with the performance of these machines and the Gloster Aircraft Company's development work on them to place a £16,000 order with the company to provide two machines for the 1925 race. It was allocated at the same time as the Supermarine order and was in keeping with government policy of promoting efficiency by competition between contractors. It is not clear whether this was a joint contract with Napier, as in the case of the Supermarine S.4, but it is significant that the commercially conscious aviation journals at the time refer to the machines as Gloster-Napiers.

Folland's new design was naturally a development of the Gloster II floatplane and the biplane configuration was the same with equal span, I-strutted wings and a ply-covered, oval section fuselage. The key to the design was of course the availability of the cleaned-up and tuned, direct-drive Napier Lion VII engine which its makers were busy developing for the Supermarine S.4. Power was raised from the 525 hp of the special Lion supplied for the Sea Lion III to 680 hp by increasing the compression ratio and lightening the reciprocating parts to permit it to run up to 2,600 rpm. This speed was made possible, without the use of a reduction gear, by Syvanus Reed's metal propeller. Incidentally the propellers chosen for the Gloster III were the cut and bent type made by Fairey from plate rather than the later, forged type which had to be imported from America at that time.

The construction of the monocoque fuselage for the Gloster III was on the same lines as that of the II

monocoque with a light ply skin, diminishing in thickness towards the tail, and longitudinal ash stiffeners. The empennage was basically that of the company's Grebe fighter with double wire-bracing picking up with the leading edge of a ventral fin which was put there as much for structural reasons as for its aerodynamic effect. A feature of the tailplane design was that the elevator hinged on a separate tube. A small increase in rudder area was obtained by filling in the tail skid cut-out of the fighter rudder. Otherwise no increase in vertical surface area was provided to compensate for the extra side area of the floats.

Wing construction was conventional two-spar with dihedral on the lower mainplane only. In common with the Bamel and the Gloster II, the upper mainplane had blunt elliptical tips, and ailerons were fitted to the lower mainplane only. The control surfaces were uncompromisingly rectangular in shape which, in combination with a straight leading edge gave the impression either that someone had fitted the wrong wing, or had forgotten to round off the tips. This was in fact one of Folland's design foibles because not only were the wings a different shape but they were of different section, the upper one having a higher lift section than the lower one and being set at a different angle of incidence. Folland had patented a system of wrapping the ribs with fabric and sewing the wing-covering to it following a frightening incident in the 1921 French Coupe Deutsch de la Meurthe, when the wing fabric of J.H. James's Bamel started to part company with the wing ribs. This method was used to attach the fabric to the Gloster III ribs.

Folland was busy developing wing surface radiators and the wing section was made intentionally thin to take them. But even at that time, two years after the Americans had shown the way, the radiators were not ready and, rather than use an untried system, he had made do with the well-tried but drag-provoking Lamblin plate radiators mounted on the leading edges of the lower mainplanes. Surface radiators were fitted after the race to N.195 and in combination with other changes, added 30 mph to the maximum speed.

Hubert Broad's brief experience with the Harden and May flotation gear of the Gloster II was not a happy one and Folland wisely went to Short's at Gloster for floats for the III. The all-metal pontoons, devised at Rochester and tested in Short's new test tank cut into the chalk cliff behind the works, had been test-flown in scaled-down form on the Short Mussel monoplane, and were further tested on the Bamel before being mounted on the new racers. They weighed a mere 386 lb each and never gave a moment's trouble from the day they were fitted. Their only drawback, not appreciated at the time and only discovered later during wind-tunnel experiments for the Gloster IV, was their inordinately high drag.

With the accident to the Gloster II at Felixstowe firmly in mind Folland gave the new machine strengthened tubular steel float struts streamlined with wooden fairings. The float chassis was diagonally braced with round wire, as was the tailplane.

Taxying trials for the first machine began at the Marine Aircraft Experimental Establishment Felixstowe on 16 August 1925 and ran through without mishap in twelve days despite bad weather. Hubert Broad, who had been loaned by de Havilland to fly the machine in the race, made the initial test flight on the 29th and reported poor directional stability. As recorded elsewhere the pilot's suggestion was that dihedral should be added to the upper wing. This would have meant building new wings and was impossible in the time available. With shipping space booked for September the only course, suggested by the RAE and endorsed by Folland, was to increase the fixed vertical area of the empennage by extending the chord of the dorsal and ventral fins. This was duly done and the machines redesignated Gloster IIIA. The second machine, still under construction, was modified in the works. This machine, serialled N.195 by the RAF and later given the civil registration G-EBLJ, was allocated to Bert Hinkler, the Australian long-distance flyer and Avro test pilot, as back-up machine to Broad. It was distinguished from N.194, the race machine and the first to be completed, by its full-depth rudder. N.194 was modified at Felixstowe and retained its original rudder. The rather rough-and-ready construction of the extension can be seen in some photographs.

After the race the machines went back to the works and N.195 was fitted with surface radiators and an enlarged, reshaped, unbraced cantilever tail with concealed control levers. Designated the Gloster IIIB N.195, it was distinguished by the slim coolant expansion-cum-header tank, mounted on the upper mainplane centre section, needed to maintain a head of water in the upper wing surface radiators. This machine was also given a new windscreen which was an extension of the wing pylons and the round rod float chassis wires were replaced by streamlined section ones. This cleaning-up process increased the maximum speed from 225 mph to 252 mph.

Both machines were returned to Felixstowe for test work in connection with the 1927 race and the development of the Gloster IV. For reasons best known to themselves the RAF used N.195, the faster machine, for propeller static tests to decide between an RAE adjustable pitch propeller of 6.75 ft diameter and a Fairey-Reed Duralumin blade of 7.75 ft diameter and 9.08 ft pitch. It is interesting to note that the engine fitted to N.195 for these tests was Lion VII, serial no. 62001, whose log book stated an output of 601 hp at 2,600 rpm.

Flight Lieutenant Oswald Worsley flew N.194 for comparative tests fitted with the same Fairey-Reed screw – Serial FR63 – that had been used in the static tests with three different Gloster detachable-blade propellers with machined blades. The engine in this case was Napier Lion no. 62015. The object was to find the most suitable propeller for Gloster IV N.224. With this in mind the IIIA was flown at an all-up weight of 2,700 lb. At 206 mph the Fairey-Reed propeller (R63) gave a rate of climb of 80 feet per minute.

It is interesting to conjecture what the outcome of the 1925 race would have been if the shortcomings of the floats had been known and N.195 had been flown in its cleaned-up state. The race speed of the only Curtiss to survive was 231 mph, well within the scope of the IIIB.

Macchi M.33

The M.33 was only the second Macchi aircraft to be conceived in its entirety by Mario Castoldi. No doubt the decision to build a flying-boat when the trend was to build floatplanes was influenced by the Italian belief that the Schneider race should rightly be a proving ground for commercial seaplanes. The rules made for the 1920 and 1921 events were evidence of this line of thinking. But the overruling factor was that Macchi, in common with Supermarine, and the Italian constructors generally, were dedicated to the flying-boat, rather than to the aeroplane on floats. No doubt Macchi felt capable of building a flying-boat able to compete on equal terms with the very fast American floatplanes.

In this context technical publications would have kept Castoldi informed of progress in America. But it was usual at the time in complacent Europe, which had been technically so far ahead of the USA in the recent war, to regard any American claim for achievement in aviation as vainglorious boasting to be taken with a very large pinch of salt. The only time the American seaplanes had flown in Europe and had been timed by European timekeepers was in 1923 at Cowes, when David Rittenhouse had won the Schneider race at a speed of 177.28 mph. No doubt Castoldi felt that this was a figure to be relied on, was the one to beat and designed his machine accordingly. Certainly de Briganti's speed in the 1925 race seemed to indicate that Castoldi's thinking was of this order. He either ignored the well publicised R2C-2 acceptance trials in September 1924 when Rittenhouse unofficially achieved 227.5 mph or maybe he simply did not believe the American claims.

The M.33, the last flying-boat proper to take part in the Schneider race, merits attention because it reflected the European trend towards cantilever monoplane flying-boats with pylon-mounted engines. Dornier and Rohrbach were already building big commercial machines of this type, which was then regarded as the ultimate in aerodynamic and structural efficiency. It was natural that Castoldi, being a European, should look in the direction of Germany for inspiration, for here the aerodynamicists and aircraft structural engineers were leaders in their field. German constructors were certainly not afraid to try something new despite having to build their machines in Switzerland, Sweden or Italy to get round Treaty regulations. Whatever the inspiration leading to the M.33 the resulting machine was one of the prettiest and aerodynamically clean monoplane flying-boats seen up to that time. Its structure was of elegant simplicity and it looks good today.

Castoldi's aerodynamic target appears to have been to create a machine with a flat plate area better than that of the Curtiss CR-3, a further indication that he considered that was the machine to beat. To keep the cross-section area and skin friction of the M.33 to a minimum, he gave the hull the minimum volume which would keep the engine and pilot afloat and combined it with a monoplane cantilever wing. The object was to reduce drag by eliminating interplane interference and bracing wires. As a result the M.33 had a lower drag coefficient* than the R3C-2, 0.036 against 0.039, but unfortunately its flat plate area** was greater because it was a bigger machine. The relative areas were 0.52 m² compared with 0.0545 m². Macchi retrospectively claim that the M.33 had a smaller plate area than the S.4, which they calculate as 0.64 m² but it is not clear whether one was measured with radiators and the other without. In the Castoldi design, as on the S.4, the radiators added considerably to the parasitic drag. The wingtip stabilising floats further added to the total drag of the Italian machine.

Built in the traditional Italian manner, the M.33 was of wooden construction throughout, the plank and ply-skinned hull, including the integral cantilever tail fin being based on multi-plywood bulkheads. These were set at varying pitch along the hull, closely spaced forward and wider aft, according to the estimated air and water loads. Castoldi personally developed the hull using his special motorboat with forward-facing derrick and spring balances. The resulting form had a vee-bottom flattening out to a step 9 ft 6 in from the bow with a small vertical stabilising fin set in the middle of the step. There was a further long, shallow fin below the rudder whose purpose may have been to keep the machine steady against engine torque in the water, since the whole of the underside of the hull was immersed at rest because of the small hull volume. The tapered cantilever wing was of conventional two-spar construction with built-up main spars having solid flanges and ply webs. The ribs, too, were cut from ply with spruce flanges. The wing section was an asymmetrical bi-convex one similar to RAF 32 but deeper in section to accommodate the cantilever spars. For ease of transport the outer panels of the wings, which included the high aspect ratio ailerons, were section made detachable. They were bolted to the fixed centre section which acted as the foundations of the engine pylon.

It has been stated that the wings were ply-skinned but photographs indicate that they were fabric-covered. Presumably Castoldi was unaware of the flutter problems being encountered at that time in the USA with the Verville monoplane racers with this form of covering.

Had he chosen plywood covering he would well have preserved the M.33 from the flutter problems which so worried the Italian pilots. Small torpedo-shaped, vee-bottom wingtip floats of the type devised by Mitchell for the Sea Lion III were attached close up to the wingtips on N-struts with transverse wire-bracing. These and the exposed, but faired, aileron levers can hardly have eased the drag problem.

Castoldi gave his design an extremely elegant wire-braced, cruciform empennage using elliptical shapes throughout. Unfortunately flight trials indicated the need for a mass balance, which somewhat marred the shape when the machines were presented at Bay Shore. Factors which must have considerably increased drag were the double, round-section tailplane flying wires and control gear exposed to the airstream.

Power was supplied by a Curtiss D-12-A engine driving a tractor propeller. It will be recalled that a number of these engines were bought by General Guidoni for study by the Italian aero-engine industry and for use in experimental aircraft like the M.33 until a suitable domestic equivalent became available.

Folklore has it that the engines allocated to Macchi had been almost worn out by Fiat in the course of testing. Bearing in mind that Fiat, at that time, were producing the fastest racing cars in Europe, had the world's best engine technology in their 800-series racing engines and engine fitters second to none, one finds it difficult to believe that they would hand over to Macchi shot-out engines for installation in machines which were to be sent to America to defend the honour of their country. It is more likely that the poor race performance of the M.33 was due to the engines being untuned, standard units giving at least 100 bhp less than the larger-capacity, highly developed V-1400s fitted to the Curtiss racers. Moreover, they were fitted with wooden propellers which were unsuited to the engines and would not permit them to be run at maximum speed and power. It would be unwise to sit in judgement without being aware of all the facts. Undoubtedly Macchi would have preferred to use Italian engines but the existing Fiat A.20s weighed considerably more than the Curtiss D-12 for the same power and the racing AS.2 was still in the design stage.

The M.33's engine was carried on a rectangular frame inside a streamlined cowling and supported by N-struts fabricated from streamlined section steel tubes. The main mounting points were on the mainspar centre section, the front tubes picking up with a double bulkhead in the bow of the hull. Engine control rods and fuel lines were led inside the rear pylon tubes. The open pilot's cockpit was located between the wing spars with the main fuel tanks in front of and behind it.

Engine cooling was by means of a pair of Lamblin plate-type radiators mounted on either side of the tail of the nacelle, looking for all the world like massive earrings. A ventral, skin-type oil radiator looked after lubricant cooling.

Three machines were built, one for static destruction tests, the other two, serial numbers MM.48 and MM.49

*A **drag coeficient** is a non-dimensional quantity in the equation of air density, surface area trand the square of air speed which may be used to compare one aircraft with another. **Flat plate** area may be used to compare the absolute resistance of two or more different bodies in the air. It equates their resistance to the area of a flat plate normal to an airstream moving at a specific speed.

Macchi M.33. Castoldi's design for the 1925 event. The drum-like device on the aft end of the Curtiss D-12A engine is one of the two Lamblin radiators. (*Macchi*)

being allocated to the race team. The whole project, including transport, was funded by Macchi themselves. But it must be remembered that Mussolini was planning a massive expansion of his Regia Aeronautica and Muzio Macchi would most certainly have had his eye on military contracts when the Schneider challenge was mounted.

Curtiss R3C-2

Faced with the prospect of less than the usual financial support for their 1925 racing programme the US Navy and Army for once got their heads together and decided to order three landplane racers from Curtiss. The first off the line was to be shared between the Navy and Army pilots for acceptance trials and then put on floats for the Schneider and flown by a Navy pilot. Of the remaining two, one was to go to the Army and the other to the Navy for the National Air Races. Afterwards they would be put on floats for the Schneider.

This new machine, christened the R3C by the Navy, was a developed version of the very successful, if unlucky, R2C of 1924. But although it differed little in appearance from the R2C it was a completely reworked design, aerodynamically and structurally, by a new

Curtiss team led by Theodore P. White. Stressed to withstand the higher speeds which were expected of the new Curtiss V-1400 engine, it also had a new Curtiss C-80 wing section and subtle changes to the nose shape to improve penetration. Structurally it followed the Curtiss tradition, having a double-diagonally planked fuselage up to the firewall; it was built in two halves on moulds and joined on the vertical seam. In common with the R2C the front portion of the fuselage consisted of a fully triangulated tubular space frame built into the forward end of the monocoque and supporting the engine, radiator header tank and providing attachment points for the wings and undercarriage.

Apart from the complete stress analysis and redesign of the main airframe components of the R2C instigated by T.P. Wright, a number of improvements over the previous year's machine were made. One of them was a change of wing profile from the Curtiss C-62 section used on the R2C to the new, slim C-80 profile which had the happy property of producing its best lift/drag ratio at the minimum drag angle. This necessitated multi-spar construction to maintain the beam strength. Five main spars were used, the front and rear ones being doubled out to the interplane strut station. The result

The Curtiss R3C-2 which Doolittle flew to victory in 1925.

was a virtually cellular wing when the planked skins were glued in place. Minor changes were to cut out small notches at the roots of the upper mainplanes to improve the pilot's view and to replace the celluloid wind-deflector panels with Triplex glass. A nice detail of the control system inherited from the R2C, called for because of the sensitivity of the Curtiss racers in particular and high-speed aircraft in general to rudder control at high speed, was the variable-rate rudder control circuit. This incorporated gear-driven parabolic pulleys to give small rudder deflections with normal control movement in the straight ahead position, but large ones if the rudder were pushed hard over. This Curtiss 'first' was later adopted by most of the other builders of high-speed aircraft who had had the common problem of needing a large rudder area to combat engine torque in the early stages of take-off with the result that they were over-sensitive to rudder control at speed. Yaw problems with the Gloster III would have been cured this way.

Although the Army was insufficiently disturbed by Pearson's accident to take steps to make their machines any easier to bale out of, the Navy thought differently and specified a jettisonable cockpit surround and wind deflector which could be quickly detached by pulling a lever on the panel. They also called for a parachute seat so that the pilot stood a chance of leaving the machine at altitude, although it did not cater for a low-level exit. The net result of the change was that the empty weight

went up by 100 lb, of which the airframe changes accounted for 60 lb. The other 40 lb was due to engine ancillary equipment.

The new V-1400 engine, one copy of which developed a freak 620 bhp on test, was a private venture by Curtiss embarked on with Navy encouragement to keep their engine department busy between contracts. In fact the Navy paid the bill for all three aircraft although the cost of a basic structure for destruction testing was shared between the services.

More power was to be provided by their chief engine man, Arthur Nutt, creator of the D-12, who did a complete redesign to produce the V-1400 *en route* to the even bigger V-1550. As the designation indicated, the V-1400 boasted a swept volume of 1,400 cu in (22.94 ltr). This was achieved without exceeding the external dimensions of the D-12 by increasing the stroke from 6 in to 6.25 in and the bore from 4.625 in to 4.875 in. When you've got twelve cylinders to go at, little increments add up to a lot!

The main change from the D-12 was to use open top liners screwed into the head in place of the old, closed top liners made from cup-like forgings with the valves seating in the steel top. In the 'open top' engines the valves operated on seats inserted into the light alloy cylinder heads. The main advantage of this form of construction was improved cooling due to enhanced heat transfer to the coolant, which in turn permitted a higher useful compression ratio; and a slight saving of weight. On its first bench run the V-1400 gave an astonishing 619 bhp at 2,520 rpm. This was obviously a spurious result although it was used for publicity purposes.

Further testing of the high compression (6.25:1) units, of which seven were built, produced the more credible figure of 565 bhp at 2,400 rpm. Later in its life the V-1400 passed a 50-hour test at 500 bhp and 2,100 rpm rating but it did not catch on with the Navy, who were moving over to air-cooled radials, and only a dozen units in all were built. This should not detract from the V-1400's virtues as a racing engine. Curtiss claimed it weighed 30 lb less than the D-12A and developed 60 bhp more. Output was 565 bhp for a dry weight (without accessories) of 670 lb giving a power to weight ratio of 1.18 lb* per horsepower. This was partly due to the availability of the new Curtiss-Reed forged propeller which allowed it to be run up to 2,400 rpm regularly and 2,600 rpm *in extremis*.

Early flights were not without their anguish. As mentioned, on 11 September 1925 Navy Lieutenant Al

*This 1.18 lb/hp ratio is remarkably good for an unsupercharged 1,400 cu in engine in 1925. As a comparison the supercharged 1,650 cu in wartime Rolls-Royce Merlin had a low altitude combat rating of 1,705 hp for a dry weight of 1,645 lb, giving a power-to-weight ratio of 0.96 lb/hp.

Williams, flying A.6978, the first machine to be finished, had a wheel disc fall off and the other one crack. Worse still Jimmy Doolittle, in the same machine on the same day, had a wingtip start to break up in a 300 mph dive; only his consummate skill saved him and the aircraft. Later on Cyrus Bettis had a nose spinner break up and damage a wing. Notwithstanding all this, Williams has to be credited with being the first American to exceed a ground speed of 300 mph in level flight. Flying A.6978 on 18 September, Williams was unofficially timed to cover a 3 km course at Mineola NY at a speed of 302 mph.

It is history that the two R3C-1s took first and second places in the 1925 Pulitzer race, the Army's First Lieutenant Cyrus Bettis winning at 248.975 mph in its silver-painted machine, which was later to become USN A.7054. Al Williams flew A.6979, painted in the Navy's blue and gold colours, into second place. Bettis won with a restrained, controlled display of flying that nevertheless resulted in a record speed and a new 100 km closed-circuit record into the bargain. Williams's speed was 241.695 mph with a failing motor due, they say, to unsympathetic engine management.

For the Schneider race the two Pulitzer machines were put on floats and joined A.6978, the first machine, which had been on floats since the end of the acceptance tests. It was allocated to Navy Lieutenant Ralph A. Ofstie, and Lieutenant George T. Cuddihy took over the A.6979. First Lieutenant James Doolittle, who had been back-up pilot to Cyrus Bettis in the Pulitzer, took the

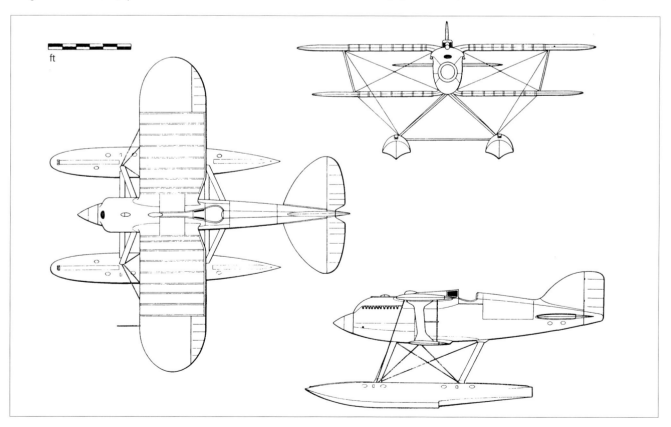

Curtiss R3C-2 (1925): Wing Span: 22 ft (6.71 m). Length Overall: 19 ft 8 in (6.00 m). Wing Area: 149 sq. ft (13.84 m²).
Weight Empty: 1,750 lb (794 kg). T-O Weight: 2,768 lb (1,255 kg). Max Wing Loading: 18.5 lb/sq. ft (90 kg/m²).
Curtiss V-12, liquid-cooled, engine of 600 hp.

Pulitzer-winning Army machine, mounted on floats and painted black and gold for the occasion.

An identification point is that the Navy machines retained their tail skids, while the Army machine was fitted with a 'bumper'.

The Supermarine S.4, 1925

It is difficult at this distance in time to assess the influences which caused Commander Bird and Reginald Mitchell to abandon the Rolls-Royce Condor-engined Sea Urchin flying-boat design in favour of a floatplane. They may have accepted the flying-boat configuration because it was the only way of housing the bulky Condor without attracting undue drag. When the RAF abandoned the single-engined night-bomber concept they could have found themselves not only free to return to the Napier Lion but actively encouraged to do so. Having seen the Curtiss racers in action at Cowes in 1923 it must have been plain that a flying-boat was not in contention so long as the seaworthiness tests were sufficiently easy for a floatplane to survive. So while the regulations favoured this configuration it was up to them to build a race-winning floatplane. What we do know is that for the first time in Britain the 1925 Schneider challengers were to be government-inspired. In the case of Supermarine it was to be a joint venture between airframe and engine manufacturer, namely The Supermarine Aviation Works Ltd and D. Napier and Son Ltd. An agreement between the two companies was ratified on 18 March 1925 to Air Ministry specification S.2/25. The Ministry agreed to buy the machine if it were successful and the undertaking was conditional on the two companies sharing the costs. It was significant that Mitchell had drawings already prepared and within a week of signing, two sets had been issued, one to the shops and one to RAE at Farnborough for construction of a wind-tunnel model.

Five months later, on 24 August, the Supermarine-Napier as it was officially known, designed by Reginald Mitchell and designated by him the S.4, flew for the first time in the hands of Henri Biard. And only three weeks after that, we find it quietly setting a new World seaplane record of 226.752 mph (364.92 km/h). So discreetly was this done that it was first revealed to the world through the medium of a supplier's advertisement in the aviation press. No doubt the record attempt was also a form of acceptance trial to justify payment by the government for the work done and so allow the machine to be loaned back to the makers for the race. It may be significant in this respect that the S.4 was never allotted a civil registration, nor did it appear with a service serial number.

All the S.4 trials took place at Calshot with the full co-operation of the RAF and the 3 km course required by the FAI was laid down by the Borough Surveyor of Southampton. Royal Aero Club observers were Captain C.B. Wilkins and Commander Perrin with A.G. Reynolds and S.D. Bidlake as timekeepers. Speeds attained on the four runs were:

Supermarine S.4 with the Napier Lion VII 680 bhp 12-cylinder 'broad-arrow' three-bank engine.

226.715 mph (364.865 km/h)
223.693 mph (360.000 km/h)
225.194 mph (362.416 km/h)
231.406 mph (372.414 km/h)

Biard was a logical choice as pilot. Apart from his job as Supermarine's test pilot, which involved flying everything from prototypes to the scheduled flights to Jersey, he was already holder of the British seaplane record. However, in common with most pilots of the day, he was a stranger to monoplanes and heartily disliked the S.4 with its almost complete lack of forward vision due to the placing of the wing. We are told that while manoeuvring for his first flight he narrowly missed the liner *Majestic* simply because he did not see it, and on landing taxied between a pair of warning posts and headed for a dredging operation, completely unaware that they were there.

But at one fell swoop Mitchell had produced an aeroplane that at least equalled the exquisite Curtiss biplanes in looks and promised to exceed them in performance as well. The only things that marred the lines were the Lamblin blade radiators protruding below the wings. Farnborough wind-tunnel results told him what they were costing in terms of performance. But surface radiators of the type used by Curtiss were still under development in Great Britain and he dare not take the risk of using them.

That Mitchell was fully aware of the importance of eliminating drag was shown by his insistence on shaft drive to the propeller of the Sea Urchin, thereby keeping the engine out of the airstream and eliminating the drag of a nacelle. He was also aware that the Curtiss racers were almost the ultimate development of the racing biplane – Gloster were to achieve the ultimate with more power in the next few years – and he would have to adopt the monoplane form if he was to gain an advantage. This was fortuitously confirmed for him in 1924 when Alphonse Bernard's HV.2 took the World Air Speed record at a shattering 278.7 mph (448.471 km/h). He cannot have failed to be impressed with the main design features of the HV.2. Its 'broad-arrow' Hispano-Suiza twelve-cylinder engine was the same configuration as the Napier Lion which was available to him. Bernard had faired the outer cylinder cowlings into the roots of the mid-wing and he had constructed the machine as three units based on an immensely strong centre-section combined with the wing mainspar. The other sections were the engine mountings and engine cowling forward and the tail cone combined with the pilot's controls and empennage aft.

In contrast with the Bernard, which had a laminated wooden centre-section in unit with the wing, the vital central structure of the S.4 was a triangulated steel, tent-shaped structure made up from a couple of A-frames joined by fore and aft tubes. It was irreverently dubbed the 'clothes-horse' by the drawing office. The legs of the A-frames protruded below the fuselage and acted as float struts while inside the fuselage there were extra transverse and longitudinal diagonals bracing the rectangles.

The portions of the legs exposed to the airstream were enclosed in streamlined wooden fairings and were originally intended to be cantilevered. But last-minute misgivings brought about the addition of a pair of spreader tubes immediately above their junction with the floats to assist in maintaining alignment.

Mountings for the direct-drive Napier Lion picked up with the forward A-frame while the wooden, monocoque, rear fuselage cone was bolted to the rear triangle. The wing was threaded through the sides of the 'clothes-horse' and was bolted to a pair of the longitudinal tubes via suitable brackets.

Apart from the tubular main frame the whole of the S.4 structure was in wood as befitted the Solent area where the main trade was boatbuilding. The two-spar wing was tapered in plan from with elliptical tips and was based on two spars fabricated from spruce flanges and plywood webs. Spanwise spruce stringers, slotted into fabricated plywood ribs maintained the airfoil section, which was Mitchell's own symmetrical form. This structure was skinned in plywood, tapering in thickness from the centre-section outwards. The whole of the trailing edge aft of the rear spar was formed by a pair of inboard flaps and the ailerons which were linked to droop when landing. The purpose of this arrangement, which was not unlike the Fairey wing, was said to have been to give the machine a reasonable attitude on the approach and thereby improve the pilot's view forward. It appears not to have appeased Biard.

As already mentioned, construction of the monocoque rear fuselage was also in wood and appears to have been on the well-proved Linton Hope system of mahogany planking on a rib and stringer foundation although the possibility of diagonal planking cannot be ruled out. The fin kingpost and the tailplane spar were built into the fuselage and fully cantilevered, there being no external wire bracing anywhere on the machine.

Forward of the rear cone joint the top half of the centre-section was skinned in wood and the belly closed in by sheet metal cowlings. The oil radiator lived between the float strut roots. The sheetmetal work in this area was particularly impressive, the long-chord flat strut fairings being made in one with the lower fuselage cowlings. The engine cowlings were all in sheetmetal and were extended under the wing roots to shield them from the fiery blast of the Lion's stub exhausts.

Supermarine's expertise in hull design was evident in the 18 ft-long floats which were of wooden construction with full-length ash keels and skinned with narrow Honduras mahogany planking screwed to multiple stringers. Watertight bulkheads provided strongpoints for the float struts, maintained the cross-section and acted to localise flooding in case of damage. Mitchell gave them deeply convex vee-bottoms both in front of and behind the step to dissipate alighting loads by 'parting' the water when arriving at speeds of 100 mph and more.

Being partners in the project, Napier produced a special direct-drive Lion VII engine to an Air Ministry specification laid down specifically for the race. The arrangement was that engines were to be made available to both Gloster and Supermarine, indicating the faith the Ministry had in Napiers. The abolition of the reduction gearbox and the consequent weight saving was made possible by the availability of British-made Reed propellers for which Fairey had negotiated a manufacturing licence. To attain the desired output Napier had raised the compression ratio to 8:1, a remarkably high number at that time, and reduced the weight of the pistons and connecting rods to allow the Lion to run up to 2,600 rpm on a diet of petrol/benzole. The penalty paid for this *joie de vivre* was a drastically reduced engine life, just long enough for practice and the race. The engine had also been considerably tidied up by moving various ancillaries away from the cleavages between the cylinder blocks. This allowed the airframe designer to tuck the skin of the nose cowling tightly between the blocks and so reduce frontal area.

Wind-tunnel results with the eighth-scale model in the Farnborough tunnel confirmed Mitchell's doubts about the radiators. Although the model-makers found difficulty in making a miniature radiator to give the right scale effect, the results in the seven-foot no. 1 tunnel showed that they were likely to account for 35 per cent of the drag of the whole machine. Mitchell's estimate had been 38 per cent. Without the radiators the S.4 had a C_D (Coefficient of Drag) of 0.0199 and bid fair to be the 'cleanest' aeroplane in the world. The radiators pushed this factor to 0.0246, indicating that it would be less efficient than the Curtiss machines it would be up against. It could be read as an indication of the influence of the Bernard V.2 on Mitchell's thinking that the Lamblin radiators he chose were of the same type and fitted in the same position as on that machine.

Other work done at Farnborough was to measure the drag of the floats and calculate the drag of the complete machine with them set at different angles relative to the fuselage. One recommendation was that the cockpit sides should be raised, although it is not certain that this was done on the full-size machine.

However, Mitchell was encouraged by the results from Napier, whose 680 bhp – they had promised 700 – was at least 120 bhp more than the best D-12A he knew about. However the direct-drive Lion weighed 120 lb more than the Curtiss V-1400 so the extra power gave it an almost identical power-to-weight ratio. Its shortcoming was the large frontal area inseparable from the broad-arrow configuration.

It is interesting, incidentally, to conjecture on the S.4 designation. Veteran employees of Supermarine told me some years ago that the Sea Lions were called Schneider Specials in the works, abbreviated to SS1, 2 and 3 and that since the Sea Urchin never got as far as the shop floor it was never given the dignity of a type number. However, a drawing of the Sea Lion III in the writer's possession depicts it as the SS II, which suggests that the Sea Urchin was either the SS III or S.3, the 'S' signifying Schneider followed by an Arabic numeral.

Looking back to the accident to the S.4 it seems somehow unlikely that the cause was wing-flutter in view of the advanced wing structure which was quite up to the standards of such aircraft as the much-later Miles Master which operated in the same speed range. Could the vibration reported by Biard have been buffet associated with high-speed stall? The turn where the accident happened was an extremely tight one. A proper conclusion seems never to have been reached although there was a full enquiry at the time. The general feeling was that the cause was wing-flutter.

Hampton Roads 1926

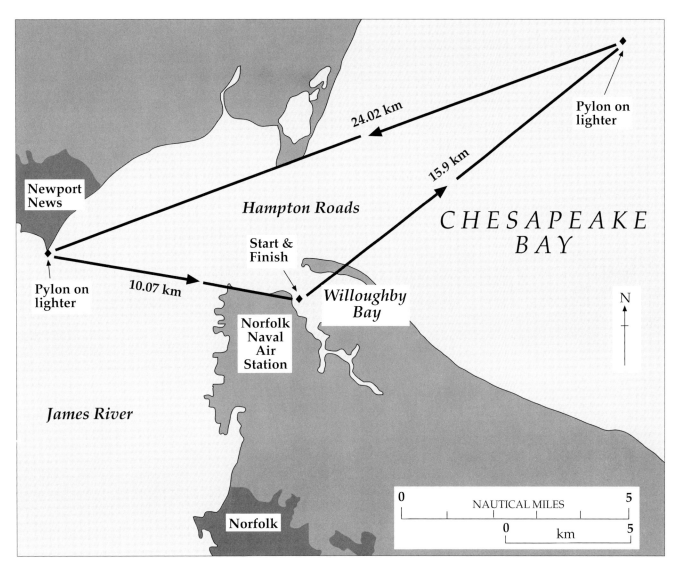

Schneider Trophy Contest Course: Hampton Roads 1926.

Run-up

The 1925 result showed more than ever that the Schneider race was now firmly established as an event in which the prestige of competing nations was at stake. Future entries would inevitably be the concern of governments rather than individual aircraft manufacturers. It was also clear that the only competing countries would be the great air powers, anxious to show off their technical expertise. This automatically restricted the takers to the American defenders and the British, French and Italian challengers. Germany was excluded because of Treaty obligations which forbade her to build machines of the required power although she was already finding ways round that restriction. Japan at that time did not have the skills and her air arm relied on imported machines.

Among the regular participants there was a shift of interest. The American defence effort was aimed at Japanese aspirations to make the Pacific a Japanese ocean and the intensive development provided by air racing had established them in a position of technical supremacy *vis-à-vis* the Occident. They were raising their heads and realising that there was much more to aviation than air-racing; that this activity, of which the Schneider contest was just one manifestation, had exhausted its immediate potential as a means of developing high-speed pursuit aircraft. They wanted to get on with the job of applying the knowledge gained. As a nation they were entering a more adult phase of aviation in which commercial air transport was clearly the only mode of transport in a country of vast distances and would have to be a main priority. The emphasis was moving from the razzle-dazzle of air race meetings to the achievement of well-planned, reliable, safe, long-distance flying.

The disciples of air power in the US Army, who had been so influential in the promulgation of air racing as a means of high-speed development in that country, had suffered a major setback from the highly publicised court martial of the previous October when their prophet-in-chief, the vociferous Brigadier-General Billy Mitchell, proponent of service participation in air-racing, had been suspended from rank and command for his outspoken views on the conduct of the US armed services. The US Navy, too, was widening its aviation interests. Admiral Moffett, who masterminded the Navy's air-racing activities, had become entranced by the strategic promise of the dirigible airship. Moreover, the American naval arm, envious of the British lead in air-cooled radial engines established by the Bristol Jupiter, was becoming increasingly interested in developing American engines of this type for carrier-borne fighters. The slim, water-cooled power units, better suited to high-speed flying, were destined to become a rarity on the flight decks of America's new aircraft carriers by the end of the decade. In the light of all this, so far as the Americans were concerned, the race for the Coupe Schneider did not have the same importance as it did in 1923. They could have been forgiven the sneaking feeling that maybe it had been the wrong thing to do to stand down in 1924. If they had not done so the Trophy would already have found a place in some American institution. Nevertheless, having won the Trophy twice in succession they were determined to win it on their own ground for the third time even if it were by a flyover.

The US Army, in disarray after the Mitchell affair, were in poor shape to make a showing in the 1926 contest. It was destined to be a strictly naval occasion conducted by the other great proponent of competition as spur to progress, Admiral William Adger Moffett. The Navy had suffered setbacks in 1925 with the loss of the airship *Shenandoah* and the tragic failure of a transpacific flight, events which had indirectly precipitated the Mitchell court martial. They badly needed the boost which a successful defence and annexation of the Schneider Trophy could give; however, lack of funds would force them to do it with existing, but modified, machines. The British Air Ministry, for their part, had become uncomfortably aware that, far from having the most powerful air force immediately after the Kaiser War, they had slipped back to fifth in the world league. Steps to redress the balance of power *vis-à-vis* other European countries had already been put in hand with the formation of new squadrons equipped with more advanced machines.

The Schneider race had been elevated by the Americans to the status of a government-sponsored contest. This had not gone unnoticed in England, where the Air Ministry had ordered Air Vice-Marshal Sir Geoffrey Salmond, the Air Member for Research and Supply, to take a long look at the conduct of the 1925 Schneider race. His report had come back stating that British high-speed technology was sufficiently advanced to be able to produce a winner in 1927 but not before. He went on to say that it was a waste of money to pay for machines out of the public purse and then hand them over to civilian pilots and ground crews to race. The maximum benefit would be achieved with service crews throughout. It would be more cost-effective and there would be an inevitable, and invaluable, spin-off of experience to the RAF. What he did not spell out, but what would be clear in his mind was that the Schneider event was an arena in which British technological progress could be compared with that of other great aerial powers. Success would be of great political value in the power struggle which was already beginning to form in Europe. So far as the Schneider race was concerned the main aim of the British would have to be to work for a postponement until 1927.

Meanwhile Italy, smarting under its defeat in 1925 and angered, it is said, by derogatory remarks in one of the US forces newsletters about its showing at Baltimore, was now in the mood for an all out government-backed effort. Benito Mussolini's Under-Secretary of Air, Marshal Italo Balbo, the great publicist of the Regia Aeronautica, had undoubtedly pointed out to his master the publicity potential of a Schneider win and it is likely that even before the decisive meeting in Paris the famous edict had gone out that the race must be 'won at all costs'. The only question was how and with what.

The Italians had traditionally regarded the Coupe Schneider as a means of developing flying-boats and while they were willing to challenge they would root for a 250 kg payload requirement in the rules. The bonus would be an increase in their chances by outlawing the all-conquering American Curtisses. So far as they were concerned the decisions made at the annual FAI rule-making meeting would be about the means to be adopted rather than whether or not they would participate.

In France the emphasis was on high-speed landplanes and for the first time the country which had given birth to this great contest would not propose an entry. With two nations in favour of a high-speed, no-holds-barred contest it was clear that the format for 1926 would be a foregone conclusion. Nevertheless the Italians argued vehemently for their kind of race and the Americans and British equally hard for theirs, the latter with the addendum that the race should be postponed until 1927. Pending ratification of virtually unchanged regulations at the annual FAI rule-making meeting in early January – in 1926 it was on the 11th of the month – the American club announced that the venue for 1926 would be the Naval Air Station at Hampton Roads, Virginia and that the contest would take place in the week beginning 24 October.

A fortnight after the FAI meeting a formal request for postponement was made by the British Royal Aero Club to the American National Aeronautic Association on the grounds that they could not have a challenger ready in time. They argued that, in common with themselves, the Italians were in the position of having no suitable aircraft and that in the circumstances a flyover would be an unsporting way to win an international trophy of the importance of the Coupe Jacques Schneider. The American response was that they had made one sporting postponement and that they were not really in the mood to do it again. One very good reason would have been that their Army and Navy, who owned the machines, were not prepared to hold them, and their crews, in readiness for another year. Also they probably took into account that, while they were at the end of their development programme, the British were just at the beginning of theirs and were about to embark on a new phase of high-speed flying which could well produce machines much faster than the American product.

At a meeting at the Royal Aero Club on 19 March it had been decided jointly by the Air Ministry and the British aircraft constructors that, as a matter of policy, there would be no British challenge in 1926 but it was hoped that new machines would be built and tested late in the summer as prototypes for definitive, and more advanced, race machines for 1927. The plan was that, should the Americans win the Trophy outright, the RAF would immediately mount a world record-breaking attempt to draw off publicity from the US victory. A month later Sir Sefton Brancker, Britain's charming, monocled Air Minister, had been despatched to the USA to try to weedle a postponement out of the unexpectedly obdurate Yankees. He returned to inform his masters that a challenge from the Italians had been received and that the 1926 race was on.

In Italy, although a design competition was suggested, there was really no time for such niceties. There were only two airframe manufacturers capable of building high-speed machines; Macchi and Savoia, although there would be the inevitable Pegna project to be taken into account. Macchi was the obvious choice, having produced the previous year's contender. Moreover, Castoldi was in the position of having been able to see, photograph in detail, measure and indeed touch – an engineer needs this sometimes – the machines with which he would have to compete. The story goes that when the Italians were in Baltimore in 1925 they had approached an unspecified American engine builder for supplies of power units for a 1926 challenge, and had been refused. In view of the facts this sounds like a publicity ploy; or maybe a manifestation of Castoldi's habit of laying false trails to fool the opposition.

In fact by 1926 the basis of a power unit for an Italian challenge already existed. Even while the Macchi team were soldiering away in Baltimore with their 'cooking' Curtiss D-12s, Fiat were busy putting into production the first of their Zerbi-designed, A.20 series power units, the A.20 and A.22. The latter was an obvious starting point. In production form it had an only fractionally greater frontal area than that of the D-12. Admittedly it was heavier but gave around 130 more horsepower in standard form. In production trim its

power-to-weight ratio of 0.61 hp/lb weight compared adequately with the 0.64 hp/lb of the standard Curtiss. A slimmed-down and supertuned racing version of the A.22 was an obvious choice and there is little doubt that the project, named AS.2, existed long before the end of 1925. This was for an engine with the same frontal area as the D-12 but giving 880 bhp for a dry weight of 800 lb (Fiat's 1926 data sheet gives 355 kg or 782 lb) compared with the then latest Curtiss V-1550's 600 bhp and 700 lb weight. To the designer the overriding factor was the high ratio of power to frontal area.

It has been suggested that Fiat lacked experience in aero-engine design. The reverse is nearer to the truth. They had, in fact, designed and built many outstanding power units, notably the mighty 52-litre, A.14 wartime engine and in 1922 one of these, installed in a Fiat R.700 biplane flown by Francesco Brack-Papa, had unofficially beaten the world airspeed record. Fiat's chief engine designer, Tranquillo Zerbi, was certainly no stranger to high-performance engines. Apart from development work on the A.14 and the design of his own A.20 series engines he had created a series of racing car engines which had put Fiat at the forefront of Grand Prix racing. His twelve-cylinder, 15,000 cc Fiat 406 racing engine produced no less than 187 bhp at 8,500 rpm. He was hardly likely to be daunted by the prospect of extracting five times that power from an engine twelve times the size.

It has been recounted that Castoldi was on his sickbed when the decree came through to put all work on one side and get on with the construction of a team of racers. To help him a senior draughtsman was seconded from the Air Ministry to oversee the operation and by the second week in February prototype drawings were being issued to the shops. A vital factor in this almost instant response would have to be that Castoldi knew exactly what was available in the way of a power unit. He was able to take for granted that an engine would be available with the same frontal area as a D-12 and a predicted power output considerably greater. Without engine installation drawings, weight, frontal area and power neither he nor the redoubtable Ing. Filipa from the Ministry would have been able to put pencil to paper.

The machine which Castoldi and his team created was a masterly distillate of what had gone before. The Italian could not have failed to be impressed by Mitchell's slim S.4 monoplane; this and the exquisite Curtiss racers must have convinced him that the floatplane was the way to go, especially because of the way it lent itself to an immensely strong, lightweight, wire-braced structure and the use of thin wings. His own, and Mitchell's, experience of cantilever wings on high-speed machines would have told him that there was much to be learnt before that route could be taken again. Not only were they heavy but the evidence showed that thin wings were more suitable for high-speed work with known airfoil sections.

It is tempting to conjecture that Castoldi saw that the easy route to a monoplane was by taking the Curtiss as a starting point and throwing away the upper wing. This would eliminate the drag of one wing, the inter-plane struts and the upper lift wires. The rigging diagram of the lower wing and floats would be the same and a known quantity. Even with an enlarged lower mainplane there would be less drag and with a more powerful engine the end result just had to be a faster aeroplane.

Castoldi, being a superstitious man who regarded thirteen to be his lucky number – in continental Europe seventeen is considered to be unlucky – type-numbered his new racer the M.39 by multiplying his lucky number by prime three. The contract from the Regia Aeronautica called for five machines; two trainers with extra wing area and three racers. The two trainers were given a span of 10.2 m (33 ft 8 in) compared with 9.26 m (30 ft 5 in) and were powered by 600 bhp engines, presumably the production A.22.

For the contest a new Regia Aeronautica high-speed flight, forerunner of Il Reparto Alta Velocità – the High Speed Detachment – was formed at the Schirrana sea-plane station on Lake Varese. This was an ideal training base for the team as the lake here is about five miles long and vaguely T-shaped, offering long take-off runs in four directions. Moreover, it was close by the Macchi factory and fitters were always available to back up the Regia Aeronautica personnel. It was also not too badly placed in relation to the Fiat factory in Turin. This elite unit of the Regia Aeronautica was led by a 26-year old Genoese nobleman, the Marchese Vittorio Centurione, a renowned long-distance seaplane pilot, with the experi-enced Major Mario de Bernardi as his second in com-mand and chief pilot. The highly decorated Captain Arturo Ferrarin, already famous for his Rome–Tokyo and Rome–Brazil flights, was also seconded to the squadron. The other pilots were seaplane expert Captain Giulio Guasconi, war veteran Lieutenant Federico Guazzetti and Lieutenant Adriano Bacula. The team began to shake-down at the Schirrana seaplane base on Lake Varese in mid-July with just four months to go before the race.

On the other side of the Atlantic Ocean the defend-ers were already preening their wings under the team leadership of Lieutenant-Commander Homer C. Wick. As a result of the general policy of entrenchment and without the Pulitzer race to act as a feeder and pro-motional exercise there were no new aircraft on the inventory. It was to consist of four machines. First was Doolittle's 1925 winning R3C-2, now transferred to the Navy and serialled A.7054; it would race using a devel-oped version of the D-12A engine with which it had won the previous year. Its sister machine, A.6978, the first R3C-2 out of the factory, flown by Ofstie in the 1925 race, was to be fitted with a geared, racing ver-sion of the Packard 2A-1500 and redesignated R3C-3. Cuddihy's mount in 1925, A.6979, was re-engined with a Curtiss V-1550 engine, taking on the R3C-4 designa-tion. A fourth machine, A.6992, the R2C-2 which, in landplane guise, had won the 1923 Pulitzer and was a team machine for the abortive 1924 race, was allocated

as a trainer. All the machines were to be fitted with new, Navy-designed floats, built by Curtiss and incorporating reserve fuel tanks. The US pilot team as originally formed consisted of George Cuddihy USN, nominated to fly the R3C-3, Harmon Norton of the US Marine Corps allocated to the ex-Doolittle R3C-2 with Lieutenant Frank Christian Schilt as his back-up, Lieutenant Frank Hersey Conant USN would fly the R3C-4. Lieutenant Carleton C. Champion and Lieutenant W.C. Tomlinson were seconded to the team as reserve pilots.

The Packard installation in the R3C, designated the R3C-3 with this power unit, resulted in what is to many Curtiss-watchers the most beautiful Curtiss racer of all. The raised shaft line resulting from single-stage gearing made possible a particularly clean, bullet-shaped, nose profile which was not only extremely handsome but showed all the signs of being aerodynamically superior to the rather beetle-browed D-12 installations. The combination of this and the extra power and reliability of the engine made the R3C-3 a potential race winner. American sources claim a wide range of speeds for it, of which 258 mph, reported to the Press by Admiral Moffett, seems the most reliable.

Unfortunately, as so often happens in government institutions, the work on the R3C-3 was finished late and there appears to have been no properly conducted flight test programme before it was handed over to the US team. It had, however, flown enough to have acquired a reputation for being difficult to handle. Being the fastest of the Curtisses, the extra speed would tend to exaggerate any inherent shortcomings in the han-dling, which were of the knife-edge variety at the best of times, with considerable stick and rudder forces required to control it in the horizontal axis. Added to this its pilots would have to contend with reversed torque reac-tion due to the single-reduction gearing causing the propeller to rotate in the opposite direction to normal. It would no doubt be for these reasons that it was allo-cated to the veteran George Cuddihy who had flown Curtisses almost since their debut.

In Britain the Royal Aero Club had received two pri-vate entries for the race, one from Colonel Bristow, a well-known and wealthy aviation consultant and the other from the redoubtable Sammy Saunders of Cowes. They were hastily summoned to the Ministry and warned that it would be unpolitic for any entries to go in from the UK in view of the Ministry's efforts to get the race postponed. As the price for his withdrawal Bristow was given the promise of a development con-tract for his machine and a place in the 1927 British team. It is believed that a Ministry flying-boat contract went the way of Sammy Saunders.

Meanwhile, in accordance with Air Ministry policy, specifications for high-speed floatplanes had been issued to Supermarine and Gloster, one for a monoplane and the other for a biplane. The main requirements set out were for speed at low altitudes and control at high speeds with a reasonable degree of positive stability about all axes in flight. Static stability on the water and seaworthiness in any conditions in which the aircraft might operate were also called for. The main ingredient was a speed of not less than 265 mph at 1,000 ft and an engine-off alighting speed of not more than 90 mph. It is interesting that tankage for 75 minutes at full throttle was originally called for; this was reduced to one hour on 12 August 1926. The full resources of the National Physical Laboratory (NPL) at Teddington and the RAE were put at the disposal of the constructors. Within a week of the specifications going out the Supermarine wind-tunnel model had been received at the NPL, to be followed by a gamut of different configurations. Meanwhile a model of the S.4 was quickly built by the RAE as a yardstick against which the results from the new designs would be judged.

In fulfilment of the Ministry's promise a specification went out for the Bristow entry. This was for a radial-engined, wire-braced monoplane mounted on floats. Midwife to the project was A.R. (Roy) Fedden, chief engineer of the engine department of the Bristol Aeroplane Company, designer of the outstanding Bristol Jupiter radial engine, who needed a flying testbed for his latest project, a small-diameter, supercharged radial to succeed the Jupiter.

Preliminaries

While the British designers and scientists were playing with wind-tunnel models, Macchi in Italy was producing aeroplanes and the Regia Aeronautica team at Schirrana was building up seaplane experience on the old M.33 and sundry service flying-boats.

The first wide-span M.39 trainer was ready at the beginning of July and Romeo Sartori took it into the air on the 6 July. His first alighting in the type was not a happy one, no doubt due to the hairline fore and aft stability of the M.39; he hit the water hard, buckling the float struts and generally overstressing the structure, calling for almost a complete rebuild before the machine could be delivered to the flight. It was followed by the other two trainers and then, on 6 August, the first of the contest machines was towed over from the factory just eleven weeks before the contest was due to take place. However, there were problems with carburettor settings and the design of the air intake was far from satisfactory, resulting in mixture variations in flight. As a consequence it was not until 30 August that Sartori was able to make the maiden flight. Between that date and 17 September he and Major de Bernardi systematically explored the whole performance envelope up to maximum speed. This, over a number of runs, proved to be a very satisfactory 257.25 mph (414 km/h), comfortably in excess of Doolittle's world seaplane record set up the previous year at Bay Shore with the R3C.

Hard on the heels of this first measure of success came tragedy. Centurione, an experienced flying-boat pilot, had left the test-flying to his three pilots de Bernardi, Sartori and Guazetti: Ferrarin and Bacula had yet to put in an appearance. Encouraged by the results obtained with the racer he decided on 21 September

that the time had come for him to put in some floatplane time on one of the trainers. His handling of the machine on the water seemed to be competent and he held the machine well against the initial propeller torque during the take-off run: he was almost at unstick speed when the machine suddenly leapt into the air 'as if it had hit a wave'. The pilot appeared to attempt a recovery with a steep turn but the wing stalled and the M.39 rolled into the water, killing Centurione instantly.

Peacetime flying is different from wartime flying, when pilots are failing to return every day. The team's immediate reaction to the death of their popular young leader seems to have been sadness and confusion. There was no flying for a week at a time when every day was vital. Moreover, even at this late hour they were without their full complement of machines or pilots. The former were delivered before the end of the month and were readied by de Bernardi and Sartori, but Ferrarin and Bacula did not arrive until 30 September. It was clear that time was running out and a request was wired to the American National Aeronautic Association seeking a short postponement of the race. The American team was not without its own problems; moreover, it was difficult for the authorities to refuse the only challenger and, despite a rather naive protest by the British, the race was put off until 11 November.

In the meantime de Bernardi, as the senior-ranking pilot, had taken over as team leader – the administrator was Major Aldo Guglielmetti – with Ferrarin as number two. Both men were exceptional pilots and they proceeded to wring the necks of the M.39s to extract the bugs. To Castoldi's horror, but wonderful medicine for team morale, they regularly engaged in aerobatics and gradually eliminated the weaknesses. One they could not get rid of was lack of straight-line stability. In common with all these high-speed seaplanes the machines had to be flown with the rudder bar braced solid by the pilot because of their sensitivity to even the slightest rudder movements at maximum speed. Like the British test pilots each man had his own cure for the problem; one wanted a bigger rudder, the other a smaller one. Castoldi saw the real reason and enlarged the area of the ventral fixed fin with beneficial results.

The team left for Hampton Roads on 12 October aboard the liner *Conte Rosso*, the tanks of their machines reputedly filled with wine to offset the effects of America's Prohibition. They docked in New York on the 20th, just four days before the original date of the race but now, thanks to the postponement, with three weeks to shake down and tune the machines. The Americans were much impressed by the efficient Regia Aeronautica turnout compared with the frugal Macchi private effort in 1925. The Italians, for their part, were delighted to find the much improved conditions at the US Navy seaplane base at Norfolk with its big permanent hangars, expansive hardstandings and proper launching ramps.

There was still much work to be done on the Macchis. Some of the engines had only been delivered a short time before departure and needed to be run in and the carburation set for the new conditions. The carburation problem in flight, which was to bug Macchi for years, still persisted and would eventually be traced to the failure to adopt proper testhouse procedures.

It was not until 9 November, with the race date only two days away that the Macchis were flown for the first time. Mario de Bernardi was the first to go. He was scarcely airborne when a couple of the AS.2's pistons burnt out and the resulting blowback ignited loose fuel in the cowlings. He quickly alighted and the fire was put out by the crew of a launch. This incident and the problems with Ferrarin's engine were apparently too much for Castoldi's inordinately suspicious nature. Fearing that the fuel specially ordered by Fiat for the engines was being tampered with, he insisted on drawing from the same supply as the Americans. It may have been good reasoning but there was every chance that theirs was a different mix; in fact from what we are told it may well have been a number of different mixes, and could very well have induced overheating.

The Fiat engineers were also finding it extremely difficult to persuade the engine of MM.75, Ferrarin's machine, to run evenly and for this reason Castoldi insisted on a change to AC sparking plugs of the same type as the Americans were using although the Italian ones had been specially developed for the engines. It must have brought tears to the eyes of the Fiat engineers.

Ferrarin's flight on the 9th was beset with dramas of a different kind. Late in the day his engine was finally judged to be airworthy and he took off straight into a line-squall backed by heavy rain and stratus. The hero of the Rome–Tokyo flight was hardly to be put off by this kind of going but his safe return from the gloom made a story for the local papers.

Despite their experience, and the advantages of flying over familiar ground, the Americans were not without their setbacks. The first of these was in September when Harmon Norton, one of the Marine Corps' most experienced high-speed pilots, fourth-placed man in the 1925 Pulitzer, had been killed instantly when his machine had stalled and spun into the Potomac River. Making an air experience flight in one of the R2C-2s, which had been allocated as a trainer, he had attempted to formate on two slow-flying Army machines; the speed differential was too great, the Curtiss's nose dropped and machine spun inverted into shallow water. It was on the 13th day of the month. Norton was replaced by Marine Lieutenant Frank Christian Schilt, a fine airman who, two years later, was to distinguish himself in a sensational air evacuation in Nicaragua in an action against the Sandino rebels; yes, in 1928!

Despite the proximity of their makers to the scene of events, or maybe because of it, none of the American race machines was ready before the beginning of October. Lieutenant Frank Conant did not begin test-flying the V-1550-engined R3C-4 at the Curtiss facility on Long Island until 26 October, two days after the original race date. He made two runs over the speed course in the sound and was credited with a published speed of 251.3 mph. The R3C-4 was duly crated for

despatch to Norfolk but sadly Conant was not there to greet it. On October 30, en route to Hampton Roads, flying a service machine, he is thought to have hit a fishing stake or wreck as he flew low over the sea near Winter Harbour. The impact destroyed the aircraft and poor Conant, a gifted pilot and career officer, was either killed instantly or, tangled in the wreckage of his machine, drowned. His place in the team was filled by Marine Lieutenant Carleton C. Champion, another experienced young career officer whose main claim to fame is that he was the first man to fly behind a Pratt & Whitney Wasp engine. These losses and the general state of unreadiness in the American camp caused team leader Homer Wick to be relieved of his captaincy and Admiral Moffett, chief of the Navy Bureau of Aeronautics took over. Meanwhile George Cuddihy, as the most experienced member of the team, had been assigned the Packard-powered R3C-3. With it he had successfully completed the acceptance trials and the machine was duly crated and shipped to Norfolk.

With all their machines and pilots successfully ensconced in the Norfolk air base hangars the American team started to shake down in readiness for the race. Once more, trouble struck when, according to Tom Foxworth, the turn came for Carleton Champion to fly A.6979, the R3C-4 with the Curtiss V-1550 engine. By all accounts Champion – one wonders if he was related to spark-plug Albert Champion – regarded himself as a fuel expert and despite the fact that the V-1550 was set up to run on pure benzole, insisted that it should be fuelled with 40/50 petrol/benzole. Curtiss engineer, Bill Wait, and the Curtiss crew chief vehemently protested but since the work was being done by Navy ratings, who couldn't disobey an order, the fuel was put in; but not until Champion had signed an authorisation. As a consequence on start-up the engine detonated horribly, overheated and the resulting steam in the cooling system bulged the wing-radiators. The engine was destroyed and had to be replaced with one of nominally lower power. Meanwhile the radiators were knocked back into shape and the machine re-allocated to Lieutenant William C. 'Red' Tomlinson. There were no witnesses to the interview between the crusty Admiral Moffett and a still-defiant Champion but the latter quietly dissolved from the scene; officially he went sick.

Meanwhile Cuddihy had flown the re-engined R3C-4 and found it so satisfactory – the engine was running up to 2,600 rpm in level flight – that a 3-in larger propeller was considered worthwhile. In the absence of a true assessment of the speed of the Italian machines A.6979 seemed a more likely mainstay for the American effort than the relatively untried R3C-3, although it appeared that Cuddihy was not quite sure. The decision that faced the American team leader was whether to keep his best pilot, Cuddihy, in the machine which was more difficult to fly but perhaps fast enough to win, or to put him in the aircraft which was a known quantity and could finish the race at a predictable speed.

Bad weather in Virginia caused the race officials to move race day back to the 13th with the 11th and 12th reserved for the navigability trials. Moffett's decision did not become known until the morning of 12 November when Cuddihy was seen to walk out to the R3C-4 and Tomlinson, inexperienced in high-speed aircraft, to the tricky R3C-3. It was hardly a fair deal for Packard, who had a great deal to lose; but it was in the American interest if the race was to be won by the US. One can only hazard a guess that Moffett was in possession of a more realistic assessment of the R3C-3's performance than we have at this distance in time.

Tomlinson was the first to go, the intention being to combine his first flight in the machine with the navigability test. He was obviously in trouble right from the start. Massive low-speed torque from the geared Packard was pushing the starboard float under while, once under way, the new floats started to porpoise. Innate airmanship got the machine into the air and he was able to fly it around to familiarise himself with the controls and handling. His first mandatory landing was baulked by a stray service machine. His second approach was a good one but, unaccustomed to the machine and with minimal forward visibility, he rounded out too high, near-pancaked onto the water, burst a float, cartwheeled and ended up inverted. He surfaced and sat on an upturned float, little the worse for wear, until a rescue boat arrived; but it was the end of the R3C-3.

In the meantime Cuddihy and Schilt had completed their navigability trials without incident. Tomlinson, not to be deprived of his race, inserted himself into the Curtiss F6C-3 Hawk which had been nominated as a last-ditch reserve – it was good for 145 mph at the most – and completed his test in readiness for the morrow.

Even before the American dramas, on the evening of the 11th, the Italians had been having their share of anguish. That evening Ferrarin had set off with the intention to complete the flying part of the navigability trials. He would then be able to leave the Macchi to ride out the buoyancy test overnight away from the diurnal wind effect. He had almost completely finished the trials with an engine which was getting rougher by the minute, when it quit with a mighty clatter and he had to put down in the middle of the steamer lane through Hampton Roads. A Navy flying-boat went to his rescue and circled him on the surface until a launch could arrive to tow him back. A quick look at the engine showed that it was scrap, with holes through the crankcase where the connecting rods had poked through following piston failure.

Only hours earlier, Champion had wrecked the R3C-4's engine: now it was Italy's turn and there was no factory with a spare engine to call on. The only chance was to build another engine using parts from de Bernardi's wrecked engine, spares and the remaining intact pistons from the Ferrarin engine. Urged on by the Italian Air Attaché Commendatore Silvio Scaroni, himself a distinguished airman, who invoked Mussolini, d'Annunzio and the Fascist cause in alternate breaths, the mechanics set to and by 2 pm the following day, had an engine installed and running. Ferrarin was able to

complete his tests before nightfall and leave the Macchi out overnight as planned for the preceding day.

The Race

Race day, 13 November, dawned with both sides able to field a three-man team but with the defenders at a disadvantage, mainly because of the unfortunate decision to choose the inexperienced Lieutenant Tomlinson to replace Champion, leading to the destruction of the R3C-3, when there were a number of veteran Curtiss high-speed pilots to draw on. Maybe Moffett was prey to the same kind of dogma which beset the Royal Air Force's Trenchard. Whatever the reason, the US team was left to defend the trophy with two racers which were in effect refinements of a 1922 design and a slow service fighter type. Pitted against them was a full Italian team equipped with machines of the latest conception.

The Italians had thought through their tactics well. Their plan was to use Bacula in MM.74, fitted for the occasion with a low-compression engine and fine-pitch propeller, as long stop with instructions to finish without straining the engine. Ferrarin in MM.75 with the rebuilt engine and using, we are told, a medium-pitch propeller, was to feign an engine start-up problem – taking advantage of a 15 minute allowance in the rules – so that Cuddihy took off ahead of him: he would then tail the American machine and if possible get ahead of it just before the finish. As senior pilot and team leader, de Bernardi, in MM.76 fitted with the best engine and a coarse-pitch propeller, was to go flat out to win. Guazzetti and Guasconi were to go out in a boat and let Bacula and Ferrarin know, with pre-arranged hand signals, if the American machines dropped out so that they could throttle back and conserve their engines. De Bernardi would go out to win and break records.

The course was laid out in Hampton Roads and Chesapeake Bay with the start line off the US Naval Air Station in Willoughby Bay. From this point the machines flew on a north-easterly heading to a marker boat anchored in the middle of the bay. There they turned sharply through 340 deg to head up Hampton Roads, clipping Old Point Comfort, to a pylon on the beach of the southernmost tip of Newport News. Here they turned back to the start line pylon. As at Baltimore the course was exactly 50 km – flown seven times for the race – making it suitable for international distance records. For this reason Odis A. Porter, the FAI-approved timekeeper from the Indianapolis Speedway, was in charge of timing using an electronic chronograph said to be accurate to 0.0025 seconds.

To allow for the possibility of a last-minute navigability test on race day the start time had to be set at 2 pm. The Italians had drawn to take off first and they had chosen to lead off with Bacula in the Muletta. He would be followed at five-minute intervals by Tomlinson in the F6C Hawk followed by Ferrarin, Cuddihy, de Bernardi and Schilt.

Adriano Bacula, using up five minutes of his allowance, was airborne at 14.35 hrs with the minimum of fuss and went winging like a red dart out into Chesapeake Bay. As he made a steep climbing turn round the first mark, Red Tomlinson was crossing the line in the Curtiss Hawk to begin his relatively slow, but very sure race.

As planned there was difficulty in firing-up Arturo Ferrarin's engine and by the time he was taxying to the line. George Cuddihy in the R3C-4 was making his take-off run. The Macchi surged across the line just a minute behind America's white hope. By this time Bacula was rounding the Chesapeake Bay pylon for the second time, leaving Tomlinson still on his first lap. Meanwhile the Italian crew readied Macchi number 5 for de Bernardi while the US Navy crew were warming up the D-12A in the venerable R3C-2 for F.C. Schilt.

Ferrarin's first round, in 7 min 56.69 sec, was the first true measure the Americans had of the Italian opposition. Until then the Macchis had been flown close to land, away from reference points, to avoid being timed. Flying according to plan, the Macchi's speed, 234.63 mph (377.60 km/h), was a mere 2 mph more than that of Cuddihy's Curtiss and almost the same as Doolittle's race-winning speed in 1926; but it was enough to get informed American observers worried. Arturo was obviously happy to maintain this speed differential, which allowed him to keep the Curtiss in sight, because his next lap, his first flying lap after take-off, was at 242.99 mph. He was passing the timekeepers just 59 seconds after his pacemaker.

It was exactly 3 pm as de Bernardi's Macchi crossed the line to be followed a minute later by Schilt in the light blue R3C-2. Briefly the spectators thronging the shores round Hampton Roads were treated to the sight of the five fastest seaplanes in the world, three from the Old World and two from the New, fighting a battle for supremacy. It was not to last for long; the note of Ferrarin's engine was beginning to take a rough edge, the thin black smoke trail typical of the Fiat engines began to thicken, and on his fourth lap the red monoplane was seen to put down in the bay. A broken oil pipe was the official explanation.

The Italians still had two machines in the contest and the latest arrival could not fail to give heart to the challengers. Bernardi's first lap off the water, a shattering 7 min 32.69 sec, was almost as fast as Cuddihy's flying laps. His next lap was naturally faster, at a speed of 397.62 km/h, faster than the straight line World Speed Record set by Doolittle the preceding year. Despite the wide, sweeping turns he was making round the pylons his next lap was faster still, a devastating 7 min 30.05 sec, a speed of 248.5 mph (399.95 km/h), as near 400 km/h as makes no difference. However he was not without his problems. The AS.2's coolant temperature was beginning to creep up and he climbed from 200 ft to 600 ft in search of cooler air. This was sufficient to stabilise the temperature and on laps five and six his speeds were high enough to gain for Macchi the International 100 km closed-circuit record at 399.422 km/h (248.2 mph).

While this record-breaking was taking place Bacula

had quietly completed the course at a speed of 350.85 km/h (218.0 mph) and taxied back to the slip. At least one Italian machine was home and dry, as planned. Cuddihy, too, was on his last lap, having had the mortifying experience of seeing de Bernardi's Macchi take off in front of him and, lap by lap, open up the gap. If the lap times are to be accepted as gospel, Cuddihy's had not been a consistent race. His fourth lap is given as 7 min 48.81 sec and his fifth as 7 min 41.87 sec: this looks suspiciously like a timekeepers' error of the 'keeping the books straight' variety. But it may be that his concentration was distracted by an impending fuel crisis. After his test flight the previous day he had complained about the functioning of the wobble-pump used to lift fuel from the float-tank to the fuselage tank. It had been replaced but the new one was now playing up and failing to lift fuel. On his final lap the last drop of fuel in the main tank was exhausted and just two miles from the finish line, on his final lap, poor Cuddihy had to put down on the sea and watch de Bernardi's red Macchi swoop overhead to complete his fifth lap.

If de Bernardi saw the Curtiss on the water it did not cause him to slacken off because his sixth, and penultimate, lap was almost his fastest, no doubt due to his intention to take the 200 km closed-circuit record, which was duly achieved at the end of this sixth round at a speed of 399.12 km/h (248.00 mph). The Italian team leader's final lap was little slower and he crossed the line 52 min 56.22 sec after take-off, a race speed of 396.70 km/h (246.50). His race average was faster than Doolittle's 1925 world record by almost one mile per hour. Meanwhile, five minutes later Schilt, a broken bracing wire streaming in the wind, brought the R3C-2 over the line into second place at a race speed of 231.36 mph, confirming victory for de Bernardi. Only Tomlinson was left, then on his sixth lap, to grind along for another fifteen minutes to become the second American home, in fourth place.

To drive the point home, and to confirm the superiority of the M.39, de Bernardi went out four days later on the speed course laid out in Hampton Roads and established a new world speed record for seaplanes with a mean speed of 416.62 km/h (258.87 mph). It was a triumphant week for Italian aviation.

De Bernardi had taxied in after the race to a typically emotional Italian reception from Air Attaché Scaroni and the ground crew. His first duty was to despatch the now famous signal to Benito Mussolini, 'Your order to win at all costs has been carried out.' It had indeed been a costly exercise, with poor Centurione dead, engines and machines destroyed and much Italian gold spent not only by the government but by constructors Macchi and Fiat. But much had been learnt which would be of benefit to all concerned in the coming years. One can be sure that every aspect of the race and details of the hardware had been carefully noted by the designers and scientists labouring away at Teddington and Farnborough in the UK.

Castoldi had confirmed a format for fast single-seaters which would finally defeat the biplane lobby and persist into the jet age. Fiat had tested their engines literally to destruction and learnt much thereby which would stand them in good stead when they came to power the fighters, bombers and flying-boats of the Regia Aeronautica. But most of all the victory put Italy into the front rank of aviation technology, sadly in the course of promoting a sordid political ideal.

The Italian win delighted the British because it brought the Coupe Schneider back to Europe and confirmed the continuity of the series for at least two more events. There must have been some gusty sighs of relief in Piccadilly and Whitehall.

It must have been clear to European observers at Norfolk that the US Army and Navy had lost interest. The 1926 event was a good opportunity to confirm their decisions about the relative merits of the Curtiss and Packard V-12 power units, but little more than that. Already the trend in the US services was towards air-cooled radials. The mood is evident in official Navy pictures of the R3C-3 on the slip at Norfolk with its well-worn paint scheme and the varnish peeling off the floats. It was a far cry from the sparkling US Navy presentation at Cowes only three years earlier.

The 1926 contest marked the end of the third era of the Schneider races. Before the 1914 war the races at Monaco had gone to prove that flight off the water was a practical proposition, that machines could be built which could raise themselves off the water and race against each other at speeds very little lower than that of their landplane counterparts. Post-war the flying-boat had dominated the scene as the result of the Savoia moral victory at Bournemouth and the Italian-only events in Venice. A British flying-boat put paid to Italian dominance only to have the cup snatched away by the swift American float-equipped biplanes. At Norfolk three years of biplane superiority had been devastated overnight. The monoplane was now poised to come into its own.

The Aircraft

The Macchi M.39 of 1926

Reginald Mitchell and Mario Castoldi had proved, to their pilots' discomfiture, but their own satisfaction, that not enough was known about the high-speed characteristics of cantilever wings to risk them again for the time being. However, Mitchell had been visionary in his assessment that a monoplane mounted on twin floats offered the smallest frontal area and the minimum drag for the purpose of surviving a seaworthiness test, lifting a pilot off the surface of the water and transporting him round a triangular course at the best possible speed. The only shortcoming of the arrangement would appear later when more-powerful engines caused float volumes to be

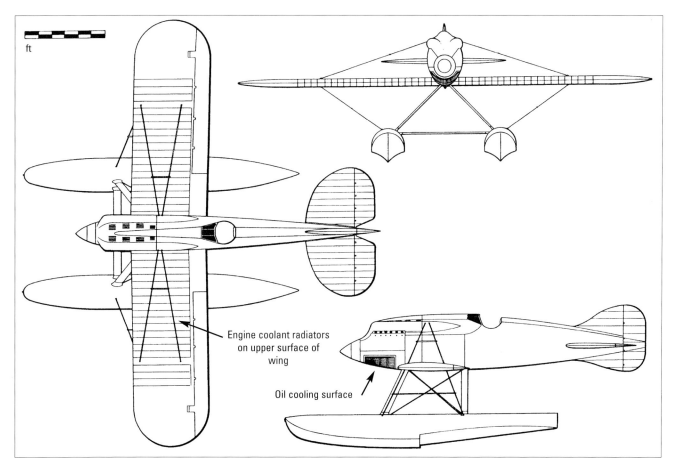

ft

Engine coolant radiators
on upper surface of
wing

Oil cooling surface

Macchi M.39 (1926): Wing Span: 30 ft 4 in (9.26 m). Length Overall: 22 ft 1 in (6.74 m). Wing Area: 156.08 sq. ft (14.30 m²).
Weight Empty: 2,778 lb (1,260 kg). T-O Weight: 3,560 lb (1,615 kg). Max Wing Loading: 22.5 lb/sq. ft (111.37 kg/m²).
Fiat V-12 engine, liquid-cooled, of 800 hp.

plussed-up for the take-off condition when engine torque tended to bury one of the floats.

It was left to the pragmatic Castoldi, saddled with an almost impossible time schedule, to accept Mitchell's lead and adapt it to known structural methods. One can imagine him standing back at Bay Shore, looking at the sleek S.4 and the smooth Curtiss biplanes alongside each other and figuring out that all he had to do was to take one of the Curtiss racers, throw away the upper wing and struts and there he would have a monoplane racer with all the stress work done for him. It has been said that he hoped for the low-wing configuration to improve the pilot's view: however he would have been more likely to choose it for the practical reason that it provided better landing-wire angles without having to resort to a pylon.

The structural solution was immaculate, though hardly new; after all the first race at Monaco in 1913 had been won by a wire-braced monoplane on floats. On the Macchi the float struts, spreaders and flying wires collectively formed an enormously strong truss with the float struts in compression and the lift wires and float spreaders in tension. The landing wires, picking up with a strongpoint on the engine bulkhead, completed the stress circuit. Bracing wires were kept to a minimum. Each wing was supported by a pair of flying wires with drag bracing and a pair of landing wires. The only other wires were double diagonals for the float struts. Lenticular-section wires were used throughout with, on the race machines, horizontal flutter dampers. With structural integrity thus assured Castoldi was able to adopt a thin wing of known characteristics with a thickness-to-chord ratio of 10 per cent, secure in the knowledge that his pilots would not be bugged by the then new and not fully understood problem of flutter. The M.39 was indeed one of the strongest of the Schneider machines, being capable of withstanding a static load of seventeen times its own weight. Moreover, because of the inherently superior aerodynamic qualities of the monoplane Castoldi was able to go for a much higher wing-loading than the Curtisses without drastically increasing stall speed.

Five machines in all were ordered. Two of them, MM.72 and MM.73 were intended as transition machines and were given a 10.6 m span. The remaining three were race machines with the serial numbers MM.74, MM.75 and MM.76 and a span of 9.26 m. All had a chord of 1.68 m. The short-span M.39s raced at Hampton Roads had an all-up weight of 1,575 kg (3,465 lb) for a wing area of 14.3 m² (153.9 sq ft), resulting in a take-off wing loading of 22.5 lb/sq ft compared with about 19.4 lb/sq ft for the Curtiss. Yet the stall speed was only 3 mph higher at 82 mph. In fact the alighting and take-off speeds were always in excess of the stall speed because the wing could not be brought anywhere near the maximum angle of attack for fear of the sterns of the floats digging in and setting up uncontrollable porpoising. This was one reason why Castoldi could go for a thin wing with less than desirable stall characteristics in the hope – not realised – that it would have a lower drag factor.

Structurally the Macchi was based on a wooden

Mario Castoldi's design which won in 1926, the Macchi M.39 powered by a Fiat AS.2 engine developing 800 hp.

The winning M.39 with its low frontal area.

The nose of a Macchi M.39 showing the less than smooth surface. The ribbed oil cooler forms under the surface of the nose.

monocoque fuselage constructed on the Béchereau-SPAD system of double diagonal wooden planking over wooden bulkheads. The wooden section terminated ahead of the pilot at a metal firewall which formed the main fuselage strongpoint into which loads from the front mainspar, the forward float struts and the engine mounting were fed. There appears to have been a short keel running down the fuselage to which the rear wing spar and float struts were attached.

The straight – some three-view drawings wrongly show it with slight sweep-back – one-piece wing with rounded tips was based on twin wooden spars and was skinned with double diagonal planking on the same system as the fuselage. Corrugated brass skin radiators, similar to those used by Curtiss were superimposed on the whole of the upper and lower surfaces of the parallel section of the wing. In addition a corrugated brass oil radiator was mounted under the nose cowling.

Being a true seaplane, rather than a converted landplane, Castoldi was able to give the M.39 an elegant unbraced cruciform tail. In common with all the flying surfaces this was also wood-skinned and with buried control linkages. It is said that split elevators with differential adjustment were fitted to counter engine torque.

For the first time in a Schneider machine the whole fuel load was carried in the floats, whose underwater form, like that of the M.33, resulted from experiments using Castoldi's special motorboat. These again were of wooden construction with steel keels and bulkheads at the chassis attachment point. They were painted and highly polished to give minimum drag on and off the water. Fuel, contained in tinned steel tanks stressed to withstand alighting loads, was pumped to a small fuselage tank located beneath the rear of the engine and then to an even smaller header tank mounted above the carburettors.

To keep drag to a minimum and reduce interference effect the float struts, spreaders and bracing-wire end-fittings picked up with internal brackets on the float bulkheads. The whole of the float chassis was constructed from steel tubing with wooden fairings and light alloy cuffs at the intersections.

All the Schneider floatplanes, with large areas of float ahead of the centre of lateral resistance, had poor directional, or weathercock, stability. The M.39 was no exception and the prototype had a strong tendency to what we would now call Dutch roll. To reduce this the area of the ventral fin was increased on the definitive machines. Castoldi also adopted the Curtiss solution of a variable-ratio pulley system built into the rudder control circuit. Even then, in line with the general experience of high-speed floatplanes, the M.39 was unstable with a free rudder and the pilots had to fly the machines with their feet braced hard on the rudder bar. In contrast aileron control was extremely heavy at speed, calling for a long control column.

It has often been stated that the AS.2 engine for the M.39 was a last-minute development by Fiat. Evidence in the form of dates on drawings would seem not to bear this out and it would not be unreasonable to conjecture that the M.33 flying-boat used in the 1925 race was designed round one of the Fiat A-series engines, possibly a boosted A.20. The holes in the A.20 crankcase brackets, by coincidence or design, were at the same 400 mm centres as those of the D-12 and thus the A.20 would fit the same bearers; it is quite within the bounds of possibility that the American engines used by Macchi in the 1925 race represented a last-minute change of plan due to the Fiat units not being ready in time. The 430 bhp A.20 with the same frontal area as the D-12 and the 600 bhp A.22 with very little more were certainly in existence in definitive form in 1925; in this light it would be interesting to have chapter and verse on the story that the Italians approached American companies for engines for the race.

While a racing version of the A.20, giving, say, 570 bhp would have been ideal for the M.33, the edict to 'win at all costs' demanded a bigger margin of power over the opposition. The A.22 was the ideal starting point and the 800 bhp AS.2 designed for installation in the M.39 was a straight development of this latter based on a lighter crankcase of slightly smaller dimensions fitted with a long-throw crankshaft and enlarged cylinders to raise the cylinder dimensions from 160 × 135 mm to 170 × 140 mm, equivalent to 31,403 cc, some 13 litres more than the swept volume of the Curtiss D-12.

Fiat engineers were able to design the AS.2 to develop maximum power at 2,500 rpm only by reason of the existence of the high-speed Curtiss-Reed propeller. By 1926 the latest forged and machined types were being made available to countries outside the USA and were an essential ingredient in the success of the challenge. For the race three different pitches were chosen, fine for MM.74, Bacula's machine, medium pitch for Ferrarin's MM.75 and coarse for MM.76 which would be flown by team leader de Bernardi. It seems likely that these pitch variations were conditioned by the fuel requirements. It is a basic tenet of air racing that the propeller pitch is tailored to allow the engine to run at the speed at which it develops its maximum power. Could it be that with the M.39 the designer, for the first time, came up against the problem of providing sufficient fuel capacity to run the whole race at full throttle? With a specific fuel consumption of 235 kg/bhp/hr the AS.2 needed 200 kg of fuel to develop its full power for an hour; with a reasonable reserve for starting up, taxying and a safety margin, about 230 kg would be needed. Oil (remember the AS.2's smoke trail) would take up a further 70 kg; this left just 50 kg (110 lb) for the pilot, bearing in mind the M.39's useful load of 350 kg. Bacula's machine was fitted with a 600 bhp engine, calling for a finer pitch; however, the less powerful engine would consume less fuel. Ferrarin's machine would appear to have an ideal propeller/engine match while de Bernardi's was possibly 'overgeared' to allow it to finish with fuel in hand. On this basis Ferrarin's times should have been faster than de Bernardi's. The fact that they were not indicates that the team leader's engine was producing substantially more power than that of his team-mate.

increasing the power by an increase in compression ratio in combination with higher-octane fuel. This particular engine is reputed to have given momentary readings of 665 bhp on the test-bed. A.7054 was assigned to Harmon Norton, an experienced racing pilot who had taken fourth place in the 1925 Pulitzer flying a Curtiss PW8B.

R3C-3

The third American defender for the 1926 race, A.6978, as already mentioned, was the machine which had been held back by the Navy for the 1925 Schneider race and in the event failed to finish. After the race it was sent off to the Navy's Philadelphia factory to receive a new Packard power unit; the geared, racing version of the 2A-1500 V-12 which had been sponsored by the Navy as a D-12 alternative. In standard, low-compression trim, it developed 600 bhp at 2,500 rpm from a swept volume of 1,530 cu in and was available in three configurations, direct-drive upright, direct-drive inverted and upright geared.

As prepared for the Schneider race the upright geared version was chosen; upright to suit the R3C-3 configuration and geared to allow it to be run up to 2,700 rpm when it developed 700 bhp. Although having slightly less frontal area than the direct-drive Curtiss V-1550 the reduction gear caused it to weigh some 160 lb more. This almost 20 per cent penalty would ultimately have to be paid for in drag. It was

Curtiss R3C-2 powered by a Packard V-12 engine developing 700 hp. (*Flight*)

Curtiss Racers for 1926

Curtiss R3C-2

This, the ex-Doolittle machine, A.7054, was retained virtually in its winning form with the exception of new Navy-designed floats. Engine development centred on

The Curtiss R3C-2 which came second at Hampton Roads in 1926 when flown by Frank C. Schilt.

nevertheless a beautifully made engine – Packard cars had the reputation at that time of being the Rolls-Royce of America – and the Navy no doubt hoped that it would be more reliable than the Curtisses. Maybe they also hoped that the more efficient propeller made possible by the reduction gear would offset the weight penalty. The one drawback of the choice of this engine was that the Allison single-reduction gearbox adopted by Packard caused the propeller to rotate in the opposite direction to normal. Pilots accustomed to the very considerable, left-wing down, torque reaction of the direct-drive racing engines during the early stages of take-off were in danger of being caught off their guard when an instinctive reverse reaction was called for.

The Packard engine had also been chosen as a test-bed for the new steel, detachable-blade propeller made by the Standard Steel Propeller Company – later to become Hamilton Standard – with the object of comparing results with the fast-running, supersonic tip, Curtiss-Reed units. The latest versions of these, first used on the US 1925 Schneider aircraft, were machined from forgings and were considerably superior to the sheet type supplied to the opposition in that year.

R3C-4

Modification of the R3C-4, allocated to Frank Conant, apart from the new, snub-nose floats were an enlarged air intake in deference to the greater swept volume of the V-1550 engine and the addition of experimental skin radiators to the forward float struts in combination with an increase in the chord of the struts to provide a larger 'wetted' surface. To boost the power of the V-1550 it is rumoured to have been modified to run on fuel with high benzole content; reports vary between 75 per cent and 100 per cent. Benzole – nothing to do with Karl Benz incidentally – in the modern sense is a mixture of benzene and toluene and would call for a substantial increase in compression ratio to take advantage of its properties.

The V-1550 was in effect a completely new engine with a strengthened crankcase designed to fit into D-12 mounting points but housing a new crankshaft with enlarged main and big end journals to withstand not only the extra power expected from a swept volume of 1,569 cu in (25,711 cc) but also the crankshaft cyclic variations which might be encountered in a geared version, the GV-1550. In common with the V-1400 it retained open-top liners and the 6.25 in stroke of the earlier engine but with the bores enlarged from 4.875 in to 5.125 in. This engine was later redesignated the V-1570, reflecting its true capacity, and later the Conqueror. While the V-1400 had been a little lighter than the D-12, the V-1550 was considerably heavier, scaling 720 lb in direct-drive form. Production engines developed 600 bhp at 2,500 rpm. With racing pistons and a compression ratio of 7.5 to 1 it was claimed to produce 736 bhp at 2,600 rpm.

Venice 1927

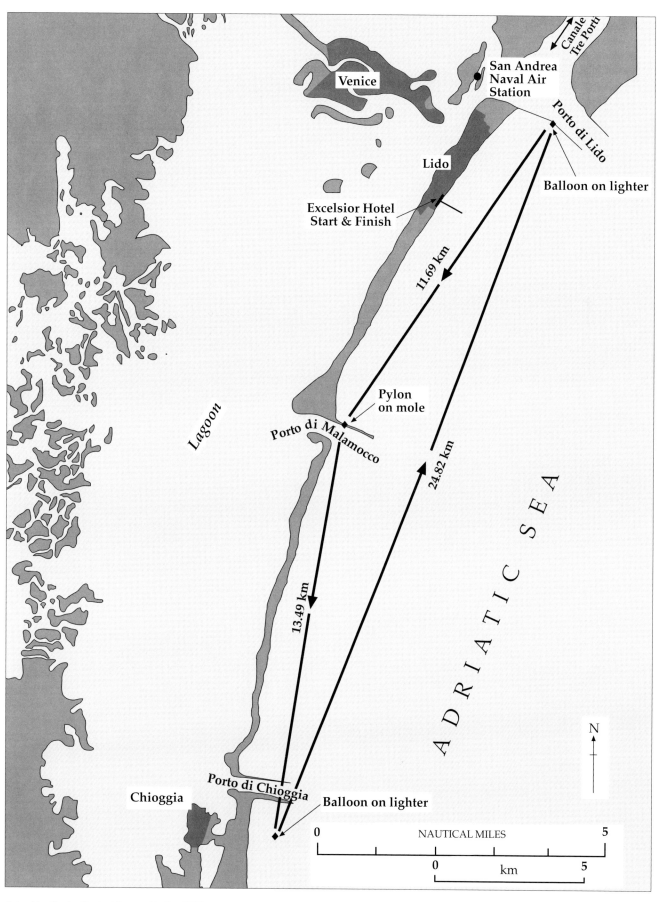

Schneider Trophy Contest Course: Venice 1927.

Run-up

Italy's win in America brought the Coupe d'Aviation Jacques Schneider back to Europe, whence it had started. It also made life potentially a good deal easier and less costly for any would-be European challenger and made it much more difficult for any attempt by the USA to regain the 'Flying Flirt'. Not that the US government had any serious intentions. Their defence of the Trophy at Norfolk had been in the nature of a final fling. After that the Army and Navy high-speed flyers had dispersed into test-flying and air racing became a sideline. The accent had shifted to transport aviation and building up an airmail network. This was evident in the work being done on blind-flying and bad-weather landings. An indication of this was that Doolittle was test-flying the first artificial horizon and was involved in a series of blind-landing tests. Congress was more inclined to sponsor the National Air Tour than air racing.

In Europe there were different attitudes. New air forces were being born in Italy and Germany. The writing had been on the wall when, in May 1925, the Paris Conference was told that with effect from 1 September that year the Inter Allied Aeronautical Guarantee Committees, whose job it was to make sure that Germany should not develop as an air power, would be dispersed. With them went the Nine Rules which forbade Germany to import or build large civil aircraft. The politicians probably saw that the regulations were fruitless because German aviation companies were already building advanced prototypes in adjoining neutral countries. And, following a treaty of friendship with Soviet Russia, the German military air arm was training military pilots at the secret flying school, jointly operated with the Russians, at Lipetsk, in exchange for technical know-how.

According to the conference the Germans would not be allowed to build large transports which could be converted to bombers; but they were allowed to train thirty-six officers from the Army and Navy as pilots. More important, permission was given to train only fifty police pilots, but there could be no reasonable limit to the number of civilian pilots, trained to fly in all weathers, to operate these civil aircraft. It was hardly surprising that the British Air Estimates for 1925/6 included a five-year plan to treble the size of the RAF with a special requirement for high-speed fighters. The Americans had shown how quickly development progressed in the white heat of sporting competition. The Air Ministry's orders for the S.4 and the Gloster III to take part in the 1925 contest was a measure of the Air Ministry's awareness. The further orders for the Supermarine S.5 and the Gloster IV early in 1926 simply confirmed the policy being followed.

Whereas Germany had other things than the Coupe Schneider to think about, there was nothing covert about Italian activity under Mussolini's Fascist regime. For the Italian dictator aviation had a dual purpose. It gave glamour to his movement and at the same time built up technical resources. The 1926 win by de

Bernardi had been a great success in both these areas.

In a review of the 1925 race, Air Vice-Marshal Sir Geoffrey Salmond, had pointed out that any future British challenge must be conducted by a services team so that both pilots and ground crews could operate with single-minded efficiency. Any experience they gained would be retained in the RAF rather than by the industry which had built the machines. Air Chief Marshal Sir Hugh Trenchard, head of the RAF, despite intense personal reservations about the desirability of service pilots taking part in races and becoming national heroes, had permitted the formation of a high-speed flight even before de Bernardi's Macchi had trounced the Americans at Hampton Roads. It was headed by the dour South African, Squadron Leader Leslie Slatter, who had been posted to Felixstowe to form a flight whose object was to test the new high-speed seaplanes that the industry was building, and accept them on behalf of the Air Ministry. Three RAF test pilots were allocated to this High Speed Flight. But there was still no assurance that the air and ground crews who tested machines and serviced them would go to Italy to challenge the Italian team.

Meanwhile, politics between the Italian and British Aero Club were in full swing to decide just when the next contest would be held. The Royal Aero Club had campaigned for a two-year interval between races because of the time needed to develop suitable aircraft, and wanted the next event to be held in 1928. The Italians, fresh from their victory in 1926, wanted it in 1927. It was logical that they would wish to keep the Squadra Alta Velocità together and in current practice. Their crew's tails were in the air and a two-year break could take the edge off their flying. Moreover, the Italian Ministry felt that the existing Macchi machines, with a little development, could eat the untried British machines. It was settled when, at an extraordinary meeting of the FAI in Paris on 25 January 1927, the Italians won a vote for the race to be held in 1927.

The British were not unduly dismayed at being outflanked. Their machines were well advanced, the shortcomings of the Italian Macchis were known and it was patent that the Americans had neither the time nor the inclination to build a new team to replace their outclassed Curtisses. Many sections of the French industry would have dearly loved to have prepared a challenge but no money was forthcoming from their government. If it had been, there was no time to build and test machines. The date was fixed for September.

In Britain, Trenchard and the Air Council still had to assure the Treasury, who feared that the aircraft industry was about to receive free publicity at the taxpayer's expense, that the advantages which would accrue to the RAF, in the shape of experience in flying and servicing these high-speed machines away from established bases, and under pressures akin to combat flying, were unique and unobtainable elsewhere at any price. On 13 May the Treasury, at that time under Winston Churchill, agreed to foot the bill.

Despite the lack of government interest there had

The score board on the Lido beach in Venice, 1927 showing the lap times of Kinkead and Webster. (*Flight*)

also been developments in the USA. The Secretary of the United States Navy Department had announced on 9 February that they would not participate in the 1927 contest because of lack of funds. He estimated that transportation of a navy team to Venice, and the construction of new machines and engines, would cost half a million dollars and there was no appropriation for such an amount for this purpose. But he had left the door open for a private entry. That entry was forthcoming a little more than a month later when news came through that a group of New York's sportsmen were raising 100,000 dollars between them to build a machine to take the world speed record from France, who held it at 278.48 mph (448.15 km/h) with the Bernard-Ferbois V.2 and to regain the Coupe Schneider from the Italians.

The Kirkham Products Corporation of Garden City, Long Island, headed by Charles B. Kirkham of Curtiss K-12 and Wasp triplane fame, would design and construct the machine for which Packard would build a new, 1,200 hp engine. Lieutenant Alford J. Williams, the great Al Williams, rivalled only by Jimmy Doolittle as an all-American aviation hero, would do the development and test-flying and pilot the machine in the contest. He had already obtained leave from the Navy and had put all his savings into the project.

The choice of Kirkham's company to build a challenger was logical. They had a great deal of experience and the most cordial relationship with Curtiss. The machine is said to have been designed by Curtiss engineers from the dispersed race engineering team, some of whom were still at Curtiss and some of whom had left. The one imponderable was the Packard engine which was to be in effect two Packard 2A-V1500 twelve-cylinder engines with the cylinder banks mounted on a common crankcase in X-configuration. It was expected to give 1,200 hp, which would make it the most powerful racing engine extant. The most important aspect of this activity was that it meant America was virtually back in the picture, especially because the US Navy was known to be keeping a fatherly eye on the project.

For once the British were well placed to mount a challenge. Their machines had been originally intended to race in 1926, the specifications having been issued early that year. Delays in the delivery of the special Napier engines had been the main cause of withdrawal of the entry. Supermarine had been given the job of building a monoplane while Gloster, who had always specialised in high-speed biplanes, would build to that configuration. Thus services chiefs would be able to assess the relative merits of the two types. Even at that stage in the evolution of the aeroplane, there was a strong anti-monoplane lobby in most of the world's air forces.

The third British entry would be the Short-Bristow Crusader, whose main function was to explore the merits of air-cooled radial engines in high-speed aircraft. Since there were three machines each on order from Supermarine and Gloster, plus the Crusader, Britain would have more machines to choose from than any country in the history of the race. There was no doubt that she meant to win.

Most of this was known to the Italians. They had less than a year to develop and build new machines for 1927 but they had a good start with the Macchi M.39. So their machines for 1927 would follow their established formula for success, a Macchi wire-braced monoplane on pontoons, powered by a Fiat engine. Mario Castoldi, with the promise of 1,000 hp from a lightened version of the AS.2 from Fiat, sat down to design a 300 mph aeroplane.

Mitchell, now a main board director, had decided, as the result of experience with the S.4, that the cantilever wing exacted too great a penalty in terms of weight. It was part of Supermarine's contract with the Air Ministry that full use should be made of the wind-tunnel and other test facilities at the RAE at Farnborough and the National Physical Laboratory (NPL) at Teddington. Therefore, early in 1926, anticipating the contract, he had caused his friends at the NPL to set up a series of experiments to determine the drag of three different monoplane configurations featuring a braced thin wing. Two of these were strut-braced and one wire-braced. It is now history that as the result of these tests the low-wing, wire-braced configuration was chosen because of the lower drag. It was followed by a whole series of experiments to establish, among other things, the best bracing-wire section, the floats with the least resistance and the drag of various forms of wing radiator.

It is human nature to debate who was first with the wire-braced monoplane. Glossing over the fact that a machine of this configuration won the first-ever contest in 1913, we know that Mitchell and Castoldi were working on the same type of machine at the same time for the 1926 contest. The difference was that with less resources Castoldi made his decision instinctively, while Mitchell, with the co-operation of the National Physical Laboratory working overtime, arrived at his decision by the process of engineering logic. In the end, the engine problem precluded the British machines from taking part in the 1926 race and gave their makers a year's breathing space in which to refine the design. This respite was also of value to Napier, who were able to

offer a choice of power units with direct drive and reduction gear. There was also a chance for P.A. Ralli, Fairey's Greek propeller designer, to calculate and test a whole series of propellers.

The Supermarine aircraft which emerged was seen to be, for the first time in the Schneider races, a stressed-skin, metal fuselage with wooden wings mounted on all-metal floats asymmetrically arranged to offset engine torque on the water and to a lesser extent in flight. To this end the starboard float was not only made bigger than the port float but was set out further from the aircraft centreline and contained all the fuel for the race. The engine was the special short-stroke Napier Lion VIIA which the makers had updated from the 7,000 hp of the Napier VII which had powered the British machines in the 1925 event to 898 hp at 3,300 rpm in 1927. At the same time they had reduced the frontal area of the engine from 5.55 sq ft to 4.25 sq ft.

Gloster had access to the same engines as Supermarine, the Napier Lion, rightly, being considered the best available British engine at the time. Folland had established his I-strutted, biplane configuration, with the Gloster III. It had the merits of low drag and immense inherent strength. H.E. Preston, under Folland, set out to refine it aerodynamically. The result was what many people, with justification, regard as the most beautiful biplane racer ever built. Of all-wood construction, except for the metal floats, it had a monocoque wooden fuselage with cantilever, cruciform empennage and planked, multispar wings clad with corrugated copper wing radiators. A special feature was the Gloster Patent Variable Control gear in the elevator and rudder control circuits.

Short Brothers of Rochester, Kent were chosen to build the Fedden-inspired, Bristow-conceived Crusader which had been proposed for the 1926 race and turned down at the instigation of the Air Ministry. Design work had, however, gone ahead under the guidance of the experienced W.G. Carter. The real object of the Crusader was to prove the feasibility of high-power radial engines for high-speed aircraft and it was in effect a flying test-bed for Bristol's completely new short-stroke, supercharged Mercury, whose only similarity to the well-tried Jupiter was that it had nine cylinders. Although of smaller diameter and capacity than the earlier engine, it gave 800 bhp at 2,500 rpm, thanks to the addition of a gear-driven supercharger and four-valve heads in L.24 alloy developed at the RAE.

Unusual features of the Crusader airframe were the wood-clad, tubular-steel framed front fuselage mated to a semi-monocoque, all-wood rear fuselage. The mainplane platform was elliptical with the wing roots picking up with short-stub wings integral with the front fuselage.

The Crusader was the focus of a big investigation by the NPL to evolve a drag-free cowling for the individual cylinder heads which protruded into an aerodynamically critical area of the fuselage. As originally designed, the drag of the fuselage alone was equal to that of the complete S.5. By the time the NPL had finished with it, the coefficient of drag had been halved although, even then, it was not as low as that of the Supermarine and Gloster machines with water-cooled engines. Unfortunately the Crusader slightly antedated the Townend ring cowling which might easily have improved its performance substantially. Certainly the machine was ready for flying ahead of the Supermarine and Gloster machines. It was delivered to Felixstowe for test flying on 4 May 1927.

Shortly after the Crusader's arrival at Felixstowe Slatter and his pilots were posted to the RAF seaplane station at Calshot, at the mouth of Southampton Water, where they and their machines could gain experience on more open and less congested water than the Orwell Estuary.

It was typical of Trenchard's way of doing things that although he did not commit himself to allowing Royal Air Force personnel to take part in the race until 1927, he had formed the High Speed Flight at Felixstowe as early as October 1926. Slatter, the South African who commanded it, did not have the flying experience of his pilots, but more than made up for it in administrative ability. One of the pilots was Flight Lieutenant Oswald Worsley, one of the most respected aviators in the RAF. He was the one pilot to stay with the High Speed Flight right through to the race in Venice.

In those days midsummer brought a special kind of madness to the RAF in the shape of the Hendon Display. It was the display of the year and gave the service the opportunity to let the public see the hardware they were paying for and the skill of the people they employed to use it. That year there were two

significant groups of foreign guests. One of them was bearded General Italo Balbo, Mussolini's energetic young Chief of Air Staff. A great showman, Italo arrived piloting his own machine, albeit with a safety pilot and navigator, having flown via Germany and Holland to avoid overlying France, who at that time took a less than kindly view of Fascist goings-on in Italy.

Also, for the first time, there was a group of German officers, who turned up as guests, again much to French annoyance, to take a look at the RAF on show. Among them was a certain Hermann Goering, who had commanded the Richthofen Squadron after its leader had been shot down. Private RAF comment on Goering was that he was 'singularly like one of our own fighter pilots and very entertaining company. Altogether our German visitors are a very good lot and we hope to meet them again...'. It was prophetic comment. French reaction was less cordial and there were mutterings about the Treaty of Versailles.

Balbo used his stay in Britain to good purpose, with visits to the Napier engine works, Gloster Aircraft, Bristol, and Supermarine, among other important manufacturers. What he saw at Supermarine and Gloster's cannot have filled him with confidence over the outcome of the race in Venice. However, the Air Ministry seemed happy enough to let him wander round and Roy Fedden was able to do some ground work on the subject of air-cooled radials which was to bear fruit at a later date.

While all this was going on the High Speed Flight at Calshot was shaking-down. Two of the original pilots

Supermarine S.5 being prepared for the 1927 competition. Supermarine and RAF personnel of the RAF's High Speed Flight conduct a test of the Napier Lion VIIA engine. (*Flight*)

Supermarine S.5 at RAF Calshot prior to being shipped to Venice for the 1927 competition. The starboard float is not only larger than the port, but is set further out from the aircraft's centre line. (*Flight*)

had been stood down. Slatter chose in their place the diminutive, boyish Flight Lieutenant Sidney Norman Webster, Flight Lieutenant S.M. Kinkead, a fellow South African, and Flying Officer H.M. Schofield. Although they were meant to fly all the machines in turn, Schofield had been allocated to the Crusader, whose enclosed, bubble canopy he hated; the diminutive Webster was a natural for the tiny cockpit of the S.5. The first of these, N.219 had been delivered on 7 June and test-flown by Oswald Worsley with the direct-drive propeller.

The new men in the flight were all landplane pilots, though very experienced instructors. Webster had 150 types in his log book. They had to find their sea-legs using first a Fairey Flycatcher and the old Bamel and then the Gloster IIIs as trainers.

The first of the Gloster IVs, N.224, was delivered in March. Although it was the first of the three machines to be constructed it bore the highest service serial. It had been built with 26 ft 7½ in span upper mainplanes and soon confirmed what wind-tunnel tests at the NPL had indicated, namely that the complete machine generated much more than the designed lift, a phenomenon attributed to the fairing of the upper wing roots into the engine cowlings. Since the design conception had been to accept 80 mph as a touch-down speed and N.224 was landing at 70 mph with a corresponding reduction in maximum speed, the span of the remaining machines N.222 and N.223 was hurriedly reduced by 4 ft. The two short-span Glosters took the works designation IVA or IVB depending on whether they were powered by a direct-drive Napier Lion VIIA or the geared version.

The Air Ministry plan was to utilise one Supermarine and one Gloster as development machines and keep the others in reserve for the race. As already said the first S.5, in works grey with silver-doped flying surfaces, was delivered in early June and Worsley's flight was under works supervision. At the end of the month it was towed across to the Supermarine works, on the other side of Southampton Water, and fitted with the first of the geared Lions, engine no. 63102. It was immediately apparent that the geared engine gave the machine an extra 10 mph. This geared engine was removed, however, and replaced by a direct-drive unit before Webster's first flight in the machine on 24 July. His flight, made in the early hours of the morning to avoid prying eyes and to make the most of the cool morning air, was over a 3 km course laid out between Calshot and Southampton with camera gun timing at both ends. The mean of the two runs showed that the machine with the direct-drive engine was good for 284 mph. That finished flying for July but during August N.219 was used for further tests with a range of different propellers flown by Webster and Schofield.

Initial flight trials of the Gloster IV, which was ready for flying in March, appear to have been carried out by the firm's test pilots. Initial tests by Gloster's indicated that the wide-span Gloster IV was good for 274 mph with the direct-drive engine. On their completion the modified, short-span IVA and IVB were found to be capable of 283 mph and 298 mph respectively. The RAF flew the Glosters only briefly at Calshot in July, Worsley as usual making the acceptance flights. Whereas the Supermarines used Fairey-Reed propellers, Gloster used three-piece propellers of their own make. The separate blades were machined from forged blanks of Duralumin with the object of reducing vibration. Only single, short

Preparing one of the Gloster IVs at RAF Calshot for the 1927 event. (*Flight*)

flights seem to have been made at Calshot before the machines were crated. The plan was to take a full complement of propellers to Venice and try them under the actual conditions in which the race would take place.

The Crusader had been delivered to Felixstowe as early as 4 May after brief taxi tests by the very experienced John Lankester Parker, ready for its first flight by Bert Hinkler, whose honorary rank as Flight Lieutenant in the RAF Reserve, plus his experience with the Gloster III in America, caused the Air Ministry to feel that he was perhaps better qualified to undertake the first flight. Hinkler's first reaction when he saw the machine was that the fin area was too small compared with the apparently vast forward area created by the helmeted cylinders of the Mercury radial. Accordingly it was enlarged before he made his first flight. The Mercury engine was, at that stage, not at its best, giving about 790 hp with the speed limited because of spark plug problems. The engine air intake was also proving unsatisfactory, causing the engine to cut-out spasmodically. However, Hinkler managed to record a true air speed of 250 mph and found that at this speed the aircraft tended to hunt longitudinally because of the overlarge fin.

Unhappily, because of the very poor view forward and the limited visibility from the Crusader's canopy, his touch-down was not one of the best. The machine hit the water heavily and buckled the float structure but rescue boats quickly got it in tow and it was whisked back to Felixstowe for repairs. After repair, and reduction of the fin to the original size, it was the subject of a whole series of trials by the RAF in co-operation with Short's.

Painted all white with navy-blue cockpit fairings, the Crusader eventually found its way to Calshot in time for a Press presentation on 9 August, when journalists saw it in company with the blue and silver 55s and the dark blue and copper Gloster IVs, lined up and glistening in the sun in readiness for the journey to the Adriatic.

The Race

One imagines that the Air Ministry decided to send the British machines to Venice in two consignments for safety reasons. The Gloster IVA, N.219 and the Crusader were shipped in the Admiralty Collier SS *Heworth* on 16 August. The remaining two S.5s – it may have been only one – and Gloster IVB N.223 left later on board the SS *Egyptian Prince*, with all the experimental propellers, bound for Malta where they were to be transferred to the aircraft carrier HMS *Eagle*. Taking a leaf out of the Americans' book, the British government had obviously decided to treat the whole episode as a flag-waving exercise.

Macchi M.52 powered by a Fiat AS.2 V-12 engine. (*Macchi*)

In Italy the Reparto Alta Velocità was reformed at Varese in early May under the command of Colonel Tecchini. His two leading pilots were Major Mario de Bernardi, who had won the race at Hampton Roads, and Arturo Ferrarin, a protégé of Fiat and the renowned long-distance pilot who had experienced such bad luck the previous year in America. New boys to the team were Lieutenant Salvatore Borra and Captain Federico Guazzetti, a veteran of the 1914 War with a fine record in bombers and fighters who had been the pilot of General Guidoni's abortive CRDA. Squadron equipment was the M.33 left over from the 1925 race and the Macchi M.39 trainers and race aircraft from 1926. Their base was at Varese and was conveniently located close to the Macchi works where the M.52 race planes were in preparation.

Delivery of the M.52 was conditioned by the availability of Fiat's new lightweight 1,000 hp AS.3 engine. Twelve engines had been laid down at Turin and six of them had blown up before Zerbi even began to get the experimental magnesium pistons, which he had designed for them, to stand up with any degree of reliability. Apart from running the engines at a higher compression ratio, Zerbi had planned to run them faster to allow them to digest more air and fuel mixture and thus produce more power. The function of the magnesium pistons was to keep the reciprocating weight as low as possible and thus avoid mechanical disaster. The reverse seems to have been the case. He was venturing into the unknown with

a new material which, as we now know, is far from ideal for the particular purpose. Engines were eventually delivered late in August and installed in the M.52 airframes waiting at Varese. Meanwhile Salvatore Borra, flying on 19 June in one of the training machines, whose stalling characteristics in turns were of the knife-edge variety, crashed into the lake and was killed. At that stage it was too late to replace him, and the team was reduced to de Bernardi, Ferrarin and Guazzetti.

On the other side of the Atlantic things were not going at all well with Lieutenant Alford Williams's Kirkham-Packard project. The machine had been completed well on time by the enthusiastic engineering team

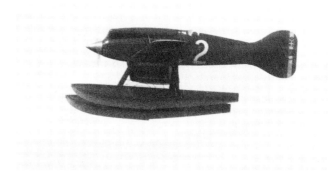

Macchi M.52. As with other competing aircraft, the pilot's forward view was limited. (*Flight*)

which included all the relevant employees of the Kirkham Products Corporation plus the aforementioned spare-time helpers form the old Curtiss race team. The idea of doubling up the Packard 2A-V1500 was on the surface a good one but needed far more development time than was available. The X-configuration for engines has always attracted aircraft engineers but has always proved to be fraught with difficulties verging on disaster. To retain reasonable bearing area one should, ideally, use two crankshafts, one for the upper two banks of cylinders, and one for the lower two banks of cylinders and gear them together. Rolls-Royce tried to do this with their World War Two Vulture engine and failed due to internecine warfare between the torsional vibrations of the individual shafts. Packard, on the X-24, tried to take the constructionally easy way out and run a single crankshaft with the master rod eyes of opposing pairs sharing common crank pins. They appear to have quickly found that their hopes of cramming a quart into a pint pot were excessively ambitious with the bearing materials and technology available to them at the time. It is doubtful whether it could be done today. The excessively narrow bearings running on large-diameter crank pins were bound to melt with great regularity. Added to this shortcoming, photographs of the machine seem to show that someone had not done their sums correctly and the floats had barely sufficient buoyancy reserve to keep the machine afloat, let alone withstand engine torque during the initial stages of take-off.

It was heartbreaking for Williams, who had put most of his spare cash into the project. It was equally depressing for the people who had devoted so much of their time to designing and building the machine and the sportsmen who had got together with the bulk of the money for the project. Just how national a project this was is shown by the fact that President Coolidge authorised the use of the cruiser *Trenton* to transport the machine to Italy with the minimum of delay, should it be ready in time. But bad weather and engine trouble delayed Williams so much that by early August he had no more than four flights in the book and the best speed he had been able to achieve was 275 mph. This was not nearly enough and the entry was withdrawn.

Williams had foreseen that time was not on his side and, as early as July, had asked the American NAA to approach the Royal Aero Club of Italy for a thirty day postponement. Eager as the Italians were to help the Americans, who had postponed their race in the past for much the same reasons, they felt that a month's postponement, bearing in mind the one-aircraft challenge from America, was not desirable. The show was already on the move and involved a great many service personnel and a lot of equipment, apart from the disruption of the diaries of a number of Italian party dignitaries. Moreover, a month's postponement would have taken the race into October, when the weather in the northern Adriatic is not of the best for seaplane flying. This had been proved in 1921.

The request was passed over to the British Royal Aero Club for a final decision which would take the ball out of the Italian court. Being committed to what amounted to a military exercise, the Air Council's reaction was emphatically negative. This decision, passed by the Italians to the NAA, created a nasty scene in the American Press at the time but reason eventually prevailed and everyone became friends again. Sensible Americans soon saw that the whole show could not stop for one very doubtful private entry.

Squadron Leader Slatter and Flight Lieutenant Worsley, together with some ground crew, had arrived in Venice on 30 August with Flying Officer 'Tom' Moon, the Technical Officer, to supervise unloading of the crated machines and their erection. The next day, SS *Heworth* docked and the crates were carefully offloaded into lighters by a highly efficient team of Italian navy dockers, and taken to the San Andrea base for assembly and rigging. They were ready a few days before the Adriatic weather, belying its reputation, calmed down enough for them to fly. Meanwhile Webster, Schofield and Kinkead had arrived and settled themselves in the Excelsior Hotel, which was to be their race headquarters.

Britain was leaving nothing to chance in her determination to take home the Trophy. Air Vice-Marshal F.R. Scarlett was in overall command of the team with Slatter in charge of flying, assisted by Tom Moon and twenty-seven RAF technicians. He was further advised by Mervyn O'Gorman from the Royal Aero Club and Major Buchanan of the Air Ministry. On the civilian side Supermarine were represented by Commander Bird, their Chairman and Managing Director, Reg Mitchell and a team of seven fitters and riggers who had been involved in building the S.5. There were similar teams from Gloster's and Short Brothers.

Bad weather held up flying until the morning of 10 September when at 9.30 am the Supermarine flying test-bed, N.219, was seen to be launched from the San Andrea ramp and towed into the channel. On this occasion it was fitted with a geared Lion VIIB – No. 63105 for the record – and a hitherto untried propeller of smaller diameter and pitch than had previously been used on the geared engine. This was a Fairey Reed FR 376 of 7.25 ft diameter and 11.43 ft pitch, which allowed the engine to run up to 3,300 rpm; about 100 rpm more than the 7.5 ft dia × 12.24 ft pitch screw that had been tried at Calshot on N.219. The engine had been ground-run and Slatter was soon making his take-off run across the Tre Porti channel for an exploratory run round the course. He was careful not to use full throttle near reference points although he did pull 3,350 rpm for eight minutes of the twenty minute flight. Kinkead in Gloster IV N.222 followed him shortly afterwards and made a series of fast runs along the beach and round the pylons at low level. Full throttle was used for twenty-five minutes of his twenty-seven minute flight, suggesting that the direct-drive engine with which the machine was fitted was an expendable, practice motor.

The next day the wind was gusting lightly with a slight chop on the water. It was Webster's turn to try N.219 with the geared engine and Schofield was to give

Venice 1927. One of special Italian lighters for moving their aircraft between the shore facility, the navigation trials course and the 'speed' course. (*Flight*)

the Crusader its first Venetian flight. Webster had already alighted after a thirteen minute flight, most of it at full throttle, as the Crusader was being readied to go. Schofield was already in the cockpit and the hated canopy was fastened down. He opened the throttle and this most docile of the British racers surged away, and after a clean run, lifted off. In the cockpit Schofield levelled off to gain speed before starting his climb when he felt the port wing drop. Instinctively he pulled it up with the stick. Instead of lifting, it dropped deeper. He gave it more correction and down the wing went, into the water and immediately the machine was cartwheeling in a cascade of spray. Fortunately the fuselage broke in half at the transport joint aft of the cockpit and he was sucked out. When he came to after a hearty crack on the head which drove the frame of his goggles into his face and shattered the laminated glasses, he found himself close to the wooden tail section, which was still floating. He clung to this, shedding shoes and trousers to make swimming easier, and waited some time for the rescue boats to pick him up. He was black and blue from head to foot but in a few days he was hobbling about on sticks. The Crusader was not so good and it took days before the remains of Bristow and Fedden's white hope was fished from the bottom of the lagoon.

There is a story that when the Mercury engine came to be examined the 'magnesium' crankcase had all but dissolved! That was the end of flying for that day. The identities of the rigger who crossed the aileron control wires and the Short's and Air Ministry inspectors who passed the machine were never divulged. The British had planned a whole series of propeller tests during their long stay in Venice, intending to try the Gloster propellers on the S.5s and vice versa. The weather decreed otherwise, and there was a shortage of machines because

HMS *Eagle* did not arrive until the 19th with the geared Gloster IVB and the other two Supermarine S.5s aboard. When she did arrive she anchored off the Lido entrance the better to offload the machines, while her escorting destroyers, HMS *Witch*, *Wren*, *Worcester* and *Whitehall* moved into the lagoon to show the flag.

It was not until the 21st that N.220 and N.223 were ready to fly and the weather was suitable. Kinkead, predictably, was put into the Gloster and spent thirty-four minutes of high-speed flying getting to know it. Webster was out that morning too, in N.220 fitted with geared engine no. 63106 and the Fairey-Reed FR 376 propeller from N.219. The same combination, Webster, N.220 and FR 376, were out again the next day, as were Kinkead and the Gloster IVB. It was clear that two of the British machines and their pilots had been chosen. Worsley would be third man because Schofield was still not fit after his crash.

Meanwhile, the Italian team had arrived and installed themselves at the Hotel Danielli. General Andreani was in charge of the Italian operation with Slatter's opposite number, Colonel Tecchini, in charge of the flying, if there had been anything to fly. The Macchi M.52s were still somewhere *en route* and there were disturbing rumours about the performance of the engines. When they did arrive at San Andrea they were quickly hustled behind locked doors for assembly.

Venice on the weekend of 25 September must have presented one of the more momentous sights since the formation of the new state of Italy. Mussolini's *Fascisti* and the energetic Italo Balbo had seen to that. The town and the long, reef-like Lido were thronged with people brought from all over Italy on special excursion trains. The streets were decked with bunting and insignia, the Schneider Trophy was on display outside the Museo

The 1927 winner, Supermarine S.5 No. N.220, is towed in the channel off the San Andrea air station. (*Flight*)

Civico. Crown Prince Umberto and his entourage were lending presence to that of party dignitaries and ambassadorial contingents. Offshore, opposite the Porto di Lido could be seen the lofty silhouette of HMS *Eagle* and her attendant destroyers anchored in line astern. She had been joined by four Italian battleships, presumably sent along to assure the natives that they had a navy too.

The course was a flattened triangle with a northerly marker on the mole of the Porto di Lido channel, a westerly one on the northern side of the entrance to the

A Macchi M.52 being attended to as it rests on a lighter. The upper surface of the inner wing is covered with a mattress to protect the cooling elements.

Malamocco channel into the lagoon, and a southerly one on a lighter anchored just to the south of the Porto di Chioggia and positioned to give lap distance of 50 km. In the event of bad weather a similar course was available in the lagoon. The starting line was an imaginary one projected from a timing hut erected on the private beach in front of the Excelsior Hotel.

For the first time in the history of the race the machines were allowed to go off to a flying start, mainly, one feels, because the direction of the race on this first leg was southerly and the prevailing winds in the northern Adriatic are northerly at that time of the year. It would have been asking too much of them to take off downwind, indeed they would have been unlikely to get airborne in those conditions. Each machine would be required to fly seven laps, a total distance of 350 km. To keep the crowd in touch with the progress of the race a huge scoreboard was erected on the beach, backed up by a loudspeaker system.

The only thing the organisers could not arrange was the weather. It had been moderately kind for the navigability trials but during the seaworthiness test, when the brightly painted machines were moored in the Tre Porti channel, a line-squall had come through, showering the machines with walnut-sized hailstones, and there were fears that the lightly skinned wing radiators might be damaged. Fortunately, all was well but the squall was the harbinger of a weather front which, although it did not prevent Webster from rerunning his navigability test on the Saturday morning, effectively prevented racing on the Sunday.

While the machines sat quietly in their hangars at San Andrea the British crews relaxed over a bottle, confident that the foul weather would ground them for at least another day. Unsure of the performance of the Macchis, they had already settled their plan of campaign, which was to fly at full throttle throughout, secure in the knowledge that the engines had been developed to do just this.

In the Italian camp things were not so relaxed. The Fiat AS.5 engines were still giving trouble on ground runs and in the air. Zerbi had rushed from Turin with yet another batch of magnesium pistons. They would have to be fitted with the engines still sealed in the airframes as was permitted by the regulations. With the AS.3 units in considerable doubt it had been decided that Guazzetti's machine should be fitted with the AS.2 engine from de Bernardi's 1926 winning machine. Like Worsley's direct-drive S.5, this would be the Italians' safety racer.

On Monday the wind had dropped and despite a heavy, overcast sky, it looked as if it would be possible to race. The organisers, mindful of the tens of thousands of people crowded into Venice and the surrounding countryside for the race, and very conscious of the dignitaries who had come to witness an Italian victory, announced that the race would go on that afternoon and ordered the machines to be in the take-off area in the Tre Porti channel by 1.40 pm. The British machines were towed over from San Andrea, the Macchis came on their special

lighters towed by tugs showering their precious charges with smuts.

On the Excelsior Hotel beach the officials and Party people all had their allotted places in a new tribune. And for the whole length of the beach the Italian crowd stood in a black mass, like flies, some of them even wading in the water. One can imagine the Italian excitement. For the first time they were to see *their* Macchis in action, racing at speeds twice that of the latest fighters and piloted by men who had, in the eyes of mere mortals, the same standing as our astronauts today. They wanted to see these heroes confirm the Italian world supremacy in speed aviation that the red machines had demonstrated at Hampton Roads.

In typical fashion the RAF had made their own timing arrangements. In addition to the Royal Aero Club timekeepers in the timing hut on the beach, a party from the Air Ministry had set themselves up on the roof of the Excelsior, where they could see the whole course. They had already observed that the view from the official timing box was limited and gave insufficient advance warning of the arrival of such fast machines and moreover, in the course of calibrating the air speed indicators (ASI) of the British machines, they had discovered the shortcomings of stopwatches for this kind of work. They had brought along with them a chronoscope which allowed the timekeeper to see the watch and a collimated line at the same time. The party was joined on the roof by the Crown Prince and his party and Rodwell Banks, among others.

Off the Lido, Venice: Kinkead in the biplane Gloster IV with Webster's S.5 overhead. (*Flight*)

The competing aircraft were given five minutes to start their engines, ten minutes to warm them up and get airborne from the take-off area in the Tre Porti channel, and a further five minutes to make a circuit and cross the line in the direction of the course.

'Kink' Kinkead in the Gloster IVB, N.223, had been allocated race number 1 and was the first to go, taking off at precisely 2.03 pm into wind and sweeping back to cross the start line and head for the Malamocco marker. On this first lap he flew at the planned altitude of 300 ft but, because of the poor visibility from the Gloster's cockpit, obscured as it was by the upper wings, he ran wide at the turn and, on the long, 25 km northerly leg, deviated out to sea before making the planned flat turn round the Tre Porti marker. Realising his problem he dived down to only a few feet from the sea for his next lap. Nevertheless, his speed for this first round was 20 mph up on de Bernardi's winning speed in 1926.

Four minutes after Kinkead had made his start de Bernardi lifted the Macchi M.52 off, banked wide round the Lido marker and swept past the Excelsior Hotel to commence his first lap, flying well above the Gloster's line. The blood-red Macchi was trailing a bigger than usual smoke trail – the Fiat engines were run rich and oily to keep the pistons cool – but it was running evenly and nobody attached too much significance to the smoke. Seven minutes later he was back again, making the Italian climbing-and-diving turn round the Lido marker. The time, 7 min 1 sec was announced and there were long faces among the Italians. The speed was less than Kinkead's first lap. But the Air Ministry team on the roof thought differently. Their chronoscope had shown a time of 6 min 48.1 sec, equal to 275.8 mph, 12 mph faster than the Italian timing. By the time they had worked all this out, Webster had taken off in N.220 – he started his run at 2.41 pm – as de Bernardi was halfway along the seaward leg. As de Bernardi made his climbing-and-diving turn round the mark Webster was only a couple of hundred yards behind him. It was a rare opportunity to compare the relative performance of the rival machines. It was plain to see that Webster would overtake the Macchi before the Chioggia turn. But the promised battle did not develop. As he approached the Porto Malamocco, de Bernardi's engine spouted smoke from a broken piston and he dropped the Macchi gently on the sea, where it rolled on the swell waiting for a rescue boat.

Webster's time for his first lap, 6 min 38.7 sec cannot have overjoyed the crowd. But there again, the Air Ministry rooftop party, with much better visibility, and better equipment, gave Webster 6 min 48.1 sec, which was slower than the Italian machine's time. Down in the official timing box, the Royal Aero Club of Italy's timekeepers had roughly the same time. So both nationalities were wearing long faces because both thought each other's machine was faster. It didn't last long.

Meanwhile, the remaining machines had got airborne one at a time. Guazzetti's 'safety' racer had followed five minutes after Webster but his first lap at 252.1 mph, though proving that the M.52 airframe was faster than the M.39 with the same engine, was 20 mph slower than Kinkead's Gloster IVB, which was steadily lapping at better than 270 mph, still flying only a few feet above the sea.

With so many machines in the air there were inevitably opportunities to compare their performance. The NPL scientists had done their first mathematical study of cornering techniques and established that the quickest way to take the turns was in a fairly tight level bank. The Italians had instinctively worked out their method, which was to climb into the turn and dive out of it to gain speed for the ensuing straight. The idea was to 'put the brakes on', slowing the machine into the turn with the climb and to use the dive to accelerate out of it.

The Italian safety racer was off ten minutes before Worsley in N.219, the British 'safety' machine, which was airborne at 2.50 pm. Worsley, in the direct-drive S.5, came round the Lido turn and past the Excelsior like a train, flying a level and precise course in 6 min 55.1 sec (269.5 mph). He was too late to see Ferrarin in Macchi no. 7 cross the line and get only as far as Malamocco before turning back over the lagoon with the engine belching smoke and flame. He could not make the base and had to put down in the channel where he waited patiently for a tow. It was a sad result for the Italians. Their two fastest machines were out and it was clear from the times that were coming through that Guazzetti's Macchi was no match for either the Supermarines or the Glosters. Ferrarin's drama had hardly played itself out when the British, watching their three machines moving like darts over the sea and praying for a one, two, three victory, were dismayed to see Kinkead, on his sixth lap, go straight on at the Lido marker and put the Gloster down in the Tre Porti channel. For his last two circuits there had been an engine vibration which got progressively worse until it reached the stage when it was only good airmanship to land. The cause of the vibration was a light-alloy closing-plate on the spinner that had carried away and wrapped itself round the root of the propeller blade.

While it had been racing the Gloster had confirmed its designer's faith in the biplane. It had lapped consistently at around 275 mph, which was only five miles per hour slower than Webster's S.5 and faster than Worsley who was, however, holding power in reserve. At one stage of the race, Webster's S.5 and the Gloster had come round the Lido turn together, the one flying high and the other flying low, and the Gloster had actually pulled away from the Supermarine. Maybe 'Kink', who had an unrivalled view upwards at least, had seen his team-mate and pushed his throttle even further against the stop. The sight of these two beautiful machines, the blue and silver S.5 and the blue and gold Gloster streaking along at nigh on 300 mph must have given the crowd value for money.

There was another thrill for them when Guazzetti, on his fourth lap, was overhauled by Webster at the acute Lido turn. As he made his climbing-and-diving turn the Supermarine, making the faster British level turn, passed right under him and came out ahead.

Maybe the Britisher put him off his line, because he came out of the turn wide and, instead of passing in front of the Excelsior, passed behind it, nearly knocking the Crown Prince's hat off in the manoeuvre. It was said at the time that he was blinded by petrol spray – one wonders where from – but the Air Ministry observers were convinced that he had stalled in the turn. On the next lap he did the same thing again, without any help from Webster, who was far in front of him, so maybe the Air Ministry people were right.

Poor Guazzetti – he was bearing the whole burden of his country's honour. Flying cautiously, apart from the aforementioned incidents, and conserving his engine, he had completed six laps and had just passed the tribune on his penultimate lap when his engine started to blow out smoke and he had to alight on the water right in front of the crowd. By the time this drama had been enacted, Webster had completed his seven laps and, unsure of his lap counting, had done one more to be sure. He landed with seven gallons of fuel left in his tank, having flown a wonderfully consistent race at an average speed of 281.65 mph (453.2 km/h). It was 35 mph faster than de Bernardi's race-winning speed at Hampton Roads and apart from being a new race record, the timing by FAI timekeepers enabled him to claim a new World Speed record for 100 km over a closed circuit. His race speed of 453.2 km/h was also fractionally more than the World Speed Record which Bonnet had established in the Bernard V.4 landplane on 11 December 1924.

Webster's ride had not been without worries. No pilot likes flying with the oil temperature needle up against the stop and the oil pressure gauge disconnected. That was the measure of the oil heating problems of

Flight Lieutenant S.N. Webster wins the 1927 event in Supermarine S.5 No. N.220. (*Flight*)

the Lion VII. More tangible was a tendency for the engine cowlings to lift due to pressure build-up from the cooling holes cut in the leading edge of the cowlings to help control that selfsame oil heating problem. He had flown the race at engine revs of 3,300 rpm, at which speed it was giving 899 bhp on the test-bed. When the cowling started to lift he eased the throttle but lap times did not suffer! Worsley used less engine speed, keeping this down to 3,000 rpm, equivalent to 826 bhp. The oil temperature did not rise above 83 degrees.

Kinkead was lucky to have landed when he did. The out-of-balance loads from the spinner had acted like a fatigue-tester and the propeller shaft was fractured two-thirds of the way through when the engine was stripped.

One of the three Macchi M.52s which competed at Venice in 1927. (*Flight*)

Although he was using 200 rpm less than Webster he reported seeing an ASI reading of 300 mph on the long straight.

For Fiat, the race was a disaster. Apart from proving that you cannot run magnesium pistons in steel cylinders, it was also the beginning of the end of the water-cooled in-line engine in Italian military aviation. Castoldi, predictably, was by turns furious and tearful. Just what the Party had to say to Senator Agnelli has to be left to the imagination. Castoldi's frustration was understandable. Whatever horsepower the engine in de Bernardi's machine was giving, it was enough to make the M.52 a match for the S.5 and it could have been a close-fought contest. Just to show what could be done with a good engine de Bernardi went out with an M.52 on 4 November and, over a 3 km course, established a new absolute speed record of 479.29 km/h (297.8 mph). Following this up, a special clipped wing M.52, the M.52R, was built to boost the record even higher and on 30 March 1928 de Bernardi took it out and established a new absolute record of 512.776 km/h (318.63 mph). It confirmed the worth of the airframe and to a certain extent vindicated Fiat, who were at least able to prove that they could produce a sprint engine. And they had the satisfaction of having built the first engine to travel at over 300 mph officially.

Fiat were lucky with their over-300 mph achievement. The High Speed Flight detachment at Calshot had been deactivated after the Venice race but reformed early in 1928 specifically for an attack on the World Airspeed Record. Kinkead had been assigned to fly the machine S.5, N.221, which had been held back from the 1927 race, presumably with a record attempt in mind. It was prepared with a boosted Lion VIIB to be the first machine to officially exceed the magic 300 mph. A measured course had been set out in the Solent off Calshot and with the FAI timekeepers installed, 'Kink' took off on the afternoon of 12 March 1928 to go for the record. Conditions were not good. A calm sea and light haze were creating what airmen call the 'milk-bowl' effect. With no horizon to help him, poor Kinkead misjudged his pull-up from the entry dive into the measured distance, hit the sea at more than 300 mph and was killed instantly.

So the honours went to Italy and were some consolation for the Venice débâcle. Flight Lieutenant D'Arcy Greig stepped into Kinkead's place but it took the whole of the year to prepare N.220, Webster's Venice machine, for a further attempt. The extent to which it was cleaned up was shown in landing speed tests in October, when speeds of 95.5 mph, and 91.5 mph at 11.6 deg incidence were reported. In the attempt on 4 November at 2.15 pm Greig's mean speed was 318.57 mph (512.7 km/h), which was enough to establish a new British record but insufficiently in excess of de Bernardi's speed to be a World Speed figure.

After the 1927 race, for the British pilots there was the fêting and hero-worship that Trenchard had dreaded. Sir Philip Sassoon, the British Under-Secretary for Air, who had flown over to see the race in a Fairey IIIF,

took the pilots off to an ambassadorial function. Webster managed to escape. When he was asked what on earth he was up to, Webster solemnly replied, 'I'm just buying Kink a drink'.

At a reception given by the Provincial Fascist Federation they presented Webster with a gold plaque, and Worsley, the only other finisher, with a silver one. In addition there was a gold ring in the shape of an eagle, set with rubies for the winner, and medals for all the other entrants. Finally there was the homecoming to Croydon aboard an Imperial Airways Armstrong Whitworth Argosy escorted by six Gloster Grebes and a DH.50, to a tumultuous public welcome.

The Aircraft

The Short-Bristow Crusader

Colonel Bristow had been one of the four members of the very influential aviation consultants, Ogilvy and Partners, on whose behalf he had revived the Handley Page air transport operation. On the dissolution of the Ogilvy partnership he had set up shop in Grosvenor Place as a fuel expert with his own research laboratory; he also provided a technical and design service to Sumet Metals. He was the catalyst in the Crusader project. Short Brothers were very quickly called in to undertake construction of the machine while the designer was to be W.G. Carter, who late in 1925 quit his post as chief designer to the Hawker Aircraft Company and was immediately seized upon by Fedden to handle the design side. The fact that Carter was not even allowed a short holiday before starting work on what was to become the Crusader dates the project as beginning early in December 1925.

The whole Bristol/Bristow/Short episode was not lacking in supporters. The operation was especially dear to Fedden, whose object was to produce a radial successor to the Napier Lion for the RAF. He felt that the only way to prove the point was to race it against Lion-powered machines, but the Bristol directors refused point-blank to fall in with the scheme, although they were happy enough to finance engine development. The Air Ministry, too, had an axe to grind, for they were interested to assess the high-speed possibilities of a radial engine installed in an airframe of approximately equal drag to that of the Supermarine. On their part Short's were very happy to take on the project as a means of getting in on the act for, as seaplane specialists, they did not take too kindly to the monopoly that their arch-rivals, Supermarine, were establishing in this field.

In brief Colonel Bristow was the entrant, the Air Ministry contract was let out to him and Carter nominally worked for him. Carter, not Bristow, conceived the original layout and the bills for the airframe and engine were footed by Short's and the Bristol Aeroplane Company respectively. By tradition the machine is usually referred to as the Short-Bristow Crusader; the type-name is said to have been derived from the helmet-shaped cylinder cowlings although it could equally well apply to the main object of the exercise.

Short-Bristow Crusader. Bristol Mercury 9-cylinder air-cooled radial engine in contrast to the in-line, liquid-cooled engines of the other competitors.

Specification 7/26, issued in March 1926 was, in effect, the fulfilment of the Air Ministry's promise of a development contract if Colonel Bristow's entry for the 1925 race were withdrawn. As we have said before, the Bristol directors were not convinced that racing was the best way to prove and promote a new engine although Roy Fedden, their brilliant engine designer, was. It was a golden opportunity for Colonel Bristow to prove his independence and foresightedness by offering to design and enter an aircraft powered by Roy Fedden's Mercury concept which, at the time of the entry, was not even in metal. It would be nice to know whether Oswald Short, who as a seaplane manufacturer, was more than a little jealous of the publicity that Supermarine were getting, prodded Bristow into making the entry. It may be that Bristow, having decided to contract the floats out to Short, succumbed to their blandishments and Oswald Short's offer to stand the cost of constructing the machine, and put the whole of the construction into the hands of the Rochester firm.

As it was, W.G. Carter was put in charge of the overall design. Later, when Bristol were appointed constructors, Arthur Gouge and C.P.T. Lipscombe were seconded from Short's to help with the detail design. One feels that their experience with seaplanes must have come as something of a relief to Carter, who was primarily a landplane man.

The design thinking behind the Crusader project was that the lighter weight of the air-cooled Bristol engine compared with a water-cooled unit would result in a reduction of about 12 per cent in the total weight of the aircraft, which alone would be worth 6 mph in maximum speed. Preliminary wind-tunnel tests of Carter's first quarter-scale model, sent to the NPL in late 1925, suggested that this gain would be more than offset by the drag induced by the engine cylinders protruding into an aerodynamically critical area of the fuselage. This disturbance to the airflow gave the fuselage alone the same flat-plate drag area as the complete Supermarine S.5. This model, which had a huge, conical spinner, streamlined fairings behind the cylinders and a Warren-truss float chassis, was hurriedly turned down by the NPL. The number two model which came next ironed out most of the problems and was almost identical to the definitive machine. It featured a smaller, more practical spinner, helmeted cylinders and all-wire bracing to the extent of replacing the float booms with wires.

The wings of this second design were elliptical in planform, like a sycamore seed's, and were hinged to short-stub wings which formed part of a tubular space frame front fuselage. This frame, fabricated from steel tubes had, at its forward end, a circular Duralumin plate to which the engine was mounted. In it were incorporated mountings for the fuel and oil tanks, the flying control assembly and the pilot's seat. It was faired to a circular section with wooded formers and an aluminium skin. A beautifully made, nine-segment cowling was provided to fair-in the engine.

The rear fuselage was all wood and consisted of a double diagonal planked skin on four longerons and wooden bulkheads. The mahogany skin, interleaved with linen and riveted with copper rivets, was a throwback to the old Linton Hope Supermarine hulls. It was enigmatic that Supermarine were at that moment in time busily constructing their S.5 with a monocoque, metalskinned hull, a method of construction which owed almost everything to Oswald Short's pioneering efforts.

The fixed tail surfaces were integral with the rear fuselage and were ply-skinned with a final covering of doped silk. The two-spar wings, which were of conventional construction with spruce and ply box-spars, were similarly ply- and silk-covered back to the rear spar but with fabric covering thereafter. The control surfaces, with the exception of the rudder, were also of wooden construction and ply-covered. The rudder was fabricated from steel sheet and fabric-covered. A metal tail-cone 'finished off' the fuselage streamlining.

Metal was used throughout the float chassis and the floats. The former were steel tubes and the latter riveted Duralumin on longitudinal steel bulkheads. Only the float-strut fairings were wood. A reserve buoyancy of 78 per cent was provided. This was more than that of any of the other British Schneider machines and yet the floats were, aerodynamically, the cleanest and ran with minimum spray on the water.

A notable innovation on this machine was the blown cellulose acetate canopy over the pilot's cockpit. It was way ahead, even, of the metal-framed devices that came ten years later and was only revived in earnest for fighters just in time for World War Two.

The NPL did a great deal of work on the cylinder fairing, discovering, for what it was worth, that removing the valve gear was more effective than any kind of streamlining. No doubt this discovery prompted Fedden's interest in sleeve valves at a later date. Unfortunately the Crusader's Mercury could not function without the valve gear and, although excellent results were obtained with modifications to the cylinder helmets – the Townend ring had yet to be invented – drag figures equivalent to the S.5 and Gloster IV were just not to be had. This, coupled with the fact that the engine was giving less power than the Napier Lion VII, was the reason why the Crusader was taken to Venice as a practice and reserve machine.

See Results section page 244.

Mercury Engine

The Bristol Mercury, around which the Crusader was designed, was the second stage in Roy Fedden's conception of a high-performance radial. His Jupiter had been revolutionary in 1919 and was a most reliable prime mover. But Fedden saw better than most that it was becoming too big and somewhat overweight for its power. He saw the need for a lighter, smaller-diameter

engine producing more power by turning over faster and with supercharging to better the sea-level and altitude performance.

Definitive design of the new Mercury project was initiated in November 1925 and the first engine was assembled and run in August 1926. Like the Jupiter it was a nine-cylinder unit but compared with that engine the stroke was reduced from 5.75 to 6.5 in, thereby reducing the swept volume from 28.7 to 24.9 litres. New cylinder heads were made with four valves in pent roof heads based on a design evolved by the RAE. The advantages were much better cylinder filling, hence higher volumetric efficiency. Also the gap between the valves permitted a free flow of air to dissipate the resultant heat. A centrifugal blower, driven at 7.5 times crankshaft speed, raised the induction pressure to 7.5 psi.

Ricardo at Shoreham ran a series of single-cylinder test heads and finally succeeded in getting 94 bhp per cylinder at 2,500 rpm. Thus encouraged, Fedden was prompted to promise the Air Ministry 800 bhp.

One of the weight-reducing features which was not a success was the use of a drop-forged magnesium crankcase. On test the material proved too soft with a tendency for the studs to pull out. It was replaced with a forged Duralumin casing machine from a Jupiter forging.

The first engine developed 490 bhp. This was quickly extended to 840 bhp at 2,500 rpm, at which output the engine test-bed shafting developed a nasty attack of the whirls and had to be redesigned. Subsequently 940 bhp was seen but never maintained for more than a few minutes because of the spark plug manufacturer's inability to provide durable means of ignition. It was eventually derated to 898 bhp, at which output it could be relied on for 30 minutes using specially developed KLG plugs. The first engine handed over for installation in the Crusader had the following specifications:

Dry Weight 684 lb without propeller hub. 714 lb complete
Bore and Stroke 5.75 × 6.5 in. C.R. 6.25:1
Power 808 bhp (nett) at 2,500 rpm
Boost pressure 7.5 psi

One can understand the British Air Ministry's interest in the Mercury and in sponsoring its installation in a lightweight high-speed airframe. The Mercury had turned out to be the lightest engine for its power anywhere in the world, comfortably exceeding the magic one pound per horsepower which had been the goal of aircraft engine designers since aviation began. This fact was not lost on the Italians either.

Gloster IV 1927

There is no doubt that the performance of the Gloster IIIA in the 1925 Schneider race was considered satisfactory by both the British Air Ministry and the Gloster Aircraft Company, bearing in mind the state of readiness of the machines. They were certainly the starting point for something much better, having provided data on

Gloster IV under tow off the San Andrea air station. (*Flight*)

flying qualities and structural strength. Napier's, the engine builders had also learnt a lot and, urged on by the Ministry, were prepared to promise an extra 150 hp for a new machine.

H.P. Folland and his chief design assistant, H.E. Preston, therefore set about a new design with a clear idea of where they were going. It was logical for them to choose the biplane configuration because not only was it the one they knew but the Ministry looked to them to produce a biplane to compare with the Supermarine monoplane. Fortuitously, Folland was always reluctant to leave a field of endeavour until he had exhausted the possibilities of the one he was working in. And he sincerely believed in the biplane configuration for racing because of the short span for a given wing area and because of the rigidity and structural strength conferred by biplane rigging.

Folland had his team set out to win extra speed three

Gloster IVB at RAF Calshot prior to being shipped out to Venice.

ways. The first was to reduce head resistance, the second was to increase the efficiency of the propeller and the third was to put up the landing speed by 10 mph and thus gain speed at the top end of the range. If the last objective seems to make operation of the machine more perilous one must remember that in those days an aeroplane which landed at 60 mph (100 km/h) was considered a pretty hot ship. Most airliners could land in a small field without danger to the hedgerows. With a seaplane the landing area was almost unlimited and it was quite feasible to raise the landing speed of the Gloster IV by 10 mph without bringing it anywhere near to that of the average executive twin of today. This was worth 4 mph on maximum speed.

Reduction of head resistance was naturally concentrated on the fuselage, floats and wings with help from the engine builders. Napiers' contribution was to reduce the frontal area of their Lion VIII engine to 4.25 ft. Consequently, the frontal area was reduced to 55 per cent of that of the III and was worth a 40 per cent reduction in drag. This alone was good for an extra 37 mph.

Working independently of Fairey, who had taken up a Reed licence, Gloster's designed their own, fully machined, Duralumin propellers with detachable blades on the lines of those fitted to the 1925 Curtiss machines. Types were designed to operate at high tip speeds for the direct-drive Napier Lion VIIA and for lower-speed operation with the later geared VIIB, which was produced as a result of propeller tests after the airframe design had been frozen. The engine design is a separate story but it is worth recording here that although Napier's promised an extra 150 bhp from the VII they actually delivered engines giving an extra 200 bhp!

Over and above the reduction in frontal area, great attention was paid to blending the wings and other main components into the fuselage. This was most apparent in the way the upper mainplane was kinked down and blended into extensions of the side cylinder cowlings, while the lower wing roots were cranked up to make a 90 deg join with the fuelage. This change increased the lift of the 152 sq ft of wing. However, in order to increase the top speed the wing area was reduced to 139 sq ft, thereby reducing drag. At the same time this increased the landing speed, as mentioned, by 10 mph. The smaller wings – the upper wing only was reduced – were fitted to the second and third machines serialled N.222 and N.223. In this wing arrangement Folland and Preston broke away from the Bamel configuration by adopting an I-strutted sesquiplane design with the ailerons in the large-span upper wing and a bottom wing of reduced chord and span. Each wing strut was machined from a pair of Duralumin forgings. Both wings had elliptical tips to match the truly elliptical tailplane and elevator. The whole empennage was cantilevered with hidden mass balance horns and – shades of the III – ample fixed vertical surfaces. The original design called for a conventional tail without ventral surfaces but for the second and third machines, N.222 and N.223, a cruciform tail was designed and built.

In common with the III the floats were mounted on steel tubular struts with wooden fairings. Spreader struts were omitted and replaced by streamlined wires which reduced air drag and water resistance and thereby helped take-off. The Duralumin floats, of Gloster design and construction, were the result of tank and wind-tunnel tests at the National Physical Laboratory. No attempt seems to have been made to carry fuel in the floats, as Mitchell did with the S.5, nor were they offset, or of unequal buoyancy, to offset propeller torque. The main 58 gallon fuel tank was in the fuselage, with a small header in the centre cylinder-block fairing. This fairing, which also housed the water header tank, incidentally, was extended through to the fin with a small break for the cockpit.

Structurally the fuselage, like that of the III, was monocoque built up on ash longerons and planked with two layers of three-inch wide spruce planks laid diagonally. Forward of the wing mountings an extra skin was laid to transmit engine mounting loads. To keep drag to a minimum a thin, RAF 25 wing section was chosen, necessitating multi-spar construction to take the bending loads. Tests showed that much of the load could be taken through the wing skin and this was planked up like the fuselage with the difference that the ply strips were laid at right angles spanwise and chordwise. The surface radiators were slipped on the wings like sleeves and secured by stainless steel bicycle spokes and nipples running through the depth of the wing. The cantilever tailplane and fin were of the same construction as the wing and were completely trouble free.

A specially ingenious feature of the control gear was a patented, variable-ratio rudder mechanism rather like that which Curtiss used in their biplanes. Pilots had complained of oversensitive directional control at high speed on previous Gloster machines – Glosters had flown more high-speed hours than any of their British competitors – caused by the need for a large rudder angle to overcome engine torque at low speed. Folland and his team solved the problem with a differential gear in the control circuit geared 2:1 for small movements of the rudder bar and 1:2 for large movements. It was eventually used in all the British Schneider machines. In 1925 Curtiss, on the R3C had introduced an extra pair of bracing wires joining the lower ends of the front float struts and the leading edge of the wing. This was in addition to the usual diagonal bracing in the wing bays and the float chassis wires. It was a belt-and-braces addition which must have done much to steady the upper wing. On the Gloster IV Folland went one better – this, incidentally, is probably the reason that the lower wing was of reduced chord and without stagger – by bracing the upper wing directly to the lower ends of both pairs of float struts. In conjunction with the float spacer wires this made a four-sided stress path of which the upper wing was the fourth member. To withstand the bending load on the upper wing he then braced the lower ends of the interplane struts to the top of the cabane. So, compared with the Curtiss, he eliminated two pairs of interplane bracing wires and two pairs of wings-to-float wires. He further reduced drag by replacing the float spreader struts with wires.

The resulting engines needed constant attention and were frequently changed. The VIIIA and B had only a three-hour overhaul life. For these reasons Preston designed fabricated Duralumin bearers supported by a triangulated tubular steel structure which gave easy access to the unit once the cowlings were removed. The oil tank was housed beneath this structure with a ventral oil radiator exposed to the airstream. Later in the aircraft's life additional oil coolers were fitted along the fuselage sides. Coolant radiators were located on both mainplanes and on the tops of the floats. They were of corrugated section with the corrugations exposed to the airstream. NPL tests showed that the drag with this type was greater than with the plain type used on the S.5 but, logically, the wing surface requirement was less.

Although N.223 was unsuccessful at Venice the RAF got full value out of all the IVs, using them as research hacks and trainers. After the race all three were shipped back to Felixstowe and stayed there until 21 February 1928, undergoing flight and handling tests. Thereafter they were returned to Gloster's for conversion to trainers for the 1929 race. On N.222 and N.223 a one-piece upper wing faired into the main dorsal fairing replaced the original cranked wing and overcame the pilot visibility problem which had caused Kinkead to miss markers in the race. With the original wing, pilot visibility forward was effectively nil, especially in the critical landing attitude. This modification called for the addition of two pairs of cabane struts and a water header tank above the wing. A further modification, to cure high-speed yaw, made in 1929, was to convert the empennages of N.222 and N.223 from cruciform to the original inverted T-configuration of the original design perpetuated on N.224.

In 1930 Amherst Villiers, the engine designer, bought N.224 with the object of fitting it with a wheeled chassis and going for the World Speed Record held at the time by a Ferbois monoplane at 278.5 mph. Power would have been supplied by a geared Lion VII. The attempt was abandoned. N.223 was written off on 19 December 1930 by Flight Lieutenant John Boothman during a landing in sea fog. But N.222 remained, making 147 flights in the course of training and perfecting 'concerning' techniques. During this time the overhaul life of the Lion was extended to 15 hours. This was the first of the Schneider machines to be rolled and looped by Kinkead.

Napier Lion VIIA

In 1918, at the same time that the Curtiss K-1, forerunner of the classic D-12 was going through the trauma of unsuccessful acceptance trials in the USA, the firm of D. Napier & Co. of Acton in England were successfully testing a broad-arrow, twelve-cylinder engine of 24-litres capacity. Weighing 1,918 lb with a frontal area of 5.68 sq ft and developing 450 bhp, it was accepted by the

Napier Lion VIIA three-bank 12-cylinder engine. Used for Schneider Trophy aircraft in ever increasing power versions from the 450 hp of 1919 to the 875 hp geared VIIB at Calshot in 1929. (*Derek N. James*)

Royal Air Force in 1918 just too late for action in the War. As a comparison the K-12 and its more reliable successors produced about 370 bhp, weighed about 670 lb and had a frontal area of 4.6 sq ft.

The Curtiss D-12 came up against the Napier Lion for the first time in 1923 at Cowes and beat it handsomely, mainly, to be fair, because it was installed in an airframe of some antiquity, design-wise. But whereas the D-12 series was never developed to give much more than 460 bhp, the Napier Lion series VII was developed to produce almost 900 bhp in 1927. At the same time the frontal area had been reduced to 4.25 sq ft, less than that of the Curtiss, and the weight had been reduced to 928 lb, very near to the magic one pound per horsepower figure.

In designing the Lion A.J. Rowledge chose the broad-arrow cylinder configuration because it made for a short, stiff crankcase, relieved him from the bugbear of crankshaft torsional vibrations and made for what was, at the period, a lighter engine. At a time when most engine designers were copying the aluminium-block Hispano-Suiza, Rowledge went his own way and gave the Lion separate steel cylinders with closed tops. Most of the cooling water, the valve gear and induction and exhaust passengers were contained in three light alloy heads, each one spanning a bank of cylinders and effectively tying the tops of them together. A novel and effective expedient was to hold down the alloy heads to the cylinders by threaded valve throats. The valves were operated by six camshafts, two per bank, which were driven by shafts from a distribution gear-box at the back of the engine. This little box, full of gears, also drove the twin magnetos, three oil pumps and the cooling water pump.

At the bottom end of the engine the relatively simple, single-plane crankshaft was supported on six bearings, five of them large-diameter roller-races and the odd one a plain bearing. Following conventional aero-engine practice a master connecting-rod and slave rods were used, the slave rods belonging to the middle bank of cylinders.

The first engine built in 1918 had a 44:29 reduction gear to allow the engine to run at 2,000 rpm while not taxing the rather limited efficiency of the propellers of the period. Power output at this engine speed was 450 bhp on a compression ratio of 5.55:1 which, at that time, was considered daringly high for an aircraft engine.

The history of the Lion is one of continual development. For service use it worked through five marks between 1918 and 1925. The engine that powered the winning Sea Lion II in 1922 was a tuned version of the service engine supplied by Napier's. Before the 1925 race the high-compression, cleaned-up, Lion VII was specially produced for the Gloster III and the Supermarine S.4. This was a direct-drive unit to save weight and some attempt was made to declutter the cleavages between the cylinders. As installed in the Gloster III it developed 700 bhp.

Captain George Wilkinson had taken over from A.J. Rowledge in 1922 when Rowledge was enticed away by Rolls-Royce. George Pate, Technical Director,

Wilkinson and their experimental engineer H.C. Tryon had been responsible for the development of the Lion. For 1927 they were called upon to excel themselves and to produce 170 more horsepower than they had extracted from the Lion VII and at the same time cut down the frontal area of the engine to less than that of the Curtiss D-12. What resulted was almost a complete redesign.

To minimise the frontal area the height of the cylinder blocks had to be reduced. To achieve this Wilkinson and Pate reduced the length of the connecting rods by one inch, designed shallower pistons, measured from the gudgeon pin boss to crown, and, a master stroke, increased the compression ratio to 10:1 which allowed him to use a considerably shorter cylinder over and above the alterations to the connecting rods and pistons. At the same time that they increased the compression ratio the design team were not at all sure that they would be able to get the engine to run at this figure!

The next thing was to remove the magnetos from the back end of the engine and to tuck them alongside the crankcase nose extension in line with the side cylinder blocks. This left room at the back of the engine to house three carburettors, one for each bank of cylinders. These two changes left the cleavages between the cylinders completely uncluttered. To make the engine even more compact especially short sparking plugs were designed by the plug manufacturers.

Finally, with the object of making the aircraft nose cowling skin tight, provision was made for fitting the nose cowling directly to the engine and special valve covers were fabricated, one type for Supermarine and the other type for Gloster's which followed the nose contour and therefore needed no separate cowling.

Initial running of the engine revealed the tendency to burn holes in the pistons and plug life was short, but active. To help them with this Tryon called in F.R. Banks, then Chief Engineer for Peter Hooker Ltd, the British licensees of Gnome Engines, to help solve the problem. Rodwell Banks helped them concoct a fuel which consisted of 25% benzole, 74.78% petrol and 0.22% lead tetraethyl. On this brew the winning engine developed 898 bhp at 3,300 rpm with a specific fuel consumption of 0.452 pints/bhp/hour. At the more modest speed of 2,000 rpm the specific consumption was 0.31 lb/bhp/hour, a remarkable figure which took many years to better.

Halfway through development it was decided that a reduction gear would not only help the engine to produce more power but would allow a more efficient propeller to be designed. Since the airframes had been designed and, in any case engines had to be interchangeable, a two-step gear was designed with a layshaft and two sets of gears to bring the shaft centreline back to that of the direct-drive engine. Reduction gearing was 0.765:1.

The ultimate development was the VIID, a supercharged version of the VIIB, which was coaxed into developing 1,320 bhp. In this form it was intended for the Gloster V and ultimately installed in the Gloster VI when it proved not only unreliable but overweight.

The former shortcoming caused the Gloster VI to be withdrawn from the Schneider team.

Supermarine S.5

On 19 March 1926 the British Air Ministry, the Society of British Aircraft Constructors and the Royal Aero Club got together to discuss whether to offer a challenge that year, and decided against it. At the same meeting Colonel Bristow and Sammy Saunders were persuaded not to go ahead with their private entries. Almost immediately specifications for the Gloster IV and the Supermarine S.5 were issued, not to mention one for the radial-engined Bristow-Fedden machine. The one issued to Supermarine called for a high-speed seaplane powered by a Napier Lion VIIA engine which had yet to be developed. The main requirements were high speed at low altitudes and controllability at those speeds. The machine was to be seaworthy on the water in any weather in which it was expected to fly and must carry fuel and oil for 1¼ hours at full throttle plus a 50% excess of oil. The duration was later reduced to one hour.

Contract performance was to be a maximum speed of at least 265 mph and a deadstick touch-down speed of 90 mph. Crew weight was given at 180 lb plus 20 lb of instruments which were to comprise air speed indicator, rev counter, oil pressure gauge and radiator and oil thermometers. In the best Ministry language it was laid down that the pilot should have as good a view as possible for alighting and that he should be adequately screened from the wind.

Foreshadowing a very fruitful relationship between Supermarine and the National Physical Laboratory, the contractor was required to provide a quarter-scale model of the complete aircraft and to have the float form thoroughly checked in the tank before construction could proceed.

R.J. Mitchell, Supermarine's technical director at the time, confirmed that Supermarine intended to have machines ready for the 1926 race. The Air Ministry decision not to race in 1926 took the heat off and he was able to devote the whole of that summer to working out a series of projects for testing at the NPL. In any case he would not have been able to make a precise design until the Napier Lion VIIA engine was ready at the end of the year. For the record Mitchell did consider the biplane configuration but dismissed it because of its greater drag. His experience with the S.4 cantilever monoplane convinced him that a brace-wing would give him a lighter machine which could therefore be made smaller and thereby make up for the extra drag of the wing bracing.

Mitchell's co-operation with the NPL started in November 1926. Supermarine sent down the three alternative configurations for testing in the Duplex

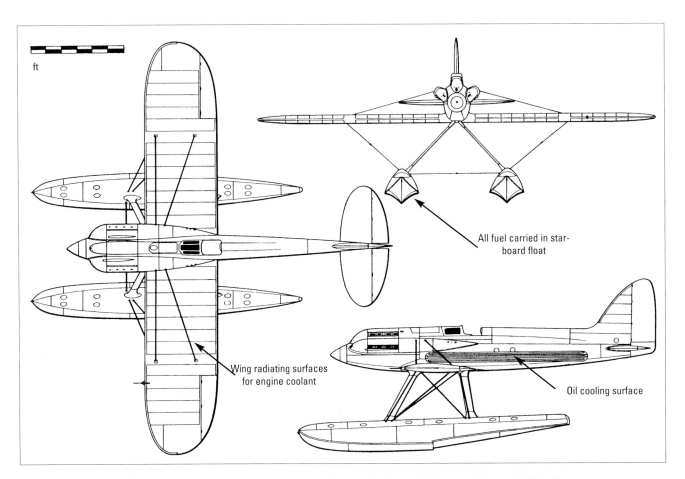

ft

All fuel carried in starboard float

Wing radiating surfaces for engine coolant

Oil cooling surface

Supermarine S.5 (1927): Wing Span: 26 ft 9 in (8.15 m). Length Overall: 24 ft 3 in (7.40 m). Wing Area: 115 sq. ft (10.68 m²).
Weight Empty: 2,680 lb (1,216 kg). T-O Weight: 3,242 lb (1,471 kg). Max Wing Loading: 28.19 lb/sq. ft (137.64 kg/m²).
Napier-Lion VIIA 12-cylinder, W-configuration engine of 900 hp.

Tunnel. One was a shoulder-wing machine with the wing roots cranked down to fair in the side cylinder fairings. The thin wing was braced to the roots of the float struts by streamlined struts – wire bracing was ruled out because of adverse bracing wire angles – and more struts were used to maintain the float track. The second model was a low-wing design with the wing braced to the float chassis by solid streamlined struts. The third design was all-wire-braced, including tension wires between the floats.

Wind-tunnel tests quickly established that the wire-braced machine was the one to go for. As an example of the thoroughness with which the NPL undertook this work, they also ran wind-tunnel tests for two different kinds of solid streamlined strut, and were able to establish that a solid one caused less drag than an identical unit fabricated from plywood. They also experimented with a new fish-section bracing wire which it was thought would give less drag than the old lenticular-section, RAF wire. The lenticular wire proved better with less drag and less tendency to vibrate, and was adopted. The same kind of attention was given to the floats with the objective of obtaining the best combination of water performance and drag. No less than eleven water tank tests were run in addition to wind-tunnel tests to establish the difference between flush riveting and snap heads. There were also wind-tunnel tests to establish the effect on handling if one float were bigger than the other and set further from the centreline. Mitchell had already decided that a smaller, lighter machine with an engine which was expected to give 170 more horsepower would suffer badly from torque effect during the initial stages of take-off, and had decided to put all the fuel in the starboard float to offset this.

Mitchell had been well aware that the Lamblin radiators fitted on the S.4 had created a lot of unnecessary drag. He did not know until the NPL tested a model of the S.4, much later, that those radiators accounted for one third of the total drag of the machine and that without them the S.4 was probably the cleanest monoplane in the world. Skin radiators were essential to the success of the new S.5 but he was not certain that the American corrugated type was best. He caused the NPL to make comparative tests between radiators with a flat outer surface and the corrugations inside the wing against the Curtiss type. His assumption was right; the smooth type gave less drag and was therefore fitted to the S.5.

Only one project was put out to contract. This was an investigation into the relative drag of different wing positions relative to the fuselage. They were carried out by Göttingen Aerodynamic Research Laboratory in Germany. The findings were that a shoulder or mid-wing layer configuration gave the lowest drag with the low-wing somewhat inferior. However, the low-wing position was chosen because it gave better pilot visibility and more favourable bracing wire angles.

In the final design the cross-sectional area of the S.5 fuselage, compared with that of the S.4, was reduced by 35%, mainly by Napier reducing the frontal area of their engine from 5.55 sq ft to 4.25 sq ft and partly by Supermarine making the cockpit fit tightly round a small pilot. Duralumin construction of the fuselage was chosen because it gave the thinnest possible skin. The change to wire bracing also reduced the structure weight from 46% to 35% of the total weight compared with the S.4. The High Speed Flight pilots journeyed to the works at Southampton to be fitted to the cockpit and Mitchell grumbled because the Air Ministry were unable to provide small pilots all of the same size.

Structurally, the machine was simple by today's standards. The metal semi-monocoque fuselage was not new. Oswald Short had been doing it for years but no-one had previously considered using it for what were then ultra-high-speed aircraft. It was based on four main longitudinal members, two of them being extensions of the engine bearers, the other being at cockpit coaming level. The transverse frames were spaced at six-inch intervals and the skin plates varied in thickness from 16 SWG at the wing roots to 24 SWG at the fin, which was a built-in unit with the fuselage and called for advanced riveting techniques in those days before the advent of explosive rivets. There were no separate engine bearers, the engine being supported in a boat-shaped extension of the front fuselage which looked rather like a prognathous jaw. Neither was there anything unorthodox about the mainplanes, which were of constant chord with double-elliptical tips and of conventional two-spar construction. The main spars were box-section, built up with spruce flanges and plywood webs with ribs fabricated from the same materials. They were covered with stressed plywood followed by doped fabric. The wing radiators were made up into detachable panels 85 inches wide and fabricated from 30 SWG copper sheet. They were corrugated on their inner surface and semicircular channels sweated to the leading and trailing edges were provided to feed the cooling water in and out. The radiators covered the whole of the wing surface apart from the tips.

The tailplane and the elevator, which were of a beautiful elliptical planform were, like the wings, of wooden construction. So was the rudder. The tailplane spars were built into the fuselage. Longitudinal steel bulkheads formed the basis for the all-metal floats. The transverse frames were attached to these at 18-inch intervals and the skinning was mainly light alloy except for the middle section of the starboard float which formed the petrol tank and caused this float to be longer than the port one. This was built up from tinned steel plate. The float struts were tubular with wooden fairings and, unusually, fitted into sleeves built into the floats.

Throughout the construction of the machine all bracing wire ends and the brackets to which they were attached were located inside the skin to get them out of the airstream.

Fuel from the float tank was pumped to a small header tank located in one of the side cylinder fairings. When the S.5 and the Gloster IV were flown it was quickly found that the Lion VII engine tended to boil its oil. Oil coolers had already been provided along the sides of the fuselage. These were extended to eleven feet long and seven inches wide but oil cooling was still marginal. Oil was pumped from the engine to one of the coolers into the oil tank and then back through the other cooler to the engine. Mitchell summarised the gains as follows: The wing radiators were worth 30 mph and the wire bracing, by permitting him to build a smaller, lighter machine, was worth 5 mph, 11 mph for the smaller fuselage and 5 mph for the reduction in float size which the light weight permitted. Incidentally, by carrying all the fuel in the starboard float he had been able to reduce the buoyancy reserve and therefore the drag of the floats. Finally the more powerful engine was worth another 30 mph.

Three machines were built according to the contract and given serial numbers N.219, N.220 and N221; the last was held in reserve. It was not test-flown at Calshot prior to the 1927 race and, although it was presumably taken to Venice aboard HMS *Eagle*, it was neither erected nor flown, being held in reserve, should disaster overtake any of the other machines. Eventually it was specially prepared for Kinkead's attempt on the World Speed Record which ended so tragically with its destruction and the death of the pilot.

Macchi 52

Winning the 1926 Schneider race put the Italians at a disadvantage. They had lobbied for an annual race at a time when it was becoming obvious to one and all that the type of machine which would win the race, with a maximum speed twice that of current fighters, needed two years to design, construct and develop. The British seem to have been the first country to appreciate this fact. When it came to 1927 the Italian defenders, who were not entirely unaware of the strength of the British challenge, found themselves with a bare 10 months, less in fact, to prepare a new machine. Obviously they had to build on what they already had.

Nevertheless the M.52, the type number was the next multiple of 13 after M.39 and perpetuated Castoldi's lucky number, was an entirely new machine. Immediately after the race at Hampton Roads, Fiat had intimated that they could boost the AS.2 to 1,000 hp and at the same time reduce the weight. With this kind of power Castoldi could set his sights on a 300 mph maximum speed.

The resulting machine differed very little in appearance from the M.39 although practically every dimension was different and most of them reduced. The

Macchi M.52. A special clipped wing version established an absolute speed record of 319 mph (512.8 km/h) on 30 March 1928.

construction was the same, being mainly of wood, making the most of the superb craftsmen in this material who inhabit the Varese area. The fuselage was once again a wooden monocoque with double-diagonal planking superimposed on multiple longerons. It was slightly longer than that of the M.39 with enlarged vertical surfaces to improve weathercock stability. In combination with larger tail surfaces and a lighter engine, not to mention shorter floats, these changes moved the CG aft, necessitating a slight sweepback of the wings. This was the main distinguishing feature.

The wings were of constant chord with semi-circular wingtips in contrast to the elliptical form favoured by the British. Again these were of wooden construction based on the conventional two-spar system. They were beautifully finished with highly rubbed red paint and French-polished wingtips. The tail surfaces were also all wood but were not built as part of the fuselage, the fin and tail plane being slotted over steel tube stubs built into the rear fuselage.

The only change to the flotation gear was to slightly reduce the volume of the floats and thus save drag at the expense of buoyancy reserve, which was reduced from 70 per cent to 43 per cent. British observers commented that the machine had a tendency to capsize backwards unless the engine was kept running. They also remarked that the floats ran very cleanly with a minimum of spray despite the retention of rigid float spreaders. Wing bracing was the same as on the M.39 with the landing wires picking up with a strongpoint on the top of the engine bulkhead and the lift wires running down to the roots of the float struts. Obviously there had been problems with bracing-wire vibration because steadies were fitted between the lift and landing wires.

Practically the whole wing was covered with radiators. The outer sections looked after engine cooling while the inner sections cooled the engine oil. The oil tank located underneath the engine was also heavily ribbed and exposed to the slip stream for further cooling like that of the Gloster IV.

It is noticeable on the M.39 and the M.52 that Castoldi did not take advantage of the pains taken by Fiat to reduce the frontal area of the engine, preferring to produce a better streamline form by making the fuselage a teardrop shape. Dr Ermanno Bazocchi gives the cross sectional area of the M.52 as 0.625 sq m compared with 0.481 for the Supermarine S.5. The colour scheme for the Italian machines was Italian racing red with the underside of the floats painted white. The Fascist emblem was carried on both sides of the machine forward of the cockpit.

After the débâcle at Venice de Bernardi went out with the quickest M.52, which was highly polished and had slightly flattened corrugations on the radiators,

Fiat AS.2 12-cylinder V engine of a Macchi M.52.

and recorded a maximum speed of 297.83 mph (479.29 km/h) which can be regarded as the maximum speed of an M.52 and confirms Castoldi's theoretical calculations.

Spurred on by this performance and with the object of getting back some past glory, a clipped wing version of the M.52, designated M.52R was built to take the World Air Speed Record past the 300 mph mark. On 30 March 1928 de Bernardi, at Venice, achieved this and a new absolute speed record with a speed of 318.57 mph (512.69 km/h) over a measured 3 km. After Kinkead's tragic attempt D'Arcy Greig slightly bettered this speed in the S.5 but not sufficiently to establish a new world record.

The M.67 – the digits add up to 13 – was structurally the same as the M.39 and M.52 with the difference that it was flown with a higher wing loading and a thicker wing, 13 per cent instead of 10 per cent of chord on the earlier machines. The tops of the floats were covered with radiators to cool the W-18 Isotta-Fraschini Asso 2-800 engine.

The aft end of a Fiat V-12 engine showing the carburettors mounted between the cylinder banks and the two magnetos for the 24 spark plugs. (*Fiat*)

Aircraft type & data Macchi	M.52		M.52R		M.67	
Overall length	7.13 m	23 ft 5 in	7.12 m	23 ft 4 in	7.15 m	23 ft 6 in
Span	8.54 m	28 ft	7.85 m	25 ft 9 in	8.98 m	29 ft 5½ in
Chord Mean	1.67 m	5 ft 6 in	1.67 m	5 ft 6 in	2.33 m	7 ft 7½ in
Wing area	13.3 m	143.2 sq ft	10.2 m	109.8 sq ft	13.3 m	143.2 sq ft
All-up weight	1515 kg	3333 lb	1480 kg	3256 lb	2180 kg	4796 lb
Dry Weight	1190 kg	2618 lb	1170 kg	2574 lb	1765 kg	3883 lb
Engine	FIAT AS.3		1000 hp		Isotta-Fraschini ASSO 2-800 1400 hp	
Propeller	Curtiss Reed	2.308 m dia × 3.415 m pitch (7.57 ft × 11.2 ft) 3-blade				
Power loading	0.66 kg/m²	1.451 lb/hp	0.68 kg/hp	1.501 lb/hp	1.56 kg/hp	3.431 lb/hp
Wing loading	1.08 kg/m²	23.3 lb/sq ft	1.36 kg/m²	29.71 lb/sq ft	1.63 kg/m²	33 lb/sq ft
Power/surface ratio	71.5 hp/m²	7.6 hp/sq ft	91.5 hp/m²	8.5 hp/sq ft	105 hp/m²	112 hp/sq ft
Floats						
Length	5.5 m	18 ft	5.5 m	18 ft	5.5 m	18 ft
Step from bow	2.2 m	7 ft 2½ in	2.2 m	7 ft 2½ in	1.76 m	5 ft 9 in
Buoyancy reserve	43%		45%		33%	

Calshot 1929

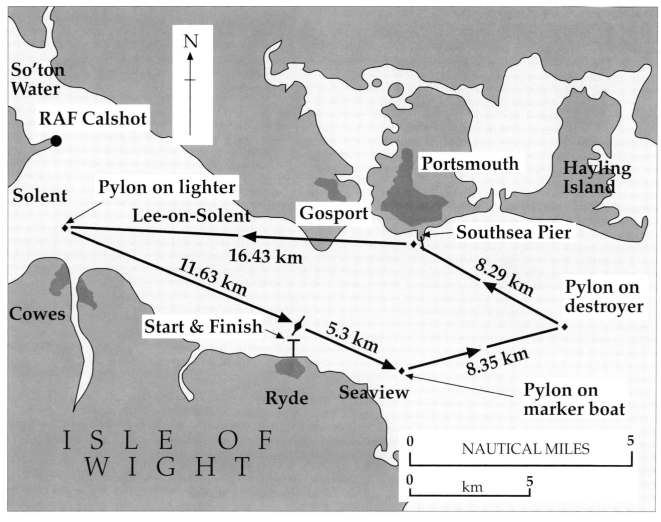

Schneider Trophy Contest Course: Calshot 1929.

Run-up

No sooner had the 1927 race been won than, inevitably, politicking began prior to the next one which, so far as everyone was concerned, would take place in 1928. Decisions had to be made quickly because any changes in the regulations would have to be made at the annual FAI meeting in Paris scheduled for January 1928 which would make the rules for the race later in the year.

Italy was naturally keen to avenge her defeat, of that there was no doubt. But she needed breathing space to build new machines and train fresh pilots. With machines nudging up to the frontiers of current technology and becoming very complicated a two-year gestation period was essential for any country, although General Italo Balbo, on one of his frequent visits to England, did not quite put it that way when, in a talk

with Sir Samuel Hoare, the British Air Minister, the subject of the Schneider Trophy races came up. He mooted the idea of a biennial race but he would have liked the British to propose it. Eventually it was agreed that Italy would make a proposal at the forthcoming meeting in Paris. There the idea was approved, apparently with little dissension, that the race should be held every two years and that any country winning the cup three times in five years would hold it in perpetuity.

There was no doubt that both the British and the Italians breathed a big sigh of relief and gratitude for the gestation period this decision gained for them. A further benefit was that it gave the French an opportunity to think about making an entry and possibly build some aircraft for a race in 1929. Lieutenant Alford Williams, over in America, must have felt much the same way because it gave him a better chance to get support for a new machine and with it achieve his ambition of beating the World Speed Record and taking the Schneider Trophy back to the USA.

Even before this the British, who were automatically hosts designate for the next race, had to indulge in the inevitable bickering between government departments. The Chief of the Air Staff, Lord Trenchard, was on the verge of retirement and, as Ralph Barker aptly remarked, seemingly almost jealous of his high-speed pilots. He was opposed to RAF participation. Ostensibly his objections were that it was against the best interests of the service to indulge in this kind of public competition. A further concern, almost Calvinistic in its outlook, was his concern about the effect of 'stardom' on his young pilots. All these objections emerged from behind the shelter of an argument that the Treasury would not help financially any way. Trenchard's attitude was that the Schneider Trophy race was a private competition and the Royal Aero Club, as representatives of the country, should foot the bill.

The Aero Club swiftly came back with the argument that the contest had become an inter-service affair, as it most definitely had, and they could not cope with the problems of entertaining official government guests and members of other air forces. In point of fact it would have been extremely difficult for them to operate without help from the services because the only suitable places with hangarage, slipway facilities and large stretches of open water were under service control.

Sir Samuel Hoare, who was fully aware that only the RAF could play host to the Italian air force and the Italian aeronautical hierarchy, not to mention representatives of the French air ministry and air force, went along to sound out Winston Churchill, Chancellor of the Exchequer, at his home. Churchill, who had not been at all helpful about the finances of the 1927 race, had obviously seen the value of the British victory in terms of prestige and technology. His surprising response was simply to ask Hoare what he was doing about running the Trophy in Britain and how much money he wanted. Obviously the stream was getting too strong for Trenchard to swim against and by the beginning of 1928 moves were being made to make machines and men available for a race in 1929.

With almost two years of preparation to look forward to, very little activity showed on the surface during 1928. That was not quite an illusion. The Italian plan for the next race was to take a leaf out of the British book and spread its options over three constructors, rather than one. Also, having seen the RAF establishments at Calshot and at Felixstowe, Balbo decided to set up a school of high-speed flying rather than relying on a single high-speed squadron and a handful of pilots. To the latter end a new base was acquired at Desenzano on the shores of Lake Garda where there was more elbow room for the long take-off runs required by the latest machines, and where any likely course could be laid out full scale for practice.

Meanwhile contracts were let out to Fiat, Macchi, Savoia-Marchetti and Piaggio for airframes and to Fiat and Isotta-Fraschini for engines. Balbo and the Italian air ministry were no longer putting all their eggs in the Macchi and Fiat baskets. Indeed Castoldi at Macchi was so disillusioned with Fiat after the 1927 Venice race that he was determined that Isotta-Fraschini engines should power the Macchis in 1929. It was not an illogical decision. Isotta-Fraschini, under the guidance of Ing. Cattaneo, was at that time the largest Italian aircraft engine manufacturer and one of the most advanced. One feels that the decision to go to Fiat for engines in 1926 and 1927 had been, possibly, because they had been the first to offer, in the AS.2, an equivalent to the Curtiss D-12 in terms of frontal area, power and weight.

France too, after an absence of years from the race, was showing signs of interest. Not only was her economy on the upgrade after a number of politically disruptive years but she had finally lost the Absolute World Speed Record of which she had been proud possessor for three years. She must have felt herself outclassed in this sphere by the perfidious British and the fascist Italians. She was suddenly in an aeronautical vacuum. Moreover, she had traditionally fielded a challenger whenever the Britons had been holders of the Coupe Schneider. Her reaction was for the Minister of Marine, M. Georges Leygues, who controlled French military aviation development, to place orders with two firms, Nieuport-Astra and Société des Avions Bernard, for suitable machines with which his country could challenge the British.

One wonders if the passing away of old Jacques Schneider at his home, Villa Minossa, at Beaulieu-sur-Mer, within sight of the 1913 Schneider Trophy course might have nudged French officialdom out of its torpor.

France was being reminded in other ways that her former glory as leader in world aviation had lost its shine. On 21 May 1928 at 10.20 pm Charles Lindbergh, flying a Ryan FYP monoplane, *Spirit of St Louis,* put his machine down at Paris-Le Bourget, 33 hours out of New York. Lindbergh was the first man to link the two great cities non-stop by air and, for good measure he did it flying solo. For 33 hours he had sat, flying almost blind, behind the 425 gallon fuel tank, changing his course at intervals to fly a great-circle route. His was an American technical achievement every bit as great as that of the Curtiss racers and confirmation of rightness of the US Navy's decision to make the marriage between the tiny Lawrence Aero Engine Corporation and the might of the Wright Corporation which had produced the immortal Wright J engine of Lindbergh's Ryan.

The salt was sadly rubbed into the French wounds because they were even then mourning the loss of their great long-distance aviators Nungesser and Coli, who had been lost attempting the same feat.

Way back in America Packard had developed their X-24 engine to a sufficient pitch of reliability to allow Al Williams in the Kirkham-Packard biplane, fitted with a land chassis, to make an unofficially timed flight at more than 300 mph. But much more development was needed and biplanes had now become erstwhile. It remained to be seen whether American aviation would produce another challenger.

The two main contenders remained the Italians and

the British. De Bernardi's brief performance with the M.52 at Venice had shown that the Fiat engines did not lack power while they were running. Had it not been for the availability of gearing on the Napier Lion VIIB, which permitted the use of a slower-turning and more efficient propeller, the Supermarine S.5 would have been slower than the Macchi. This fact had not been lost on the British, who could see that the Lion engine was nearing the end of its development and that they had better look round for something new.

One Briton to whom this engine problem was very much a matter of commercial life and death was Commander Bird, the Chairman of Supermarine, who had been forewarned that machines would be required of him. He knew that the only hope of building another race-winner was to find a more powerful engine with the right characteristics of low frontal area and light weight. At the Air Ministry Directorate of Technical Development the same problem was taxing the mind of Major G.P. Bulman who had taken over from Colonel Fell. Major Bulman (George to the aviation world), not to be confused with Flight Lieutenant Paul Ward Spencer Bulman, Hawker's illustrious test pilot, could see that the only alternative was the new Rolls-Royce Buzzard, only then going into production.

The Buzzard, type name H, had been designed as a

Lion replacement and was developing, in service form, some 825 bhp, weighed 1,450 lb and had a frontal area only a little more than that of the Napier. Its great advantage was that it was a big engine, 36.7 litres against Napier's 22.5 litres and it was supercharged and geared. It was quite within the bounds of possibility to develop it to give the same volumetric efficiency as the racing Napier, to wit 40 bhp per litre, when it would be good for better than 1,500 bhp without a substantial weight increase, if any.

Bulman put this to Bird and Reg Mitchell. The latter was initially a little apprehensive about Rolls-Royce, who he did not know, but Bulman patted his hand, assured him that they knew what they were about, and it was decided that he and Bird should go to see Henry Royce at West Wittering. There the great man had been put out to grass by the farsighted Claude Johnson for the benefit of his health and to get him out of the hair of the Derby factory, where his interference, in his eternal quest for perfection so often led to stoppages. From Wittering he very much retained control of all that went on at Derby and even retained his own design office in his coastal home, with A.G. Elliot in command, but nevertheless physically out of the way.

Bird's and Bulman's appeal to Royce was on the grounds of national prestige, apart from the publicity it

R. J. Mitchell (left) with Henry Royce. (*Flight*)

would bring to Rolls-Royce if the engine should win. Despite his antipathy to racing, Henry Royce gave his immediate approval; but his board of directors was not so happy. One strong dissenter was Basil Johnson, brother of the great Claude, the hyphen in Rolls-Royce, who thought motor cars were better business. Fortunately, for reasons recorded elsewhere he soon ceased to exercise a strong influence and was replaced by Arthur Sidgreaves as Managing Director. The new engine, which would be a beefed-up and heavily super-charged Buzzard, was given the factory designation 'Racing H'.

Royce and A.J. Rowledge, his chief designer, decid-ed that the design should be a joint venture between the West Wittering and Derby design teams. On 3 July 1928 Des. 917 Preliminary Racing Installation Drawing: Racing-H, was issued from the Derby drawing office. It would be many months before a contract would be forthcoming from the Air Ministry but it gave Reg Mitchell a weight and something to sketch an airframe round. With it went forecast fuel consumption figures and a laconic, and private, message from Henry Royce to James Bird saying that he would be able to give him about 1,800 horsepower to play with. Mitchell was able to get to work on his drawing board but in common with Rolls-Royce, no metal could be cut until the gov-ernment came forward with contracts.

At this stage of the aviation game the Napier Lion, designed in 1918, was beginning to lose its teeth. Napier had hoped that the sixteen-cylinder, 1,000 horsepower Cub engine of which they produced six prototypes in 1919, would take over as their main product when the Lion was eventually phased out. But the Lion was such a good, successful engine that they had fallen into the trap of beginning to think that it would go on for ever, and so neglected promotion of the Cub or a direct replacement. One factor was that the RAF concept for a very heavy, single-engined bomber for which the Buzzard had also been designed, was dropped in favour of multi-engined types, and orders for the Cub were just not forthcoming. So Napier let themselves drop into a vacuum. However, so far as the 1929 Schneider Trophy race was concerned there was still enough development left in the Lion for George Pate, their Technical Director, to suggest a supercharged version. This, Napier reckoned, would produce about 1,300 horse-power at sea level. It would require a smaller airframe but it was an engine with which the Air Ministry could hedge its bets in case the new Rolls-Royce power unit was a flop.

While the British effort slowly rolled into motion the Italians were busy establishing their high-speed school. Lake Varese, where the pilots had trained previously, was far from ideal for the new, faster aircraft envisaged, being barely seven kilometres long and surrounded by high ground. Lake Garda at that time, had very little waterborne traffic and the right meteorological conditions. It was not only big enough for the extensive take-off and alighting runs of the latest aircraft but was sufficiently capacious to allow a full-scale course to be simulated if need be.

The new Reparto Alta Velocità base proposed, and achieved, at Garda was an ideal one. Apart from accom-modation for the machines and lavish slipping facilities there was a heavy-machine shop, instrument and photo-graphic laboratories, a small hospital and a medical research centre which would investigate the physical and psychological effects of high-speed flight on the pilots.

Pilots, carefully selected for their skill and daring, had to be less than 30 years old and with more than three years' experience. They would first of all be taught sea-plane handling on old Savoia S.59s with a maximum speed of about 280 kilometres an hour. They would then graduate through the M.33 high-speed flying-boat to the M.52 floatplanes left over from Venice. One imagines the M.39 trainers and the M.39 race machines would also be valuable stepping-stones in the education of high-speed pilots. The base was built during the win-ter of 1928/1929 although the first high-speed flight, a flag-wagging exercise by an M.52, took place in April 1928. Pilots in the first course during 1929 were Giuseppe Motta, A. Carnaveri, Giovanni Monti, Remo Cadringher, Tommaso Dal Molin and Francesco Agello.

It is difficult to set exact dates to the beginning of French involvement in the 1929 race. It is probable that Georges Leygues, the French Minister of Marine, placed the order for two Nieuport-Astra NiD 450 racers, two Bernard racers and two trainers and two SPAD racers in May or June of 1928. At the same time orders for train-ers which were eventually code numbered HV.40 and HV.41 were also placed. By the time news leaked out to the Press Georges Leygues's responsibility for aviation had ceased and a separate, autonomous ministry of com-merce and aeronautics had been formed under Maurice Bokanowski. Unfortunately M. Bokanowski was killed in a flying accident on 2 September 1928 and there was yet another reshuffle with a ministry of air being created twelve days later.

André Victor Laurent d'Eynac was President Poincaré's nominee for Air Minister. He was to hold this post almost to the end of French involvement with the Schneider Trophy. So far as the Schneider entry was con-cerned he took over where Leygues left off. With his arrival a few details of the French involvement started to leak out into the Press. It was learnt that these orders were tied in with a development contract for a new, all-wood, monoplane fighter christened the Bernard Jockey 20-C-1. One imagines that the Ministry reckoned that the floatplane racers would provide valuable high-speed data. The French entry was sent to the Royal Aero Club of Great Britain in the first days of January and was ini-tially for four aircraft; two Nieuports and two Bernards. At the same time it was announced that the USA would be sending one aircraft, Italy four and the UK three.

On 23 January entries were fully confirmed by the Aero Club. They had now changed to three from France, Italy and the UK and one from the USA. The entries were announced after a Royal Aero Club Committee Meeting on 10 January. At that same meet-ing it was decided that the event would be held on 6 and

7 September, weather permitting. This date made it the final aviation event of the year so far as the UK was concerned.

It is generally believed that the RAF High Speed Flight was produced like a hat out of a box, popping up a few months before the Schneider race and being put away shortly after that event. In fact a minimal High Speed Flight was maintained throughout the years at RAF Felixstowe for training and research and occasional flying of outdated Schneider machines. Before the end of 1928 three of the pilots assigned to fly in the 1929 race had arrived to strengthen the Flight. All of them were instructors from the Royal Air Force Central Flying School (CFS) at Upavon. The CFS traditionally instructs the instructors, and all three pilots, Flying Officer Atcherley, George Stainforth and D'Arcy Greig, were at the peak of their flying ability and at the start of brilliant careers in the RAF. It was generally recognised at that time that under the Smith-Barry Gosport system, the CFS trained some of the finest pilots in the world. These were the best men that the CFS could find.

On 24 January their numbers were further strengthened by the arrival of their team captain Squadron Leader A.H. Orlebar. This lean, aquiline-featured, good-humoured administrator was an ideal choice. In the 1914 War he had been wounded at Gallipoli as a soldier, and shot down as a pilot in France after transferring to the Royal Flying Corps. When war ended he was granted a permanent commission, spent a period as a test pilot at Martlesham Heath and then moved on to become the Director of Organisation of Staff Duties at the Air Ministry. His new title was Officer Commanding the High Speed Flight, at RAF Felixstowe. Apart from his ability as a pilot he was a leader of exceptional quality.

D'Arcy Greig was a Scotsman, born near Elgin, and had joined the RAF in 1918, qualifying as a pilot four months before the war ended, long enough to be shot down behind enemy lines and to make his way back to his unit through the enemy trenches. After the war he was posted to Iraq, where he was awarded a DFC, an unusual 'peacetime' decoration, for his services there. Later he moved on as an Instructor at the CFS before being appointed Flying Examining Officer in the Fighting Area of Home Defence. He volunteered to join the High Speed Flight after Sam Kinkead's death in the S.5 early in 1928 and flew that machine to a new British record that year.

Flying Officer R.L.R. 'Batchy' Atcherley, a practical-joking Yorkshireman from Mitchelgate had joined the RAF as a cadet in 1922 and had been posted to 29 Fighter Squadron after graduating from Cranwell. Later he became an instructor with this squadron, ultimately returning to CFS in 1926 as a flying instructor. He joined the High Speed Flight in October 1922. He and Stainforth were to gain air racing honours before the Schneider, that same year, by winning the King's Cup Air Race in a Gloster Grebe fighter.

The RAF High Speed Flight in 1929. Left to right: Flying Officer H.R.D. Waghorn, Flying Officer T.H. Moon (Technical Officer), Flight Lieutenant D'Arcy Greig, Squadron Leader A.H. Orlebar, Flight Lieutenant G.H. Stainforth, Flying Officer R.L.R. Atcherley.

Atcherley's contemporary at Cranwell had been Flying Officer Waghorn, then a cadet, the only one of the team who was a Londoner. A keen rugby football player and a good skier, H.R.D. Waghorn had been posted to 17 Fighter Squadron as a pilot and was then sent for an instructor's course to the CFS. His flying ability was such that the CFS kept him there as an instructor until he joined the High Speed Flight in February 1929.

George Stainforth had started as a regular soldier and saw much foreign service before taking to the air with the RAF with a short-term commission in 1922. He had been a flying instructor at the No. 4 Flying Training School in Egypt before moving to the Central Flying School in 1927. He joined the High Speed Flight in the autumn of 1922. Somewhat withdrawn, he was one of those people, not so rare as one might imagine, who was a superb pilot and an absolutely hopeless car driver. Incidentally, all of these pilots, as a team with one other pilot, were nationally famous as members of the RAF Formation Aerobatics Team.

The first tangible sign of 1929 Schneider hardware of any description or nationality appeared at the 1928 Salon de L'Aeronautique in Paris, in August, when Société des Avions Bernard displayed a clever combined cantilever monoplane wing incorporating the middle section of the fuselage as part of the wing structure. Of multi-cellular wooden construction, it was the brainchild of that doyen of French designers, Louis Béchereau, creator of the fabulous Deperdussin racers and the SPAD fighter. Shortly after the formation of Société des Avions Bernard from the crumbling ruins of André Bernard's Société Industrielle des Métaux et du Bois (SIMB), the chief designer, John Hubert, had been killed in a car crash. With important contracts pending, the Bernard board was at a loss to find a new designer and Louis Béchereau had been called in as engineering consultant. This wing was his first creation for Bernard and was shown as a component of the new Bernard Jockey 20-C-1 fighter which was part of the contract for Schneider machines.

An exhibit at this show which was of the greatest interest to the Bernard company was the M.52 seaplane racer on the Macchi stand. Their engineers lost no time, burning midnight oil carefully dimensioning and picking off the lines of the floats of this machine. The dimensions were taken back to the factory, a tenth-scale model made, and flotation tests were carried out in the little river Morée close to the Courneuve factory.

Construction of the Bernard HV.40 started at the end of 1928 and was completed in the spring of 1929 at the Courneuve factory, where it lay for many months waiting for the engine builders to produce the promised power output from the Gnome et Rhône Mistral engine. Meanwhile the HV.41 trainer designed to take a souped-up, 450 hp Hispano-Suiza engine, from which 900 horsepower had been promised, was completed. It in turn had to await the pleasure of the engine constructors. The two racers to the original contract, first designated HV.47, were also put in hand. They

were intended to fly in the contest powered by the new Hispano-Suiza R18, W-configuration engine of 1,500 horsepower. The first of these engines was not delivered until some months after the 1929 race, by which time the HV.47 had been changed in detail and redesignated HV.120.

While the French were waiting for their engines the British government stirred itself into activity and, in February 1929, finally gave the go-ahead for Rolls-Royce to start on the Racing H project. By May detailed drawings of the first engine had been produced and an engine was running and giving 1,540 bhp at 2,750 rpm; but only for 15 minutes. After that time it began to overheat and tighten up. The date of this first test was 4 May, by mid-July Rolls-Royce had got the speed up to 3,000 rpm and the Racing-H was pushing out 1,614 bhp running on a diet of pure benzole. But there was still trouble in the combustion area of the engine. Valves were burning and distorting and the engine would not run slowly without sooting up the plugs. Once again Rodwell Banks, now a member of the technical sales department of the Anglo-American Oil Company, came to the rescue. He joined the test team at Derby and, working on the fuel by diluting it with Romanian petrol and adding a touch of lead tetraethyl, not only succeeded in getting the engine through its acceptance test but eventually helped to extend its overhaul life to some five hours. It should be said that the five-hour life was a full-throttle life and by Rolls-Royce standards that was *full* throttle.

Inhabitants of Derby knew all about the Rolls-Royce effort because apart from the mighty roar of the 'R' exhaust, three Kestrel engines, of 400 horsepower each, were running at the same time as ancilliaries driving fans and the supercharger test rig. For the record by the end of July the engine was giving the promised 1,800 horsepower at 2,850 rpm with an installed weight of 1,530 lb. During the last four weeks of the engines' existence their output was increased further to 190 bhp at 3,000 rpm. Incidentally the 1929 British Schneider machines were civil-registered and had to have certificates of airworthiness (C of A). The C of A for the 'R' type gave it a five-hour life before complete overhaul!

At the same time that the engine order went to Rolls-Royce a specification and contract had already been issued to Supermarine for the construction of the two contest machines. Mitchell, with all the data for the S.5 in front of him, and nearly a year to decide what he was going to do, had no hesitation in adopting the S.5 configuration once again. But this time the machine was of all-metal construction rather than having a metal fuselage and wooden flying surfaces like the S.5. Supermarine, now owned by the great Vickers combine, were rapidly developing metal-working expertise at the instigation of the British Air Ministry, who could see that, in a future war, metal construction would be essential because not only was it more amenable to mass production and unskilled labour but the aircraft manufacturers during World War One had used up almost the entire world supply of seasoned spruce. Apart from its metal construction the new S.6A had also to be a much larger machine to carry the heavier 'H' engine and the big fuel load required to assuage its thirst. This new beauty from Rolls-Royce drank petrol at the rate of 3.6 gallons per minute and would require 160 gallons of fuel, weighing half a ton, to complete the race at full power. Compared with the diminutive S.5 which scaled 3,000 lb, the S.6 weighed 5,771 lb fully laden and had a wing area of 145 sq ft compared with 103.5 sq ft for the 1927 machine. But the main conception was the same with a low wing and asymmetrical floats with the main fuel load carried in the starboard float, which was set further out from the centreline of the machine.

Writing his diary at the beginning of August, Orlebar commented that here they were, barely a month before the race, and there was still no sign of the S.6. However, Rolls-Royce had delivered engines a week before this was written and only four days later, on 4 August, bank holiday Monday, the first machine, N.247, was towed over from the Supermarine Works at Woolston for flying. At least that was the idea but when Orlebar took it out it resolutely refused to leave the water. The trouble was a combination of the pilot's unfamiliarity with what was, after all, the most powerful single-engined machine ever built, floats with too small a buoyancy reserve and the massive torque effect of the coarse-pitch propeller. From standstill the propeller was trying about seven times as hard to turn the S.6 over as it was to pull it forward. Until the machine reached a speed of 20 mph

the port float was almost submerged.

It took Orlebar two or three days to develop a take-off technique with a light fuel load to get N.247 airborne. The procedure, for the record, was first of all to find a ruffled path of water, then to visually make sure that the take-off area was clear. The machine was then turned 45 degrees to the right of the wind and the pilot would open the throttle and at the same time duck his head under the windscreen to keep his goggles clear of spray. As soon as the S.6 got under way the spray would clear and he could raise his head. He had already pulled the stick right back and applied full right rudder. Rudder was essential to keep the aircraft straight against torque and the tail had to be kept down to prevent porpoising. Normally when the machine got up on the step it would level out and overcome the elevator, which took over again once it became airborne. Speed at this stage would be about 40 mph. If porpoising did start but the machine continued to accelerate it would work itself out of it but if the porpoising were violent enough to slow the machine down it would increase in violence until the S.6 leapt out of the water. That was the time to throttle-back and start again.

Orlebar records that immediately after becoming airborne the stick had to be kept right back to maintain the angle of attack of the wings. Otherwise the machine would sink back onto the water. It was longitudinally unstable at these low speeds and at all speeds if out of trim or with any aft movement of the C of G. Owing to

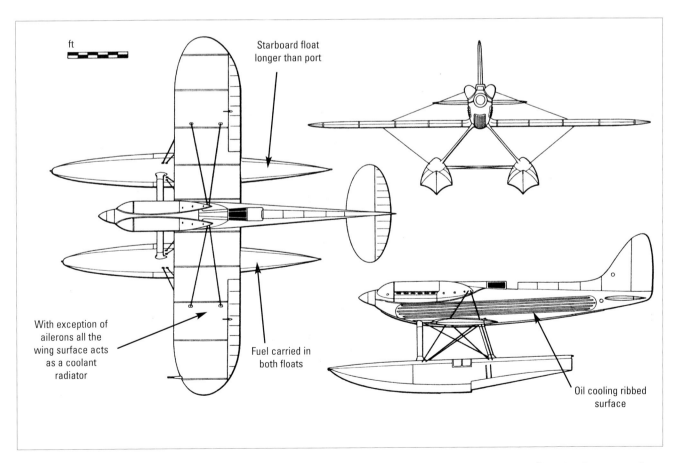

Supermarine S.6 (1929): Wing Span: 30 ft (9.14 m). Length Overall: 26 ft 10 in (8.18 m). Wing Area: 145 sq. ft (13.47 m²). Weight Empty: 4,471 lb (2,028 kg). T-O Weight: 5,771 lb (2,618 kg). Max Wing Loading: 39.8 lb/sq. ft (194.32 kg/m²). Rolls-Royce 'R' engine of 1,900 hp.

the poor forward visibility it was necessary to start the alighting run across wind to get a good sight of the landing area, and choose an unobstructed run and then turn onto a line and stick to it. The approach speed was 160 mph with touch-down at 110 mph.

Even by modern standards these approach and round-out speeds were in the jet category. In those days they were phenomenal. The approach speed was as high as the maximum speed of the fastest fighters. In the eyes of the public the pilots had the same stature as the astronauts of today simply because they were venturing far beyond the known barriers.

Orlebar had certainly tamed the S.6 sufficiently for it to be shown to the assembled press at Calshot on 10 August. The knowing ones had an inkling of the problems that the team were having with the machine and hardly expected the demonstration flight the team captain laid on for them. It was, in fact, a chance to get a little precious flying time on the machine and the opportunity was taken to do some speed runs over the Calshot speed course.

In America the Mercury Flying Corporation, a non-profit-making organisation had been formed to provide funds for Alford Williams's Schneider challenger. Although there was no official backing for the challenge the aircraft was designed by the Navy Department's Bureau of Aeronautics and the wind-tunnel models were tested in the Washington Navy yard tunnel. Construction was at the naval aircraft factory in Philadelphia under conditions of utmost secrecy. It is not quite clear whether the secrecy was to keep the project details away from the British, the Italians or Congress. The end product was an all-wood, mid-wing monoplane mounted on twin pontoons and wire-braced like the British and Italian participants. Power was provided by a developed version the same Packard, 24-cylinder X-type engine that had powered the Kirkham-Packard and which was expected to give 1,100 to 1,200 horsepower or more.

Construction of the machine was not complete until the beginning of August 1929, when news came through to London that the Mercury high-speed was on its way to the Annapolis Naval Academy for testing. From the outset the project was dogged by propeller damage from spray and, one would judge from photographs, an insufficient buoyancy reserve. This was really the root of the propeller problems because the floats, time and time again, would bury their noses and kick up spray into the propeller disc. Williams found, as Orlebar had discovered in England, that excessive use of the rudder created drag which prevented the machine getting on the step, and that the best way to get it on the move was to point it at 90 deg to the take-off run and let propeller torque pull it in line. But even though he eventually managed to get the machine over the 'hump' it was reluctant to take to the air, so much so that it only ever made one attested flight. This was only a matter of a few hundred yards. Williams had to put the machine back on the water because of low fuel pressure and a bent propeller.

Although the machine was built in great secrecy its trials were attended by nation-wide publicity. There is no doubt that the nation took Alford Williams to its heart in his attempt to represent it. Packard were developing an engine giving 200 more horsepower, which might have solved a few problems, and it was proposed to install this on the journey to England which was to be made in a Navy destroyer. Unfortunately the machine had not flown by the time it was due to leave for England and not unnaturally the US Navy withdrew its support. In the ensuing period a reassessment of the machine was made and it was found to be some 400 lb overweight compared with the Navy Bureau's calculations. It would have been a very welcome visitor to Great Britain, where a hangar had been specially set aside for it at Calshot. In the event the Italian team took the hangar over for their mobile aircraft exhibition.

Although the flight of the Macchi M.52 in April 1928 had opened the Reparto Alta Velocità at Desenzano with a bang the facilities were not fully available until May 1929, when intense preparation for the race began. Early announcements gave the names of de Bernardi and Ferrarin as pilots of the Italian machines but the Italians were obviously taking a last-minute leaf out of the RAF book. The British High Speed Flight had a completely new set of pilots on the basis of spreading experience among as many pilots as possible. The Italians, on the other hand, had used de Bernardi and Ferrarin for the 1926 and 1927 races and were now proposing to utilise their services once again for 1929. Colonel Bernasconi, who had been put in charge of the new project, clearly saw that this was not such a good idea. So in June 1929 it was announced that de Bernardi, Ferrarin and a previously unmentioned name, although one famous in the annals of Italian aviation, Brack-Papa, would not after all take part in the race but that the Italian effort would be in the hands of pilots chosen from the first course to come out of Desenzano. The method of choosing this first course had been a selective one. The fifty most likely pilots in the Italian air force had been summoned to Turin for a preliminary seeding. Of these, twenty were chosen for tests in fast seaplanes. The six team members came from these twenty.

Fiat had been put on their mettle by Macchi's decision not to use their engine for 1929 and the first machine from any country to appear was the diminutive Fiat C.29 which was delivered to Desenzano in June 1929. Tiny, perky little Francesco Agello took the CR.29 on its maiden flight. Apart from being one of Italy's best pilots and therefore the most suitable one for knocking a high-speed prototype into shape, Agello was probably the only member of the team who was small enough to fit into the tiny cockpit. He made the first flight in early June without incident but found the machine laterally unstable due to lack of fin area. Modifications were put in hand on a second machine which was then under construction. Meanwhile Agello made a number of short flights in the prototype until on 11 June, coming in to land, he hit the wash of a boat, the machine shot into the air, stalled and dived vertically into the water. Fortunately the cockpit enclosure carried away and Agello was thrown out to be picked up by one of the rescue boats, very little the worse for wear. This prototype, works serial number 129, was quickly replaced by the second machine, no. 130, which had been practically completed at the Fiat works when the incident happened. It differed little from no. 129, except in having enlarged tail surfaces to correct the instability reported by Agello, and a lower windscreen. Testing procedures on this machine went on until 18 August, when Agello was due to demonstrate the C.29 to a representative of *The Aeroplane* magazine. Two attempts to fly were made in the morning but the little machine refused to get off. A second attempt was made in the afternoon and this time Agello managed to get the Fiat airborne and had reached a height of 45 feet when it sank back onto the water, tripped up over the toes of its floats and turned over in a cloud of spray. Agello was lucky to extract himself from the debris but the machine was a write-off. Parts of it were recovered but the engine sank in 300 feet of water and was never found.

Italo Balbo immediately ordered a new machine to be built; 130bis, which was identical to the one lost and had to be sent directly to England without having previously flown.

The most revolutionary and contentious of the Italian aircraft, the Pegna Pc.7, was almost ready by August. It was sent along to Desenzano for trials by Warrant Officer Dal Molin. As we have said this machine was expected to rise onto its hydrofoils into a take-off position, urged on by a water propeller. When the propeller was clear of the water, the pilot was expected to set it in motion by operating a clutch in the propeller shaft. Hopefully the machine would then raise itself onto a take-off attitude and climb into the air. Diagrams of the machine show that the water propeller and air propeller clutches were mechanically operated. It is quite probable that the pilot, who would have his work cut out getting the machine into motion at all, would need a third hand and much strength to operate a mechanical clutch having the necessary clamping loads to transmit 1,000 hp. Dal Molin was a skilful and very brave man, but one imagines that the thought of putting that machine down onto its hydrofoils if ever it did get airborne would have daunted even the most bold. In the event history repeated itself; like the British Burney X-boats of 1914, the Pc.7 never did get further than raising the propeller clear of the water and dragging it, tail submerged. So the Italian fourth string was a non-starter right from the beginning.

The other Italian seed was the Savoia-Marchetti SM.65, a twin-float, push-pull monoplane mounted on floats with the tail surfaces supported by twin booms. It was powered by two Isotta-Fraschini 1,000 hp engines driving a tractor propeller and a pusher propeller. Although the machine was completed before the race, and had done acceptance tests on Lake Varese in the hands of Giuseppe Motta, it was barely raceworthy before the team was due to leave for England. In the end

it was simply taken along to Calshot for window-dressing.

Macchi, however, had been able to get delivery of one of the Isotta-Fraschini engines and delivered the first of the M.67 race machines late in July. It was successfully test flown by Lieutenant Giuseppe Motta, the second in command of the flight, before weather clamped down on the lake and prevented further high-speed flying until late in the month. It was 22 August when the next flight took place. Once again Motta was the pilot and he took off in the same kind of 'milk-bowl' conditions, haze and no horizon, in which Kinkead had met his end. His assignment that day was to discover the high-speed possibilities of the machines. He had made a number of high-speed runs flying flat out at 100 metres above the surface of the lake when suddenly the M.67 was seen to dive into the water and disappear in a huge show of spray. There was no hope for poor Motta although rescue boats went out and searched for wreckage. The reason for the crash will never be known. The pilot may have been overcome by fumes, which were known to pour into the cockpit in banked turns. Or maybe he had been the victim of a high-speed stall in a turn. It was poor consolation for the Italians that the only positive thing that had come out of this tragedy was the sure knowledge that the machine was fully competitive. The timekeepers' sheets showed that the machine had made two runs at 362 mph.

With the tragedy heavy on their hearts and the knowledge that the other two Macchis were not even completed although the advance party of their team were already at Calshot, the Italian authorities immediately telegraphed the Royal Aero Club in London to ask for a postponement of the race. Reluctantly, because of the huge organisation involving not only the Royal Air Force, but also the Admiralty and shipping up and down a very busy channel, the Royal Aero Club were not able to accede to this request.

Long before the Italians' tragedy the French had to give in. They had got off to a late start and their École de Haute Vitesse had not been formed until June 1929. The location, which was the choice of their first pilot Sadi Lecointe, was the naval air base at Hourtin in the Gironde. Sadi chose it because of the loneliness of the setting and the flat topography of the surrounding countryside. The six pilots who began training there on 1 July were, apart from Sadi Lecointe, Warrant Officer Florentin Bonnet, the Absolute World Speed Record holder, Lieutenant Maurice Vernhol and three other pilots, NCOs Lepreux, Jacques Fickinger and Jean Francoise Lagadou. Lagadou was the only member of the team from L'Aviation Maritime and was a fighter instructor at L'École St Raphael. There was an unconfirmed back-up team of four naval airmen, one of whom was Marie-Jean Demougout, a naval catapult specialist who had officially been named after Lecointe and Bonnet as the third team pilot. The naval airmen were not meant to appear at Hourtin until later in the training programme to give the land-lubbers time to get their sea legs on the old Schreck FBA flying-boats with which

The Gloster IVB of 1929. The radiator surfaces are visible on the tops of the floats. (*Flight*)

the resident squadron was equipped. The transition from getting out of one of these antiques into a high-speed floatplane would have been rather like getting out of a horse and cart into a Grand Prix racing car. However, the Ministry of Air had sent down a squadron of the latest Nieuport ND 62 high-speed fighters in which the pilots could practice high-speed turns.

Sadly, one of these machines proved the undoing of Florentin Bonnet. Taking off one day on a practice flight, he attempted a loop immediately after take-off, failed to recover and the machine dived vertically into the ground and was wrecked, killing poor Bonnet instantly. This was not the foolish pilot error that might have been suggested but, it is thought, was due to a known fault in the attachment of the seat-back causing the pilot to lose control. Bonnet's loss was a tragic blow for French hopes, but, had he survived, the aircraft were not forthcoming. The Bernard HV.40 Radial engine trainer – the first to be completed – had not even flown by mid-July, by which time rumours started to arrive in England from France that the French might not compete. To be fair to them when d'Eynac had announced that France should participate in the 1929 race he hedged his bets by saying that the preparation would require 'long adjustments and trials'. When, with the race only two months away, not even a trainer had flown and the new HV.120 racers were sitting in the factory

at Courneuve waiting for engines, the rumours were hardly surprising. There was no sign of the Nieuport and Dewoitine machines. However the HV.41 had been delivered to Hourtin and, ever hopeful, the French Minister put in a request for a postponement of the race to give them the chance to field a challenger. This request came long before that of the Italians and had to be rejected for the same reasons.

The Société des Avions Bernard's test pilot, Antoine Paillard, who himself had to go to the École Schreck for tuition in flying seaplanes, finally got the second HV.41, in-line engined trainer airborne in August but, although it immediately showed that it was capable of exceeding 400 km/h, it was equally incapable of reaching the contract speed of 430 km/h. However, there were thoughts of sending it over to England, if only to recover the 200,000 francs (£1,500) entry deposit. But apart from the fact that the machine would have been outclassed, its fuel load was insufficient for it to complete the race even if it had started.

Although the British Air Ministry order for new racers from Gloster's was not forthcoming until November 1928, design and some construction work began as early as May 1928. Folland had wanted to build a Gloster V biplane again but the extra weight of the Napier Lion VIID engine meant that the upper mainplane would

A Gloster IV biplane in front of a Gloster VI monoplane at RAF Calshot in 1929. (*Flight*)

have had to have been mounted right on top of the middle cylinder-bank. Apart from aerodynamic problems associated with this location, servicing under racing conditions would have been made extremely difficult and it was therefore a case of Hobson's choice that forced the Gloster design team to go for a monoplane configuration. The end product was what has been said to be the most graceful monoplane ever built. Two machines were built, N.249 and N.250. They were of mixed wood and metal construction, the fuselage and floats being metal and the flying surface wood.

Difficulties with engine development at Napier delayed delivery until August. N.249 was delivered by road to Calshot on the 12th of the month and N.250

followed five days later. When they were assembled and shown to the press they attracted a great deal of admiration. N.249 had blue floats and an old-gold fuselage and wings and was promptly christened 'Golden Arrow'. N.250 had gold wings and tailplane, Cambridge Blue fuselage and white floats. They must have been a stirring sight lined up on the tarmac at Calshot with the blue and silver Supermarines as a foil. Bad weather during the middle of August delayed the first flight until 25 August when Orlebar got N.249 airborne but had engine failure almost immediately afterwards, when he had reached a height of 20 feet. While the engine constructors started what was to be a four-week stint to sort out this problem, N.250 was flown by the same pilot on the evening

Gloster VI N.250 under tow in Southampton Water. (*Flight*)

of 31 August. The Gloster flew well enough in a straight line but the engine was cutting out badly in turns. D'Arcy Greig and George Stainforth both tried the machine in the course of the next few days but neither of them was able to track down the problem, which later transpired to be due to fluctuations in the engine intake duct because of poor siting of the inlet. At the time it was put down to a faulty fuel pump.

During the month of August the Royal Aero Club announced the arrangements for the Navigability Test. The area chosen for the tests was close to Calshot and was bounded by imaginary lines drawn from Cowes to Stone Point in the New Forest, from there to the Agwi oil tanks, across to Hamble, along the coast to Lee-on-Solent, to Kings Quay on the Isle of Wight and thence to Cowes. It was a big area but these fast machines covered a lot of ground once they got airborne. The taxying tests were due to take place in an area near the Calshot lightship where a buoy would be moored to mark the centre of an imaginary circle half a nautical mile in diameter. Whatever the direction of the wind, the machines would be able to taxi half a mile along the diameter of this circle, the course being marked with buoys according to the direction of the prevailing wind. The machines could be taken out to the trial course any way their owners wished. Having been out on the water and the engines started, they had to taxi across the start line on the periphery of the circle, take off and fly a marked course of 10 miles, during which they had to alight twice and taxi across the full diameter of the circle at a minimum speed of 12 knots. Having done this, they had to alight in the circle and cross the finishing line.

Having successfully completed the test, the machines had to be either towed or taxied across to a small bay to the north of the Calshot base where they would be moored for six hours to test the watertightness of the flotation gear. The test was scheduled to begin at 7 am when there was the best chance of calm water. Should the weather not be good, three alternative locations for laying out the circle were provided for at Cowes off the Royal Yacht Squadron, a further site to the east of Cowes and off Lee-on-Solent.

The race itself was scheduled to start on Saturday, the following day, at 2 pm, the starting ship being a Royal Navy monitor, HMS *Medea*, moored off Calshot. The signal for each machine to take off was by the firing of the gun and by hoisting the national flag of the competing machine. On receipt of the signal each pilot was allowed ten minutes to take off and cross the starting line at Ryde pier. The course itself had been publicised for some time and had four legs with turning points after passing the line at Seaview, at a marker boat moored due South of Hayling Island, a third turning point off Southsea pier and a fourth in the middle of the Solent off Cowes, opposite the Royal Yacht Squadron. The start and finish line was on a line projected from Ryde pier. The course would be flown anticlockwise.

On 22 August the advance party of the Italian contingent arrived at Calshot bringing with them two M.52 trainers. For this purpose they were fitted with the more reliable AS.2 engines. Indeed one of them, christened by its ground crew the *Moro di Venezia* ('Moor of Venice') because of the smoke grime that almost obscured its red dope finish, could well have had a Fiat A.20 powerplant because it was said to have clocked up 400 flying hours.

Even while they were erecting these machines the sad news came through of poor Motta's death in the M.67. Almost immediately the Italian Air Attaché, Lieutenant Monti, no relation to the Monti in the Italian team, applied to the contest committee for a postponement of the race for thirty, or at least twenty, days. His point was that the team had lost its best pilot and that their new machines were virtually untried because of unfavourable weather on Lake Garda. Motta's death was directly attributed to these conditions. After a whole day's consultations the Schneider Cup committee issued a statement in which they reluctantly, but very firmly, told the Italians that this was impossible and that the British machines would fly round the course on the chosen date whether there was any opposition or not. They explained, quite rightly, that the race date was the culmination of massive arrangements which included not only the RAF but the Navy and the railways, who had for months been taking bookings to bring down thousands of spectators. Moreover, shipping lines all over the world had arranged sailings to leave the Solent and Southampton Water, one of the world's busiest shipping areas, free of traffic on the appropriate days. Finally the date had been chosen because of the known meteorological conditions at that time.

For a day or so it appeared from Italian Press reports that the team might withdraw. But in fact they were already committed. Their contest machines were already packed and on the way, while the personnel were on the point of departure. But the Anglophilic Italo Balbo announced on 28 August that the team would participate after all. The following day the team arrived at Calshot under the command of Colonel Bernasconi. He was accompanied by Lieutenant Giovanni Monti, Lieutenant Remo Cadringher, Warrant Officer Tommaso Dal Molin, Sergeant-Major Francesco Agello, and the team medico Doctor Marocco. In an interview that evening to the Press in RAF Calshot Officers' Mess, Colonel Bernasconi told representatives of the technical and national Press that Italian hopes for victory were in the hands of the pilots rather than the machines. He remarked that he and six others had all exceeded de Bernardi's Absolute World Speed Record over the three kilometre course, referring to the record taken at Venice in the M.52R early in 1928.

The two M.52 trainers were by then ready and waiting to be flown. The remainder of the Italian contest machines arrived on Saturday, the last day of August. This second consignment comprised the one surviving Fiat C.29 number N.130bis, de Bernardi's record-breaking Macchi M.52R and the two Macchi M.67 race machines. General Balbo arrived at the same time, made himself comfortable at the Gloucester Hotel in Cowes and then went down to see Giovanni Monti flying the old M.52 trainer. He also was able to watch Orlebar in the Gloster-Napier, N.250, still patiently trying to sort out the carburation problems, which seemed insoluble. Meanwhile D'Arcy Greig and Stainforth flew two of the 1927 Gloster-Napier IV biplanes round the Solent to work off the frustration that Gloster-Napier troubles were creating. With only a week to go before the race it seemed unlikely that Napier's would be able to solve the carburation problem on the beautiful little golden Glosters and that the old Supermarine S.5 would have to be brought in to take their place. In fact it was already at Supermarine being worked on.

Orlebar's test-flying in N.247 had revealed a number of shortcomings. The engine was overheating and fuel consumption with the first 'R' engine was higher than expected and was bound to be higher still with the latest, 1,900 bhp version. It is a measure of the pace everyone was working at that, after Richard Atcherley made his first flight in days and she was ready for full-load flight trials on 28 August, changes included a new starboard float with a bigger tank section, larger skin radiators on the floats and a new engine of the latest type.

It was fortunate that the Supermarine works was virtually on the spot for modifications of this type. Rolls-Royce were not so well placed. With engines lifted at a mere five hours between overhauls and frequent changes to be made, they built a special Phantom I lorry to transport them to and from Calshot. A typical time was five hours to cover the 160 or more miles between the works and Woolston. E.W. Hives, a fearsome driver, on one occasion got it down to 4 hr 15 min.

Unfortunately the day N.247 came back was a bad flying day but Atcherley managed one 24-minute flight in her the following day and seemed happy with the results although he fouled the slipway when towed in. Work had already started on N.219 to get her raceworthy, should the second Gloster VI prove as troublesome as the first. This machine, N.250, was erected and ready to fly by that evening but she had to wait until the morrow for her first flight because of rough water.

The Southampton Water and Calshot area was a hive of aviation activity in those weeks. If the contest machines were not in the air, various dignitaries would be coming and going in all kinds of aeroplanes ranging from coupe and amphibious Moths to Supermarine Southampton flying-boats. 'Boom' Trenchard had landed close to RAF Calshot in such a one and had inspected the High Speed Flight quite early in the proceedings.

On 31 August Italian machines were in action for the first time, with Lieutenant Monti airborne in the 'Moor of Venice'. Orlebar also made the first flight in the Gloster N.250. In the course of a gentle flight he found her less prone than her sister to the fuel feed problem. This was the day for Waghorn to make his first three-quarter load take-off with N.247. It was a fruitless exercise, the floats dug in and she would just not get up enough speed to get on the step. Finally he came back and it was found that one float had taken in about 300 lb of seawater through a displaced float-strut seal.

There were some worried faces around but they brightened the following day when he got N.247 airborne with the same load. Both Cadringher and Agello made their first British flights that day in the grimy M.52R trainer.

The following Monday, 1 September, it was Atcherley's turn to fly the Supermarine S.6 with a full fuel load. He landed after 20 minutes' flight with one of the float struts dented and partially stripped.

It was assumed at the time he had hit a seagull. Fortunately the works was only 'across the road', and a new fairing had been made in time for flying the following day. On that day, 2 September, Orlebar finally handed the Gloster-Napier VI to D'Arcy Greig for test flying and his opinion. A number of runs were made over the three kilometre course between Calshot pier and the Agwi pier to calibrate the air speed indicator. It was noticed that every time Greig made a turn the engine was popping and cutting out intermittently but ran clean as soon as the machine got back on a straight course. It began to look as though the Gloster VI would not be representing Britain after all.

It was a measure of the importance of the event that 3 September was the occasion of a royal visit from the Prince of Wales, whom we knew later as the Duke of Windsor. Both teams were presented to him and he was able to inspect all the machines. The M.67s had done their ground runs while the Fiat C.29, number 130bis and the Savoia-Marchetti SM.65 had been erected to prove that they did exist even if they were not going to fly. However, the engine of the Fiat, and one of the engines of the Savoia, had been in the air only briefly.

During the final week both teams spent time getting the feel of their machines and putting the final touches to them. On Wednesday Monti went out in one of the M.67s to make the first flight. Despite interference from an informal encounter with a passing motorboat, which churned up the water just as he was leaving the slipway, and with the liner *Majestic*, which slowed down to allow him to cross its bows, Monti was able to get the M.67 airborne without incident but alighted again almost immediately with a broken lift wire.

The same day N.248 was towed across from Woolston, where she had been fitted with horizontal vanes on the floats in an endeavour to cure the machine of the tendency to sit back on take-off. As was his rule with any modification Orlebar flew the machine first before handing it over to his pilots. At least he attempted to fly it but on the take-off run it pitched so violently that he had to return and have the vanes removed. Indeed the only properly completed flight of the day was by Dal Molin in the old M.52 hack. Later that day Waghorn went out again with N.247 and a full fuel load. This time, in spite of a tendency to porpoise, he got the machine airborne after a 40-second run. Unfortunately he misjudged his height when putting the machine back on the water, stalled it and struck the water so heavily that the engine stalled. Before his tow launch could get to him the machine had drifted onto a passing tug, damaging the wingtip and the propeller.

A Macchi M.67 at Calshot. The oil cooling radiator can be seen under the nose and coolant radiating surfaces along the sides of the fuselage and on the upper surface of each float. (*Flight*)

HRH The Prince of Wales with the Italian team pilots for the 1929 competition in front of a Fiat C.29. (*Flight*)

Fiat C.29. The fuselage is a tight fit around the engine. (*Flight*)

Supermarine S.6. The starboard float is larger than the port float to counteract the anticlockwise torque reaction of the propeller. (*Flight*)

Waghorn quickly got out on the float and managed to fend the machine off the next obstacle, a moored barge, as he was carried along by the swift current. That was about all for that day although, in the twilight, Atcherley went out for taxying practice in N.248, the second Supermarine S.6, and Cadringher was out in one of the

Macchi 67s for the same purpose. Neither of them flew.

There was similar activity on the Thursday but with the Italian team getting down to some serious flying. In the morning Dal Molin took up the M.52R machine for a run-round up coast. On take-off, unfortunately, one of the floats hit a piece of debris making a gash seven or eight inches long. Luckily, plenty of rescue boats were to hand, otherwise the machine might have overturned and sunk after alighting. The Italians were certainly not at all happy with the virtually untried Isotta-Fraschini W-18 engines in the M.67s. The only one of these machines to go out that day was the second aircraft, fitted with a three-bladed propeller. Cadringher was again at the helm, but the aircraft failed to get airborne.

It was interesting that the British team still persisted with the Gloster-Napier. Stainforth had N.250 out that afternoon with a full fuel load, made a quick take-off but landed almost immediately. The machine was taken back into the hangar to join its sister, N.249, on which a Gloster and Napier team had been working night and day for almost the whole of the week. It was all in vain because Orlebar had obviously made up his mind to field the Supermarine S.5.

That evening old N.219 was towed out for D'Arcy Greig to fly. In the event the engine started but stopped

Gloster VI. This clearly shows the coarse pitch of the propeller. (*Flight*)

quite suddenly and the flight was aborted. Meanwhile Stainforth had appeared with his little pet – he had formed a real attachment to the Gloster-Napier – and made a full-load take-off just as the sun was setting. This time the Napier engine appeared to be running smoothly, both at full throttle and part throttle setting, and after a perfect landing in the gathering dusk, the machine was put away and Napier announced that they had finally traced the trouble to the fuel pump. However, the cure had come too late. When the starting order was announced that evening it was seen that first away would be Waghorn flying the Supermarine S.6, followed by Dal Molin in the Macchi M.52R, then D'Arcy Greig would go off in the Supermarine S.5, followed by Cadringher in an M.67, Atcherley in an S.6, and Monti in one of the Macchi 67s would bring up the rear, so to speak. Reserves were Stainforth in the Gloster-Napier VI and Agello in one of the M.52 trainers.

Navigability Trials

The fine weather which had been such a feature of the week preceding the race was still on its best behaviour in the early hours of Friday 6 September, the day fixed for the navigability trials and water-tightness tests. By the time 7 am came round the three Supermarines, two S.6s and the S.5, and the three blood-red Macchis were already on their pontoons, ready to go out to the Calshot light vessel for the trials. These pontoons, which had attracted scepticism from the British when they had seen them for the first time in Venice in 1927, had been

enthusiastically copied by the RAF because they allowed the high-speed machines to be taken out to the start of whatever they were going to do without having to use up any of the precious fuel load or have the propellers damaged by spray while they were taxying. Moreover, engines could be started while the machines were still on the lighter, it was easier for the pilot to get into his cockpit and the whole thing could be turned into wind ready for take-off. The only difference in the British approach was that they used individual pontoons whereas those used by the Italians carried two or three machines.

As the pontoons were towed out to their stations General Italo Balbo could be seen aboard the lighter carrying Lieutenant Monti's Macchi M.67 which was wearing competition number 10. Waghorn's S.6 had been allocated number 2, Atcherley's S.6 was given number 8, which was coincidentally the last figure of its service number N.248, and D'Arcy Greig's S.5 had number 5. Of the remaining Italians, Dal Molin's M.52R had number 4 painted on it and Cadringher's M.67 was race number 7.

A line of boats marked the lane down which the machines would take off, alight and do their taxying tests. Unfortunately a change of wind came just as the tests were about to start and the whole armada had to be moved to reorient it. The clock showed 9.15 am before proceedings could start, when it was Waghorn's turn to initiate. There was little chop where the Southampton Water and Solent tides met at this point, which probably helped Waghorn's take-off by breaking the floats clear of the water. But it didn't help his taxying tests because, after a very good landing the floats 'dug in' and he completed his taxying run in a cloud of spray. He had no problems in taking off again, made a big circuit passing over the Isle of Wight and, on his second alighting, kept his speed up on the water to well above the regulation 12 knots. Dal Molin in the M.52 was next, followed by Batchy Atcherley in N.248 and D'Arcy Greig in the little Supermarine S.5. Both of these pilots completed the air and water tests in a thoroughly professional manner. Monti in the M.67 would have done the same had his activities not been interfered with by HMS *Iron Duke*, which took it upon itself to steam sedately across the middle of the alighting lane as he was taxying. The signal lamp on HMS *Medea* broke into a frenzy of Morse as race officials signalled to the warship to get out of the way as smartly as possible. Meanwhile Monti, in the Macchi, had to divert among the small craft to avoid the naval encounter. As soon as the course was clear he completed the test without further incident.

The last machine to go, Cadringher's Macchi M.67 with the three-bladed propeller, which had failed to get airborne the previous day, actually made its maiden flight on this occasion. There were a few anxious faces among the Italian contingent but Cadringher got the machine off without incident and successfully completed the taxying tests at a smart clip. All the machines were duly towed back to Calshot and moored out in the bay. By six o'clock they had all successfully completed a mooring-out test.

During the mooring-out test there were anxious moments for Orlebar when it was noticed that the starboard float of Atcherley's S.6, N.248, was taking in water. Mitchell was able to put his mind at rest because the rate of intake was not fast enough to endanger the machine before the end of the six-hour period. In any case the float would have been unlikely to fill completely because each float was divided into three watertight compartments by the petrol tank which, even if full, which it wasn't, would have contributed some buoyancy. This was not nearly as serious a problem as the one they found when the machines were taken ashore and into their hangars for routine maintenance ready for the race on the morrow. Stan Orme was the Rolls-Royce fitter-tester allocated to Waghorn's machine. One of his jobs was to remove the Lodge XK170 plugs from the engine, examine them and replace them with a fresh set that had been run in an engine and then rebuilt by Lodge. Examination of the plugs is an essential, and skilled, chore when operating any high-performance engine. It was particularly important in this case because the 'R' engine was prone to fill the supercharger volutes with neat fuel when idling and when it was opened up, this wet petrol would swill into the cylinders and proceed to wash the lubricant off the cylinder walls and cause the pistons to pack up. This very thing had happened when Waghorn went out for his navigability test. Lovesey had started the engine before Waghorn got aboard. When the pilot opened up, precisely what Lovesey had feared happened. The engine hesitated,

belched out flame and smoke and then ran rough for a few seconds until the plugs cleared.

Stan Orme was therefore specially on the lookout for specks of molten aluminium on the plug electrodes. At 10.00 pm that evening he found them on just one cylinder. He at once showed the plug to Tom Moon, the technical officer, who had been with High Speed Flight since Venice in 1927. Lovesey saw it too and immediately summoned Hives.

In common with Supermarine the Rolls-Royce company had made sure that the people who had worked so hard on the machines were present at the race to see them perform. One such party from Derby were the racing-shop engine fitters whom Hives had lodged at the Crown Hotel in Southampton. One can't help feeling that Hives had seen to it that they were there, and in one group, just in case of this kind of emergency. First of all he had to make sure that the rules allowed them to change a piston. The rules were quite clear that they could. But the race committee had to be consulted, as had the Italian team captain. This took time and it was midnight before Hives could go into town and rake the fitters out of bed. As probably the finest team of fitters in the country at the time there was no delay when they did start. Within ten hours they had lifted the block, replaced the offending piston and tucked everything up again. It was a near thing.

The Race

The weather men at the Meteorological Office had told the Air Ministry and Royal Aero Club that the weather was always fine on the Solent during the second week in September. That beautiful morning of 7 September, with the wind raising a ripple on the sea and a light film of stratus cloud which would burn off before 10 am, proved them right. Not only was the 1929 Schneider Trophy race *the* aviation event of the year, it was *the event* of the year for the British public. For weeks the daily Press and the technical Press had been giving blow-by-blow accounts of the preparations. Meanwhile, the railway companies offered special cheap excursion rates to key points. South Coast Radio added a new dimension. Those who could not get to the race could listen to an eye-witness account by two expert commentators. Squadron Leader Helmore and Flight Lieutenant Ragg, who had been set up in a canvas enclosure on top of Ryde pier pavilion. On top of this same building the official timekeepers had installed themselves with sighting wires on the seaward side and landward side just in case a pilot should decide to go behind them. The sighting point was the weather cock on top of Ryde Parish Church.

The Press were accommodated here too. But most of the official guests were to be found aboard SS *Orford*, an ocean-going liner which had been chartered by the Royal Aero Club as a large and luxurious grandstand. On a less pretentious scale the technical staff of Vickers Supermarine had chartered the SS *Monarch* while the works were accommodated on board a lighter towed by

COMPETITORS NUMBER		COMPLETED LAPS TIME IN MINUTES & SECONDS. SPEED IN M.P.H. DECIMALS OMITTED							SPEED OF RACE M.P.H.
		1	2	3	4	5	6	7	
U.S.A. 1	TIME			17·2					
	LAP SPEED								
GREAT BRITAIN 2	TIME	5·45	11·25	16·5	22·43	28·22	34·4	39·42	328
	LAP SPEED	324	329	331	328	330	327	331	
ITALY 4	TIME	6·30	13·0	19·32	26·8	32·43	39·18	45·54	284
	LAP SPEED	286	287	285	283	283	283	282	
GREAT BRITAIN 5	TIME	6·34	13·10	19·47	26·24	33·2	39·39	46·15	282
	LAP SPEED	284	282	282	281	281	281	283	
ITALY 7	TIME	6·34							
	LAP SPEED	284							
GREAT BRITAIN 8	TIME	6·9	11·54	17·33	23·10	28·50	34·28	40·5	325
	LAP SPEED	302	324	330	332	328	331	332	
ITALY 10	TIME	6·11							
	LAP SPEED	301							

The score board for the 1929 event with the space for the entry of Al Williams and his Mercury empty. (*Flight*)

a small and fussy tug which towed them out to the middle of the course. It was said at the time that two million people watched the race. Every vantage point, every beach and every yacht in the Solent was pressed into service as a viewing point.

As laid out in the regulations starting signals would be given by HMS *Medea* which had been positioned, after consultation with the team captains, at the entrance of Southampton Water off the Calshot buoy. From this point the machine could take advantage of the southerly wind, with a touch of east, which prevailed that day. By midday the Italian machines were on station and ready to go, followed by the British machines. The last to go was Waghorn's S.6 which was being run-up on the Calshot slipway long after the Italians were on the move, with the Rolls-Royce mechanics checking the results of their nocturnal activities. But by 1.30 it was out by the *Medea* on its individual pontoon and ready to go.

Orlebar's race strategy was conditioned by three factors. Because of the relative inefficiency of the surface radiators in the S.6 the Rolls-Royce engines could not be held at full throttle for any length of time without overheating. Even, had this been possible, the fuel load was insufficient to take them through the race at full power.

Moreover, there had been no chance to assess the Italian performance. All he knew was that Motta's M.67 had shown itself capable of 360 mph during the speed runs before the fatal crash. The only course was to send Waghorn out first with instructions to 'go fast slowly', to keep the coolant temperature down and to fly to finish.

As Dal Molin was the Italian safety racer it was logical to follow him with D'Arcy Greig and save Atcherley until last, delaying his take-off as long as possible within the regulations – a delay of 15 minutes after the starting gun was allowed – so that he could assess Cadringher's speed in the first of the M.67s. If need be he could then instruct Atcherley to make an all out effort at the risk of the machinery. He had to assume that Monti, in the latest M.67, with the three-bladed propeller, would not be as fast as Cadringher, in the older Macchi, which had at least flown more than once. So far as the Colonel Bernasconi was concerned he could only play on the British nerves and hoped to provoke them into pressing their machines to the point of mechanical failure. But his heart must have been heavy because he knew that the untried Isotta-Fraschini engines were most unlikely to last the course.

The first machine was due to leave the take-off area

Macchi M.67 on the slipway at Calshot in 1929. Italian mechanics are testing the 18-cylinder (three banks of six cylinders) Isotta-Fraschini engine. (*Flight*)

at two o'clock. With 20 minutes to go, N.247 was filled with hot Castrol oil – the grade was henceforward to be known as Castrol R in honour of its use in this engine – and Cyril Lovesey fired-up the engine and ran it for two minutes to get the oil circulating. Leaving the engine turning over quickly, he changed places with Waghorn, standing there in white overalls on top of swimming trunks and wearing a navy-blue flying helmet. His take-off run started immediately he was winched off the pontoon, which had been towed out of line with the wind so that the machine could turn itself into wind without using undue rudder to counter engine torque. Watched anxiously by Orlebar, he gained speed in a gentle curve with the port float almost submerged and the machine shrouded in spray; then the floats started to get onto the step, the spray dispersed and he was running cleanly, directly into wind. It was a copybook take-off and, at

14.02 and 5.2 seconds to be exact, he swept past Ryde pier and headed for the Seaview marker boat, swung round it using the level RAF turn and headed for Hayling Island. In a little over half a minute he had found the pylon, made the acute turn and was swinging back towards Southsea and Calshot. For the first time British spectators had the sensation of seeing an apparently silent high-speed machine with sound following later. While the speed of the machine was apparent to everyone, the rumble of the Rolls-Royce 'R' engine and the geared propeller turning over almost lazily, so that at certain angles the blades could be seen by close observers, was something of an anticlimax. But the speed announced over the loudspeakers as he swept past Ryde pier for the first time was anything but an anticli-max. The speed announced, 324 mph (521.43 km/h), was 24 mph faster than the Absolute World Speed

Macchi M.67 taxying off its float. (*Flight*)

Record set up by de Bernardi in the M.52R, which at that moment was being warmed up on the big Italian three-machine pontoon for take-off.

Waghorn's second lap, in 5 minutes 39.8 seconds – 5 seconds faster than his first lap – indicated that he was finding his marker more accurately, after initial confusion because of the mass of boats around the markers. It was equivalent to 329.16 mph (529.73 km/h). He was flying the machine beautifully, lapping in under six minutes with the speeds coming over the speakers at 331 mph for the third round, 328 mph for the fourth.

As Waghorn was streaking across from Southsea to Cowes on his fourth round with the S.6 looking as if it was pulled along by an immensely strong, invisible piece of elastic, Dal Molin was airborne after a relatively short, clean take-off run and passed Ryde pier ahead of Waghorn with the twelve-cylinder Fiat engine screaming defiance. Comparing it with the Rolls-Royce it was difficult to imagine that the two V-12 engines could make such a different sound. With a red machine in the air it began to look like a race to the crowds and they were given a view of two years' aviation progress as the S.6 relentlessly overhauled the red Macchi. There were 20 seconds between the two machines as they passed along the Hampshire coast between the Hayling and Southsea

markers; at the west Cowes turn Dal Molin was still 100 yards ahead, flying close to the sea but by the time they came to Ryde pier, Waghorn's S.6 had rumbled ahead on its penultimate lap. Nevertheless it was good to see at least one of the Italian machines going so well and being flown so precisely by stocky Dal Molin. It was interesting to compare his cornering technique with that of the British pilot. Two 'chasers' from the RAE had worked out that it was best to take the turns at a steady 3G and to let the machine gain a little height as it came out. The Italian technique, completely different from that used at Venice two years ago, was inspired by the RAF turn but was different in that the course flown was a parabola and was initiated by a slight gain in height before the turn. It was christened by the Italian crew the '*Curva Garda Parabolica*' and was subsequently used by them when they took Coupe Blériot records in the M.67 the following year.

As the M.52 speeds started to come through it was clear that it was no challenge to the S.6. Dal Molin's first lap speed of 286.2 mph was fractionally slower than his second lap but thereafter his lap speeds dropped into the 283 mph region. Dal Molin had covered two laps and was on his third as Waghorn, in N.247, completed his final lap. Inexplicably the British machine thundered off in the direction of Seaview as if he were going to continue.

While Waghorn was on that southern leg, D'Arcy Greig, in the little S.5, had taken off from alongside *Medea* to start his time trial. Meanwhile Waghorn's S.6 was seen to round the Seaview marker and head for Hayling, gaining height, much to the consternation of the officials, who expected him to turn and alight in the take-off area. He rounded the Hayling marker at a height of about 470 feet, headed for Southsea and finally succeeded in rounding the west Cowes pylon before alighting on the sea. Just as Webster had done at Venice he had failed to punch his lap counter on one lap, and imagined that he had a lap to go before the finish. While he sat in his cockpit, despondently trying to work out what he had done wrong, the crowds all round the Solent were jubilant in his performance. But a launch from *Medea* was soon alongside to take him in tow and wipe the sorrow from his face. His time for the seven laps had been 39 minutes 42.8 seconds, equivalent to a speed of 328.63 mph (528.88 km/h). It was a full 50 mph faster than Webster's speed at Venice and every lap had been better than 30 mph in excess of the Absolute World Speed Record.

While this episode was unfolding Cadringher's M.67 was seen to be taking off, just as D'Arcy Greig started on his third lap. This was the moment of truth for

the British and hundreds of stop-watches were on the machine as it shot past Ryde pier with the 18 cylinder Isotta engine emitting a staccato scream even more piercing than that of Dal Molin's Fiat AS.3, whose M.52 had preceded Cadringher across the line, on its final round, flying low and followed by a trail of black smoke which experienced observers had come to expect from the Italian machine, the M.67. On his first lap he passed Ryde pier still astern of his compatriot at a speed of 284 mph, barely that of the S.5. On the ensuing round he navigated the Southsea mark quite successfully but at Cowes with his windscreen obliterated by black, oily smoke from the engine and dizzy with fumes despite the fresh air supply the ground crews had hastily rigged up in the cockpit, he failed to see the turn. He realised he must be past it and made a sweeping left hand turn over the Isle of Wight, passing three miles inland before, almost unconscious, he turned back and put the machine down on the water between *Medea* and Calshot. It was a sad blow to Italian hopes and put the ball entirely into Monti's court in the second untried M.67.

D'Arcy Greig was flying the S.5 flat-out to try to match Dal Molin's speed in the M.54R which had been given to him just prior to take-off. The geared Napier Lion VIIB fitted to N.219 for the race was giving all it had got and running like a sewing machine but as he

Supermarine S.5 taking off. The propeller torque reaction is forcing the port float low in the water. (*Flight*)

Supermarine S.5 with its Napier Lion VII engine obstructing the pilot's view ahead. (*Flight*)

crossed the line shortly after 3.25 pm and his speed came through at 282.11 mph, it was seen to be 2 mph less than that of the M.52R.

As D'Arcy Greig crossed the timing strip for the last time Richard Atcherley was airborne and heading for Ryde pier. Batchy's take-off run must have felt like an eternity. As the afternoon had worn on the wind had freshened a little and, running against the tide, had created a slight chop superimposed on a swell rolling in from the sea. These were conditions that the S.6 definitely did not like and Atcherley's heavily laden machine started to porpoise in a cloud of spray and adamantly refused to get up on the step. The pilot had kept his head down under the cockpit to protect his goggles for the prescribed number of seconds at the start of take-off but each time the aircraft pitched he had to put his head up to see what was happening. Immediately his goggles were covered with spray. He had to push them above his helmet to see at all; immediately the propeller slipstream whipped them off. As Orlebar had found when he tested the machine it would eventually porpoise right out of the water and flop back again. In any other circumstances Atcherley would have aborted the take-off and started again but he was in the race now and he had to live with the problem. Eventually the machine made one big leap which got it over the hump. It landed back on the water but fast enough to start the floats planing. One more leap and it was in the air and heading for Ryde pier with Atcherley vainly trying to push his spare

pair of goggles up with one hand. The other pair had disappeared into the Solent, taking the retaining straps with them. Fortunately there was a small eye shield fitted to the extremity of the left hand side of the windscreen. By pressing his head against this he was able to see a little to the left but absolutely nothing to the right.

Within seconds of take-off he was over Ryde pier, passing between the timekeepers and Ryde Church on his way to Seaview. Flying low and almost blind, he almost knocked the British and Italian observers off the top of the canvas-covered pylon mounted on the old destroyer, HMS *Urchin*, which marked the turn. In avoiding them he passed inside the turn and by that act disqualified himself without knowing it. His next problem was to find the Hayling Island marker. He longed for a compass and he headed vaguely in the direction of West Wittering, where Henry Royce had his home. Eventually he spotted the marker far over to his left and swung round well to the outside of it to head back to Cowes via Southsea. He had resigned himself to flying without goggles but on his third lap he again missed the Seaview turn, passing well inside of it again. Thereafter he flew a correct and accurate race, keeping an eye on the engine temperature gauge hovering around the 98°C mark. Atcherley's speed for the first lap, 302.46 mph, proved that he had flown many extra miles in the course of finding the Hayling marker, because his speeds progressively rose to 324.57 and 329.74 mph as he got the hang of the course. In 40 minutes and 5 seconds he had crossed the finish line for the seventh and last time, having established not only a new speed record for the Schneider Trophy race but on his fourth, fifth, sixth and seventh laps new 50 km and 100 km world records over a closed circuit. Meanwhile he had landed off Lee-on-Solent and had been picked up by Earl Howe, who was acting as steward in his own motor yacht, and revived himself with the earl's champagne. Even as he drank it the announcement was being made that he had been disqualified for cutting the turns. But his closed-circuit record stood because, on the specific laps claimed for the record, all turns had been correctly made. However, the British crowd was jubilant because while Atcherley's drama was being enacted, on his fourth lap, the last of the Macchi M.67s had successfully taken off, piloted by the experienced Giovanni Monti for the second time in its life. Trailing a cloud of steam in addition to the usual black smoke it had passed the start line, reached the Seaview turn and had then hurriedly alighted on the sea with clouds of steam coming from the cockpit and a badly scalded pilot aboard. A cooling water pipe had fractured, the last of the Italians was out of the race and while launches rushed to his assistance the crowd was celebrating the winning of the cup for the second time in succession. It was a sad day for Italy but the results were not unexpected, especially by their team. But they had tried hard and shown wonderful sportsmanship.

Next came the junketing and banquets. But these were not allowed to interfere with one more formality – it was almost a tradition – which had to be enacted while the High Speed Flight was at Calshot and all the machines on top line. This was to have a go at the World Speed Record. On the very eve of the Schneider race the Napier mechanics reckoned that they had finally got to the bottom on the fuel feed problems that had been bugging the beautiful Gloster-Napiers.

It was therefore decided that George Stainforth, who had been so disappointed by not being able to race, should go for the officially timed speed record on the measured 3 km course which the High Speed Flight maintained in Southampton Water. After he had made his runs Orlebar would take the S.6 out and have a second try at the record. These attempts went off without incident. Stainforth's four runs were timed at 351.3 mph, 328.3 mph and 329.3 mph, giving an average speed of 336.3 mph. Thereby he beat de Bernardi's record by 17.7 mph in spite of poor visibility over the water which made it difficult to keep a straight course. Shortly afterwards when Stainforth had alighted, Orlebar got into N.247, Waghorn's winning machine, fitted with the standard engine, and made four runs up and down the measured course. His times, in order, were 368.8, 365.5 and 343.7 mph, an average speed of 355.8 mph. Thus Stainforth's short-lived record had been broken by 19.5 mph and de Bernardi's by a staggering 32 mph.

Looking back at the 1929 Schneider race a number of things stand out. One of them was that although the firms concerned had two years to build the machines,

government delays in placing the orders deprived them of half of this time. In the two years since 1927 progress in engine design had allowed the engine builders to produce motors pushing out nearly 2,000 hp, more than twice that of the engines of 1927, without appreciably increasing their frontal area. However, cooling was becoming a very serious problem because the whole of the surface area of these tiny machines was insufficient to provide a radiating surface which would dissipate the heat from 2,000 hp. To help with the cooling the engines were run rich, which meant that the aircraft had to be made that much bigger to carry the extra fuel load but even then the radiating surface was not enough. Another factor was that the massive torque from these engines applied to fixed-pitch propellers made the machines difficult to handle in the initial stages of take-off and the floats now had to be made that much bigger than they need be simply to prevent the aircraft from turning over at this stage in the proceedings. That the Italian designers appreciated this was shown in the Savoia-Marchetti SM.65 with its contra-rotating propellers which did not have to contend with torque effects and could therefore be flown off smaller, low-drag floats.

The Aircraft

The Bernard Racers

Adolphe Bernard was an entrepreneur who seemed to have a gift for mixing with the right people, and initiating action. He came from the Paris suburb of Asnières, in that loop of the Seine which housed the northern industrial complex of the capital, close by the Hispano factory at Bois-Colombes and a host of engine and aircraft manufacturing establishments in that area. In the light of this it is not unnatural that he had associations with two other 'B's; Louis Béchereau, the Deperdussin and SPAD designer and Marc Birkigt, the talented designer of Hispano-Suiza engines, both of whom were working in that area during the closing stages of World War One. It is said that they were known as *'Les Trois Bs'*. But there was a fourth 'B' who was probably the most important of all, namely shrewd Louis Blériot, the guiding light of SPAD, who also had factories in that area. One is tempted to feel that the original *'Trois Bs'*, were in truth Blériot, Béchereau and Birkigt, the legendary trio who created the immortal SPAD fighter, and that Bernard was the *quatrième* 'B'.

The success of the SPAD XIII created an enormous demand for this aircraft and Blériot put Bernard in charge of his assembly plant at Levasseur, one of the nine plants building SPADs. Out of this grew the first Société Avions Bernard (SAB). Just who put up the cash to form SAB is not clear. Be that as it may, in the closing stages of the war SAB were in a position to build a short series of biplane fighters to their own design, one of which was displayed at the Paris Air Show at the Grand Palais in 1919.

SAB appear to have languished and died in the postwar slump. However Bernard reorganised his finances and a new company, Société Industrielle des Métaux et du Bois (SIMB) was formed in 1922 to build fighter aircraft exploiting the exciting new aluminium alloy Duralumin devised by the Germans in the recent war. The French, with their huge reserves of aluminium ore in the south, were keen to exploit this material and the 1921 Salon de l'Air saw an enormous display of construction methods, many quite impractical, using this material.

Jean Hubert, Bernard's designer was caught up in the trend and produced a complex fighter design, way ahead of its time, which made clever but complex use of the new material. The design was developed but the French military were more interested in steel lattice structures. More capital was needed and Bernard conceived the idea of building a high-speed machine which would win the well-endowed annual Coupe Beaumont air race and then go on to take the world airspeed record for which the French government of the day was offering a handsome reward.

In the event two high-speed machines were built, designated V.1 and V.2, the first to be powered by a Modèle 14, 500 hp Lorraine-Dietrich motor and the second to have the new, broad-arrow, Modèle 50 Hispano-Suiza 620 hp geared engine. Both of these were wooden, ply-skinned, mid-wing machines, lovely to look at and beautifully built. However, their designer had drastically underestimated the tailplane area required for stability and V.1 crashed on its maiden flight, almost killing its pilot, the illustrious Florentin Bonnet. After a little belated wind-tunnel work in the Eiffel tunnel, this shortcoming was corrected on the V.2, which on 8 November 1924 went on to take the French national speed record at a speed of 393.40 km/h. On 11 December in the same year, after a reduction in span and a change of mainplane incidence, plus revisions to the cowlings, Bonnet established a speed of 448.171 km/h over a 3 km course at Istres, a new world record which was to stand until 1928.

The Société Industrielle des Métaux et du Bois lasted until 1927, when Bernard's dabblings in the financial markets, using the firm's capital, caused it to be wound up. The Société des Avions Bernard was formed out of the remains on 14 September 1927. Jean Hubert remained as chief designer with Georges Brunet and Roger Robert as assistants. Sadly, Hubert was killed in a car accident near Caen only weeks after the formation of the new company. At a loss for a designer of authority, Bernard hired Louis Béchereau as a consultant. It was a good move because although Brunet and Robert were first-class engineers, Bernard were, after all, in the upper echelons of high-speed aircraft manufacturers, with the world speed record under their belt. To have someone of the calibre of Béchereau as a consultant was expected of them. Moreover, he was a man who could be innovative without his every move being questioned.

Exactly a year after the formation of the new SAB the French government moved to rationalise the multitude of departments which administered aviation. Hitherto there had been aviation sections in the ministries for the Army, the Navy, the Colonies, Public works and the rest.

From 14 September they were regrouped in a single Air Ministry under the jurisdiction of M. André Victor Laurent d'Eynac. Only a month later it was announced that orders for high-speed aircraft to contest the 1929 Coupe Schneider had been allocated to Bernard, Nieuport-Astra and SPAD. Details of the contracts are lost in the mists of time but it is known that the one to Bernard called for two trainers, one with a Le Rhône radial and the other with a Modèle 50, V-12, 600 hp Hispano engine, and two contest machines which were to be powered by a new 1,800 hp Hispano engine. Along with this went a development contract order for the Bernard Jockey 20-C-1 fighter.

The wooden Jockey had already been displayed at the Paris Salon in the summer of 1928. Its construction set the pattern for all the wooden Bernard HV (Haute Vitesse) machines for the Schneider. It broke new ground in having a one-piece, multi-cellular wing incorporating most of the front fuselage in its centre section. The cross-section of this wing was like a huge fishbone with the pilot sitting with his legs through a hole down the fish's spine. The rear fuselage and pilot's cockpit were attached to the rear face of this wing and the engine bearers to the front of it. The sandwich was held together by four massive tiebars. Structurally the wing was enormously torsion-resistant being made up of at least thirteen box-spars. These were made up on long tables and when finished assembled with spanwise spacers between each sub-spar. After gluing, the steps between the spars were planed off, the nose and tail cap ribs fitted and the whole wing covered with plywood diminishing in thickness towards the tips. The width of this substantial cellular mainspar was approximately half the full chord of the wing.

One would have expected a monocoque rear fuselage from Béchereau, but here again the multi-cellular theme was perpetuated with two deep, double-box longerons which had metal fittings to pick up with the main tiebars at the front end. They extended back to the tail and were fabricated with the outer surface curved to conform with the fuselage line. These spars were based on ash stringers with internal elements arranged to act as a Warren-truss. The pilot's seat, headfairing and cockpit floor were formed in the forward end of this rear section. Machines intended for in-line engines had fabricated, sheet-metal engine bearers shaped rather like the protruding chin of the Supermarine S.5. Bracing tubes connected it to the upper ends of the centre-fuselage tie bars. The one radial-engined machine, the HV.40, had a welded tubular engine mounting.

The empennage consisted of a pretty, elliptical tailplane of wooden construction skinned with ply and based on the D-spar which formed the leading edge. The elevators were similarly ply-skinned with seals to the tailplane. The fin and rudder were of similar construction following the methods established on Bernard fighters.

The machines were supported on their floats by tubular steel struts cased in load-bearing wooden fairings which replaced longitudinal bracing wires. Lateral bracing was by two sets of streamlined wires, each consisting of a float track wire and two bracing wires to the wings. Since the wings were structural members in their own right and were in effect given the extra job of preventing the float assembly from collapsing sideways, Béchereau conceived the idea of allowing them to flex naturally. This insulated them from water shock loads, by anchoring the ends of the float-bracing wires on stacks of Belleville washers contained in little cylinders. (Belleville washers are double-turn spring washers.) Thus the wing could live a life of its own and follow its normal flex pattern.

The floats were fabricated from flush-riveted Duralumin and housed steel fuel tanks located forward of the step. French know-how on high-speed float design was at that time virtually non-existent and, it is said, Bernard draughtsmen spent their night hours during the 11th (1928) Paris Salon, after closing hours time, picking off the dimensions of the floats of the Macchi 52 then on display. Tenth-scale models were then water tested using a towing rig motivated by a device strongly reminiscent of a Wright Brothers launcher. The end result was evidently satisfactory during the limited flying done by the HV (Haute Vitesse) racers and, in any case, provided a practical basis for development rather than being simply a carbon copy.

It is an interesting sidelight on cross-fertilisation of ideas between Bernard and Supermarine that while the HV landplane record-breaker no doubt inspired Reginald Mitchell to create the S.4, equally the HV.120 with the outer banks of the broad-arrow engine faired into a mid-wing provided inspiration for the Bernard designers when they came to establish a configuration for their wooden floatplane with its broad-arrow engine. At first glance the HV.120 could well have been a carbon copy of the Supermarine S.4, even to the one-piece wing in unit with the middle section of the fuselage.

In all, three engine types were used during preparations for the 1929 contest. For the HV.40 trainer, the first machine to be delivered, there was the Bristol-based Gnome et Rhône Mistral from which 900 hp was promised but never realised. For the HV.41 trainers with in-line engines there was a special version of the Hispano-Suiza V-12, geared Modèle 50 tuned to give 1,000 hp by raising the compression ratio and running it faster, thus reducing its life to 15 hours. For the HV.120 contest machines Hispano-Suiza were to provide what was given a temporary designation of 18R Special. This was a supercharged and geared broad-arrow engine from which 1,800 hp was promised.

The water-cooled engines used a variety of radiator configurations. The one 1929 HV.41 trainer started with a belly-mounted Lamblin radiator between the float struts. This was changed to more generous Lamblin cuff-radiators mounted round the roots of the float struts. A similar arrangement was used on the three HV.42 trainers for 1931. The contest machines were endowed with rectangular, flat-panel, Curtiss-type wing radiators attached to the upper surfaces of the wings.

For the 1931 contest, contracts were let out to Lorraine-Dietrich and Renault for engines developing more than 2,000 hp. There was a further contract awarded to Farman for a 1,300 hp engine, two of which were meant to power a proposed Bernard twin-engine, high-speed flying-boat.

The very pretty HV.40 radial-engined trainer was the first to be delivered, in the spring of 1928. However it sat around for two years awaiting the promised high-power replacement for its standard 650 hp Gnome-Rhône Mistral. It was taken to Berre when the team moved from Hourtin, as part of their baggage. Eventually someone got bored with seeing it lying around, ordered it to be checked, and it made its first flight in July 1930. Not only was it found to fly more willingly than any of the other Bernard Schneider racers but it proved to be better than good for aerobatics to the extent that the Air Ministry ordered a short series of metal versions of it, presumably landplanes.

For the purposes of clarity here is a list of Bernard aircraft and their engines.

1929 contest

HV.41 trainer	Hispano-Suiza Modèle 50 V-12 high compression special. 900/1,000 hp 15 hr life.
HV.120-1	Hispano-Suiza 18R broad-arrow eighteen-cylinder direct-drive, supercharged. 1,500/1,680 hp. Given the civil registration F-AKAK for acceptance trials.
HV.120-2	Hispano-Suiza 18R as above but with geared drive. Civil registration F-AKAL.

1931 contest

HV.40	Gnome-Rhône 9 Mistral. Special 900 hp promised but never materialised. Delivered July 1929 but first flown with standard 650 hp engine January 1931.
HV.41	Hispano-Suiza Modèle 50 Special. Donated serial no. 4. The only trainer available during training for the 1929 race. First flown August/September 1929.
HV.42	Hispano-Suiza Modèle 50 Special 900/1,000 hp. Three built and given serial nos 1, 2 and 3. HV.120 cockpit enclosure, cuff radiators, trailing edge of cylinder fairings cut back to improve view during take-off and landing. Longer fuselage oil radiators than the HV.41.
HV.120-1	Hispano-Suiza Modèle 18R Special 1,500/1,680 hp. Direct drive.
HV.220	All metal construction. Lorraine 12RCR Radium 2,000/2,200 hp engine.
HV.330	All-metal Renault 12 Ncr 2,000 hp.

Antoine Paillard, Bernard's chief test pilot was an artist at his trade. A veteran airline pilot, he had to take a course on waterborne aircraft at the École Schreck before he went on to test the Schneider racers. He made the maiden flight of the HV.41 at the Hourtin base at the turn of September 1929, after the race for which it was intended had been run.

Roger Robert, who was chief designer on the HV project, told how he went out in a launch with Madame Paillard hoping to witness the first take-off. As Paillard opened up the engine to start his run Madame Paillard produced a revolver from her handbag, pointed it at Robert, and announced, 'If this aeroplane of yours kills my husband, I shall kill you.' Fortuitously the HV did fly well, watched not only by Robert but also by M. Megaud, Managing Director of SAB and a group of his engineers. Service observers were the Commandant of the base, Adelus, and Jean Amanrich, who was later to become Captain of the French high speed flight for 1931. Incidentally, this was not the first outing of the HV.41. It had earlier been mounted on the shorter floats from the HV.40 which dug in when attempts were made to taxi the machine while the wingtips touched the water due to torque effect when the engine was opened up.

By the end of 1929 the HV.41 had made ten flights in the hands of Paillard but so far had not attained its contract speed of 430 km/h despite the change to cuff radiators. The machine was reported to handle well, but the best speed attained was 410 km/h. Throughout this period the engine team had a hard time replacing burnt and deformed valves and suffering continuous plug trouble.

While testing was going on at Hourtin the two HV.120 contest airframes had been completed at Bernard's La Courneuve works. The first of the Hispano 18R engines, the alternative direct-drive version, was delivered in January 1930. Having overcome their initial shock at the gargantuan proportions of this noble engine, the engine team installed it for ground-running in the factory yard. It is on record that the Hispano engine fitters struggled for a whole day to fire it up until they eventually discovered that the plug leads were crossed. This machine, works serial HV.120-1, civil registration F-AKAK, made its first flight in the hands of Paillard on 25 March 1930 and by December of that year it had been worked up to 510 km/h.

The Testing

At the prompting of Sadi Lecointe the Air Maritime base on the large Bassin de Hourtin, in the Gironde, was chosen for the training of the 1929 team. Well away from main centres of population, it was safe from prying eyes, an essential, bearing in mind that the French challenge was to be veiled in official secrecy. Hourtin was also the base for the École Schreck, a training establishment for flying-boats. Here the landplane pilots could have their first taste of maritime aviation.

Fiat C.29

Fiat have made many successful aeroplanes in their time. One wonders whether the C.29 can truthfully be numbered among them. It may be significant that the letter R, for Rosatelli, is always omitted from the type prefix. Maybe this is a tacit admission that Celestine Rosatelli was not inordinately proud of this particular creation.

Designed at the instigation of the Italian Air Ministry as one of the four options to challenge for the Schneider Trophy in 1929, the C.29 was tiny compared with Rosatelli's last racer, the mighty R.700 which Francesco Brack-Papa had campaigned in the early twenties. It was the smallest entry in the 1929 race with a wingspan of a mere 21 ft 9 in (6.6 m) and an all-up weight of 1,160 kg (2,556 lb). The design objective was to achieve the best possible power-to-weight ratio and to this end it was designed round a new, lightweight engine of 25.5 litre capacity – the AS.2 and AS.3 were designed to develop their power by running up to 3,300 rpm, almost 1,000 rpm more than the early engines.

Structurally it was something of a sheep in wolf's clothing. Beneath its sleek, metal-covered flying surfaces were to be found wooden spars and ribs. The two-spar wings and the empennage were both of composite construction with Duralumin skinning on spruce and poplar spars. The floats were also composite to the extent of having metal keels and frames with a planked wooden skin of silken smoothness.

In contrast, the fuselage was all metal but, eschewing the monocoque principal, Rosatelli designed a lattice frame consisting of machined, light-alloy longerons braced by steel tubular formers, with stranded-wire bracing, on which was superimposed the Duralumin skin.

However, the most significant design feature was the use of the engine mounting as the structural stress focus of the whole machine. This was fabricated from steel tubes and light alloy with two sidemembers in the form of Warren-trusses united by the engine firewall at the rear end and by what appears to have been a tubular crossmember at the front. The engine itself consolidated the structure. The float struts and wing spars picked up with suitable attachment points on this frame and the tail cone, comprising the pilot's cockpit and rear fuselage were built on the back of it.

While, to the purist, the use of wooden spars with a metal skin sounds, to put it mildly, a little unusual, the C.29 was an immensely strong aeroplane, being stressed to a load factor of 19.

Tranquillo Zerbi collaborated closely with Rosatelli in the design. As befitted the creator of a number of world-beating racing-car engines he was not afraid of running the engine fast to get the required horsepower. Consequently the AS.5 was rated at a continuous 1,000 bhp at 3,200 rpm with a maximum of 1,050 bhp at 3,300 rpm for a dry weight of 348 kg (767 lb) which gave it the outstanding power-to-weight ratio of 1.36 bhp per pound of weight, which compared more than favourably with the 1.24 bhp per pound of the Rolls-Royce 'R' of 1929. Its one drawback was the lack of a reduction gear to bring the propeller tip speed within bounds. Incidentally the weight of such a gear would have brought its power-to-weight ratio to about the same as that of the Rolls-Royce unit. As it was, the small, 2.35 m diameter, forged Curtiss-Reed propeller with which the machine was fitted was expected to operate at a tip speed of 406 m/sec (908 mph) when other designers felt that 350 m/sec (782 mph) was tempting providence. Supermarine's experience with the direct-drive Napier of the S.5 showed a considerable loss of efficiency at tip speeds of more than 335 m/sec.

Engine cooling of the C.29 was effected by surface radiators mounted on the upper and lower surfaces of the wings and represented a total cooling surface of approximately 4.3 sq m, or 46.2 sq ft. Oil coolers were fitted under the wing roots and in the nose of the machine, while there were further coolers on the upper float surfaces. One is left with the impression that, unless Fiat had developed an ultra-efficient type of surface radiator, the machine would have overheated badly in much the same way as the French Bernard racers if it had been persuaded to fly for any length of time.

Savoia-Marchetti SM.65

It is difficult at this late stage to ascertain whether Alessandro Marchetti's inspiration for the SM.65 was the push-pull nacelle which was the trade mark of his flying-boats. It most probably was, because his twin-engined flying-boat designs with the engines mounted high above and a low cantilever wing, depended to some extent for their stability on the lack of torque provided by the propellers rotating in opposing directions. It was a simple enough concept to take one of these nacelles, separate the engines sufficiently to accommodate a pilot between them, and mount it on top of a monoplane wing. There was no problem in supporting the tail plane on long booms on either side of the rear propeller. This twin-boomed fuselage was mounted on long slender floats with a very low frontal area which, as well as being, with the struts, part of the lateral bracing structure, also acted as part of the fore and aft structure. No doubt concerned by the possibility of tailplane flutter, Marchetti braced the tail booms with a pair of slim steel struts, in the formation, to the tail of the floats, which were extended for this purpose. The wing and tail plane were of constant-chord, rectangular planform, the wings having rounded tips. The single fin and rudder was mounted in cruciform in the middle of the tail plane and braced with streamlined wires.

Structurally the SM.65 was enormously strong. Marchetti was an instinctive designer rather than a technician and, just for good measure – so an old workman who had worked on the SM.65 told me – the main spars were made of walnut. The wings were of all-wooden construction and were planked with double-diagonal strips of thin mahogany. Almost the whole area of the wing top and bottom surfaces were covered with surface radiators. The tail-booms and empennage were also made of wood, this being the traditional material in the Varese area. In contrast the engine nacelle was of all-metal construction based on a steel tubular frame of Warren-truss construction skinned with light-alloy panels. The oil radiators were mounted on either side of the pilot's cockpit. The float struts were steel tubes of streamlined section with internal pipes to feed fuel from the floats, where it was contained in cylindrical tanks, to the engine.

With a wing area of 167.23 square feet and a weight of close to 3 metric tonnes the SM.65 had the highest wing loading of any aircraft in the 1929 race. Allied to a thin, sharp-edged wing with the airflow disturbed by wing radiators, it showed every promise of being a difficult aeroplane to fly. That promise was fulfilled in a tragic way. The apparent drawbacks of the design were the multiplicity of float struts which must have added considerably to the drag of the machine compared with the conventional configuration. Furthermore, the size of the tail plane was imposed by the clearance between the tail booms, and thus by the size of the rear propeller rather than by the true design requirements of the machine, and could also have added some drag. The machine served one useful purpose. That was to impress upon Castoldi the merits of contra-rotating propellers.

Calshot 1931

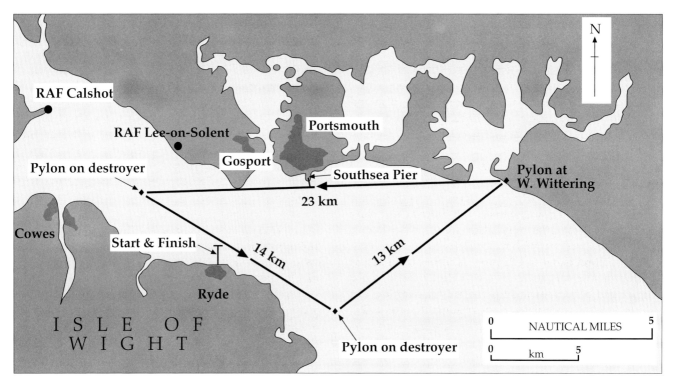

Schneider Trophy Contest Course: Calshot 1931.

Run-up

Almost as soon as the cheers and the tears had faded after the 1929 race, plans were afoot for 1931. In England, inevitably, approaches had first of all to be made to Lord Trenchard, the Chief of the Air Staff, apropos of the 1931 race; at that time, literally on the eve of his retirement. On the very day that Orlebar and Stainforth were breaking the Absolute World Speed Record, he produced a predictable reaction, bearing in mind that he had been manoeuvred into approving RAF participation in the 1929 event. All he had to say was that he could see no value in the Schneider Trophy race and that high-speed flying was better developed by properly organised scientific programmes. Moreover, he felt that the whole affair was bad for service morale and that was that. One wonders how so great a man could be so wrong. Worse still, his sentiments were confirmed by a Cabinet meeting in late September 1929 when the decision was minuted that an RAF team would not again be entered and that British participation was best left to private enterprise. This, despite the pronouncements of the Prime Minister immediately after the race.

It was a reasonable and logical reaction because the echoes of the Wall Street Crash were reverberating throughout the civilised world, and right on the Cabinet's own doorstep the Hatry financial empire had only recently fallen in ruins, taking with it the savings of many Britishers. There was no doubt that a lot of people in the RAF felt that they had got everything they wanted out of the Schneider contest, just as the Americans had done in 1926. It seemed to be scarcely their concern that just one more successful effort on their part would retain the Trophy in the UK for keeps.

In Italy the approach was different. The Italians had appeared at Calshot in 1929 as a matter of honour and in a spirit of sportsmanship, knowing full well that only a miracle could win them the race. They were determined to change all that and in the October following the race Colonel Bernasconi, who continued to command the Reparto Alta Velocità, convened a meeting with Italian designers to discuss plans to retrieve the Trophy for Italy. The conclusions they reached were heavily influenced by Italo Balbo, who had decided that the 1929 idea of spreading the options over a number of companies had been a mistake after all, and that for 1931 they should fall back on the expertise of Macchi and Fiat. Only the Savoia-Marchetti push-pull floatplane was considered to show any promise because of the way its engine layout eliminated torque from the design equation. It would therefore be retained. As a result of this decision the third Fiat C.29, number C-130bis, is said never to have taken to the air and was, sadly, scrapped.

Whatever the internal politics of British participation might be, the race had to go on. The rules of the Trophy stipulated that a meeting of the FAI sporting commission should be held before the end of January of the year preceding the race to decide the rules. Two proposals put forward by the British Royal Aero Club, as the host nation, were approved at this meeting in January 1930. One, which had been discussed between the British and Italians immediately after the 1929 race, was to combine the navigability trial with the race so that the whole event could take place on one day. The idea was that this did not rely on getting two days in a row with fine weather. Added to that it drastically reduced the disruption of commercial traffic in the area where the event was likely to take place, namely the Solent. The rules called for a 'getting off', and alighting test immediately prior to the speed test with which it would be combined.

The second decision was more controversial because it struck at the very roots of the thrifty instincts of the French and Italians. It was to increase the entry deposit which had been required of every entrant since 1921, from 5,000 francs to 200,000 francs. It was a sum equivalent to £1,600 sterling or $8,000 at the time. The object was to discourage frivolous entries; it was approved. This threw the Italian and French clubs into a frenzy of pseudo-legal activity to get the decision reversed, and they very nearly did so in the middle of 1931, by a subterfuge. But in the end the higher entry deposit was upheld and the end result was a loss of time and effort which could have been more usefully employed in getting on with preparations for the race. The general confusion certainly detracted from the Royal Aero Club's lobbying efforts in aid of government participation. The politics which ensued have been chronicled in fascinating detail elsewhere.

The important thing was that both countries placed entries for three machines. Sadly, when it was almost too late, a message from Rear Admiral Moffett announced that there would be no entry from the USA. Nevertheless, everyone at the time was overjoyed that it was to be a three-cornered contest. French participation was especially welcome.

Reg Mitchell of Vickers-Supermarine and Arthur Sidgreaves of Rolls-Royce had ample experience of the way governments could change their minds at the last moment. Rolls-Royce were sure that there was a lot more power left in the 'R' engine. Mitchell, for his part had to be prepared to design a machine to defend the Trophy whether or not it was government backed. Accordingly a discreet approach was made to the Air Ministry early in 1930 to ask if development costs of the 'R' engine could be included in the routine Air Force engine development programme. This was agreed and a first step had been made. Rowledge of Rolls-Royce had told Mitchell privately that he could expect much more

than 2,000 bhp from the engine without affecting its silhouette, so he was able to quietly plan a new machine based on the S.6, but incorporating all the lessons learnt in 1929, as well as adapting it to a greater fuel load to assuage the thirst of a more powerful motor.

An interesting revelation in Parliament during April 1930 was that the cost of the Schneider machines to that date had been £230,000 and that since they were part of the Research Establishment, they were being reconditioned and brought up to date for further use. Only a month later the Air Ministry were offering the loan of the machines to anyone who was prepared to defend the Trophy. But the machines had to be insured, and it was well known that insurance for the kind of activity they were designed for was non-existent. This was difficult, but just possible economically, if a major firm like Supermarine had taken up the challenge. There were certainly a few very gifted test pilots outside the RAF who could well have done the job.

This statement must have been made before the Depression started to bite, or maybe Scrooge-like little Philip Snowden, the Chancellor of the Exchequer, put his oar in because, in January 1931, there came yet another about-face. Without any preliminary warning he blurted out that in no way would the machines or pilots of the High Speed flight – it still existed at Felixstowe – be loaned for the defence of the Trophy, nor would the services of the Navy or Air Force be available to help with the running of it. Nothing could be more final than that. It was a typically British emphatic denial of something that was about to happen. No sooner had the words been said than the Prime Minister, Mr Ramsay MacDonald, had ordered a feasibility study with the industry and had come out with the offer to loan the machines and men if £100,000 could be found from private funds to underwrite the cost to the country.

Almost immediately £20,000 was forthcoming from various industry sources, which seemed a good start. But while everyone was debating where the next £80,000 was coming from, a magic fairy appeared and publicly offered to make up the difference. Although one could hardly describe Lady Lucy Houston, widow of a shipping millionaire, as a fairy; maybe only P.G. Wodehouse could, properly, have done her justice. An ardent and arrogant Tory of the old brigade, one can see her waving her parasol and declaring that her only object was to save the dignity and sporting name of Great Britain from the petty meanness of a Labour government. All her public statements at the time, and there were more than a few of them, were good, red-blooded stuff aimed at rubbing the government's nose in the dust. The real truth of the matter was that her late husband, a tax exile in Jersey, owed the Chancellor of the Exchequer a large amount of income tax which the Inland Revenue was endeavouring to recover from his widow. Someone at the Exchequer made a confidential approach to the lady and suggested that if she were to make a £100,000 contribution to the cost of entering a Schneider team the matter would be forgotten; and so it was. To their credit, thankful for getting the Schneider problem out of their hair, the government ministers stood back and let her get on with it.

From that time on things started to move. At the beginning of February Squadron Leader Orlebar, who had been such an outstanding leader in 1929, was very rightly, and to his huge delight, assigned to lead the 1931 team. Concurrently it was announced that Flight Lieutenant John Boothman, Flight Lieutenants E.J. Linton Hope and F.W. Long, who were already engaged in high-speed flying at Felixstowe, would join the team. Another interesting and worthwhile appointment outside the RAF was that of Commander Bird, head of Vickers-Supermarine, to be chairman of the Royal Aero Club Schneider Trophy Committee.

A month later the Air Ministry announced that they had ordered two new contest machines from Supermarine to be powered by developed versions of the Rolls-Royce 'R' engine, Arthur Sidgreaves having confirmed to the Ministry that he could give them 2,350 hp. Additions to the High Speed Flight were also announced. The most notable of these, and a sympathetic choice, was George Stainforth who, because of the under-serviceability of the Gloster VI had not got a ride in 1929. It had also been thought wise to include a naval man in the team. He was Lieutenant R.L. Brinton, a fighter specialist serving with No. 407 Fleet Fighter Flight in the Mediterranean. Aged 26, he was the youngest, and least experienced, of the team. Others were Flying Officer L.S. Snaith, a gifted pilot, who had worked his way up from being a boy entrant in 1917, passing through the engineering branch and gaining his wings in 1923. He had been snapped up by the Central Flying School and had ended up as a seaplane test pilot at Felixstowe in early 1931. An even older hand from Felixstowe was Flight Lieutenant F.W. Long, who had joined the RAF in 1917 and since 1925 had been test-flying at Farnborough and later, since 1929, carrying out high-speed research flying at the Marine Aircraft Research Establishment. Finally there was Flight Lieutenant H.H. Leech, another Farnborough test pilot, whose name was well known to the public as an air-racer and as a polished aerobatic pilot in the prototype Miles Martlet light plane.

John Boothman, incidentally, was probably the most adventurous of the team. Educated in France, he had gone straight from school at the age of 16, falsifying his age as a matter of course, and joined the French Red Cross as an ambulance driver in the Balkans. For his efforts he had been awarded the Croix de Guerre. Joining the RAF in 1921, he became an instructor at the CFS in 1924 with, in common with Snaith, A.1 grading which means, in simple terms, the best. He was posted to Felixstowe in 1930.

Over in France things were not going well despite the best of intentions. In autumn 1930 a new unit, the Section d'Entrainement sur Hydravions de Grande Vitesse had been formed under the command of Jean Amanrich, an organiser and leader of the calibre of Orlebar, who was given a free hand to choose his own team. Of the original 1929 team only Maurice Vernhol

was retained because of his experience of air-racing. Amanrich also specially requested the services of Georges Francois Bougault, who was at that time commanding a fleet-fighter squadron aboard the aircraft carrier *Bearn*. A fully qualified aircraft engineer apart from his flying qualification, Bougault had been one of the heroes of the first Paris–Madagascar–Paris long-distance flight. The six other members of the Section were Captain Marty from the 32ème Regiment d'Aviation at Dijon, Lieutenant Paul Retourna from the 34ème Regiment d'Aviation at Le Bourget, Warrant Officer Doerner and Sergeant-Major Baillet of the 2ème Regiment d'Aviation stationed at Strasburg, Sergeant Dumas of the 3ème Regiment, Sergeant Goussin of the 30ème Regiment and finally Chief Warrant Officer Raynaud, the Chief Flying Instructor at the Istres base. It was a long list of pilots to only too few aircraft.

Headquarters of this new section were at Étang de Berre, the huge salt water lake a few miles to the northwest of Marseilles. There the section was more likely to find steady winds to ruffle the water which would make take-offs easier, without any attendant sea-swell. An additional bonus was the high salinity of the lake, giving a gain in buoyancy reserve which would help fledgling high-speed pilots with their initial hops. The team were quartered in the naval seaplane base which borders the civil airfield at Marignane. Training equipment still consisted of the venerable FBA-Schreck flying-boats despite pleas by Amanrich to be allocated a few, or even one, of the much faster Gourdou-Lesseurre GL810 boats which had just come into service as naval scouts. At least they would have been forty miles an hour faster than the 80 mph Schrecks, which were little different from Burri's FBA in the 1914 race.

The sole high-speed equipment, to start with, was the one and only Bernard HV.41 and the first HV.120 serial no. 01, with direct-drive Hispano engine. The only pilot with real experience on these machines was Antoine Paillard, Bernard's chief test pilot. However, they were due to receive three improved versions of the HV.41; the HV.42 and the first of these was promised for November. The second machine, painted bright red – actually a mock-up – was exhibited at the 12th Salon de l'Aéronautique in Paris in November. Neither of them flew until 10 March 1941 when Paillard made an uneventful 25 minute flight in HV.42-01 at Berre. His take-off time, 17 seconds, and the 430 km/h he realised, showed that S.A. Bernard had ironed out some of the problems affecting the HV.41. Unfortunately Paillard was occupied with a closed-circuit, long-distance record attempt at Oran which delayed test flying of the remaining HV.42 for some weeks.

The availability of aircraft at Berre was so bad that in April the pilots returned to their squadrons to make up their flying time and did not return until June, when all of them were able to pass out on the HV.41 and HV.42 trainers which at last were ready for them. Even then their flights were restricted in duration. All the machines were overheating badly and the most they were allowed to do was to take off, make a circuit and alight. The average training flight lasted almost five minutes.

In June there came a further setback for French aspirations. On the evening of the 15th Antoine Paillard, who had gone into hospital for a simple appendix operation, died of internal complications. His company immediately appointed a replacement, Roger Baptiste, who had been with them for eight months as Paillard's deputy, making the flight trials of the Bernard 20-C-1 Jockey fighter. Although Baptiste had a seaplane licence, for some inscrutable reason Bernard chose not to second him to Berre but handed over the test-flying of the HV.120 to Amanrich and Bougault. The first prototype, HV.120-01, with direct-drive propeller was literally the only high-speed racing floatplane available to the French at that time. Its top speed of 510 km/h (317 mph) was well behind the speeds being attained by the British and Italians. Nevertheless the two pilots built up experience during a series of short flights testing propellers.

Meanwhile the Nieuport-Delage ND 450 resolutely remained at Hourtin defying the attempts of the veteran Sadi Lecointe to get it off the water, while the Dewoitine HD.410 which had been the beneficiary of the very first production Lorraine Radium engine at the end of July was doing ground runs. But the manufacturers were still unable to clear it for flight. The two, all-metal Bernard airframes for the HV.220 and HV.320 stood waiting in the factory at Courneuve. Only the HV.220 had an engine installation from Renault, and that was a mock-up consisting of cylinder casting devoid of internals.

On the other side of the Alps the more experienced Italians were making good headway with their Macchi-Fiat project. Mario Castoldi had seen quite clearly that the limiting factor, now that engines of more than 2,000 hp were called for in machines with power-to-weight ratios of the order 0.6 kg (1.32 lb) per horsepower, was the size of floats necessary to give a buoyancy reserve big enough to prevent the machines winding round the propeller during the early stages of take-off. He had the example of the SM.65 before him which, because its two propellers turned in opposite directions, was entirely free from this torque effect and was able to make do with relatively small, low-drag flotation gear.

What he wanted to do was to build a machine similar to his classic low-wing, wire-braced floatplanes but with this facility. He knew that Rolls-Royce would give Supermarine 2,500 bhp in the next race. His problem was first of all to find an Italian engine of that power – Fiat didn't have one – and fit it with a torque eliminating device so that he could use smaller floats. His own contra-rotating propeller had already been experimented with. The previous year he had built a floating pontoon with, mounted on it, two Fiat A.20 engines facing each other, one fitted with a pusher and one with a tractor propeller, and brought together so that the propeller discs were parallel and in close proximity to each other. It was a typically simple empirical Castoldi rig which enabled him to run the propellers at differential speeds and at different distances apart and so thoroughly investigate the problem. The results he got proved that

not only was the idea valid but that there was gain in efficiency because the 'rear' propeller was operating in a stream of air which had already been accelerated by the front one. Therefore it could develop useful thrust when the machine was at a standstill without the dreaded torque effect.

The next problem was a 2,500 hp engine and the necessary gearing to drive two propellers in opposing senses. Here Fiat came to his rescue with an immaculate conception. This was to take two AS.5 engines, boosted to 1,250 bhp each, and mount them nose to nose in a subframe. Both would have reduction gears to bring propeller speeds down to a practical level. The reduction gears would serve a dual purpose because they would allow the drive line of the rear engine to be sufficiently offset to drive a propeller shaft running forward in the vee of the front engine and passing through the hollow propeller shaft of the front engine. The drive line of the front engine was naturally offset by its own reduction gear, mounted at the back of the engine, to allow this to happen. Since the vee of the forward engine would be full of propeller shafts it was proposed to mount the carburettors, which normally occupied this space, at the back of the engine, and distribute the air/fuel mixture by means of a supercharger. This would not only ensure fairly even distribution of the mixture but would also give a modest increase in power. The first sketch, produced by Zerbi and Vaghetti, shows an estimated power of 2,350 hp and a weight of 690 kg (1,521 lb).

It was a good solution to the problem because it absolved Fiat of the necessity to design and develop a new, big engine in an impossibly short space of time. It also gave them a power unit with a very small frontal area which, while being abnormally long, was not so lengthy that it was beyond the wit of Castoldi to design an airframe round it. Work on the design started early in 1931 and on 20 April the first engine ran for an hour at 2,000 bhp. It is a measure of the work put in by Fiat and Macchi that the first machine of the new type, designated MC.72, was delivered to Desenzano and ready to fly on 22 June.

Meanwhile the work of the Reparto Alta Velocità had not been without its tragedy. On 18 January Dal Molin, who had taken over development of the Savoia-Marchetti SM.65 after the death of Motta, had gone out to Lake Garda for further speed trials. This time they were to be officially timed with an eye on the outright speed record. He had started his run when the machine dived into the water and disappeared in the inevitable gigantic cloud of spray. Some of the lighter parts of the machine floated to the surface and were recovered but the engine nacelle and poor Dal Molin were never seen again. It was a sad start to a bad year for the Reparto.

Dal Molin was one of the most experienced pilots at Desenzano and his death was a sad loss. He left behind him the equally experienced Agello, also a warrant officer, and Lieutenants Cadringher, Monti, and Carnaveri from the 1929 course. They were joined later in the first half of the year by a new intake who were assigned to contest the 1931 race. The most senior of these was

Lieutenant-Colonel Casinelli, who was accompanied by Lieutenants Lippi, Scapinelli, Buffa, Neri, Bellini, Nicelli, Captain Baldi and Warrant Officers Fruet and Gari. Of these Carnaveri, Gari, Cadringher and Lippi were later posted elsewhere, the last two to the Altitude School at Ortobello.

As in previous years the two months preceding the race were the climax of all the engineering activity aimed at bringing the racers to the line and fit for the contest. In Great Britain the High Speed Flight had moved quarters to Calshot, displacing the resident flying-boat squadron which moved north to Stranraer. But their machines did not arrive until mid-July because of development problems with the boosted 'R' engine.

It seems to be generally assumed that development of the 'R' engine stopped between the end of the 1929 race and the go-ahead for the 1931 engines. This was not so. Not only were engines supplied to the High Speed Flight when it moved back to Felixstowe but during 1930 an intense development programme was carried out on two new direct-drive engines, R17 and R19 for Sir Henry Segrave's water speed record boat, *Miss England III*. These were paid for by Sir Charles Cheers Wakefield, head of Castrol Oil Company, who was backing the attempt. We owe it to him that at the end of 1930 there were in existence 'R' engines capable of developing 2,053 bhp at 3,000 rpm.

To gain the promised extra 400 hp for the 1931 race it was proposed to gear the supercharger to run faster and so increase the induction pressure, enlarging the air intakes accordingly. At the same time they would run the engine faster and change the reduction gearing to bring the propeller speed to the same as before. It sounded very simple but meant a complete redesign of most of the reciprocating parts of the engine and some of the crankcase castings too. There had been oil consumption problems as a result of the high cylinder pressures being achieved – at one time it was at the rate of 125 gallons per hour – and fuel consumption was abnormally high because the air-fuel ratio had to be set very rich to keep the exhaust valves intact. As late as April engines were lasting only 20 minutes at full power but by mid-July they were lasting half an hour under full power and, of course, much longer at part throttle. As a standby the rebuilt S.6s, now designated S.6As, had been fitted with 1929, 1,900 hp 'H' engines and had been with the High Speed Flight ever since they moved to Calshot in May. But Orlebar obviously wanted his team to have experience on the actual race machines and in mid-July it was decided to issue the 'Half-hour' 'R' engines to Vickers-Supermarine to enable them to deliver the S.6B. At the same time the Rolls-Royce high-speed tender was put back into service to ensure a steady flow of serviceable engines.

Pumping fuel into the float tanks of a Supermarine S.6. (*Flight*)

Supermarine S.6B No. S.1596 of 1931. The aileron horn balances can be seen on the upper surface of the wings. (*Flight*)

Early in the training period, when the first of the reworked S.6As, N.247, was delivered, Orlebar had taken the machine for a test flight and encountered the first ever case of rudder flutter with the S.6. It first occurred in a mild form on the climb-out under full power, and stopped when the throttle was eased back. But later in the same flight, when the machine was flying near its maximum in a speed test, the flutter came back to an uncontrollable degree and Orlebar was forced to make what looked like becoming a crash landing. The vibration stopped only on the approach to the water. Cyril Lovesey, the Rolls-Royce development engineer, who was watching, told Orlebar afterwards that he could actually see the rudder and fin fluttering. Examination of the structure afterwards showed that the skin forward of the empennage was badly buckled, necessitating the return of the aircraft to Woolston for repairs. It was too late in the day to embark on structural alterations to the machines – the S.6Bs had already been built and were awaiting engines – so Mitchell temporised by fitting mass balances on the rudders and, for good measure, the ailerons of all the S.6s.

During its stay at Calshot the High Speed Flight had the use of the two S.5s from 1927, the old faithful Gloster IV with raised upper wing, the two Gloster VIs from 1929 and the reworked S.6As, initially with the 1929 engines and then, just before the contest when they became reserve race machines, with the 2,350-hp 'R' units. In the case of bad weather, and there was plenty of that during that August, there were service floatplanes like the Fairey Firefly and Fleetwing or the Armstrong Whitworth Atlas, for the Flight to disport

themselves in. It is hardly surprising that the standard of flying in the Flight was higher than it had ever been. None the less, inevitably there were incidents. In one of them Flight Lieutenant E. Linton Hope was taxying an S.6A, N.248, in Southampton Water when a passing liner, ignoring the speed regulations, set up a wash that capsized the Supermarine, almost writing it off, and putting that pilot out of flying with a damaged eardrum.

As a result of this mishap, R.L. Brinton, the naval pilot, who, with Leech, had been sent back to his unit because of the adverse ratio of men to machines in the Flight, was recalled. This happened in mid-July and the machine was not returned from Supermarine until 1 September.

In mid-July the first of the S.6Bs, S.1595, was delivered for acceptance trials. It was powered by the definitive 'R' contest engine giving the full 2,350 hp promised. Thanks to the use of sodium-cooled exhaust valves, an innovation from the USA, it was also using less fuel because it could be run with a leaner mixture. Orlebar, as usual, did the test-flying. Initially the machine refused to get anywhere near what the pilots called the 'hump speed', when the floats got up on the step. Instead it literally water-looped, chasing its tail because of insufficient rudder control. The only variable at that stage was to play with propellers. S.1595 had been delivered with an 8 ft 6-in diameter propeller. The practical aerodynamicists from Farnborough and Fairey's, the propeller manufacturers, soon realised that the whole of the slipstream was exerting a turning moment on the fin which was quite beyond the limited movement of the rudder to control it. Their answer was to specify a larger-diameter propeller so that a smaller component of the thrust 'cylinder' would impinge on the fin. In the absence of a completed 9 ft 6-in unit, one of the 1929 propellers, which had been damaged and cut down to 9 ft 1½ in was pressed into service. It cured the problem at once and test flying was able to proceed using the offset take-off procedure adopted in 1929 and a 30/90 port to starboard fuel load ratio.

It was found that the new floats, which had snub noses for aerodynamic reasons, were also better in the water, with a lesser tendency to dig in and porpoise than hitherto, although the problem was not completely cured. As a result take-off was a more predictable procedure. Further flight trials revealed an unacceptable degree of longitudinal instability due to the C of G being too far aft. The ever ready Mitchell promptly cured this by towing the machines back to Woolston and fitting lead ballast in the noses of the fuselages and floats, coupled with reducing the amount of oil carried in the fin to the minimum required to run the race.

With the uprated engines came a change of fuel. The first of these engines was fitted in N.248, the second S.6A. On its first flight Orlebar had the engine begin to stutter and cut out. It was found that the new fuel was dissolving the sealing compound from the Superflexit fuel pipes and depositing it in the filters. The problem persisted despite cleaning the filters after every flight. Snaith had a particularly unpleasant example of this while flying over the Isle of Wight when the engine cut out a number of times. Mitchell's remedy was typical; 'You will just have to bloody well fly them until all that stuff comes out.'

At the beginning of August the date of the contest was finally fixed for 12 September and the regulations were announced. For 1931 the course was to be a triangular one, in the Solent, as before, but moved slightly to the east so as to position the easterly turning point on dry land, at West Wittering, near to Sir Henry Royce's home. The real reason was to give the pilots Chichester harbour entrance to aim for from the southerly turn, which was positioned off St Helens Fort on the easterly tip of the Isle of Wight. The third and most westerly marker was located between the Ryde West and NE Middle buoys. Ryde pier was once again chosen as the most convenient starting and finishing point.

The choice of the Solent as the venue was not ideal; the Italians hated it because of the amount of shipping compared with their tranquil and well-policed Lake Garda and because of the enormous amount of driftwood and floating debris inseparable from a busy shipping lane. But from the British point of view, apart from the foregoing objections which affected them equally, it was ideal because of the proximity of the big naval base at Portsmouth from which they could draw a ready supply of launches and seamen to police the course as well as time-expired destroyers on which to mount marker pylons. Moreover, the harbour authorities in the area were adept at keeping the most authoritarian master mariners – and there were not a few of these in charge of the transatlantic liners – firmly in their places.

The flying regulations were quite new for the Schneider as the result of combining the navigability test with the race. After the starting signal from the mother ship, HMS *Medea*, which was once again pressed into service, the machines had thirty minutes in which to take off, climb to approximately 50 metres and then alight in a prescribed area. This would be followed by a taxying test, after which the aircraft would cross the start line, either on the water or in the air. It was assumed that they would naturally do the latter. They were allowed to include the take-off run in the taxying test. If they finished the navigability test before the three minutes was up, the beginning of timing for the speed test would be taken from when they crossed the line. If they took longer than 30 minutes their starting time would be taken as the end of the 30 minutes.

It was fully appreciated that the navigability test area should be kept clear of the alighting circuit and to this end a stretch of water between Calshot and Lee-on-Solent was allocated for this purpose.

The Race

The contest date gave the competing countries just five weeks to get their teams and their flying machines contestworthy. Over in Italy, on the beautiful Lake Garda, things were not going well with Mario Castoldi's latest creation. The MC.72 had been delivered to the Reparto Alta Velocità on 22 June, as already mentioned, and the first flight had been assigned to Giovanni Monti, now promoted to the rank of Captain, the most senior of the two pilots on the project. The other was the diminutive Warrant Officer Francesco Agello.

The MC.72 was a beautifully compact monoplane, bearing in mind the amount of machinery packed inside it. Of composite wood and metal construction, it was fractionally bigger but 17 per cent heavier than the S.6B, having a wing span of 9.50 m (31 ft 2 in) and an all-up weight of 2,907 kg (6,408 lb).

Monti had successfully got the machine off the water on its maiden flight when a series of backfires in the induction manifold almost stopped the engines and forced a precipitous alighting. It was an in-flight engine phenomenon which had not reared its ugly head within the Fiat test house. Moreover, it defied all attempts to eliminate it and was destined to dog the machine for months to come. Fiat were well aware that there might be problems with their, to be frank, long-winded induction arrangement, which relied on a high-speed, centrifugal compressor driven by the rear engine, drawing air through four double-choke carburettors and forcing the resulting mixture along an inordinately long induction tract running the full length of the two engines. The carburettors, for their part, were fed with air under pressure picked up by a forward facing intake on top of the nose. On the face of it it was ready made for induction pulses.

In the still air conditions of the test house the phenomenon certainly did not manifest itself but every flight with the machine was an adventure for the pilot, and was accompanied by explosions in the induction tract, which on one flight burst.

Sadly for Monti, in a flight on 2 August which included a slow-speed pass in front of the base to give visiting Fiat technicians a demonstration of what was happening, the MC.72 prototype stalled and dived into the lake, killing the plucky Giovanni Monti instantly. The official story was that the propellers had touched but the slight nose-up pitch and the quarter-turn spin into the water supports the stall theory.

Until that time the Italian team had been looking forward to being at Calshot by 12 August and arrangements had been made there for their reception. Already they had achieved speeds of 375 mph and Fiat were working on a new induction system with the compressor blowing air through a series of smaller carburettors mounted on the cylinder heads, which they felt sure would solve the problem. They even considered fuel injection directly into the cylinders but abandoned the idea because of lack of development time.

On the Étang de Berre the fortunes of the Section d'Entrainement Haute Vitesse were no better. There was no sign of the all-metal Bernard HV.220 and HV.320 racers, and HV.120-02, which by rights should have been delivered two years previously, was not delivered until the beginning of July. After the death of Antoine Paillard it was being flown by Captain Amanrich and Lieutenant Bougault testing propellers for the geared Hispano R18 whose development had been one cause of the delay.

On the morning of 30 July HV.120-02, bearing the civil registration F-AKAL, had been readied for flight to try a four-bladed Chauviere-Reed propeller which it was hoped would give sufficient tip clearance to minimise spray damage. After the inevitable airframe checks, engine checks and ground run the machine was on the line just before lunch and Georges Bougault decided to make the test flight, which would take only a few minutes, before joining his comrades in the Mess. He took off without incident, made his long, sweeping turn onto the downward leg and opened up the Hispano for a high-speed run. He was partway through it when the duty boat crew who were following were shocked to see the machine suddenly dive into the water in a huge cloud of spray. There was nothing they could do for poor Bougault and it took days to salvage the remains of the HV.120.

At the official enquiry the reason for the crash was given as a sparking plug blowing out of the engine, piercing the windscreen, which in turn detached itself and hit the tail. There were few practical pilots who agreed with these findings. A more likely explanation was that one of the cowlings blew off, Bougault ducked to avoid it and involuntarily flew the machine into the water. He was flying at an altitude of only a few feet at the time. It was significant that one cylinder bank of the engine was found some way from the rest of the wreckage. It is just possible that the engine had blown up just like Jake Gorton's at Cowes in 1923.

Whatever the reasons, France was deprived of one of her most experienced high-speed pilots and her fastest aircraft.

Subsequent to this accident the HV.120-01, with a good many flying hours behind her, became France's one hope. Accordingly she was sent back to Courneuve for a 'quickening-up' operation which consisted of removing 0.6 metres from each wingtip and redesigning the surface radiators to suit. It was hoped the speed might thereby be pushed up to 355 mph (571 km/h). The work was carried out in less than a week but test flying took a little longer. Alarmed by the loss of Bougault, the Direction Générale Technique of the Air Ministry in their wisdom, decided that although they had the most suitable man for the job in their ranks in the person of Captain Amanrich – he was the only living person who had flown the original – the first flights should be made by a civilian. The problem was to find one. Bernard certainly would not let their own test pilot, Roger Baptiste, take on the job, such was their confidence in their own product. It was even rumoured that Nieuport would release Sadi Lecointe for the job since the ND 450 showed no sign of getting airborne.

It was left to veteran Jean Assolant, one of France's most illustrious long-distance aviators, the hero of the Bernard L'Oiseau Canari Atlantic Flight, to volunteer for the job. He had recently joined Esso-Essence, the petrol company, as chief pilot and aviation advisor and there is no doubt that the company would have been happy to release him for this episode. As described elsewhere on 25 August he quickly familiarised himself with the Bernard HV.42 trainer but the mistral started to blow and delayed him for three days before he could give the HV.120-01bis its first flight. This went off without incident but over-prudent Hispano technicians had recommended him not to use more than 1,850 of the engine's 3,000+ rpm and the best speed he saw was 500 km/h, about 300 mph. Assolant made a number of flights in the Bernard, enough to show that there was a basic overheating problem if the full performance of the engine were used, but also indicating that the machine had a speed potential which would have made it competitive, given the autonomy.

Fully aware of the situation with the Bernard machines, the French Minister of Air was forced to put his faith in the Nieuport-Delage, or Nieuport-Astra ND 650, the developed version of the ND 450 with which Sadi Lecointe had been fruitlessly struggling for some months. He was given until 3 September to make a successful flight. Moreover, the British journal *Flight* reported the arrival in England of a quantity of aviation fuel for the French machines.

Meanwhile tragedy had struck the British. On 18 August after training flights in the Gloster IV and Gloster VI which were being used as trainers, it was Jerry Brinton's turn to fly the S.6A. The machine was N.247, the winner of the 1929 contest. An area of water two miles off Calshot at the junction of Southampton Water and the Solent was chosen for take-off and the machine was towed out in the evening, when conditions were usually ideal. Orlebar and Snaith were in the launch

Supermarine S.6B No. S.1596 is towed by an RAF launch. (*Flight*)

which accompanied the machine, and gave Brinton a thorough briefing before he got into the cockpit for take-off. Shortly after 8 pm Brinton started his run and all seemed to be going well until the machine started to porpoise with increasing amplitude until it leapt out of the water. Brinton should have aborted the take-off at that point. Instead he persisted. Twice the S.6A got off and hit the water again. But the third time it nose dived into the water, turned over and sank to the bottom.

Snaith, Flight Lieutenant Castanoldini, one of the Felixstowe establishment and Aircraftman Candy tore off their clothes and with ropes round their waists dived in to attempt to save the pilot. Snaith did manage to get down to the machine and thought that he could feel the body of the pilot but was quite unable to get him out. Later when the machine was recovered it was found that the rescuers' attempts would have been fruitless. Poor Brinton had been forced back into the rear fuselage by the pressure of water and he died of a broken neck. It was a sad blow for the Royal Navy and for British hopes.

But the show had to go on. With Brinton and Hope out of the running the British training effort centred itself on four pilots, Stainforth, Long, Snaith and Boothman. During August the weather on the Solent was bad and unsuitable for high-speed flying. All the pilots had to content themselves with flying the service machines, with only the occasional flip in race machines. During the third week in August the draw for starting order took place at the Royal Aero Club and the UK, France and Italy drew to start in that order. The British machines would be numbered 1, 4 and 7, the French machines would have numbers 2, 5 and 8 and the Italians were allocated numbers 3, 6 and 9.

On 1 September N.248 was returned to the Flight from Supermarine after repairs following Linton Hope's ducking. It was now fitted with the latest type of engine in readiness for the race on the 12th. Even at that late hour the British were confident that the French and the Italian competition would be forthcoming. They were cheered by *Daily Telegraph* reports from their Paris correspondent that Sadi Lecointe had made two flights in the ND 650 at Hourtin and that the machine was on its way to England. *Flight* magazine pondered whether the Bernard racer known to be at Berre would also be shipped. Meanwhile the Italian machines were rumoured to be on their way by rail to Zeebrugge and were indeed expected at Harwich on 1 September. However, hopes of competition were dashed when on 3 September came simultaneous French and Italian proposals for a six month postponement of the race. Otherwise, they said, they would have to withdraw their aircraft. Incidentally, they did not seem prepared to put that threat into writing. The reasons they gave for their request were bad luck with the weather, the loss of their best pilots and aircraft and the difficulty of developing modern high-speed machines in the time available. There was very little the Royal Aero Club could do for them. The arrangements for the race had been on a massive scale and it would have cost many tens of thousands of pounds to unravel them. The British team was prepared and ready to race, and the government, after a poor start, had given every support to the project. It was doubtful whether they would be prepared to do so again in six months' time. Regretfully, the Royal Aero Club had to refuse the request.

These requests for postponement were made by the

French and Italian air attachés in London. It was enigmatic that, because of postal delays, lists of pilots in the French and Italian teams came through the following day. For the record they were Lecointe, Assolant and Vernhol for France with Lieutenant Retourna as reserve. The Italians had proposed to send Colonel Casinelli, Captain Scapinelli, Lieutenants Bellini and Neri with Warrant Officer Francesco Agello as the final but not the least important team member. This was a great and real disappointment for the British team. Obviously they were happy to fly the course and the Trophy would become the permanent property of Great Britain. However, the public had to be considered because much accommodation had been booked in the whole Solent area, special trains had been arranged and the British crowds loved any outdoor entertainment of this kind. It was therefore announced that one of the British team machines would fly the course and endeavour to establish a new, higher speed for the race. This would be followed by an attempt on the 100 km closed-circuit record currently held by Flight Lieutenant Atcherley in the S.6, which had been established during the race of 1929.

The British team captain continued to play his cards close to his chest. Right until the last moment the choice of pilot for the flyover ceremony was a dark secret.

Meanwhile Snaith and Long seemed to be doing most of the test flying in the S.6Bs while Stainforth was spending a good deal of time in the S.5.

On 7 September S.1595 was launched with Long at the controls testing a new engine. The aircraft was then put back in the hangar ready for the race. At the same time Snaith went out in S.1596, trying out propellers. It was finally decided to use the old, cut-down 9 ft 1 in propeller for the official ride round the course. A strengthened 9 ft 6 in propeller was fitted to S.1595, which had been fitted with the latest 'R' engine for an attempt on the Absolute World Speed Record, which it was then announced would be made on the day of the flyover, after the Schneider formalities. That way it would give the crowds more value for their money. The attempt on the 100 km closed-circuit record would run concurrently with the official flight round the course.

When the day came it was seen that the pilot chosen to represent the United Kingdom in this last of the Schneider contests was John Boothman. He would fly S.1595 round the course and attempt to set a new 100 km closed-circuit record. George Stainforth had been chosen to fly S.1595 in the record attempt while Snaith, in N.248, would stand by in case Boothman should fail to complete the full Schneider distance.

The wisdom of holding the whole proceedings on

Supermarine S.6B No. S.1596 about to take to the sea assisted by RAF aircrafthands in waders and flotation jackets. (*Flight*)

one day was confirmed by the weather on the intended race day, 12 September, which was quite impossible for flying. The contest had therefore to be put off until the following day, Sunday 13 September. That day dawned with satisfactory weather. The wind, coming from about 040 deg, was kicking up a slight chop in Southampton Water. The only swell which could make an emergency alighting dangerous was in Chichester Bay.

HMS *Medea* was ready in position at the entrance to Southampton Water, and before midday the British contest machines, each on its own pontoon, had anchored alongside her ready for the start of the formalities. As usual Lovesey fired-up the machine and warmed the oil through before the pilot got into the cockpit. At 12.55, S.1596 was winched off the pontoon and made its preliminary take-off with a run of 37 seconds into 10 mph wind. Although it was said to be Boothman's first fully laden landing there were absolutely no problems when he put the weighty S.6B down on the water to begin his taxying test. He taxied for 1 minute 45 seconds before starting his take-off run which, consistent with his first, was in 36 seconds and then headed for Ryde pier and, with strict instructions not to fly inside the pylons,

The ultimate Schneider Trophy winner, in Supermarine S.6B No. S.1595, Flight Lieutenant J.N. Boothman. (*Flight*)

started his flyover. Observers at the time remarked how wide he took the turns, but the RAE 'X chasers' Messrs Hardy and Wright had fitted the machine with recording instruments in practice and found that a gentle turn of about 3 G, allowing the aircraft to gain height naturally as it came out of the turn, made for the fastest times. However, Boothman's turns were even wider than this. But although he appeared to be flying in a leisurely but careful manner his lap speeds were all better than 10 mph up on the 1929 figures, as well they might be with another 400 hp to play with.

It was a perfect day and, flying the machine, he could see the next pylon as he made each of his turns. There was very little instrument observation to worry about. The oil gauge, boost gauge and fuel pressure gauges were all blanked off and the only instruments he had to worry about were the air speed indicator, rev counter and, most important of all, the coolant inlet-temperature gauge. At the start of the flight the air speed indicator was indicating 378 mph at an engine speed of 3,200 rpm. At this regime the water temperature was steady at 98°C. But after one and a half laps at almost full throttle the temperature started to rise fairly sharply and he had to throttle back to 3,100 rpm, which brought his lap speeds down from 342 mph to the region of 339 mph. Running the engine at 3,100 rpm the air speed indicator fell back to 360 mph but the water temperature dropped too and stabilised at 95°C which was the maximum temperature he had been given in the briefing before the race.

For his third and fourth laps he decided, as he put it in his log book, 'to give Southsea a miss owing to bumps'. Obviously the beach and the people in the hot weather were creating thermals. On his fourth lap he turned in too much to the left at Southsea and to make up for it made a sweep over the Ryde pier pavilion on the Cowes to St Helens leg. On his sixth lap the SS *Homeric*, the liner which had been chartered by the Royal Aero Club for the use of its members, blew off a cloud of black smoke as he was passing Ryde pier and he thought for a moment that he had miscounted the laps as Waghorn and Webster had done before him. Despite this and an initial worry about the fuel supply he opened up wide as he turned round the Ryde Middle buoy for the last time and shot over Ryde pier.

After the race the machine was drained and it was found that there was 20 gallons of petrol left in the floats but only half a gallon of oil in the fin tank, which had started with Mitchell's prescribed quantity in it.

So it was all over. Eighteen years after Maurice Prévost's Deperdussin monoplane had whirred across the line on 16 April 1913 to win the race at a mere 60 mph, speeds had risen 700 per cent and the race had developed from a contest between gentlemen flyers, in frail wood and wire machines, into a technological battle between nations waged by technicians and highly qualified service professional flyers.

These thoughts must have been going through the minds of many of the elder statesmen of aviation aboard the SS *Homeric* as they watched the scene being set for

The winning team 1931. Left to right: Supermarine S.6B No. S.1596, S.6 No. N.249 and S.6B No. S.1595. (*Flight*)

George Stainforth's attempt on the world absolute speed record. It took time to transfer the timekeepers and their paraphernalia, not to mention their assistants, across the Solent to the speed record course, which extended from a point about 1,000 ft south-east of Solent pier to Hill Head. The distance had been checked by the Borough Surveyor of Portsmouth, who guaranteed its accuracy with 6 inches in the 3 km length. The line of flights for the attempts was on a line extending north-west to Ryde pier and south-east to the Spithead Forts. Marker buoys to indicate the approach limits were located 500 metres from each end of the course. This was in accordance with new regulations governing aeroplane speed records which were aimed at limiting the speed dive which had been the preliminary to record runs in the past. The regulations stipulated that the machine was not allowed to dive from a height greater than 400 metres and was to fly the course at an altitude of not less than 550 metres, which had to be attained at least 500 metres before entering the course. The buoys were there to mark this point at each end of the speed course. To ensure that the 400 metre approach height was not exceeded an Armstrong Whitworth Atlas fleet spotter, serial J.9988, was sent up to cruise around at this altitude with an FAI observer on board to report any misdemeanours.

While the preparations were being made Snaith, in the Fairey Firefly seaplane, got himself airborne and gave the crowd one of the aerobatic displays for which he was so well known. At four o'clock Stainforth was airborne in S.1595 and Snaith went back to Calshot to watch the proceedings. Five runs in all were made, three against the wind and two with it, the speed of the aircraft carrying it over the Isle of Wight and over the town of Southampton at each end of the run as he made his turns. Contrary to opinion at the time, the aircraft was fitted with the same type of 'R' engine as that fitted to Boothman's machine.

Timing of record runs was by two methods, hand-timing with stop-watches and a combined movie camera and chronograph developed by the RAE. Hand-timing gave his second and best run downwind to be 404.2 mph (651.9 km) but the automatic timing more accurately gave it as 388.67 mph. The first four of the five runs were best as the average, based on the automatic timing, was 379.05 mph (610.0 km). It was a new world record, beating Orlebar's record set up in the S.6 in 1929 by more than 21 mph. But it was an unsatisfactory result for Hives of Rolls-Royce, who had set his sights, determinedly, on 400 mph.

Just as soon as the high-speed weekend was over and done with, the RAF started moves to get Calshot back into its normal routine as a flying-boat base and pack the noisy, glamorous High Speed Flight off to its lair at RAF Felixstowe. But Hives was intent on having just one more go at the record, with 400 mph as the target. With that in the bag they could sit back. The RAF thought differently and it needed a personal appeal from the ailing Henry Royce to the Air Minister to change their minds for them, albeit temporarily.

Rolls-Royce had already prepared what they called the 'sprint' engine, no. R27, which had been modified to run on a fuel with a high methanol content devised by Rodwell Banks. The only modifications to the engine were to open up the carburettor jets and passages and to run the fuel pumps faster to cope with the rich mixture that alcohol calls for. As a precaution, beefed-up connecting rods, pistons and cylinder studs were also fitted. In the time available there was not time to get the carburation right and the engine had to be kept turning over fast, even at warm-up, if it was going to run at all. For this reason a new take-off drill was devised which called for the engine to be warmed up at fairly high throttle on the lighter. It was then shut down, to allow the pilot to get aboard, and all the radiators quickly covered over. The pilot – once again Stainforth had been chosen for the attempt – would then get aboard, the covering would be removed, the engines would be started up and the machine would start its take-off from the lighter.

It was originally intended to use S.1595 and S.1596 for the attempt but on 16 September Stainforth capsized S.1596 while testing a propeller and the onus of taking the record attempt fell upon S.1595. Again with George Stainforth at the controls the second attempt at the record was made at 7 pm on 29 September. The weather was far from ideal with light visibility deteriorating at that time of the year. But time was of the essence and as the future weather forecast was uncertain it was decided to make the attempt. Taking off at an all-up weight of 5,830 lb with 100 gallons of fuel aboard, S.1595 made five runs, commencing proceedings at the Spithead Fort end. In each case it exceeded 400 mph comfortably, the best being the first run at 415.2 mph and the worst, the last, which was discarded at 404.5 mph. On 14 October the record was homologated by the FAI at 407.5 mph, being the mean of runs 2, 3, 4 and 5.

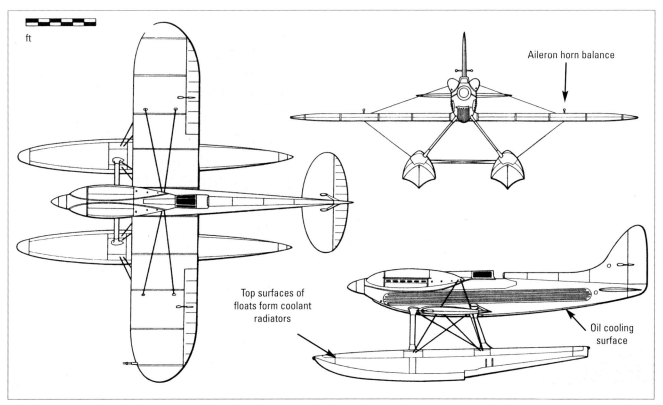

Supermarine S.6B (1931): Wing Span: 30 ft (9.14 m). Length Overall: 28 ft 10 in (8.79 m). Wing Area: 145 sq. ft (13.47 m²). Weight Empty: 4,590 lb (2,082 kg). T-O Weight: 6,086 lb (2,761 kg). Max Wing Loading: 41.97 lb/sq. ft (204.91 kg/m²). Rolls-Royce C12 engine of 2350 hp.

Engine Developments 1915–31

The Curtiss D-12 and its Derivatives

Although the Wright brothers established the USA as the birthplace of heavier-than-air aviation, the outbreak of World War found America way behind the rest of the Western World in airframe and engine technology. Moreover, so fast was the pace of aviation development in Europe, forged in the white heat of conflict, that American efforts to catch up quickly revealed that they were shooting at a moving target.

As early as 1915, it was realised that the main shortcoming was in engines. One response was to build European engines under licence; the Wright Aeronautical Corporation, after a number of tries, successfully produced and eventually improved on the V-8 Hispano-Suiza engine. Duesenberg were less successful with the untried Bugatti sixteen-cylinder, double-bank engine. On the domestic side a multimillion dollar programme to evolve a United States Standard Engine had produced the 400 bhp, 806 lb, V-12 Liberty, which was put into production in large quantities just as the war finished. One result was that the market was flooded with large numbers of these worthy but bulky engines which were to be as much a drag on the American postwar aviation scene as large stocks of the Hispanos were in France.

The Liberty was not the only engine to emerge from the wartime melting pot. In 1917 Charles B. Kirkham, Glenn Curtiss's chief engineer and confidant, had drawn out a new V-12 engine as a replacement for the company's ageing OX-5 V-8. Kirkham was part visionary, part commercial in his anticipation of the future power requirements of a military engine. He knew that the Hispano being built by Wright was, in 1915, giving about 150 bhp in direct-drive form and that its output was about to be raised to 200 bhp by increasing the crankshaft speed and incorporating a reduction gear.

Therefore, the Curtiss concept, designated the AB, was designed to develop 300 bhp at 2,250 rpm on the same principle of using gearing to match best engine speed to best propeller speed. Moreover, Kirkham set out to build an engine which would have a smaller frontal profile than the Hispano. Fortuitously, by using twelve instead of eight cylinders he was not only able to obtain the increased power – by adding cubic inches – but the 60 degree cylinder angle essential to the V-12 configuration gave him an engine which had 'narrower shoulders', a smaller frontal area, than the V-8 Hispano which was restricted to a 90 degree cylinder angle for the same reasons of firing order and mechanical balance.

Structurally, the AB followed the Hispano concept in the use of monobloc, light-alloy cylinder castings. But whereas Hispano designer Birkigt used separate blocks with integral heads, Kirkham broke new ground by forming the blocks and the upper half of the crankcase as a single casting and using detachable cylinder heads. And whereas the French engine had the whole length of its liners screwed into the blocks, only the upper ends of the American engine's liners were screwed and shrunk into the heads. This head-and-liner assembly was then assembled into the cylinders, which were in effect no more than water jackets with seals at the bases of the liners to prevent coolant entering the crankcase. Thus the coolant was in direct contact with the liners. Although this offered a slight advantage in that weight was saved and cylinder-wall cooling somewhat improved, the all-important hot end of the cylinder was no better cooled than that of the French engine. Both engines used closed-end liners – liners with a lid – to provide satisfactory valve seats, seat inserts not being properly developed at the time. The drawback of this arrangement was that heat transfer into the coolant would be inhibited by the clearance, however small, between the top of the liner and the metal of the head. Kirkham was obviously aware of this, for on the later D-12 engines a stud, machined on the top of each liner, was arranged to protrude into the water space to improve heat transfer to the coolant.

In common with Birkigt, the American designer opted for a single overhead camshaft per bank of cylinders but used it to operate four valves per cylinder. The AB was unusual in having the pairs of inlet and exhaust valves set across the heads, rather than in line along them, calling for complex cored inlet and exhaust tracts.

The AB was briefly tested and produced 300 bhp at 2,250 rpm from a weight of 725 lb. This power-to-weight ratio was obviously not good enough, moreover there was news from France that a 300 bhp Hispano was in the offing. Kirkham promptly revised his estimates and from this prototype quickly progressed to the larger 400 bhp, 4.5 × 6 in, 1,145 cu in, K-12 – officially the Kirkham-Curtiss D-1200 which was to be the real grandaddy of the D-12.

The main mechanical change was to improve the porting by fitting two overhead camshafts per bank of cylinders and setting the inlet and exhaust valves in line, the exhausts on the outside. A single cam operated each pair of valves by means of a T-shaped follower. Both the AB and K-12 engines featured four-bearing crankshafts – the K-12 had an extra outrigger bearing – and articulated connecting rods. Pressure lubrication was provided, drawing oil from a wet sump. A GM supercharger was also planned for the K-12 but the installation was found to be unsatisfactory and it was not used. A design quirk of the AB and K-12 was that each of the two magnetos fired two plugs per cylinder on one bank; thus a magneto failure halved the power output by cutting out six cylinders.

The K-12's operating speed was fast for a 1917 aero-engine; rated output was 400 bhp at 2,500 rpm from a swept volume of 1,152 cu in. Complete with the reduction gear it weighed 625 lb, an outstanding power-to-weight ratio for the period which, combined with the outstandingly small frontal area, put it away ahead of the opposition. A prototype unit installed in the Curtiss-Kirkham Wasp triplane achieved 162 mph, faster than any fighter then in service, causing a great deal of interest in military circles.

But Navy and Army tests quickly revealed innumerable engine problems, mostly with the bottom end of the engine, mainly due to the difficulty of casting the complex crankcase, combined with an apparent failure to fully understand the destructive effect of crankshaft torsional vibrations on the overhung first motion wheel of the reduction gear, which had a life, at the best, of about twenty-five hours despite the use of a friction clutch in the drive.

Frustrated by the troubles with the K-12 and reputedly prepared to blame everyone but himself for its failure, Kirkham left Curtiss in 1919 after a disagreement with company President John North Wyllis. His successor, Finlay R. Porter, took over the design and rationalised it by separating the blocks from the crankcase, incorporating the cylinder water jackets with the head and sleeve assemblies and increasing the number of main bearings to seven without, however, lengthening the crankshaft to maintain the original bearing area. Being a practical man, he also fitted twelve-cylinder magnetos, each firing one plug per cylinder. Rechristened the C-12, the reworked engine retained its reduction gear and wet sump lubrication. Tested by the Army at McCook Field in November 1921, the C-12 developed 427 bhp at 2,250 rpm with an installed weight of 712 lb.

Porter, in company with Wyllis, left Curtiss in 1921 in the middle of the CR-1 aircraft programme to return to the motor industry and build automobiles under his own name. After a short hiatus his post as chief engine designer was given to Arthur Nutt, a 26-year-old development engineer who had been with Curtiss for five years.

Having lived with the K-12 and C-12 problems, Nutt had already decided where the trouble lay. He could see that most of the durability problems with the C-12 were caused by running it too fast; by reducing the speed and accepting a lower output he could at one fell swoop throw away the troublesome reduction gear, thereby lightening the engine by some 50 lb, and increasing reliability at the same time. A bonus would be that the power previously absorbed by the reduction gears – at least five per cent – would come his way.

With encouragement from both the Navy and the Army a single modified unit was built. Designated CD-12 (D for direct-drive), this historic engine was successively tested by the Navy for 10 hours and the Army for 50 hours in April 1921 when it was calibrated at 383 bhp at 2,000 rpm. The Navy promptly ordered two engines for service use, which eventually found their way into the specially built Navy Curtiss CR-1 racers, one of which was Bert Acosta's winning mount in the 1921 Pulitzer race.

Encouraged by but not satisfied with the CD-12's performance, the US Army, who were doing most of the testing at their McCook Field research centre, were still critical of its reliability. They disliked the seven 3-in dia × 1-in main bearings of the C-12 and demanded more bearing area, especially in the middle of the engine. Dry sump lubrication was also called for and the Claudel carburettors adopted by Porter were frowned upon. It was a measure of the thoroughgoing Army approach that with their report they provided a full set of stress calculations and bearing loads for all the Curtiss engines from the AB onwards plus a set for a theoretical direct-drive K-12.

It was agreed that the only way to gain bearing area was either to revert to the K-12 four-bearing crankshaft, which would provide a satisfactory 375 bhp engine running up to 2,000 rpm, or lengthen the engine to give the stipulated bearing area and achieve an engine capable of development to greater outputs. Nutt and the Curtiss directors chose the latter and more farsighted alternative. The resulting D-12 engine, still with the cylinder dimensions of the K-12, had a centre main bearing 1.75 in wide while the remainder were enlarged to 1.5 in. Main journal and crankpin diameters were 3 in and 2.5 in respectively.

This new engine was in reality a complete redesign. Nutt was destined to be one of the great figures in American aeronautical engineering and the D-12 was the measure of his ability. A born engine man, he fully realised that any engine is only as good as its bottom end. For this good reason he built around the new crankshaft a stronger and more compact crankcase of cylindrical section. Split on the bearing centreline, its main bearings were supported by full-width diaphragms and the forged Duralumin bearing caps were each retained by four studs and located by keys and keyways.

An interesting detail was that the steel-backed bearing shells were attached to the housings and big ends by countersunk brass screws. Later in the life of the engine these screws were replaced with brass rivets. The object would appear to be as much to conduct heat away from the bearings as to locate the shells. Even at that early date there was a growing awareness in the USA of the importance of providing a good heat path away from the bearing material.

A refinement was to enclose the camshaft and ancillary drives in a separate, detachable, gearcase driven by a single bevel gear on the rear end of the crankshaft. An upper vertical shaft driven by a half-speed bevel wheel provided the magneto and the camshaft drives. A lower vertical shaft drove the ancillaries. The gear-type oil pumps, two to scavenge and one for pressure, were located in a tiny cylindrical sump at the rear of the engine, driven by spur gears off this shaft, which also operated the water and fuel pumps.

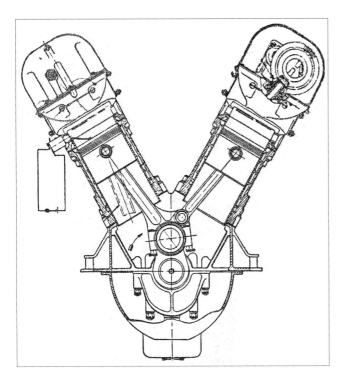

Curtiss sectioned engine.

Carburation was provided by twin Stromberg NA-Y5 downdraught carburettors specially tailored to fit between the cleavage of the cylinders. Ignition was by Splitdorf SS-12 or Scintilla AG-12D magnetos, the starboard magneto firing plugs located below the exhaust ports and the port magneto handling plugs on the inlet side.

The Navy immediately ordered a dozen of the new engines, christened the D-12, before it had passed its acceptance test. In April 1922 two of this contract were delivered to the Army at McCook Field for testing. Initially rated at 350 bhp at 1,800 rpm and then 375 bhp at 2,000 rpm, the performance spectrum was progressively explored until D-12 output was standardised at 435 bhp at 2,300 rpm.

The power obtained from the racing engines was considerably more than this. Installed in Curtiss R-6 airframes, high-compression D-12s, thought to develop 440 bhp (one source says 427 bhp) at 2,250 rpm and driving special wooden high-speed propellers, carried Lieutenant Russell Maugham and Lieutenant Lester J. Maitland into first and second places in the 1922 Pulitzer race. Behind one of these engines installed in a Curtiss PW-8 fighter, Maugham also made the classic 'Dawn to Dusk' San Francisco–New York flight in June 1924.

The major event in the progress of the D-12 came in 1923 with the advent of Reed's sheet Duralumin propeller operating at tip speeds in excess of Mach 1. This great advance in propeller technology made it possible to run the D-12 up to 2,310 rpm, at which speed the engine installed in the 1923 Schneider-winning CR-3 floatplane was reckoned to be pulling 475 bhp.

For the 1924 Pulitzer race Nutt built a short run of engines designated D-12A with bores enlarged from the standard 4.5 in to 4.625 in, raising the output to about 500 bhp. These engines were installed in the CR-3s which gave demonstrations and broke records at Bay Shore in 1924. Incidentally, Hugo T. Byttebier, whose monograph on the D-12 for the Smithsonian Annals of Flight series is such a prolific source of authentic material on the D-12, states that the Macchi M.33s in the 1924 race were powered by D-12As. If this were so it scotches once and for all the folklore that the machines were powered by standard D-12s worn-out by Fiat testing.

A first generation derivative of the D-12A was the V-1400, the first step towards the V-1550 and the geared Conqueror. In this major redesign the swept volume was further increased to 1,400 cu in by opening up the bores to 4.875 in and increasing the stroke to 6.125 in. A major improvement was to abandon closed-top liners in favour of the open-top type and to seat the valves on aluminium bronze inserts. Heat transfer to the coolant was thereby much improved, making for longer valve life and allowing a higher compression ratio for a given fuel. Frontal area was also reduced by introducing a third gear in the crossover drives between the overhead camshafts. The consequent reduction in the size of the gears allowed for more compact camboxes and reduced the width of the engine by 2 inches.

The standard V-1400 delivered 510 bhp at 2,100 rpm from a stated dry weight of 685 lb; tuned versions would give about 7 per cent more, about 565 bhp at 2,400 rpm. Dry weight is variously stated as 660 lb or 685 lb. This should be compared with 680 lb, plus or minus 10 lb for the regular D-12 without accessories.

A story, rife at the time, claimed that one of these engines pulled 619 bhp at 2,525 rpm on the brake encouraging claims of 1.1 lb per bhp, or even one pound per horsepower. However, 510 bhp and 1.34 lb/hp seems more rational. Nevertheless, it appears to have been a very good engine, getting through its 50 hour test without trouble in seven days, although it suffered from an abnormal thirst for oil. It was instrumental in winning the 1925 Pulitzer and Schneider races for Curtiss.

Only a dozen V-1400s are stated to have been built, five of them reserved for race aircraft. It was really the forerunner of the V-1550 (later the V-1570) with bores enlarged to 5.125 in to raise the capacity to 1,570 cu in. All the mechanical changes explored in the V-1400 were retained, plus an increase in main bearing sizes to 3.5 in without any enlargement of the crankpins. However, the connecting rods were beefed up to cope with outputs of the order of 600 bhp and more. Geared versions were once more in the Curtiss catalogue. The GV-1550 was officially rated at 575 bhp at 2,500 rpm and the direct-drive model at 600 bhp at the same speed. As flown in the 1926 Schneider race, the direct-drive, high-compression racing version is said by Page to have given 708 bhp at 2,600 rpm with a dry weight of 725 lb.

In its home country the D-12, which was as successful commercially as it was around the pylons, was the instrument of its own downfall by establishing too much of a monopoly. It did not please service chiefs to have only one engine supplier: moreover, they were not entirely happy with the water-cooled concept which, while it made for low frontal area, added some 200 lb to the installed weight* and was susceptible to battle damage. They hankered after air-cooled radials of the same power, and got them in the Wright Whirlwind and Pratt & Whitney Wasp, which were products of the same services sponsorship which had brought the D-12 to fruition. In 1927 the US Navy sounded the death-knell of the D-12 when it declared that henceforth it would buy no more water-cooled engines. The US Army held its ground a little longer but the writing was on the wall.

The American yen for the radial was undoubtedly spawned by envy of the world lead Britain had taken in radial engine design with the 445 bhp Bristol Jupiter, and to a lesser extent the 300 bhp Armstrong-Siddeley Jaguar, for their fighters. The D-12 was one of the designs intended to match the power of these engines and it did, with considerably less frontal area but greater installed weight. That minimal frontal area was more important than light weight when speed was the essential was brought home to the British with stunning effect when the US Navy brought its team of floatplanes to Cowes in 1923 to show off the fruits of its labours.

The ensuing shock to British composure was exacerbated by the creation of an experimental squadron of D-12 powered Fairey Fox day-bombers, Charles Fairey having bought the manufacturing rights for the UK. These could outperform any of the radial-engined fighters then in service with the RAF. The RAF's determination to have a similar but even more powerful engine of domestic manufacture for their new day-bombers was behind the creation of the Rolls-Royce FX engine, which eventually became the Kestrel and was the basis of the immortal Merlin. Inevitably low-profile water-cooled engines eventually found their way into fighters culminating in the Hurricane, Spitfire and Mustang. It could be said with all truth that in the D-12 started a trend away from the radial in Britain at just the moment that the Americans were starting to move towards it.

The Fiat AS Engines

The Fiat AS.2

The success of the American Curtiss D-12 engine in the 1923 Schneider Cup race had the same kind of purgative impact on the Italian aero-engine industry as it did in Britain. The farsighted General Guidoni imported a

number of D-12s for study by Fiat and Isotta-Fraschini. The end result was lighter and more compact power units from both companies. The influence of the D-12 was written large on the Fiat A.20 and its progressively larger derivatives, the A.22 for reconnaissance, and the A.24 and A.25 for bombers. These three engines were destined to replace the old A.14 and A.19 wartime designs. Meanwhile the Americans, because of Navy influence, were busy, and misguidedly, abandoning their in-line vee engines in favour of radials. This thinking came to Italy too late to affect the A series.

V-12 engines were not new in Turin. Fiat had produced an outstanding V-12 wartime engine for bombers and airships. But the influence of the compact Curtiss unit stimulated their aero-engine department and set new design targets which were quickly beaten. Both the Curtiss and Fiat A.20 engines were 60 deg V-12s designed into similar dimensional envelopes; both utilised mostly cylindrical crankcases, articulated connecting rods and twin overhead camshafts operating four valves per cylinder.

Above the crankcase the Curtiss influence on Fiat was curtailed. Rather than opting for the Curtiss light-alloy, monobloc, cylinder construction Fiat went for separate fabricated steel cylinders with the heads of each bank structurally united by cast aluminium cam casings. This difference in approach gave them flexibility and allowed them to quickly build a family of engines of progressively larger sizes on the A.20 pattern.

The decision by Fiat to build their D-12 inspired A-series engines round European-style fabricated steel cylinders has been regarded as retrogressive. It did, in fact, represent a shrewd assessment of their production capabilities in relation to predicted engine requirements. Moreover, it was a proven technique and offered the possibilities of altering cylinder sizes quickly, without major engine surgery and away from the development problems associated with linered, light-alloy, monoblocs.

It was not by coincidence that Daimler Motoren Gesellschaft, Rolls-Royce and others chose this labour-intensive method of cylinder construction for aero-engine cylinders. The thin water jackets and cylinder walls, combined with the accuracy with which they could be fabricated, made cylinders with a large swept volume within very tight overall dimensions possible. Evidence of this was that the 30.95-litre Fiat AS.2 engine had very little more frontal area than the 18-litre Curtiss D-12.

Fiat, in the AS.2 which powered the Macchi M.39 that brought the Coppa Schneider back to Europe, were able to get six 5.5-in. (later 5.7-in. in the AS.3) bore cylinders into a 'block' length of 38.75 inches, whereas Curtiss needed a monobloc only 4.5 inches shorter to accommodate six 4.875-in. bores in the V-1400 development of the D-12 which the AS.2-powered M.39 beat so conclusively at Newport News in 1926. The same logic caused Mercedes-Benz, as late as 1954, to opt for this cylinder construction for their successful M.196 racing-car engine.

---

*It was US practice to quote the weight and the power-to-weight ratio of their engines without ancillaries such as cooling systems, exhaust pipes or electrical equipment other than the magnetos; the opposite of European practice. Consequently, although the paper figures could be sensational, problems could arise when the engine was installed in an airframe. The poor showing of the Liberty engine is an example.

It was below the cylinder joint line that the D-12 parentage of the A.20 series was more apparent. The crankshaft, with hollow pins and journals, was supported on seven main bearings with an extra steady-bearing at the propeller shaft end with a ball thrust-bearing between the two. Incidentally on the AS engines – S for 'Spinto' (Thrust) – the bearing metal was poured directly into the big-end eyes to improve the heat flow. It is believed that the idea was pioneered in the Duesenberg auto-racing engines.

On both the Fiat and Curtiss engines the camshafts were driven by bevel gears and three quill shafts in Y-configuration from a gear on the rear end of the crankshaft. A vertical shaft drove the oil and water pumps at the bottom of the accessory drive housing. The only difference was that the Curtiss water pump was driven directly off the bottom of the shaft and the oil pumps indirectly by gears; on Fiat engines the oil pumps had priority. Both engines used articulated connecting rods, while at the top of the engine each pair of valves was operated by a bridge-piece from the cams of an overhead camshaft.

In this area the Fiat design differed, the camshafts being supported by a bearing between each pair of valves and operating the bridge-piece by a pair of narrow cams on either side of the bearing to balance the loads. Fiat saved reciprocating weight by forming their bridge-pieces as miniature cross-heads working on fixed vertical slides formed as part of the lower camshaft bearing housings. The Curtiss bridge-pieces were tee-shaped with the vertical leg acting as a plunger working in a bushing in the head, thereby increasing the reciprocating weight of the gear. The Fiat camshafts were rifle-drilled from end to end and carried lubricant to the cam faces and to vertical tubes carrying cooling oil down the exhaust valve stems.

When the AS.2 came to be designed Fiat had in production the A.20, the equivalent of the D-12, and the larger A.22. The A.24 and A.25 engines were yet to come. As mentioned elsewhere Zerbi turned to the A.22 as the basis for the AS.2. The A.20 was too small as a starting point for an engine which was intended to win decisively.

Comparing the dimensions of the A.22 and the AS.2 on Fiat drawings, we find that the all-important forward portion of the AS.2, excluding the rear accessory drives, was reduced from a height of 93.8 cm to 85 cm and the width from 72.5 cm to 72 cm, this being achieved with new, squatter, Fiat carburettors mounted low in the cleavage of the cylinders and more-compact camshaft covers. To avoid increasing the height of the cylinders in line with the increased stroke, shorter connecting rods and shallower pistons were adopted.

As an experienced high-performance engine designer Tranquillo Zerbi set to work on the classic premise that the more oxygen the engine could consume, the more power it would develop. Starting with the A.22 he proceeded to ensure this by increasing the bore and stroke as already described and lightening the reciprocating parts to enable it to run faster. Thus by enlarging the

cylinder dimensions from 135 × 160 mm to 140 × 170 mm, thereby increasing capacity from 27,920 cc to 30,955 cc and raising the operating speed from 2,200 rpm (A.22R with reduction gear) to 2,500 rpm, he increased the pumping capacity from 61,424 to 77,387 litres per minute, or some 26 per cent. Further to gain power, he upped the compression ratio from 5:1 to 6:1 and ran the engine on 50/50 petrol/benzole.

With these changes he could reasonably expect to achieve 800 bhp so long as the greater reciprocating loads could be contained and the inevitable increase in internal friction kept to a minimum. All this had to be done while at the same time reducing the size and weight of the engine.

Retired Fiat engineers who worked on the AS project told the writer that the Achilles' heel of the AS engines was Zerbi's magnesium pistons. At that time this was a relatively new engineering material and Zerbi took a chance with it, obviously with the one aim of reducing reciprocating weight and thereby raising the engine's operating speed. We now know that this material has a number of drawbacks in this application because of its softness and liability to excess ring groove wear; this would call for a piston change after only two or three hours' operation. Also its modulus, its stiffness, is lower than that of conventional piston alloys. Moreover, its thermal conductivity is inferior to that of aluminium and it does not 'wet' with oil like that material and is likely to 'pick up' in the bores. This last problem would be exacerbated by the increased side thrust on the pistons due to the shorter connecting rods.

One cannot help feeling that from the outset Zerbi lost as much as he gained in piston weight by giving the pistons inordinately thick, 14 mm crowns with no ribbing on the undersides and making them virtually solid from the crowns to the gudgeon-pin bosses. The AS.3 piston was much more complex, with finely set ribs normal to the gudgeon-pin, across a much thinner crown. Lessons learnt were apparent in the AS.5 piston, which had more widely spaced transverse ribs and was of the slipper type, permitting longer thrust faces. The heights of these pistons are of interest, the AS.2 measuring 89 mm for a 140 mm bore (64%); the AS.3 had a height of 70 mm in a 145 mm bore (48%) while the AS.5 piston scaled 78 mm for a diameter of 135 mm (58%).

The drawings also depict the steps taken to combat the excessive thirst for oil which gave the Macchi racers their characteristic smoke trail. The AS.2 started with a set of three plain rings per piston; the AS.3 progressed to a plain upper ring, two narrow rings in the middle groove and a lower oil control ring with drains. The AS.5 used three compression rings plus a grooved oil control ring.

With hindsight, it is clear that Zerbi built into his engine a problem which was to dog the AS.2 and AS.3 throughout their brief lives. It would be interesting to discover whether the low-compression, safety engine fitted to Bacula's M.39 in the 1926 race had aluminium pistons. While on this subject Ing. Vaghetti, who conceived the AS.6 configuration, described to the writer the panic at the Turin factory in 1927 when the AS.3s started to burn holes in the pistons and how Zerbi had to make a panic dash to Venice with replacements.

Fiat AS.3

The AS.3 was a direct derivative of the AS.2 built to power the M.39 for the 1927 race in Venice, the main change being to extend the stroke, again without increasing cylinder length, from 170 mm to 175 mm and the bore from 140 mm to 145 mm. At the same time the compression ratio was increased to 6.7:1. The main detail changes seem to have been in the piston area and the reduction of the connecting rod length by 2.5 mm, from 28 cm, to keep engine height the same as the AS.2. Running on straight aviation petrol the AS.3 developed 1,000 bhp at 2,400 rpm.

Comparisons are invidious and should only be taken as a measure of progress. In this light it is interesting to note that the dimensions of the 1921 D-12 (and the V-1400) cross-sections forward of the accessory drives were 79.57 cm and 71.76 cm. Thus at the expense of 5 cm in the vertical dimension, Fiat, with their pre-1914 cylinder construction, gained 13 litres and some 300 bhp. However, the AS.2 was heavier by 240 lb but in terms of weight-to-capacity ratio it was at an advantage with 2.89 lb/ltr compared with the D-12's 3.5 lb/ltr. The best Curtiss engine was the V-1400, weighing in at 2.87 lb/ltr but this again was outclassed by the later Fiat AS.5 scaling 2.47 lb/ltr.

Fiat AS.5

With competition from the British becoming hard to live with in the forthcoming 1929 Coppa Schneider, Fiat sought to counter the Gloster and Supermarine aircraft built round bulky, high-output Napier and Rolls-Royce engines, with the diminutive, minimum-frontal-area Fiat C.29. For this machine they built the AS.5. This was a true competition engine designed on a clean sheet of paper rather than being an adapted service power unit, and set completely new dimensional standards for a 1,000 bhp engine.

In designing the AS.5 Zerbi stuck to established Fiat structural techniques but designed a smaller engine with a higher volumetric efficiency, using motor-racing technology.

In this he was remarkably successful. Weighing 767 lb (348 kg) dry and developing 1,000 bhp at 3,200 rpm from a swept volume of 1,589 cu in (25,545 cc), 73 per cent of that of the AS.3, it was by far the most efficient engine of the period with a power-to-weight ratio of only 0.77 lb/hp. Dramatically smaller than the D-12, it fitted into a nose cowling measuring a mere 65 × 80 cm. The overall height of the whole engine, from front to back was only 68 cm, giving a frontal area of 4.5 sq ft.

The main changes made to achieve this were to shorten the stroke to 140 mm, permitting a smaller crankcase and to use drastically shorter (230 mm) connecting rods; the bore was also reduced to 138 mm. The compression ratio was 8:1, very high for the period,

The Fiat AS.5 12-cylinder V-engine, based on motor-racing technology, that powered the Fiat C.29 entered in 1929.

Propeller end of a Fiat AS.5 as used in the Fiat C.29.

Fiat AS.5 engine developed for the Fiat C.29.

calling for special fuel, a 50/50, petrol/benzole mixture laced with lead tetraethyl. One likes to think that Zerbi reverted to aluminium pistons; as already mentioned, they were slipper-type to cope with a master connecting rod/stroke ratio of 1.64.

An important factor in achieving the low frontal area was a pronounced step up at the rear of the sump which allowed the water and oil pumps to be tucked up tight under the accessory drives beneath the step. The forward portion of the sump was swept sharply upwards to match the shape of the C.29 cowling.

The AS.5's major shortcoming was the high speed at which its power was developed, calling for the ultimate in propeller technology, bearing in mind that the design did not incorporate a reduction gear. Fitted with the standard Fiat reduction gear, it would have weighed approximately 845 lb and still given the outstanding power-to-weight ratio of 0.935 lb/hp. It achieved the much needed reduction gear in the AS.6, and when it went into production as the A.30RA.

The Fiat AS.6 Aero Engine

The defeat of the Macchis at Venice in 1927 before a huge crowd had been an enormous setback to Italian national pride and an unwelcome loss of face for the Fascist party and its Regia Aeronautica. The immediate reaction had been to look to Isotta-Fraschini for engines for the 1929 race and, while retaining the experienced Macchi, to commission additional airframes from Savoia and Fiat. The latter company, emulating Curtiss, provided a complete airframe and engine package, creating the outstanding AS.5 engine in the process. The end result was again failure.

In 1931, after two consecutive British victories, there was only one more chance for the Italians or any other challenger. It was considered that only Fiat had the technical and financial resources to build a new engine quickly. For the airframe they would solo on the Macchi–Castoldi combination. The engine contract,

issued in 1929, was for an engine to give 2,300 hp for one hour.

Tranquillo Zerbi, Fiat's chief engine designer, and his team realised from the start that two years was far too short a time to produce anything completely new and that they would have to rely on what they had. They decided, as a first step, to set their own target of 2,800 bhp. They also decided that any new engine would employ the low-altitude supercharging technique pioneered by Rolls-Royce with the 'R' engine. Fiat were quite familiar with the principal systems in their very successful racing cars.

Lacking a big engine like the Rolls-Royce Buzzard to develop, they first contemplated attempting to double the output of the 1,000 bhp AS.5 by heavily supercharging it, running it faster and fitting a reduction gear. It was quickly realised that even this expedient would not give anywhere near the 2,300 bhp required by the contract.

The pressing problem was to decide on a configuration, and equally important, to make a decision about propellers. The Reed metal propellers used on their high-revving, direct-drive engines were working at tip speeds well in excess of the speed of sound with resulting loss of efficiency. But they knew also from the Supermarine experience that if they used a reduction gear the resulting propeller would be so big that they could be in trouble with spray damage and even the possibility of swamping the propeller.

It is to one of the design team, Ing. Vaghetti that the solution must be credited. Very conscious of the fact that they had in the AS.5 an engine with the best ratio of frontal-area-to-power output in the world and anxious to utilise this asset, he sketched on a scrap of paper the idea of mounting two of the AS.5 engines on a common base with each of them driving one component of a contra-rotating propeller via gearing and concentric shafts. He proposed to increase the efficiency of both engines by supercharging them with a blower driven by the rear engine.

Vaghetti's layout drew on the experience of Savoia with the S.65 on which the two propellers, driven by separate engines at either end of the fuselage and rotating in opposite directions, got over the torque problem of the single propeller and allowed the airframe designer to use smaller floats. Moreover, the S.65's propellers were small enough, since the total output was split between two, to get the out of the spray. He went one better. By placing the propellers in close proximity he made use of the phenomenon, demonstrated by Castoldi, that when two propellers are rotated in opposite directions on the same axis the total efficiency was better than that of the individual units.

It was an elegant solution. Apart from retaining the small frontal area of the AS.5, by mounting the engines back to back with the two reduction gearboxes in the middle of the combination, the reduction gears could be used to raise the shaft line so that the propeller shafts lay in the cleavage between the blocks of the front engine in the space normally occupied by the carburettors. These

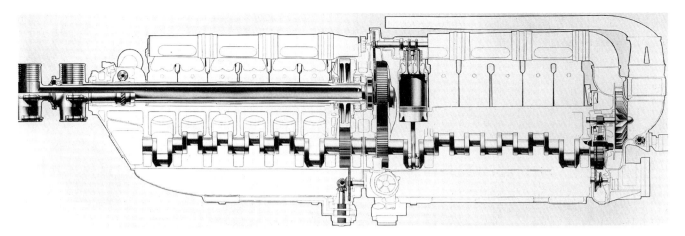

Fiat AS.6 24-cylinder engine with concentric shafts from double, centrally mounted, reduction gears. The forward engine drives the rear propeller and the other drives the front propeller.

would be mounted on the supercharger at the back of the engine.

In the definitive engine, power was taken out of the same end of the crankshafts as the camshaft drives. In line with the original concept the crankshafts of the engines were not coupled, thereby avoiding the enormous torsional problems inevitable with a twelve-throw crankshaft. Nevertheless the two cylinder groups were mounted on a common crankcase, split in the middle for access to the reduction gears. These single-step, straight-tooth, propeller reduction drives were not only called upon to perform their major function of driving the concentric propeller shafts but, to save space, acted as the lower component of the camshaft drives.

If the minuscule frontal area of the AS.5 were to be retained there was little alternative to the decision to drive the supercharger off the rear engine, thereby reducing its output by some 250 bhp. Engine speeds had therefore to be synchronised by the crude but effective method of setting the pitch of the rear propeller, driven by the front engine, coarser than the rear one.

Simultaneously with building the special AS.5 engines a massive rig-testing programme was mounted. At least one finding was encouraging. It had been anticipated that the tubular propeller shafts might present massive torsional problems and that cush-drives, of the type used on Fiat production aero engines, would have to be developed. Happily the shafts, respectively 1.334 metres and 1.77 metres long were just the right length to act as torsional couplings and the cushion-drives could be abandoned.

There was also doubt about the roller-bearings used to separate the inner and outer shafts. They were of large diameter and were called upon to operate at 4,000 rpm. Fortunately Fiat had already investigated large-diameter, high-speed, anti-friction bearings for another application and the choice of bearing was no problem.

A preliminary consideration had been whether to use a low-pressure supercharger blowing into a high-compression engine or vice versa. They reasoned that the high-boost option favoured by Rolls-Royce would call for over-rich mixtures to reduce charge

temperatures in the transfer pipe and thus make for a thirsty engine.

Experiments on a variable-compression test engine using compressed air from the workshop system showed the high-compression-ratio, low-boost option to be the right one. This work also enabled the team to decide on the best fuel, bearing in mind that the maximum permissible consumption was 260 grams/hp/hour (0.652 pt/bhp/hr), if the aeroplane was to fly the race at full throttle. They opted for a petrol/benzole mixture used in 1927 for the AS.3 with the addition of tetraethyl lead (TEL).

Compared with the exotic supercharger on the Rolls-Royce 'R' engine, which operated at a working pressure of 17.5 psi, the straight-blade, dual-rotor blower chosen by Fiat was a relatively low-efficiency device delivering the mixture at 5 psi. The drive was by a simple, two-gear system. Operating speeds of 17,000, 19,000 and 21,500 rpm were tried on the test-rig. It was found that at the highest speed efficiency tailed off and the 17,000 rpm gearing was chosen for practice, the race and the long-distance records. The 19,000 rpm option was kept in reserve for an attempt on the world airspeed record.

It was calculated that the blower would absorb about 250 bhp and rig-testing was carried out first of all with an electric motor of this power and later from the free end of a 400 hp aero-engine to submit it to the torsional vibrations it was likely to meet in service. The design of this compressor broke new ground for Fiat and they freely admit that, with hindsight, it was the weakest part of the engine, with an adiabatic efficiency of only 0.55. Nevertheless, to be fair, it was good enough to raise the output of the individual AS.5 units, whose cylinder size was unchanged, from 1,000 bhp to 1,550 bhp at the end of the AS.6 development programme.

A new fuel system to withstand cornering forces up to 6 G was also required. This gravitational pull was enough to drain the fuel out of the engine into the float tanks and stop the engine. The solution was to divide the four double carburettors feeding the blower into two groups, each with its own, individual fuel system

How to get up to 3,100 bhp and avoid the torque reaction problem: merge two 12-cylinder engines to form the Fiat AS.6 driving contra-rotating propellers.

consisting of a small header tank located above the carburettors and fed by an engine driven pump with a return system to one of the floats. There was a further pump between each header tank and its group of carburettors to maintain a constant pressure at the float chamber needles irrespective of aircraft attitude. There was no connection between the systems.

Right from the start a major problem was to strike a balance between the amount of heat transferred to the coolant and that going out of the exhaust, taking into account the cylinder material, the compression ratio, the shape of the inlet and exhaust tract, the boost rate and the type of coolant.

It was accepted that the steel cylinders passed less heat into the cooling water than any comparable material. The heat had to go somewhere and that somewhere was into the exhaust valve which overheated and stretched when the engine was finally running. This was emphasised when glycol was tried as a cooling medium on the single-cylinder test engine. It certainly allowed the engine to be run hotter, in fact so hot that it seized; this could have been overcome but glycol was ruled out because it called for bigger coolant pumps and was too viscous to run through the wind radiators when it was cold.

A move which improved the situation considerably,

was to fit Kuprodur, copper-alloy valve guides and to take individual water feeds to each pair of exhaust valves. Salt- and sodium-filled valves were tried and discarded because the filling tended to set in the stem of the valve and in one case, the valve heads blew off. Oil jets down the valve stems on the lines of the AS.2 and AS.3 were also tried and abandoned. However, good results were obtained with Duralumin inserts down the valve stems which were increased in diameter to accommodate the alloy.

Finally the cylinder was redesigned with reshaped exhaust tracts, giving improved water flow around the exhaust valve guide area. After that the valves 'ran black', too cool to measure the temperature with an optical pyrometer. As part of this exercise an extra water pump was fitted to double up the capacity, and the water pipes were increased in diameter to enable the pumps to work within their stability range.

Incidentally, when the time came to fly the engine it was found that the water flow was fluctuating badly. It took four feverish days' work to discover that the trouble was caused by air locks which could be overcome by carefully filling the system. But long before this came about the Fiat team were destined to live through complex engine problems which would cost the lives of men and machines.

Macchi-Castoldi MC.72. Problems with the 24-cylinder Fiat AS.6 engine kept it out of the 1931 Schneider Trophy competition.

Having established the main parameters experimentally, Fiat built an engine and put it on the test-bed. Initial test running of the double engine was without a compressor and, presumably, with the AS.5 arrangement of three double carburettors per engine. However the definitive design called for two inlet tracts running like a dual carriageway the whole length of the two engines. Each of these main galleries had six branches feeding three pairs of cylinders in the front engine and three pairs of cylinders in the rear engine.

When these and the compressor came to be fitted, all hell was let loose when the engine was fired up. Fiat engineers described the mixture distribution as cataclysmic, with some cylinders starved of mixture altogether and others pumping burning fuel out of the exhaust pipes. Allied to this phenomenon came catastrophic backfiring which was quite capable of stopping the engine. In one case a connecting rod broke and a compressor casing split. A check through the systems revealed broken ignition distributor brushes in the newly adopted AC-Delco coil ignition system and it was soon found that they were breaking within seconds of start-up. The problem was so acute that only four minutes' consecutive running was achieved in the whole of March 1931.

Stroboscopic inspection revealed that torsional vibration was once again the problem, this time in the drive to the distributor. It was known that the shafts were satisfactory with magnetos, so, rather than attempting to redesign the drive, a change was made back to this form of ignition and the backfiring problem went away. It was simply that the flywheel effect of the magneto armatures took the natural frequency of the drive out of the danger zone.

As ever, investigation of one shortcoming revealed others. On the first stripdown after the backfire troubles it was assumed that various broken connecting rods and bent slave rods were the result of detonation loads. However, further examination of folds in the metal of the bent rods showed that they were just not strong enough for the job. As a consequence new main and slave rods had to be designed and all stocks replaced. Since these parts were virtually hand-made, calling for much chiselling and filing, it took three whole months to make good this one snag.

Before testing proper could start a new induction system had to be designed. Many variations were tried, not only in configuration – one of these looked like a family tree – but also in a variety of materials from fabricated sheet steel to cast aluminium. Also, apart from fitting flame traps in the main manifolds, investigations had been made into fitting twenty-four pressure carburettors – in effect port injection – with a blower on the upstream side. Direct injection into the cylinders was also considered but never tried.

The eventual layout had the four double carburettors

mounted upstream of the compressor, which blew into a single main collector pipe with branches for each pair of cylinders. A new compressor casing was designed at this time, the old one having been found to have a badly formed outlet.

Because the lower was driven off the free end of the crankshaft of the rear engine it had been expected that there might be torsional problems, not to mention the problem of blower overrun. A friction device had to be designed to bring to rest a heavy rotor turning at 17,000 rpm; it was soon found that without this the blower gears lasted only seconds.

The first friction device slipped so much that the engine gave just as much power without the blower as with it. A beefed-up friction clutch added 15 mm to the overall length and was unacceptable to Castoldi, who had already designed the airframe. The next experiments were with a spring hub which gave the gears a four-minute life before disaster set in. A rubber cushion drive gave 17 minutes.

The eventual solution was a multiplate clutch in which the clamping load was increased with rotational speed by a set of steel balls operating in radial grooves in the clutch hub. This allowed the engine to run for 30 minutes before the gears broke up. The rest was up to the gear designer. After experiments with curved-tooth and Wurst-type gears, the problem was solved by simply widening the teeth.

With only a few months to go before the race, the revised engines, magneto ignition, new induction systems and stronger connecting rods, not to mention the redesigned compressor casings began to operate properly. A one-hour acceptance run was achieved on 20 April 1931 with an engine giving 2,300 bhp on a compression ratio of 6:1 (not the 7:1 originally contemplated) and with the blower turning at 17,000 rpm. This engine was rebuilt and despatched to Macchi to mount into an airframe. But the troubles were far from over. When this first engine came to be stripped there was general dismay when it was found that two exhaust valves were badly burnt. There seemed to have been a change of the characteristics of the metal close to the seat, causing a lip to form on the valve seat, allied to some melting of the rim of the valve.

This set off a massive investigation into alternative materials and into the whole characteristics of the valve gear. A crash research programme was mounted which involved testing of three different Italian valve materials and four foreign ones, and required the manufacture of 1,000 valves, apart from calling on the services of the research laboratory of the Turin Polytechnic for metallurgical tests.

As usual, more than one shortcoming was brought to light. One of them was a tendency for the valves to flutter, another was inherent camshaft torsional vibrations and a third was variations in the way that the valves had been machined. Some of the valves in the test engine had been made by Fiat and others had been made by a supplier. Fiat were big enough to admit that they had left a small forging inclusion unmachined on their valves

while their supplier had not. That was where the trouble had started.

The valves were finally persuaded to operate satisfactorily using the material, but operated by redesigned camshafts. However, it took from 20 April 1931 to the end of June that year to reach this solution. During that time twelve different types of valves, springs and camshafts were tried on five different engines.

Flight trials began on 22 June at Desenzano with Monti and Agello as the test team. As soon as the aircraft began flying there was yet more trouble with backfires and, to make things worse, fuel feed problems. The latter was traced to defective fuel pumps but the former problem had to be sweated out. One can only admire the extraordinary courage and skill of the two test pilots who had to fly this brand new, extremely heavy aircraft with unknown handling characteristics, whose engine would pop, bang and misfire as soon as flying speed was reached, and not infrequently stop altogether in flight. Despite this they persevered, while the Fiat engineering team, justly filled with an admiration akin to hero worship for the pilots, worked desperately day and night to solve the mixture problem.

Monti, particularly, seemed to be getting on top of the handling of the aircraft and on 2 August flying was sufficiently advanced for him to give a demonstration of the problem to the higher echelons of Fiat and the Air Ministry. Sadly, as we know, this flight ended in disaster with loss of the pilot. This delayed flying until 19 August when two new test pilots, Lieutenants Ariosto Neri and Stanislao Bellini, went into training under Agello in readiness for the race. But it was already too late. New fuel pumps were ready to be fitted and could have been put on the engines in England, but the weather was too bad for test-flying, there were spark plug problems and a snag with the flying controls. Moreover, General Balbo insisted that he should personally witness a flight test before the machines were shipped to England. It could not be arranged in time.

As a contingency in case of a withdrawal it had been planned to make an attempt on the World Air Speed record on 13 September, the day that the RAF would be annexing the Trophy in permanence with a fly-over (by Flight-Lieutenant Boothman) in the Supermarine S.6B. On 10 September an MC.72 was prepared, with Bellini as the pilot. This to be a practice run before the attempt proper and was intended to match speeds already attained by Neri.

Bellini made two passes and then lined up the aircraft for his full-speed run over the measured course. The Macchi flew at a speed estimated at 394 mph but instead of pulling out at the end it flew straight on, into high ground on the other side of the lake and disintegrated completely. A burnt sleeve of poor Stanislao's uniform, found three miles from the accident, seemed to prove that the crash had been preceded by either a severe engine fire or an explosion.

It is said that after the Bellini accident Mussolini decreed that the record attempt would be made but there were to be no more accidents. In 1932 General

Macchi-Castoldi MC.72 nose showing the exhaust ports of the two Fiat AS.6 engines mounted in tandem.

Crocco, a well-known Italian aviation engineer, through Fiat's Italian fuel suppliers, made an approach to Rodwell Banks, then with the Anglo-American Oil Company, to help sort out the problems of the AS.6. Obviously they knew that Banks was one of the few people outside the Rolls-Royce organisation who had been deeply involved in the development of the 'R' engine. With that programme at an end Rod Banks was given permission to help Fiat sort out the AS.6's problems.

He arrived in Turin to find the contest engine was giving 2,400 bhp on the bed in the Fiat test house at Caselle Torinese. The spring engine had given 2,850 bhp for just one minute. He recalled that the water brake used for measuring output was connected directly to the town water supply without header tanks and how the engine speed would rise suddenly in mid-morning as the Torinese housewives turned on the taps to prepare the midday meal!

An initial problem was the American-made sparking plugs being used by Fiat were coming out of the engine covered with fresh oil and were obviously not up to the job. Their use was despite the fact that Banks had already

requested that Fiat used the Lodge and KLG types cleared for the 'R' engine. It took a little time for him to get his way.

This hurdle overcome, it was discovered that while Fiat had tried the Rolls-Royce-developed forward facing pressure intake on the aircraft, they were not using it on the bed where the carburettors were set up. Thus in the test house they were working in still air at maximum pressure differential (the difference between atmospheric pressure at the carburettor intake and the depression at the carburettor exit). Installed in the aircraft, the ram effect of the pressure intake drastically reduced this differential, weakened the mixture and caused backfires in the long inlet manifold.

Banks persuaded Fiat to set up an installation similar to that used by Rolls-Royce to simulate in-flight conditions in a 400 mph airstream. The Fiat test-rig was, if anything, more comprehensive than that used at Derby, but in principle the same, and made use of a slave engine driving a pusher propeller to blow a 700 km/h wind into a volute, identical to that used in the aircraft, surrounding the carburettors.

Sub-Lieutenant Francesco Agello and the MC.72 in which he gained the World Absolute Speed Record for seaplanes at 470.4 mph (702.2 km/hr) in 1934.

at the beginning of development. This necessitated feeding inlet pressure to the carburettor float chambers, the carburettor slow-running systems and the fuel tanks.

Using the new test techniques and a pressure intake they finally achieved even-running in flight early in 1932 and on 26 February they were able to fly a series of test-runs to a simulated record flight pattern to prove to the State Aeronautics Control Board that the MC.72 installation was sufficiently airworthy to go for international records.

From that point on the Reparto Alta Velocità at Desenzano worked on the World Speed Record project. Neri was the first of the pilots to achieve 700 km/h; the date is not certain but we do know that he perished on 6 September 1932 flying one of the five MC.72s to be built. Finally, on 10 April 1933, after a year of training, Agello went out in MM.181 at Desenzano and established a new 3 km absolute speed record at 423.82 mph (682.078 km/h). At the end of the flying season, on 8 October 1933 Lt-Col Guglielmo Casinelli flew the same machine over a circuit laid out on the Lake at Ancona and established a new 100 km record at 391.07 mph (629.274 km/h) and later in the same month Lieutenant Scapinelli went further and won the Blériot Cup for a half hour flight at a speed in excess of 600 km/h. His speed over a closed circuit was in fact 384 mph (619.374 km/h).

The foregoing records were taken with the 2,400 hp installation. In October 1934 Francesco Agello went out yet again and with a spring engine giving 3,100 bhp at 3,300 rpm pushed the Air Speed record to 709.07 km/h (440.69 mph), a seaplane record that stands to this day. Thus, three years after the race for which it had been designed, the final chapter in the story of the AS.6 and Castoldi's sensational MC.72 was written.

Fiat, however, went their own way with the carburettor end of the installation by utilising the pressure carburettors they had designed for the 'downstream' installation when they had induction problems right

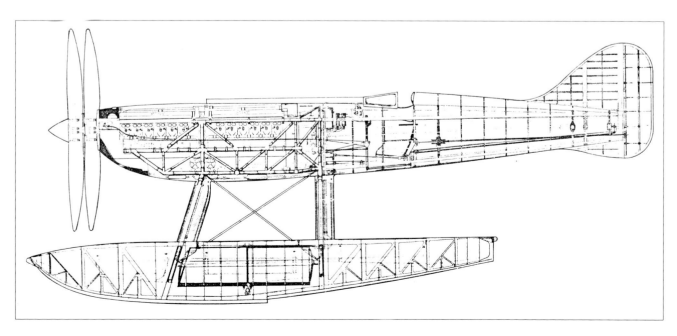

Macchi MC.72. In 1934 Francesco Agello flew an MC.72 at 440.69 mph.

The Rolls Royce 'R' Engine

The development story of the Rolls-Royce 'R' engine must go down in history as a prime example of the way pressure of competition in racing can force development. As recorded elsewhere in this book the basis of the 'R' engine or 'Racing H' as it was first called in the Derby design department, was the 6 × 6.6 in, 36.7 litre, 60° V-12, 830 hp type 'H' Rolls-Royce Buzzard engine. As a production engine it had found few takers. It had been conceived to complement the Kestrel in the Rolls-Royce inventory and as a rival to the 900 hp Napier Cub for single-engined night-bombers and very large flying-boats. By the time it became available the trend to multiple engines for bombers had set in on the score of safety. Consequently, Rowledge's smaller Kestrel or Fedden's Jupiters were being increasingly used in multiple installations.

Nevertheless, the Buzzard was a first-class foundation for a racing engine. It was ideal because of its modern conception with steel cylinder liners in light-alloy cylinder blocks, because it was a V-12 with inherently low frontal area in relation to its capacity and because it was designed from the outset to be supercharged and to run at high speeds with a reduction gear to limit propeller speed. Furthermore, all the ancillaries were well tucked away, giving it a clean outline.

The Buzzard was not light at 1,540 lb for 830 hp; its main virtue was that it had the scantlings to withstand more than double that power without materially increasing the weight. Structurally it followed the same lines as the Kestrel in having detachable light-alloy cylinder blocks with integral heads, the cylinder liners being closed-end steel forgings with four valves per cylinder operated by rockers and a single overhead camshaft. The camshafts, one per bank, were driven by bevel gears and shafts from a gear cluster at the back of the engine which also provided a power take-off for the highly efficient, Ellor-designed, centrifugal supercharger.

Three connecting-rod arrangements are possible with a vee engine, in which the motion from two opposing pistons has to be transmitted to a single crankpin. The connecting-rod big-ends can work side by side, they can be mortised into each other – called 'blade and fork' – or they can be articulated. The last arrangement utilises a master connecting-rod with a smaller slave-rod pivoted on a pin mounted above the master-rod big-end eye. The first option calls for staggered cylinder blocks and is used mainly on automobiles. The latter two are more expensive to produce but make for a shorter engine because the blocks need not be staggered. They were favoured by aero-engine designers, most of whom favoured the articulated system; Rolls-Royce opted for the blade-and-fork-type because of its more favourable geometry.

Apart from the connecting-rod set-up, Curtiss-watchers could claim with some justification that there was a lot of D-12 in the Kestrel and Buzzard. On the other hand there was little that was revolutionary in the construction of the D-12, it simply worked better than well and made a lot of good ideas respectable. The main point was that with the Buzzard as starting point, Rowledge's aero-engine design office at Derby saw no major obstacles in the way of producing one

Rolls-Royce V-12 Kestrel: the progenitor of the 'R' engine that powered the Supermarine 6s. (*Rolls-Royce Heritage Trust*)

Buzzard V-12, the ancestor of Rolls-Royce engines, developing a specific power greater than one horse power for each pound of weight. (*Rolls-Royce Heritage Trust*)

horsepower for every pound of weight, which would make the 'R' a better-than-1,500-horsepower engine.

The design team is inseparable from the story of any engineering project. The Rolls-Royce legend was based around the fact that Frederick Henry Royce, an invalid almost since the creation of Rolls-Royce Ltd, worked with a design office remote from the factory, first of all at Ramsgate then at Le Canadel in France, with summer quarters at West Wittering in Sussex. The great Claude Johnson – the hyphen in Rolls-Royce – sought to perpetuate the myth that all major schemes stemmed from this fountain-head. All new designs were meant to originate here, from Henry Royce and prepared under his supervision by A.G. Elliott, his chief draughtsman. In 1931 Royce was approaching his eightieth year.

The facts differ somewhat from the folklore. After World War One Royce went back to his motor cars and a separate aero-engine design office was established in the Derby works under A.J. Rowledge, the brilliant designer of the Napier Lion, who was brought in to produce Britain's answer to the Curtiss D-12. This was the 'F' engine which became the Kestrel; the Buzzard was a bigger engine on the same lines. Although Royce was kept informed, and his opinion invited, on every step in aero-engine development, the 'R' engine development memos, which were on loan to the author for a

number of years, clearly show that this was a 'Derby job' with the main decisions being left to Rowledge and Hives. Both Royce's and Rowledge's offices passed schemes on to the detail drawing office under Harvey-Bailey where drawings for the shops were produced and, as Royce's activity grew less, major redesigns were created.

When the parts for a new product had been made they were passed to Ernest Hives, nominally experimental shop manager and one of Royce's most trusted lieutenants, for assembly and testing. This was almost the most important part of the process, so much so that Rolls-Royce cars were once described as the '... triumph of development over design.' The author of that remark was obviously not a true engineer, for, especially with aero-engines, development is of the essence.

On the development side Hives's team included the brilliant A. Cyril Lovesey, during the Schneider period the Rolls-Royce representative at Supermarine. In charge of engine test was Vic Halliwell, later tragically to lose his life with Sir Henry Segrave in *Miss England*, assisted by Ray Dorey.

For those who wonder why all 'R' engines bear odd serial numbers, this was in accordance with Rolls-Royce time-honoured tradition. Odd numbers were allocated when the propeller revolved anticlockwise viewed from the front of the engine. Clockwise engines had even numbers. Incidentally the propellers of Rolls-Royce direct-drive engines rotated in the same direction as the geared ones due to the use of a two-shaft reduction gear.

Once Royce's formal approval of the general configuration had been obtained, the first installation drawing of the 'Racing H' was produced by T. Shelley, of the Derby design team, on 3 July 1928. This enabled R.J. Mitchell at Supermarine to proceed with the layout of his racing monoplane. There was complete co-operation with Mitchell right from the outset. As just one example he was allowed to design the cam covers to conform with the lines of the machine and thus do away with the need for cowlings in this area, as he had done on the Napier in the S.5. And of course there was complete co-operation over the size of wing radiators required.

The new engine was a major redesign. All engine castings were specified in the new Hiduminium R-R.50 series of high-duty alloys developed by Horace Campbell-Hall in the Rolls-Royce laboratories. The new, beefier wet-liner cylinder blocks of reduced height to give a higher compression ratio were in this material, as were the new sump and crankcase and a revised reduction-gear casing profiled to fit into the slim nose of a racing monoplane. Inside the engine the blade-and-fork connecting rods peculiar to Rolls-Royce were retained in strengthened form, in spite of the more general adoption of the master-and-articulated-slave-rod arrangement by other manufacturers. The reduction gears were also strengthened and redesigned to give a reduction of 0.605:1 compared with that of the production Buzzard's 0.477:1.

It is not clear who conceived the idea of the back-to-back supercharger although folklore has it that Royce sketched it out on the sand at Wittering. Certainly without it the engine's extraordinary performance would not have been possible. The likely alternative source was James Ellor, the genius wooed from the RAE, who had provided the centrifugal supercharger for the Kestrel with the then unheard of 70 per cent efficiency.

The double-supercharger layout had the minimum effect on the frontal area of the engine and yet gave more than double the pressure. Geared at first to run at 7.019 times engine speed, a ratio of 7.47:1 was adopted for the 1931 engines. Right at the end of development, for the speed record engine, a 7.94:1 ratio was tried but abandoned. This massive unit, requiring more than 300 bhp to drive it, drew mixture from two multiple-choke, updraught carburettors, one feeding the forward-facing eye of the blower and one the rear-facing one. A huge air trunk drawing air from an intake between the cylinder banks swept down the back of the engine to feed a plenum chamber beneath the carburettors.

A procedure fundamental to the success of the project was initiated on Hives's instructions in mid-June 1929. It called for 'R' engines to be tested with an airstream equivalent to the speed of the aircraft directed into the air intake. Not only did this make it possible to eliminate any air intake pipe problems, it provided substantial extra power. Known to the test house as

'double-boost', it made use of a specially designed fan driven by a Kestrel engine with its reduction gearbox turned back to front to act as a step-up gear. Air speeds of up to 400 mph could be simulated. While the engine was running a water spray was directed at the sump to provide the same cooling effect as the air provided at 350 miles per hour. Later on, air ducts were provided for this purpose.

Everywhere there was clever improvisation, like the intake air-cooler constructed from half a dozen Rolls-Royce car radiators mounted in series.

Superchargers were tested on a separate rig driven initially by a Rolls-Royce Phantom II car engine, Hives having calculated that the power requirement of the supercharger would be about 112 bhp. It was quickly found that something like 300 bhp was actually required and yet another Kestrel engine was pressed into service.

Inevitably there were problems when it came to developing an engine intended to give twice the power of any engine the company had ever built. An early snag was exhaust gas feeding back into the intake and causing false power readings. This was overcome by mounting one more Kestrel engine with a shielded propeller at the entrance to the test house and running it whenever testing was in progress. Apart from curing the original problem it provided the test-house crew with much-appreciated fresh air during that hectic summer.

On 7 April R1, the first engine, was put on the bed and run on neat benzole fuel. No power figures were taken but by the 25th of that month it had accumulated eight hours and was beginning to show signs of the problems to come. The chief one of these was excessive oil consumption, the other was build-up of fuel in the supercharger volute during warm-up. Dorey put this down to troughs which were formed on either side of the main bearing webs; they were promptly reduced by machining.

On 1 May Dorey was able to report that he had seen 1,400 hp after 13½ hours' running and that crankcase modifications had reduced over-oiling by 75%. He optimistically set out to tackle the remaining 25% with a new design of scraper-ring. There was also a distribution problem which Dorey put down to the new design of manifold and he suggested going back to the original Buzzard arrangement.

It was a measure of the pace of development that only six days later R1 was giving 1,500 bhp at 2,750 rpm and had been briefly run at 3,000 rpm when 1,686 bhp (corrected) was shown. A strip of this engine showed cracks in the forked rods. Strengthened rods were quickly designed by Rubbra and the crankcase machining modified as a temporary measure.

By mid-June production of these special engines was beginning to build up. Engine number R3 had been built and on 15 May completed a quarter-hour acceptance test, giving 1,500 bhp at 2,750 rpm with a blower pressure of 8.4 psi running on 11/89 mixture of aviation petrol and benzole with the addition of 2 cc of tetraethyl lead (TEL) per gallon. Oil consumption was recorded as 68 pints per hour. The third engine, R5,

Rolls-Royce 'R' type racing engine of 36.7 litres capacity. For the 1931 Schneider entries the 'R' developed 2,350 hp at 3,200 rpm. (*Rolls-Royce Heritage Trust*)

was completed on 18 June with standard liners, modified crankcase and scraper-rings below the gudgeon pin.

While the aim throughout all 'R' engine development was to meet the contract requirement for a one-hour full-throttle run, the Air Inspection Directorate seem to have devised a less stringent acceptance test to help Supermarine to get aircraft flying. It called for 15 minutes at 1,500 bhp and 2,750 rpm at full throttle prior to a strip and thorough inspection. The engine would then be put back on the bed and spot readings taken at 3,000, 2,850, 2,750, 2,650 and 2,550 rpm running for three minutes at each of these speeds. The gas starter would then be demonstrated and the fuel consumption, compression ratio and fire protection checked. The petrol pumps were rig-tested separately. Thus it was possible to issue R7 to Calshot on 6 July for test-flying with the minimum use of full throttle.

The major breakthrough came on 7 August when R5 completed the first one-hour full-throttle run, developing 1,568 bhp at 3,000 rpm with 7.01:1 blower gearing; the fuel was 22/78 aviation petrol and benzole with the addition of 2 cc of TEL per gallon.

This, incidentally, was one of the earliest tests made with what the test house then called 'double boost',

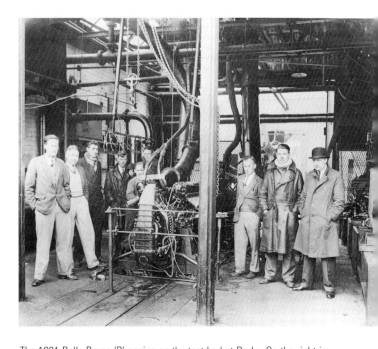

The 1931 Rolls-Royce 'R' engine on the test bed at Derby. On the right in the bowler hat is F.R. (Rod) Banks (later Air Commodore) whose special fuel 'concoctions' contributed so much to increasing the power of the Schneider engines. (*Rolls-Royce Heritage Trust*)

namely with the high-speed air blast directed into the engine air intake. Hives calculated that this created a pressure rise in the intake equal to 1.7 psi. Confirmation of progress came on 23 July when R5 ran for one hour at 2,750 rpm, giving 1,537 bhp without breaking. A supercharger ratio of 7.4:1 was used and the fuel was a pre-Banks mix of 11% aviation petrol, 89% benzole and 2 cc of TEL per gallon. Boost pressure at this output was 9.2 psi. Things were beginning to move. Cyril Lovesey, who was to gain fame as the on-the-spot Rolls-Royce engineer at Supermarine and Calshot, and Hall, a fitter, were already at Woolston superintending the installation of R7 in an airframe. Meanwhile R9 had been sent down to Calshot for installation in N.247. It was first flown by Orlebar on 10 August 1929. R9 incorporated all the modifications to date.

In view of what has been written about these engines, the Rolls-Royce final power curves for R9 make interesting reading. Maximum corrected power was 1,685 bhp at 3,000 rpm with 1,545 bhp at 2,750 rpm. Power figures for R15, the other race engine, were to all intents and purposes identical.

When installed in the race aircraft they were actually run up to 3,100 rpm during take-off. After the race when R9, the power unit of Waghorn's winning machine, was stripped it was found that white metal had been squeezed out of the big-end eyes of the first and last cylinders on each bank. Dorey comments that the engines were good for several hours at 2,750 rpm but for only one hour at 3,000 rpm.

Looking back at the 1929 event it will be seen that seven engines of the 1929 type were built. The highest number was R15 and for obvious reasons the R13 serial number was not used. R1, R3 and R5 were development engines and were not flown in 1929. R7 was the 'first engine for Supermarines' and passed its acceptance test on 6 July 1929 when it gave 1,552 bhp running on 11/78/2 cc petrol/benzole/TEL and a compression ratio of 6:1 and Lodge X112 and X115 plugs. Rolls-Royce records show that R9 was installed in N.247 on 4 August and powered the first flight of this machine on 10 August flown by Squadron Leader Orlebar. It was returned to Derby on 22 August, having run 4 hr 33 min on the ground and 2 hr 52½ min in the air.

After overhaul R9 was returned to Hythe and put back into N.247, Waghorn's winning machine, for the race. R7 was fitted to N.248 for Atcherley's speed record attempt after the race. R11 was a development engine and was worked on throughout 1930 on experiments with moderate boost and low rpm. It is not certain how R15 was used; most probably it was installed in Atcherley's N.248 for the race.

Ray Dorey's post-race report on the engines states that the race was run, and won, on a mix of 22/78 aviation petrol/benzole with the TEL content increased from 4 cc to 6 cc per gallon as a precaution. The aviation petrol referred to was napthalenic-based Romanian spirit. In his report Dorey described this mix as being their own and preferable to that submitted by the Anglo-American Oil Company. In the absence of

information to the contrary, one has to assume that the 11/89 mix with 2 cc of TEL used in much of the early development work was the Anglo-American suggestion.

In 1931 straight-run California gasolene replaced the Romanian petrol but, in fact, all the engines were run on a variety of fuels and the choice was conditioned not only by the power output of the engine but by the specific fuel consumption with a particular fuel and the specific gravity of that fuel. The aim was to find a fuel which was light enough, and would give a low enough consumption, for the aircraft to lift off and run the whole race on full power. It was never found.

It was obvious that more than 2,000 horsepower would be needed to win the 1931 contest if the rumours of what Fiat and Macchi were doing were correct. There was no doubt that 2,300 horsepower would be needed.

The 1931 Rolls-Royce Race Engines

It seems to be generally assumed that development of the 'R' engine stopped between the end of the 1929 race and the go-ahead for the 1931 engines. This was not so. Not only were engines supplied to the High Speed Flight when it moved back to RAF Felixstowe but during 1930 an intensive development programme was carried out on two new direct-drive engines, R17 and R19 for Sir Henry Segrave's water speed record boat, *Miss England III*. These were paid for by Sir Charles Cheers Wakefield, head of Castrol Oil Company, who was backing the attempt. We owe it to him that at the end of 1930 there were in existence 'R' engines capable of developing 2,053 bhp at 3,000 rpm.

Over and above this work R11, redesignated R-MS-11, was used as the 'mule' for development of the Buzzard MS (moderately supercharged) 1,030 hp engine for the proposed Supermarine 179 giant flying-boat. This helped to justify an agreement with the Air Ministry that racing engine development costs could be set against the ordinary RAF development budget.

It was during this period that 7.7:1 supercharger drive gears were developed for the Segrave engines and tubular connecting rods in place of the H-section rods used to that date. Tests were also made on a fuel containing 33.5% methanol and equal quantities of benzole and aviation spirit supplied by BP. This was later modified to 25% methanol and benzole and 50% aviation petrol, and provided valuable experience in running the engines on methanol.

From their work on the Segrave engines Rowledge and Hives knew that 2,000 bhp was available using the high supercharger gear ratio and a fuel containing a high percentage of methanol. The problem was to persuade the engine to stay in one piece. At the end of 1930 the 'R' engine was structurally at the end of its tether. New, articulated connecting rods and a balanced crankshaft would be needed to handle another 300 bhp, bringing with them the requirement for a new crankcase to overcome the cracking problem. And there was the ever present problem of exhaust valve life; to extend this the engine would have to be run very rich, which in turn would call for a bigger fuel load and higher take-off speeds. Rough estimates showed that the S.6B would not be able to lift enough fuel to run the race at full power if 2,300 horsepower was called for. However, the first thing was to get the horsepower and go on from there.

Within three weeks of the confirmation of Lady Houston's gift R3 and R5 were running on the test-bed with 7.47:1 supercharger gears. On 26 February Dorey was able to report a spot reading of 2,300 bhp at 3,200 rpm. Following this, R5 was run for short bursts with 7.03:1 and 7.47:1 blower gears and on 12 March outputs of 3,300 bhp at 2,200 rpm and 3,300 bhp at 2,360 respectively were recorded. But when the centre main bearing was stripped it was in poor condition. There was blower surge and fuel was building up badly in the supercharger volute.

At this stage the main object was to obtain performance data for the Air Ministry on behalf of Supermarine to ascertain the power available for take-off, and flying conditions at speeds from 90 to 350 mph. All testing was now done with the 'double-boost', 350 mph airstream into the intakes using the 1929 R-R fuel blend of 22% aviation spirit, 78% benzole and 3 cc of tetraethyl lead.

It was during one of these tests, on 25 February, that the connecting piece between an engine and its reduction gear burst at 3,200 rpm with the engine developing 2,000 bhp. The engine ran away and wrecked itself when the load came off, providing interesting data in the process. It was a straightforward fatigue failure; the coupling had run 80 hours and should have been replaced. It was historically significant because this failure caused Hives and Dorey to lay down a rule which was the basis of the 'life of parts' principle which became established practice in the Rolls-Royce aero-engine division.

On 21 April the first test with articulated rods and an interim unbalanced crankshaft was run on R3, on which the lower end had been built to 1931 specification with a strengthened crankcase, lateral bolts and saddle studs. The new crankshaft featured wider journals and thinner webs. The first high-speed test took place two days later, when engine speed was progressively increased to 3,200 rpm and held there for 17 minutes at 1,900 bhp. No engine with the old fork-and-blade rods had survived more than ten minutes at this speed and Dorey was able to report that it was '...the best engine of this type we have ever run'. Nevertheless oil consumption was 50 gallons an hour and there were signs of fretting on five of the main bearings.

Optimistically R3 was rebuilt exactly as before in preparation for the one hour at 3,200 rpm acceptance test on 25 March but after 22 minutes loss of oil pressure caused a shut-down. Power at the start of the test had been 2,210 bhp and 205 pints of oil were used, of which 102 pints were collected from the crankcase breather. Dorey noted that numbers 4 and 7 main bearings were showing signs of fretting and wryly commented that this was where they ought then to put the balance weights.

A balanced crankshaft was duly ready during the first half of May and by the middle of that month Rowledge had decided that the combination of articulated rods, balanced crankshaft and white metal bearings would be satisfactory. But oil consumption had risen to 606 pints per hour of which 180 pints was pumped out through the breather by the balance weights until the test house was dripping with castor oil. It took until mid-June and many hours of rebuilding and testing various piston and ring combinations in combination with crankcase baffles to reach an acceptable 130 pints per hour.

But the contract output of 2,300 horsepower at 3,200 rpm had yet to be achieved. The team was still in trouble with overheated exhaust valves and were having to 'pour' fuel through the engine to cool them. Rowledge knew all about sodium-cooled valves, having considered them for the 1929 engines, but none was available in the UK. However, Sam Heron was doing work on them in America and Rowledge asked Rodwell Banks, who was due to make one of his regular visits to America, to bring some samples back with him.

In the meantime the first true 1931 engine, R21, had been built and was 'finalled-off' on 6 July. It was found that the 2,300 horsepower was just 8 horsepower out of reach. At this output fuel was going through the engine at 0.634 pints/bhp/hour, a figure which would be quite unacceptable in the race. It was put on one side to await sodium-cooled values.

The day following the semi-abortive run on R21 it was discovered that the addition of 10% of methanol to the 22/78 fuel mix reduced the exhaust valve and induction temperatures without affecting the fuel consumption. It precipitated a flurry of tests during the early part of July with fuel containing methanol.

Meanwhile, engines were desperately needed at Supermarine to test the modified S.6. With the collaboration of the Air Ministry, R9 was built up to 1931 spec., given a restricted AID acceptance test and sent down to Calshot cleared for short full-throttle bursts. It was giving 2,165 bhp at 3,200 rpm.

The sodium-filled valves arrived from America at the beginning of July, were quickly copied in the R-R toolroom and by the 14th were running in R3 and showed an immediate improvement. It was test-house practice to measure exhaust valve temperatures by pointing an optical pyrometer up the exhaust ports. Whereas previously the exhaust valves had been running at white heat, the testers now saw the valve heads 'running almost black' with the cherry-red stems feeding heat back into the cooled guides. The result was a reduction in combustion-chamber temperatures and the modification also permitted a weaker, hotter-burning mixture and promised increased full-throttle endurance.

In this test, using the newly discovered 10% methanol addition to the fuel, R3 did its longest 'double-boost' run of 22½ minutes at full power. A fortnight later an attempt to run it a full hour at 3,200 rpm failed after 34 minutes when the crankshaft broke. This shaft had run for 71½ hours and should have been scrapped; it was decided that a new crankshaft would see through an hour at full power – this broke after 58 minutes. But the power output was an encouraging 2,360 bhp at 3,200 rpm falling to 2,335 bhp just prior to failure.

The crankshaft problem still had to be beaten. Rowledge quietly decided that what was needed was a new shaft with reduced-diameter lightening bores through the pins and main journals to leave a greater thickness of metal. It was the Friday before August bank holiday and all England had downed tools for a weekend in the sun. This did not deter Coverley, the head of the engine build shop, from getting his car and driving up to the English Steel Corporation in Sheffield, the Rolls-Royce crankshaft forgers. It did not take long to dig out the manager, who promptly got together a team and, such was the spirit of the times that everyone worked right through the holiday to forge a new batch of crankshafts.

The first of these was duly machined and on 12 August the engine ran for the full hour for the first time, giving 2,350 bhp at 3,200 rpm. The actual engine was a rebuild of R9, back in the shop from Calshot. After the run it was stripped and found to be internally better than the 1929 entries after the race, whereupon it was rebuilt for further testing at higher speeds.

Rolls-Royce were now able to honour the contract with engines capable of 2,400 bhp at 3,200 rpm with confidence. An average engine used fuel at 0.597 pints per brake horsepower per hour and oil consumption was 66 pints per hour. Engine weight had risen to 1,627 lb. These definitive engines had balanced crankshafts with weights at numbers 4 and 7 main journals, sodium-cooled valves, deep crankcases and sumps and newly calculated outer valve springs to take care of the extra weight of the sodium-cooled valves. To ensure precise slow-running settings each engine was set up with a propeller and run in the hangar before delivery.

Delivery of the actual race engines started on 30 August with R23 being delivered that day for immediate installation. R25 and R29 went off four days later. Incidentally Rolls-Royce were intentionally 'just in time' with their deliveries. Hives reckoned that it was best not to have them lying around in the Supermarine works, or at Calshot, where they might fall prey to inquisitive fingers. This was one reason for the existence of the special Rolls-Royce Phantom II high-speed engine tender, which enabled engines to be delivered hot from the oven.

It was enigmatic that having achieved the required power the next move was to decide not to use it. It was a fact of life for the team that the S.6B, despite extra tankage, did not carry a big enough fuel load for a full-throttle race. It was therefore decided that the race engines should run throttled-back, one to 3,000 rpm and the other to 3,100 rpm. At these speeds the outputs would be 1,900 bhp and 2,090 bhp respectively.

Once the race engines were out of the way, work began on the R15 sprint engine, running on a mainly methanol mix, in preparation for a world speed record

attempt immediately following the race. To increase the dynamic compression ratio it was proposed to fit 7.94:1 blower gears – the race engines used a 7.47:1 ratio – and use a methanol-based fuel to prevent detonation. Methanol has to be used as a very rich mixture and it was necessary to open up the carburettor jets and increase the fuel pump output. For the attempt both float tanks would be filled and both feed pumps kept running all the time instead of the normal procedure of using one pump and one tank at a time.

Using the 7.94 gears and a 30/70 benzole/methanol mix with 5 cc of TEL per gallon, the all-time-high output of 2,783 bhp at 3,400 rpm was achieved. However, it was decided to revert to the 7.47:1 blower ratio, not only because the higher ratio was proving too much for the cylinder holding down studs but also because the fuel change alone would take the output from 2,330 bhp to 2,600 bhp, which was in excess of the Air Ministry requirement for 2,550 bhp at 3,000 rpm.

Fuel

From a start using neat benzole, Rolls-Royce had developed a mix of 11% aviation petrol, 89% benzole and 2 cc of tetraethyl lead fluid for the early development work and the first flying on the 1929 engines; this was later modified with higher 22% petrol content, 78% benzole and 4 cc of tetraethyl lead fluid (TEF) (equivalent to 2 cc TEL). In August 1929 an extensive series of tests in conjunction with the Anglo-American Oil Company convinced Halliwell and Dorey that their brew was better than anything the petrol company could come up with and the race and the record-attempt were flown on this blend but with the TEF content increased to 6 cc as a safety measure.

Incidentally, in Ray Dorey's test-house memos the writer notes, on 24 March 1930 that, prior to that date the quantities of TEL quoted in fuel formulae were in fact tetraethyl lead fluid (TEF) which contains 52 per cent tetraethyl lead. Thus we have to assume that the 22/78/4 cc mix quoted for the 1931 engine actually contained twice the amount of lead of the 1929 brew. Whichever way it was, this formula was persisted with until June 1931 when it was discovered that, by introducing methanol in the proportion of 10% to 90% of the 22/78/4 cc mix there was a gain of 20 bhp, while at the same time the fuel had a lower specific gravity. Initially the specific fuel consumption was higher but this was reduced by increasing the compression ratio. The cooler burning conferred by the alcohol and the use of sodium-filled valves made this possible; this was the race fuel. However for the 1931 speed record with a 7:1 compression ratio Rodwell Banks, now with the Ethyl Gasoline Corporation, came back into the picture. He solved the problem of odd cylinders cutting out intermittently by incorporating acetone into a brew of 60/30/10 methanol and TEF.

Plugs

After trying a vast selection of plugs from Lodge and KLG the Lodge X170 was finally selected after having run for 80 minutes under double-boost conditions. It was found that testing the insulation of these plugs presented a real problem and that an engine run was a more severe test than anything the makers could produce. It was therefore decided to give all the plugs an endurance run before sending them to Calshot. *En route* they were diverted to the manufacturers for the micas to be repolished and new bodies fitted. A few suspects were found this way but no more plug trouble was experienced throughout.

Aircraft Developments 1931

The Supermarine S.6 and S.6B

In the few months between the decision to participate and the 1931 race itself there was no time to design totally new aircraft so the S.6B was built as a development of the S.6 to take the uprated, 2,250 bhp Rolls-Royce 'R' engine and to comply with the 1931 race regulations. As a backup the 1929 machines were brought up to S.6B specification and given the 2,250 bhp engines – they started training with the 1929 1,800 bhp engines – and new floats for increased tankage and buoyancy reserve as well as to provide more cooling area. Some differences, however, remained and the modified S.6s were given the designation S.6A.

Contracts for the 1929 aircraft were let out early in 1929. Specification 8/28, issued the previous year, had given the manufacturers due warning. Four machines were called for, two from Supermarine to Contract S.27042, powered by the yet untested, uprated Rolls-Royce Buzzard engine, the 'Racing-H' or 'R' as it was eventually designated, and two from Gloster. These latter were to be powered by the Napier Lion VIID, supercharged for the first time. The two Supermarine machines were issued with service serial numbers N.247 and N.248; the makers designated them the S.6. For the 1931 race the contract for the S.6B did not come through until January 1931; service numbers S.1295 and S.1296 were allocated.

The Rolls-Royce was a bigger and more powerful engine than the Napier Lion which had propelled the S.5 to victory, and called for a completely new and larger airframe because of its greater weight and frontal area. Bigger aircraft weigh more, and more-powerful engines consume a greater weight of fuel. Moreover, an engine with twice the power of the Lion generated twice as much heat and required double the radiator area, for which read wing surface. So, from the outset Mitchell had to contemplate a much bigger machine than the S.5 for his 1929 defender. In the event the wing area of the S.6, at 145 sq ft, was 30 sq ft more than that of the S.5 and the empty weight, 4,471 lb, 1,791 lb more than that of the earlier machine.

Reg Mitchell foresaw that race speeds approaching 400 mph could be expected if Rolls-Royce gave him more than the 1,500 bhp he had asked for. His design parameters for the S.6, based on that figure, were a straight-and-level speed of 360 mph, 520 mph in a shallow dive and a rate of climb of 5,000 feet a minute. All-up weight was reckoned to be 4,600 lb but eventually turned out to be 5,120 lb fully laden (another source says 5,771 lb); empty weight was 3,976 lb. (The S.5 weighed 3,250 lb as raced at Venice with a 160 lb pilot and 380 lb of fuel.) The S.6 had a fuselage length of 25 ft 3 in, a 30 ft wingspan and a mainplane area of 145 sq ft.

The configuration of the S.6 was identical to that of the S.5 in that it was a wire-braced low-wing monoplane with twin floats and cantilever empennage. But, in view of the official policy of all-metal construction, light alloy with steel fittings and tanks was used throughout in contrast to the S.5, of which only the fuselage and floats were metal.

One of the most interesting features of the S.6 was the wing radiators, which formed the entire surface of the wing apart from the rounded tips and the ailerons, and at the same time were a load-bearing part of the structure, a first in any Schneider aircraft, and probably elsewhere. The main structure of the wing, which was of RAF 47 section, was conventional with two box-spars formed from channel section webs and flat-strip flanges. The bracing wires picked up with trunnions bolted to the webs so that the whole rounded end of the wire was within the wing skin. The ribs were fabricated in the usual way from sheet Duralumin with large flanged holes in the webs. They were unusual in that they had extra-thick, extruded-alloy flanges into which holes were drilled and tapped to attach the wing radiator panels.

The radiator panels were each 6 ft × 2 ft using standard size sheets of 24 SWG (0.022 in, 0.56 mm) Duralumin. Two sheets per panel were used, spaced $\frac{1}{8}$ in apart by swaging the fixing holes and then separating them with $\frac{1}{16}$ in brass eyelets through which the fixing screws passed. The edges were sealed with cork jointing and jointing compound. These panels were mounted fore and aft on the wing and picked up with water 'troughs' formed in the leading and trailing edges. Coolant passed from the trailing to the leading edges, having first passed through a steam separator mounted above the water header tank in front of the pilot. It would have been naive of the designer to expect the radiators to be completely watertight once they were exposed to flexing loads in flight. They did leak and this was overcome in the traditional way by the use of an automobile leak stopper procured from the local Halford's shop.

When it came to fly the S.6 engine overheating was still a problem. It was partially overcome by cutting louvres in the roots and tips of the wings on an *ad hoc* basis to allow air to flow over the inner surfaces of the radiators, and extra surface radiators were mounted on the floats. This solved the problem and the S.6 was able to operate at full power. But it was a different story with the S.6B and its more-powerful engine. Part of the 1931 wind-tunnel research was aimed at getting the maximum airflow through the inside of the wing; slots cut in the leading edges of the wings were even considered.

The eventual solution was to construct small intake nozzles in the wingtips and exit slots in the trailing edges. This resulted in an airflow of 35 mph through the wing and no increase in drag. Furthermore, water radiators covered the whole of the upper surfaces of the floats. Despite this the engine still overheated if run at full power. For the flyover in 1931 Boothman flew at reduced power with instructions not to exceed a safe engine temperature.

The fuselage, in common with that of the S.5, was a monocoque structure just large enough in section to accommodate the engine and pilot. Fortuitously, because the engine was larger in cross-section than the Napier Lion it did mean that beefier members of the RAF could fly the S.6. Structurally, the S.6 used the same prognathous, clam-shell engine-mounting as the S.5, which was an extension of the fuselage. The frames were flanged channel section (top hat) spaced about six or seven inches apart. The only longitudinals aft of the firewall were two vestigial members along the fuselage sides, and the belly oil cooler, which was load-bearing. Mitchell remarked that the only real longitudinals were the engine-bearers although deep intercostals were fitted into the engine bed to stabilise the frames and the shell.

Fuselage skinning was in 18 SWG (0.0480 in, 1.22 mm) and 16 SWG (0.064 in, 1.63 mm) Duralumin which was doubled or trebled at stress points. Plate web frames were used at the stub spar, float chassis, tailplane and engine mounting stations. The engine bulkhead, located immediately aft of the engine, was asbestos-faced on its lower section to protect the pilot from engine heat; the upper half formed the front end of the water header tank, which was built into the fuselage and acted as part of the windshield fairing. To allow for the difference in the torsion rigidity of the fuselage and the engine, the latter was bolted down hard at the front mountings, while the rear bearers rested on rubber pads and were bolted down through slotted holes.

The fin, which doubled up as oil-cooler and oil tank, was an integral part of the fuselage. It was fabricated from tinned sheet steel to allow it to be load-bearing and at the same time to have sweated and riveted joints for the ribs and internal oil gutters. These latter were sweated to the inside surface parallel to the leading edge of the fin. Three oil-coolers ran almost the full length of the fuselage. Hot oil from the engine was conveyed under pressure from the engine along the coolers mounted along the sides of the fuselage. It was then piped to the fin through internal pipework and sprayed onto the inner surface of the fin and thence through further pipes to a third fuselage-cooler. This, a stressed member, ran along the belly of the fuselage on the centreline and took oil back to the engine. These fuselage coolers were fabricated in the same way as the water radiators, but with copper outer surfaces, and were of much greater cross-section with corrugated outer skins. On the S.6B, after considerable research, and taking advantage of the different cooling characteristics of oil as distinct from water, myriads of tiny copper tongues were

sweated to the inner surfaces of the outer skin of the coolers to present the maximum volume of oil to the air. This increased the effectiveness of the radiators by some 40 per cent.

Construction of the tailplane, elevators and rudder were on the same lines as the wing and ailerons except that the tailplane was cantilevered instead of being wire-braced. To avoid the bad area of turbulence endemic to the vee cut-out of elevators, the rudder was mounted above the tailplane and the elevators were made to operate with the minimum clearance to the rear fuselage extension.

Being practically all metal, and only a few inches deep at the most, all the control surfaces presented construction problems on the shop floor. The solution was to plate them in sections, one rib and its adjacent plating being completed before the next one was added. As a result of an incidence of aileron flutter with the S.5 and excessive rudder flutter during an early test flight of the S.6A, the ailerons and rudders of the S.6A and S.6B were mass-balanced with streamlined bob weights mounted on extensions of the aileron and rudder control arms. Incidentally, there is a *Flight* photograph with a 1929 negative number showing an S.6 with mass balances. To keep balancing weight to a minimum the trailing portions of the ailerons and rudder were fabric-covered: Mitchell noted that there was no measurable increase in drag. Fine adjustment to aileron trim was attained by fitting inch-wide, bendable, Duralumin tabs to the trailing edges of the control surfaces. This is believed to be the first ever use of this remedy which is now to be found on almost every light aeroplane in the world.

As with the S.5 great attention was paid to the shape of the S.6 floats to achieve the best combination of water performance and aerodynamic form while bearing in mind the prime requirement of keeping the propeller out of the way of solid water at all times. Aerodynamic and tank testing were carried out at the NPL at Teddington while the water performance was checked in the Vickers Duplex tank at St Albans, now available as a result of the takeover of Supermarine by Vickers in 1928.

For 1931 the contest rules for the navigability test were changed and the machines were no longer allowed to refuel after the test. This on its own called for a greater fuel load. To this had to be added the fuel requirements of the more powerful 'R' engine. Thus, for the S.6B, 161.5 gallons was called for against 115 for the S.6, a weight increase of 350 lb. To this had to be added the greater weight of tanks, coolers and radiators. Furthermore, Mitchell had decided that the buoyancy reserve of the S.6 floats was too meagre and with the S.6B he would go for a buoyancy reserve of 60 per cent and improved fore-and-aft stability. All these factors meant much bigger floats. This was achieved by making the floats slimmer and longer; the length of the S.6B floats was 24 ft. This compares with the 22 ft floats of the S.6A and the estimated 20 ft of the S.6. For the record the float volumes of the three types of S.6 were

Supermarine S.6A. The air intakes for additional cooling of the wing surface radiators can be seen on the underside close to the wingtip. (*Flight*)

as follows. The S.5 is included for comparison.

	cu ft
S.5	37.25
S.6	59.4
S.6A	71.0
S.6B	79.4

The floats were the main area of development of the S.6B and an intensive programme was once again mounted at Teddington and St Albans to determine the best combination of air and water performance. As a result of model testing at Teddington of five different basic shapes, and a series of modifications to the nose shape of one of these, the resulting floats had improved water performance and reduced drag compared with those of the S.6.

Structurally all the S-series floats followed the same pattern. They were based on a three-piece diaphragm keel, the mid-section being constructed from tinned steel where it passed through the steel fuel tank (where it doubled up as a baffle) while the end sections were Duralumin. Apart from the ends of the steel tank, which acted as bulkheads, they were framed and skinned, in light alloy.

On the S.6 the fuselage and wings were covered with oil and water radiators with the addition of small water radiators on the floats; N.247 had two of these on sides of the floats while N.248 had them on the top. On the S.6B the problem was exacerbated by the extra horse-power of the engine. For the 1931 machines it was

initially proposed to save weight by double-skinning the tops of the floats like the wings and using the whole surface as radiators. This had to be abandoned because of the difficulty of access to the float chassis fittings, and the radiators were eventually made as five separate units fitting into recesses in the upper surfaces of the floats. Extra clearance was given to the middle three, mounted above the tanks, to avoid heating the fuel.

Despite the favourable experience with asymmetric float loadings on the S.5, the S.6 carried equal quantities of fuel in each float with a 50 per cent buoyancy reserve. However, when Orlebar attempted the first flight in N.247 on 10 August it chased its tail to port due to the massive torque of the 'R' engine, equivalent to a weight of 500 lb, pressing the port float into the water. Take-off was only possible when half the fuel had been pumped out of the port float tank. As a result Mitchell increased the length of the starboard float to support a fuel load of 90 gallons and to restrict the capacity of the port tank to 25 gallons.

One improvement on the S.5 configuration was to attach the upper ends of the front float struts to the front engine-mountings, where they provided better support for the longer and heavier engine. In common with the wings, the float bracing wires were anchored on trunnions inside the floats, out of the airflow. It appears, too, that the fuselage float-chassis mountings were stressed to allow the machine to be flown without the transverse bracing wires for the duration of the race as had been done with the S.5 at Venice.

Supermarine S.6 No. N.248 with horn balanced ailerons. The ribbed panel along the fuselage is part of the oil cooling system. (*Flight*)

As before, Fairey's, who held the Curtiss-Reed manufacturing rights for the UK were called on to supply a family of propellers, first for the S.6 and later for the S.6B. Right from 1929 the decision was made to go for propellers made from light-alloy forgings rather than the original type twisted from flat-plate blanks pioneered by Dr Reed. For the S.6, P.A. Ralli of Fairey prescribed propellers of around 9.5 ft diameter with a variety of pitches to match the 0.060/1, 1929 'R' engine. In practice it was found that the screw with the best pitch for speed would not lift the S.6 off the water with its full fuel load, so one of finer pitch had to be used and the engine speed restricted to conserve fuel.

In the intervening period between the 1929 and 1931 contests Ralli, a brilliant practical mathematician, died and Hollis Williams stepped into his shoes and became responsible for the design work. He eventually produced nine different types, ranging in diameter from 8.5 ft to 9.5 ft. Initially, in the hope of providing maximum efficiency at high speed with good static thrust, and possibly to keep tip speeds down with the slightly lower-geared 1931 engine (0.605:1), he opted

for a basic 8.5 ft type, designated the 'K', with very wide blades, in appearance almost like a marine propeller. When it came to fly the aeroplane it was found that the concentration of vortex behind the small-diameter propeller, close to the fuselage, set up side-forces on the fin which could not be controlled by the rudder, and the machine turned uncontrollably in circles.

Fortunately this happened early enough for a change to be made. Six propeller forgings had been made and two of them were committed to the 8.5 ft type, another was partly finished and was converted to 8.83 ft; the remainder were lengthened to 9.5 ft by reforging the tips. Meanwhile, a damaged 9.5 ft propeller from the 1929 series, which had been reduced to 9.125 ft after an accident, was tried. When tested on S.1595 it not only gave a powerful take-off with controllable swing but also gave the highest speed of any with the racing engines. It was put on one side as first choice for the race and was actually used for Boothman's flyover. However it was considered insufficiently strong for the first record attempt and this was made with a strengthened 9.5 ft propeller, as was the second, 400 mph-plus record. One

The ultimate Schneider Trophy winner. Supermarine S.6B with Rolls-Royce 'R' engine of 2,350 hp. (*Flight*)

flight was eventually achieved in S.1596 using a modified 'K' type. Not only was its take-off performance poor, full right rudder and right aileron were needed, but maximum speed was of the order of 10 mph down; it was scrapped.

What came out of the theoretical and practical work was that the large-diameter propellers with wide tips gave the best results, on the water because of the large-diameter vortex clearing the rudder, and in flight because of the greater efficiency of the tips operating close to, but not at, the speed of sound. It is interesting that despite the publicity given by Reed and Curtiss to the supersonic tip performance of the Reed propeller, those fitted to the Schneider S.6 and S.6B, including the record-breakers, never operated in excess of the speed of sound. A further finding was that flight-testing was essential when looking for the last drop of speed. Outwardly similar propellers gave marginally different performances.

Flying the S.6

Orlebar was a team leader in every sense of the word. Like Worsley, one of the RAF's finest airmen, he did all the acceptance flights and weighed up the characteristics of each aircraft before he would let his pilots touch them. His handling notes on the S.6 are enshrined in section 8 of R & M 1575. In his preamble he remarks that the notes are disconnected and incomplete because of the prime necessity of preparing the machines for the contest, rather than carefully preparing operational data. Nevertheless they make emotive reading.

Of the machines he says that all the high-speed aircraft were easy to fly but experience was needed for take-off. At the moment of take-off the S.6 was unstable in pitch and needed careful handling to keep the nose up and maintain the angle of attack of the wings. This was aggravated if the C of G was not kept well forward. In fact the machines were modified to achieve this during the training period.

He remarks that, taking off in a light wind, the aircraft would turn cleanly in any direction with the engine throttled-back but yaw was difficult to stop without a burst of engine. Throttled-back, there was a danger of fuel building up in the supercharger if this was maintained for any length of time. The aircraft swung left if the engine was opened up and was very blind because of spray. With narrow-tipped propellers the left wing dipped very badly, especially on the S.6A with its smaller floats.

Because of the foregoing a drill for take-off was adopted. The aircraft was positioned well to the right of wind while the pilot ensured that he had a clean run into wind. He then applied full right rudder and full elevator control – stick right back – bent his head well-forward and down under the windscreen to shield his goggles, and opened the throttle fairly rapidly. In this way he went through the first one or two seconds while the aircraft was swinging left and could get his head up with clear goggles to apply rudder control as soon as it became available.

It was necessary to keep the stick hard-back right through this period since, on coming up onto the step, the aircraft tended to porpoise due to the attitude changing because of the flatter running angle. If the acceleration continued the porpoising would stop, but if it became sufficiently violent to prevent acceleration it would continue and eventually cause the machine to jump clear of the water without sufficient flying speed. At this point one started again. Once the aircraft had got through this period, which was at about 40 mph, the S.6 ran very smoothly, but it was essential to keep the elevator right back, otherwise porpoising could start again.

The aircraft would become airborne at a steep angle, and the initial acceleration would be quite slow. But it was essential to maintain the angle of attack of the wings, otherwise the machine would sink back onto the water. Poor Brinton was the victim of what would be a natural reaction with any pilot unfamiliar with the machine.

On the score of controls it was remarked that they were very effective at all speeds except that lateral control disappeared rather suddenly at the stall.

Longitudinal instability was very noticeable if the machine was at all out of trim, especially with any backward movement of the C of G. This was particularly marked at take-off, in bumpy weather and at high speed. Yet, when properly rigged, the S.6 would fly, hands and feet off, at a speed just below flat-out. Lateral changes of trim due to uneven distribution of fuel, such as more fuel in one float than the other, caused uncomfortable control loads when landing, and correction was very tiring at high speed.

There is a foretaste of the curved Spitfire landing approach in the note that it was best to approach cross wind due to blindness ahead, and once having chosen a line clear of obstruction, to stick to it. Approach speed was 160 mph and the machine touched-down at 110 mph. At 160 mph the machine sank quite rapidly. On flattening out, which involved pulling the stick well back, due to the lack of flaps and its aerodynamic cleanliness the aircraft would 'float' for about a mile before touchdown. Once on the water the control column had to be held well back to prevent one or other of the floats digging in and causing a swing. After touchdown the rudder had to be applied coarsely to prevent a swing. On one occasion Stainforth caught the heel of his shoe between the rudder bar and the slide, causing the aircraft to cartwheel and sink.

It was impossible to operate when there was any swell or wake from passing ships. Choppy water was less of a problem so long as the distance between crests was short. Conditions were usually unfit if the wind speed was in excess of 15 mph or if there were white crests on the waves.

Even with light loads and an efficient propeller an area two miles long into wind, and three-quarters of a mile wide was necessary for landing and take-off. With inefficient propellers an even greater area was called for.

The Design Team

A design is not created by one man alone. Mitchell led a team which included Alan Clifton, later to become head of the technical office, and Arthur Shirvall who, as Harald Penrose remarked, conferred good looks upon Supermarine aircraft whenever allowed to. Chief draughtsman Joe Smith, later to step into Mitchell's shoes when cancer finally overcame the great man, undoubtedly had a say in the proceedings. And Penrose records that Trevor Westbrook was temporarily transferred from his job as assistant works manager at Brooklands to Woolston to supervise the construction of the machines.

What really set the seal on the whole operation, and was fundamental to its success, was the enormous amount of work carried out in a very short time by a few scientists at the NPL at Teddington. Their findings, their guidance to Supermarine, and the meticulous reports they prepared, undoubtedly laid the foundations of high-speed monoplane design, world-wide, for the next decade.

The Macchi MC.72

The key to the whole MC.72 conception was Fiat's brilliant AS.6 engine consisting of two AS.5 engines married together, nose to nose, on a single crankcase casting, each unit driving one of a pair of propellers mounted on concentric shafts.

Mounting an engine of this extreme length called for the closest co-operation between the engine and airframe manufacturer because it is doubtful whether the engine would have been self supporting at full power in flight conditions. It was therefore up to the airframe manufacturer to design the surrounding structure to withstand engine and air loads. Maybe the inspiration for the combined structure that Castoldi conceived was inspired by the central 'chassis' on the little Fiat C.29.

Castoldi developed this idea and produced a beautifully engineered engine cradle built up from high-tensile lugs, machined from solid blocks of nickel-chrome steel, and round steel tube. It extended the full depth of the engine with the upper and lower members aligning with the four main fuselage longerons. It provided anchorages for the wings and landing wires and for the float struts, and a good deal of support for the engine, which was solidly mounted to it at crankcase and cylinder head level.

Following traditional Macchi practice, the fuselage and tail cone were of wooden, monocoque construction based on four main longerons and ten bulkheads, skinned with double diagonal planking and finally fabric covered. The empennage was also of wooden construction with the tailplane surfaces slotting onto steel tube stubs. This unusual arrangement was first noticed on the M.52 at Venice and was presumably to make the tailplane easily detachable for transport.

For the first time on a Macchi racer the wings were of metal construction based on twin box-spars with fabricated ribs at close pitch. The fact that the spars were diagonally wire-braced with tubular spreaders suggests that the copper wing radiators may have formed part of the skin. They consisted of flattened copper tubes aligned chordwise and fed by manifolds in the leading edge and behind the rear spar.

Wooden floats were used on all the record breaking machines although an experimental pair of metal floats was built and tried. Unfortunately they were built with protruding rivet heads which, not unexpectedly, cost some 15 km/h in top speed. The wooden ones were built round fabricated metal, full-depth keels and metal bulkheads. Fuel was stored in cylindrical steel or Duralumin tanks located on the C of G of the aircraft. It was drawn from them by the usual arrangement of pipes running inside the tubular steel float struts. The float chassis was of conventional configuration and, in common with the tops of the floats, was entirely covered with surface radiators. Compared with the massive flotation gear of the Supermarine S.6B, the MC.72 floats were almost dainty, with a buoyancy reserve of only 19 per cent, thanks to the torque-free propeller arrangement.

The cooling system was a complex one requiring the services of four engine-driven pumps for the water system alone. The water radiators entirely covered the wing, with subsidiary surfaces on the tops of the floats forward of the struts, and on the struts themselves. But the main part of the float surfaces between the legs and aft of them was taken up with oil radiators. It should not be forgotten that oil acts as an engine coolant as well as being a lubricant! A large oil tank was built in forward of the engine with its outer skin forming the lower part of the nose section.

Once the technique of getting the floats up on the step had been mastered the machine flew well by the standards of high speed technology at the time. Recent wind-tunnel tests on a model of the MC.72 show that it was laterally unstable and that the rolling moment due to yaw was destabilising. It cannot have been an easy aeroplane to fly, even if given predictable engine behaviour. Unfortunately, for much of the proving period this was not available. Because of the carburation problems and an insufficient understanding of the airflow in the intake duct, the fuel/air mixture would ignite in the lengthy engine intake manifold and cause frightening and sometimes disastrous explosions.

Captain Monti was lost in the course of trying to demonstrate the phenomenon to Fiat technicians, not because of the explosions but because of flying too slowly, it would appear, and stalling. Others followed him.

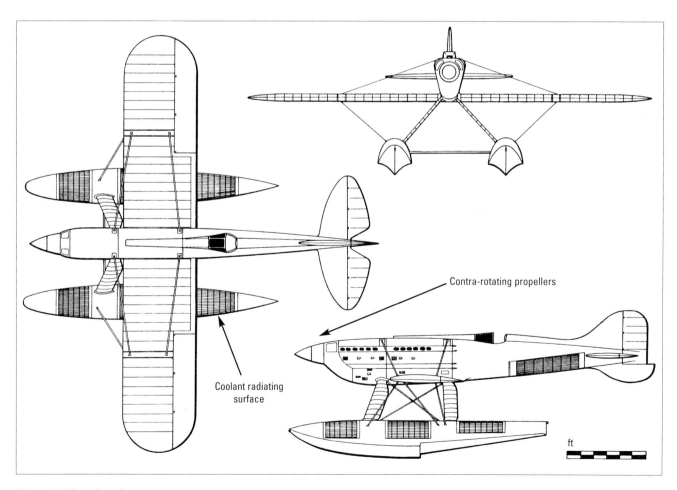

Contra-rotating propellers

Coolant radiating surface

ft

Macchi MC.72 (1931): Wing Span: 31 ft 1 in (9.49 m). Length Overall: 27 ft 6 in (8.40 m). Wing Area: 165.76 sq. ft (15.4 m²).
Weight Empty: 5,512 lb (2,500 kg). T-O Weight: 6,409 lb (2,907 kg). Max Wing Loading: 38.66 lb/sq. ft (188.75 kg/m²).
Twin Fiat A5.6 engines (2,500 hp) driving contra-rotating propellers

Lieutenant Stanislao Bellini was killed only three days after Boothman's flyover at Cowes, testing the MC.72 prior to an attempt on Stainforth's world record. A year later, almost to the day, Lieutenant Ariosto Neri's MC.72 flew into the hills which surround Lake Garda. There was evidence that it had caught fire and exploded before hitting the ground.

Initially the engines had been tested without the air intake. After publication of the Rolls-Royce test procedures following the 1931 race Fiat fitted an intake on their test bed with a high-speed air blast into it. This did not help them to solve the problem and it was presumably at this stage that they considered multiple carburettors or fuel injection. Eventually they fitted transparent windows to the intake duct and watched what actually happened. This helped them to the final solution.

Another positive factor was help from Rodwell Banks, of the Anglo-American Oil Company, who was free to help them after the Supermarine-Rolls-Royce win in 1931. It is said that he suggested fitting the high-speed nozzle into the intake but Fiat records indicate its use before his arrival in Turin. What he did do was to concoct a fuel for them which helped the engines collectively to develop as much as 2,800 bhp.

The object of all this further development, after the Schneider Cup had found its final destination, was to prove that the MC.72 could have won if it had been ready, and to take the Absolute World Speed Record. On 10 April 1933 Francesco Agello took the MC.72 out over a measured 3 km course on Lake Garda and successfully recaptured the record for Italy with an outstanding 682.078 km/h (423.82 mph). Six months later Colonel Guglielmo Casinelli lifted the 100 km closed circuit record at 628.37 km/h (391.07 mph) and in the same month Pietro Scapinelli went through the ritual of the Coupe Blériot, which is considered a more severe test than the Schneider Race, at an average speed of 619.274 km/h or 384.96 mph. Finally little Agello went out again on 23 October 1934 and rounded the job off once and for all with a superb 709.07 km/h (440.60 mph). The record, for floatplanes, stands to this day a memorial to the men who died and the heartbreaks of the aerodynamicists and engineers.

It was appropriate too, that the Schneider races, and the preparation for them, gave the Italians, who had put so much effort into high-speed flight, the privilege of having been the first to cross the 400 km/h, 500 km/h and 700 km/h boundaries of speed.

Appendices

1913 Results
Monaco: 16 April 1913

Course

A 28 lap, each of 10 km, polygonal circuit in Monaco Bay. The start off the Tir aux Pigeons Monaco with turning points at Cap Martin and Pointe de la Vieille. A first leg of 240 m, a long base leg of 4.5 km ENE, then a sharp turn to the west onto a 3.8 km leg followed by a SSW leg of 1.4 km to the start/finish line. Total course distance for 28 laps was 280 km (151.2 nm).

Regulations

Each country represented was allowed to bring three aircraft to the start line. The French club decided their representatives by means of a qualifying test over the 10 km Monaco Grand Prix course. (The original regulations mentioned a course laid out between Beaulieu-sur-mer and Cap Martin.) The French entries had to start the test by taxying across the line and continuing for 5 km on the surface before taking off and completing four laps, a total distance of 40 km. For the race itself all competitors had to demonstrate the seaworthiness of their craft by taxying on the surface for the first five kilometres of the first lap.

Competitors could start at any time between 8 am and legal sunset but they were allowed only one start. Before crossing the start line each pilot had to declare his intention to compete by handing to the commissioners a signed, duplicated set of regulations.

Results

Place	Aircraft	Pilot	Speeds
1st	Deperdussin II (Gnome 160 hp)	M. Prévost, France	73.57 km/h (45.72 mph)
2nd	Morane-Saulnier (Gnome 80 hp)	R. Garros, France	55.24 km/h (34.43 mph)
	Nieuport II (Gnome 160 hp)	C. Weymann, USA	Only completed 25 laps. 100.5 km/h (54 mph) for 20 laps.
	Nieuport II (Gnome 100 hp)	G. Espanet, France	Only completed 7 laps.

1914 Results
Monaco: 8 April 1914

Course

As in 1913. Monaco, Cap Martin, Pointe de la Vielle, Monaco. Course distances and turning points and headings as in 1913.

Regulations

Pilots had to make their take-off run and cross the start line on the surface. During the first lap they had to alight and take off twice in two measured areas on the course, each indicated by a pair of marker boats. The French rules specified *'en deux points'* which the author translates as in two places. However, the Royal Aero Club's translation was 'at two points'. Espanet's experience when he had to go back suggests otherwise. At the end of the first lap and on finishing the race the aircraft had to cross the line in full flight before alighting on the course. On the intermediate laps the aircraft had to turn round the markers at either end of the line. The duration of the competition was from 8 am until legal sunset. Only one start was allowed but aircraft were permitted to stop during the time trial.

Results

Place	Aircraft	Pilot	Speeds
1st	Sopwith SS (Baby) (Gnome 100 hp)	H. Pixton, Britain	139.9 km/h (86.78 mph)
2nd	FBA Flying Boat (Gnome 100 hp)	E. Burri, Switzerland	80.63 km/h (51 mph)
	Nieuport II (Gnome 160 hp)	P. Levasseur, France	Completed 16 laps and classed as having finished the course.
	Nieuport II (Gnome 160 hp)	G. Espanet, France	Retired after 16 laps.
	Deperdussin (Le Rhône 160 hp)	Lord Carbery, Britain	Retired with crossed plug leads
	Deperdussin	M. Prévost, France	Failed to start.
	Morane-Saulnier	R. Garros, France	Failed to start.
	Nieuport II	C. Weymann, USA	Failed to start.
	Deperdussin	W. Thaw, USA	Failed to start.

1919 Results
Bournemouth: 10 September 1919

Course

Triangular with the base along the foreshore of Bournemouth. Flown anticlockwise. The start and finish line across the extended line of Bournemouth pier. From the start to the first turning point off the Old Harry Rocks in Swanage Bay was 6 nm (11.11 km). The next leg was of 9 nm (16.68 km) due NE to a marker boat anchored off Hengistbury Head then a sharp turn to the west and 5 nm (9.27 km) to the finish line. Total lap distance 20 nm (37 km). Race distance of ten laps 200 nm (370.6 km).

Regulations

As at Monaco the aircraft had to make two 'landings' and take-offs at set points during the first lap. The alighting and take-off areas were indicated by marker boats.

Results

Place	Aircraft	Pilot	Speeds
	Savoia S.13 (Isotta-Fraschini 250 hp)	G. Janello, Italy	Completed 11 laps but they were disallowed.

The other entries either failed to start or retired after first lap.

1920 Results
Venice: 21 September 1920

(Originally scheduled for 20 September but postponed because of high winds.)

Course

Triangular laid out over the open sea off the foreshore of the Lido. To be flown, as with all previous races, anti-clockwise with the start and finish line extending out from the northern end of the built-up part of the Lido. The turning points were marked by tethered balloons flown at about 50 m. The SSE base leg, which included the start/finish line, was 11 km (5.94 nm). The next leg, due east, was 13 km (7 nm) out to a balloon flown from a moored boat. The third leg was NW for 13.1 km (7 nm). The nominal course distance was 20 nm to be flown ten times to achieve a total of 370.37 km (200 nm). However, Foxworth suggests that the distance may have been 375.56 km. The marker boat with balloon at the end of the second leg may have dragged its anchor.

Regulations

All entries had to carry 300 kg of unusable ballast. The navigability test required a take-off and 'landing' between markers but there was no flotation test.

Results

Place	Aircraft	Pilot	Speeds
1st	Savoia S.12bis (Ansaldo 550 hp)	L. Bologna, Italy	170.19 km/h (105.75 mph)

The above speed of 91.9 knots was based on a distance of 200 nm (370.37 km).
Over 371.17 km the speed was 92.03 knots (170.544 km/h, 105.8 mph).
The other entries were withdrawn.

1921 Results
Venice: 7 August 1921

Course

Triangular off the foreshore of the Lido. The start/finish line extended out from the Excelsior Hotel. The first leg was 11.1 km (5.99 nm) to the first turning point marked by a tethered balloon at Alberoni, close to the Porto di Malamocco at the southern end of the Lido. The next leg of 11.3 km (6.1 nm) was NE to a balloon flown from a boat moored off the south side of the Porto di Lido mole. The third leg was only 2.6 km (1.4 nm) NW to the final turn onto the base leg. The nominal distance cited in the regulations was 25 km (13.5 nm) per lap, giving a total distance for 16 laps of 400 km (216 nm). The course was not surveyed accurately. The true lap distance was 24.632 km (13.3 nm), a total distance of 394.11 km (212.8 nm).

Regulations

The 300 kg ballast of the 1920 race regulations was dropped. The navigability test, held on 6 August, used the start line off the Excelsior Hotel. Aircraft had to take-off and alight twice between buoys set 0.5 nm apart and then take off and fly two laps of a triangular course with turning points marked by a pylon at the northern tip of the Lido, a balloon flown from a lighter moored in the San Andreas channel and onto the third turning point marked by a balloon flown from a boat moored offshore 3.5 km (1.89 nm) to the south of the start/finish line.

Results

Speeds based on race distance of 394.1 km (212.08 nm).

Place	Aircraft	Pilot	Speeds
1st	Macchi M.7bis (Isotta-Fraschini 250 hp)	G. de Briganti, Italy	189.6 km/h (117.86 mph) *Revista di Venezia* published a speed of 189.703 km/h.
	Macchi M.19 (Fiat 680 hp)	A. Zanetti, Italy	208.74 km/h (129.7 mph) for 11 laps.
	Macchi M.7bis (Isotta-Fraschini 250 hp)	P. Corgnolino, Italy	208.74 km/h (118.14 mph) for 15 laps.
	Nieuport-Delage (Hispano-Suiza 300 hp)	S. Lecointe	Failed navigability test.

N.B. Although speeds shown are to two decimal places they have to be regarded as approximate. The official figures show all the signs of inaccurate timekeeping but they are the best available and come from Foxworth's research.

1922 Results
Naples: 12 August 1922

Course

Triangular in the Bay of Naples. The start/finish line and turning point was between marker boats moored off the seaplane base at Villa Communale. The other turning points were marked by balloons flown from lighters moored off Capo di Posillipo and Torre del Greco. The first leg was 3.73 km (2 nm) SSW. The second leg was 12.84 km (6.9 nm) due east and the third leg 11.95 km (6.5 nm) WNW. Each lap was of 28.52 km (15.4 nm). The total distance for the required 13 laps was 370.77 km (200.2 nm).

Regulations

On 10 August aircraft had to remain afloat for six hours unattended and without any bailing. The navigability test that followed required five traverses of the Villa Communale to Torre del Greco leg. During the test the aircraft had to cross the start/finish line on the water, take off and, during the course of the flight, alight and taxi for 0.5 nm. They then had to take off once more, alight before the finishing line and taxi across the line.

Results

Place	Aircraft	Pilot	Speeds
1st	Supermarine Sea Lion II (Napier Lion 450 hp)	H. Biard, Britain	234.51 km/h (145.721 mph)
2nd	Savoia S.51 (Hispano-Suiza 300 hp)	A. Passaleva, Italy	229.57 km/h (142.649 mph)
3rd	Macchi M.17bis (Isotta-Fraschini 260 hp)	A. Zanetti, Italy	213.653 km/h (132.757 mph)
4th	Macchi M.7bis (Isotta-Fraschini 260 hp)	P. Corgnolino, Italy	199.6 km/h (124.03 mph)
	Savoia-MVT (SPA 280 hp)	Guarnieri, Italy	Failed to start.
	CAMS A.36 (Hispano-Suiza 290 hp)	Teste, France	Failed to start.
	CAMS A.36 (Hispano-Suiza 290 hp)	Vroman, France	Failed to start.

1923 Results
Cowes: 28 September 1923

Course

Triangular laid out in the Solent. The start/finish line was indicated by two marker boats anchored 300 yards off Victoria Pier, Cowes. The three turning points were: at the end of the first leg of 34.299 km (18.52 nm) and marked by a white cross on Selsey Bill; 18.496 km (10.23 nm) to the turn north of a marker boat anchored

off the end of Southsea Pier, and then 15.649 km (8.45 nm) to the final turning point round the two start/finish line marker boats off Cowes Pier. This gave a lap distance of 68.89 km (37.2 nm) and for the required five laps a total distance of 344.47 km (186 nm).

Regulations

The navigability test on the 27 September required the aircraft to cross the start/finish line on the water, take off and alight, taxi on the surface for 0.5 nm at a minimum speed of 10 knots; again take off and alight and taxi for 0.5 nm, take off for the third time, fly round the full course, landing at the end of the third leg and taxi between the finish line marker buoys. Immediately after these tests the aircraft had to be towed to moorings in the Medina River. There, without any further attention or repairs, they had to remain afloat for six hours unattended and without bailing.

Results

Place	Aircraft	Pilot	Speeds
1st	Curtiss CR-3 (Curtiss D-12 465 hp)	D. Rittenhouse, USA	285.303 km/h (177.279 mph)
2nd	Curtiss CR-3 (Curtiss D-12 465 hp)	R. Irvine, USA	278.975 km/h (173.347 mph)
3rd	Supermarine Sea Lion III (Napier Lion 550 hp)	H. Biard, Britain	252.772 km/h (157.06 mph)
	CAMS 38 (Hispano-Suiza 360 hp)	Hurel, France	Retired after first lap.
	CAMS 38 (Hispano-Suiza 360 hp)	Pelletier d'Oisy, France	Failed to start after a collision.
	Blackburn Pellet (Napier Lion 550 hp)	R.W. Kenworthy, Britain	Crashed during navigability trials.
	Latham L.1 (Two 400 hp Lorraine-Dietrich)	J. Duhamel, France	Failed to start.
	Navy TR-3A (Wright 300 hp)	F. Wead, USA	Withdrawn.

1925 Results
Baltimore: 26 October 1925

Course

Triangular in Chesapeake Bay, off Bay Shore Beach, SE of Baltimore. To be flown anticlockwise over seven laps each of 50 km (27 nm) with a total race distance of 350 km (190 nm). From the start/finish line at the Bay Shore pier the first leg was due south for 17 km (9.18 nm) to the first turning point, marked by the lighthouse east of the southern tip of Gibson Island. The second leg ENE was of 14.1 km (7.62 nm) to a pylon on a barge moored south of Huntingfield Point. The third leg was 18.9 km (10.2 nm) NW toward the start/finish line. Maps published at the time show three legs measuring 9.6 nm, 8.3 nm and 10.6 nm, giving a lap distance of 28.5 nm (52.7 km).

Two start/finish lines were provided. With the wind between north and west the start line was on a line projected at right angles to the course from a lighthouse sited one nautical mile before the Bay Shore pylon, with the judges observing from the lighthouse. If this line were used the aircraft would take off into wind and then turn left through 45 degrees onto the first leg. If the wind was in the sector SW to SE the start line was immediately after the Bay Shore pylon on a line extending from the end of the pier to a boat anchored off the pier. The judges would be stationed on the pier.

Regulations
Navigability tests were completed on 23 October over a small triangular course laid out along Bay Shore and using part of a three kilometre course marked out for the speed record attempts which followed the Schneider Cup race. Aircraft had to cross the line on the surface, take off and fly two laps of the main course during which they had to alight twice, navigate on the surface between two marker boats for 0.5 nm at a minimum speed of 12 knots. The remainder of the course had to be covered in flight but competitors had to alight before the finish line marked by the two judges' boats, and cross the line on the water. Immediately after the navigability trials the aircraft had to be towed to moorings where, without any attention or repairs, they had to remain afloat for six hours unattended and without bailing. Any machine that required attention was eliminated.

Results

Place	Aircraft	Pilot	Speeds
1st	Curtiss R3C-2 (Curtiss V-1400 600 hp)	J. Doolittle, USA	430.725 km/h (232.573 mph)
2nd	Gloster III (Napier Lion 700 hp)	H. Broad, Britain	368.863 km/h (199.170 mph)
3rd	Macchi M.33 (Curtiss D-12 435 hp)	G. de Briganti, Italy	311.951 km/h (168.444 mph)
	Curtiss R3C-2 (Curtiss V-1400 600 hp)	T. Cuddihy, USA	Retired on 7th lap.
	Curtiss R3C-2 (Curtiss V-1400 600 hp)	A. Ofstie, USA	Retired on 6th lap.
	Supermarine S.4	H. Biard, Britain	Crashed during navigability trials.
	Gloster II	H. Hinkler, Britain	Crashed during navigability trials.
	Macchi M.33	R. Morselli, Italy	Withdrawn with engine trouble.

Reserve aircraft

Curtiss R2C-2	F. Conant, USA	
Gloster I 'Bamel'	Not erected.	

Proposed Italian aircraft
Piaggio P.4 A Pegna design (Pc.3) for a low-wing cantilever monoplane powered by a Curtiss D-12A engine. Construction said to have been started but not completed. Dornier-Italiano. Design exercise only. Probably of twin float configuration.

1926 Results
Hampton Roads: 13 November 1926

Originally scheduled for 24 October. Put back to 11 November at request of Aero Club of Italy. Delayed by weather until 13 November.

Course
Seven laps of a 50 km (27 nm) triangular course, flown anticlockwise, to make a total distance of 350 km (189 nm). The start/finish line was off Norfolk Naval Air Station in Willoughby Bay. The first leg of 15.906 km (8.59 nm) was NE toward a lighter-mounted pylon in Chesapeake Bay. The second leg of 24.02 km (12.97 nm) was SW to a pylon on a lighter moored off the southern tip of Newport News. The third leg, of 10.72 km (5.79 nm), was due east back to the finish line.

Regulations
The navigability trials took place over part of the course and the requirements were as in 1925. The flotation tests were the same as those of 1925.

Results

Place	Aircraft	Pilot	Speeds
1st	Macchi M.39 (Fiat AS.2 800 hp)	M. de Bernardi, Italy	393.698 km/h (246.496 mph)
2nd	Curtiss R3C-2 (Curtiss V-1400 600 hp)	C. Schilt, USA	372.345 km/h (231.364 mph)
3rd	Macchi M.39 (Fiat AS.2 800 hp)	A. Bacula, Italy	350.847 km/h (218.006 mph)
4th	Curtiss Hawk (Curtiss D-12 435 hp)	G. Tomlinson, USA	220.406 km/h (136.954 mph)
	Curtiss R3C-3 (Curtiss V-1550 700 hp)	T. Cuddihy, USA	Retired on 7th lap.
	Macchi M.39 (Fiat AS.2 800 hp)	A. Ferrarin, Italy	Retired after 3 laps.

Non-starters
Curtiss R3C-3 A.6979: badly damaged in heavy landing on 12 November after first flight with W. Tomlinson USN due to pilot's lack of familiarity with the types.
Curtiss R3C-2 A.6692: destroyed in spinning accident

into Potomac river on 13 September, killing pilot H.J. Norton USN.

Supermarine S.5: design not finalised and engine not ready; entry withdrawn.

Gloster IV: design not finalised and engine not ready; entry withdrawn.

Bristow: entry withdrawn.

Saunders: entry withdrawn.

1927 Results
Venice: 25 September 1927

Course

Triangular, flown anticlockwise over seven laps, with legs of 11.69 km (6.3 nm) SSW, 13.49 km (7.3 nm) due south and 24.82 km (12.6 nm) NNE. The 50 km (27 nm) course was laid out in open sea roughly parallel with Venice's Lido. The start/finish line was a transit between the timekeeping booth on the roof of the Excelsior Hotel and the Porto di Lido marker balloon* The turning points were: first at a pylon erected on the northernmost mole of the Porto de Malamocco; the second at a balloon tethered to a lighter moored to the south of the Porto di Chioggia and the third a balloon tethered to a lighter moored alongside the southern-most mole of the Porto di Lido.

Regulations

The navigability tests took place inside the Venetian Lagoon. Two lines 0.5 nm apart marked by buoys were laid out in the Tre Porti channel. The aircraft had to taxi over the first line, take off for a circuit not exceeding five minutes, alight before the first line and then taxi at not less than 12 knots from the first to the second line. They then had to take off once more for a second circuit and alight anywhere. As in 1926, aircraft were towed after the navigability tests to moorings and, without further attention or repairs, had to remain afloat for six hours unattended and without bailing. Any machine needing attention was disqualified.

Results

Place	Aircraft	Pilot	Speeds
1st	Supermarine S.5 (Napier Lion geared. 875 hp)	S. Webster, Britain	453.2 km/h (281.65 mph)
2nd	Supermarine S.5 (Napier Lion ungeared. 875 hp)	O. Worsley, Britain	439.5 km/h (273.07 mph)
	Macchi M.52 (Fiat AS.3 1,000 hp)	A. Ferrarin, Italy	Retired on 4th lap.
	Macchi M.52 (Fiat AS.3 1,000 hp)	M. de Bernardi, Italy	Retired on 2nd lap.

*In Airlife's Ralph Barker book *The Schneider Trophy Races* the start/finish line is given as: 'a line extended out to sea from the Lido's Excelsior Hotel'.

Gloster IVB (Napier Lion geared. 875 hp)	S. Kinkead, Britain	Retired after 5th lap.
Macchi M.52 (Fiat AS.2 800 hp)	S. Guazzetti, Italy	Retired on 6th lap.
Short Bristow Crusader (Bristol Mercury 808 hp)	H. Schofield, Britain	Crashed on 11 September.

1929 Results
Calshot: 7 September 1929

Course

The course was four sided and flown anti-clockwise. The start/finish line was in line with Ryde pier, then 5.3 km (2.86 nm) to a marker boat pylon anchored off Seaview, Isle of Wight, then a turn to port of 30 degrees on to ENE for 8.35 km (4.5 nm) and heading for a destroyer-mounted pylon moored off Hayling Island, followed by a sharp turn on to a NW heading 8.29 km (4.48 nm) aiming for Southsea pier, then due west for 16.43 km (8.86 nm) towards another destroyer with pylon moored off West Cowes, followed by a sharp turn to the SE for 11.63 km (6.28 nm) towards the finishing line. Total lap distance 50 km (26.98 nm). Race distance of seven laps 350 km (188.85 nm).

Regulations

The navigability test area was off RAF Calshot and bounded by imaginary lines from Cowes to Stone Point, from there to the Agwi oil tanks, across the Solent to Hamble, along the shore to Lee-on-Solent, to Kings Quay on the Isle of Wight and finally to Cowes.

A buoy near the Calshot lightship indicated the centre of a circle of diameter of 0.5 nm. Whatever the direction of the wind the aircraft were able to taxi for half a mile along the diameter of the circle. The course was marked with buoys according to the wind direction. Entries has to taxi across the start line on the periphery of the circle, take off and fly a marked course of 10 miles during which they had to alight twice and taxi across the full diameter of the circle at a minimum speed of 12 knots. Finally they had to alight within the circle and cross the finishing line. After the navigability test each aircraft had to be towed to a small bay north of the RAF station on the Calshot spit where they were moored for six hours to test their watertightness.

Results

Place	Aircraft	Pilot	Speeds
1st	Supermarine S.6 (Rolls-Royce 'R' 1,900 hp)	H. Waghorn, Britain	529.9 km/h (328.6 mph)
2nd	Macchi M.52R (Fiat AS.3 1,000 hp)	T. Dal Molin, Italy	457.4 km/h (284.2 mph)
3rd	Supermarine S.5 (Napier Lion 875 hp)	D. Grieg, Britain	454 km/h (282.1 mph)

4th	Macchi M.67 (Isotta-Fraschini 1,800 hp)	R. Cadringher, Italy	456.8 km/h (284 mph). Retired on 2nd lap.
5th	Supermarine S.6 (Rolls Royce 'R' 1,900 hp)	R. Atcherley, Britain	523.9 km/h (325 mph). Disqualified for cutting inside a pylon.
6th	Macchi M.67 (Isotta-Fraschini 1,800 hp)	G. Monti, Italy	485.2 km/h (301 mph). Retired on 2nd lap.

1931 Result
Calshot: 13 September 1931

Course

The start and finish line was off Ryde pier, Isle of Wight. The first turning point at the end of the SE leg was a pylon erected on a destroyer anchored off St Helens. The next leg was 13 km (7.1 nm) across the Solent on a NE heading towards a pylon erected on the coast at West Wittering. The next leg, which was of 23 km (12.5 nm), was west towards a point midway between Cowes and Lee-on-Solent, marked by a pylon erected on an anchored destroyer. The final leg was 14 km (7.7 nm) SE towards the finishing line. The total distance was 50 km (27 nm). The course had to be flown seven times.

Regulations

Changes to those applied in 1929 included completing navigability, take-off and alighting tests immediately before the speed test. The entry deposit was raised from 5,000 francs to 200,000 francs to discourage frivolous entries.

Result

As there were no challengers to the British team of two Supermarine S6.Bs and one S.6A. J.N. Boothman piloted an S.6B along the complete course of 350 km (162 nm) at an average speed of 340.08 mph (547.3 km/h), thus retaining the Schneider Cup in perpetuity for Great Britain.

Conclusions

At the time other nations were critical of Great Britain for not postponing the 11th Schneider Trophy so that the contest could be perpetuated. With hindsight there may have been some justification for this because if it had been postponed and the Italians had won the next contest, which would presumably have been staged in 1932, the contest after that would have taken place in the era when Nazi Germany was setting out to establish its technical superiority, and a great deal of technical innovation might have been expected, even if it had been inspired by the wrong people.

Baron Trenchard of Wolfeton is rightly regarded as the father of the modern Royal Air Force. He had to rescue it from the chaos of its transformation from the RFC and RNAS, and developed it into a fighting force which was capable of protecting not only the British Isles but the whole of the British Empire against any known enemy. It was he who started the system of training boys as aircraft apprentices, building beautiful accommodation for them and their instructors. Having laid the foundations of the service he established the Central Flying School and at Cranwell the RAF College for officer cadets. He was a great man but he could easily have gone down in history as the man who destroyed what he had wrought because, if he had had his way about the Schneider Trophy races, modern fighter development in the United Kingdom could well have been set back five or six years and deprived the British of the Spitfires and Hurricanes that were so vital to them in the 1940 Battle of Britain.

The Schneider Trophy races, in the last decade of their existence, undoubtedly developed aircraft which set the pattern for fighters of the future. The Supermarine racers particularly 'wrote a Bible' from which the clone that produced the Spitfire and the Rolls-Royce Merlin was drawn. Vickers-Supermarine learnt a great deal about metal construction from the S.6A and many of the lessons learnt can be seen in the Spitfire, reproduced virtually rivet for rivet. The Rolls-Royce 'R' development programme taught the Derby firm much about rapid development and introduced new alloys which would have taken much longer to come into use. More important, it caused them to appraise their own skills and see the rewards which came from the application of them.

On the airframe side both Macchi and Supermarine learned a lot about metal construction which was to stand them in good stead in the coming years, although the Schneider races helped neither of them to develop the thin, all-metal cantilever which was a feature of wartime fighters. This was where the floatplane configuration was a disadvantage because it lent itself too readily to wire bracing.

But the Schneider races were really most important because of what they brought out of the men and put into them. Designers like Nutt and Gilmore of Curtiss, Reg Mitchell and Mario Castoldi were given a peep over the horizon into the future of aviation design. They learnt to think within the parameters of performance as it would be ten years hence. It put them head and shoulders above their contemporaries. The pilots, too, were given a taste of what every service pilot would have to face in the coming war when the speeds at which 1929 machines flew would be commonplace. Though not the first pilots to be subjected to heavy G-forces, they certainly were the first pilots to experience blackouts in turns as a matter of course and learn how to cope with it. The year 1931 was the end of the glorious era in maritime aviation. It was difficult to believe that era lasted only eighteen years.

Schneider Trophy Regulations

Les congressistes se réunissent ensuite en assemblée plénière. Prennent place au bureau: prince Roland Bonaparte, president; comte Castillon de Saint-Victor, secretaire; comte de La Vaulx, député; Montu, baron de Zuylen de Nyevelt.

La séance est ouverte à 10 heurs; la première question présentée a trait au règlement de la Coupe d'Aviation Maritime.

Règlement de la Coupe d'Aviation Maritime Jacques Schneider. Cette Coupe a été remise à l'Aéro-Club de France, par M. Jacques Schneider, dans le bout de stimuler l'ardeur des constructeurs d'hydravions et de les encourager à établir le modèle le plus parfait et le plus rationnel d'aéroplane marin.

Le règlement est adopté à l'unanimité. En voici les clauses principales:

Règles générales. M. Jacques Schneider remet à l'Aéro-Club de France, sous les conditions ci-dessous exposées:

1° Un objet d'art de 25,000 francs, a transmettre à la Fédération Aéronautique Internationale, a charge par elle d'en doter une épreuve challenge d'aviation inter-clubs, nommée <<Coupe d'Aviation Maritime>> qui devra être ouverte aux appareils d'aviation de toute nature, disputé par voie de cartel international selon le règlement approuvé par la F.A.I.; mise pour la première fois en compétition par les soins de l'Aéro-Club de France, qui devra accepter les premiers défis;

2° L'engagement de verser une somme de 25,000 francs avant chacune des trois premières mises en compétition de la Coupe, au club adhérent de la F.A.I. chargé de l'organisation de l'épreuve. Cette somme devra être remise en espèces au pilote concurrent qui aura rendu son club détenteur de la Coupe ou qui la lui aura conservée.

La Coupe sera une épreuve de vitesse dont le parcours, déterminé à l'avance, sera tracé soit en ligne droite, soit en ligne brisée, soit en circuit fermé.

La longueur du parcours ne pourra être inférieure à 150 milles marins. (Le mille marin est de 1,852 m.) L'épreuve sera ouverte aux appareils d'aviation de toute nature. (Classe C.)

Tout club adhérent à la F.A.I. a quantité pour relever le cartel du club détenteur et disputer la Coupe. Tout club engagé s'oblige, au cas où il deviendrait détenteur de la Coupe, à assurer l'organisation de la prochaine épreuve.

Tout club qualifié voulant disputer la Coupe au club détenteur devra lui notifier cette résolution avant le 1er mars par une lettre recommandée adressée à son président, en indiquant le nombre de concurrents qui disputeront la Coupe. Cette lettre constituera un engagement qui devra être accompagné d'autant de fois 500 francs qu'elle ind quera de concurrents.

Il sera remboursé, après l'épreuve, autant de fois la moitie de cette somme qu'il y aura eu de partants du club engagé.

Chaque club pourra engager chaque année trois concurrents au maximum, et désigner autant de suppléants qu'il y aura de concurrents titulaires. Les concurrents titulaires et leurs suppléants devront obligatoirement appartenis à la nationalité du club adhérent à la F.A.I. qui les engage ou à un pays non représenté dans la F.A.I.

La Coupe pourra être disputée tous les ans, entre le 1er avril et le 15 novembre. La date devra être fixé par le club détenteur de la Coupe avant le 1er mars. Elle devra être courue dans le pays détenteur.

Le pouvoir sportif du pays organisateur homologuera la Coupe.

La club reconnu par la F.A.I dont un représentant à gagné la Coupe en est le nouveau détenteur. Le club qui, en cinq ans, sera sorti trois fois victorieux du défi, deviendra possesseur définitif de la Coupe. La Coupe deviendra la propriété définitive du club détenteur s'il n'a pas été défié pendant cinq années consécutives.

Le club détenteur qui se sera abstenu de concourir et qui n'aura pas cependant été dépossédé de la Coupe bien que défié, ne sera pas considéré comme ayant gagné une nouvelle fois l'épreuve challenge.

Prix accessoires. En dehors des trois primes de 25,000 francs remises par M. Jacques Schneider et des autres prix qui pourront être offerts, le montant des droits d'inscription non remboursés réparti entre les concurrents de la façon suivante:

La moitié au deuxième, un tiers au troisième et le reste au quatrième tant que les trois prix de 25,000 francs prévus à l'article premier n'auront pas été attribués. Lorsque ces trois prix auront été attribués, le concurrent classé premier recevra la moitié; le deuxième, les tiers et le troisième, le reste du montant des droits d'inscription. Il en sera de même dans tous les cas si les concours ne comportait que trois concurrents ayant effectué le parcours.

Si le parcours ne comportait que deux concurrents avant effectué le parcours, le premier recevrait les deux tiers et le second, le tiers des droits d'inscription.

Enfin, dans le cas où un seul concurrent prendrait part à l'épreuve, il recevrait le total des droits d'inscription.

Au cas où la Coupe ne serait attribuée à aucun des concurrents les droits d'inscription seraient conservés par le club détenteur et viendraient s'ajouter l'année suivante aux droits d'inscription perçus pour la nouvelle épreuve.

Conditions générales pour 1913. En 1913, la Coupe d'Aviation Maritime se disputera sur la distance de 150 milles marins.

Cette épreuve aura lieu *exclusivement en mer* sur un circuit fermé présentant un développement minimum de 5 milles marins et tracé en dehors de tout port ou rade fermés. Les escales sont permises.

Les départs seront pris à volonté par chaque concurrent, à partir des 8 heurs du matin l'épreuve sera clôturée à l'heure légale du coucher du soleil. Pendant cette période, les concurrents auront le droit de partir à volonté, mais ils ne pourront prendre qu'un seul départ, et, avant de partir, ils devront déclarer aux commissaires leur intention de disputer la Coupe d'Aviation Maritime Jacques Schneider. Au moment où le concurrent se présentera pour prendre le départ, il remettra, signée et approuvée par lui, une des deux collections des règlements particuliers et des décisions éventuelles prises par les commissaires sportifs et à lui remises par ces derniers. Après avoir satisfait à ces prescriptions, le concurrent passera la ligne de départ en naviguant. Il continuera ensuite à naviguer sur deux milles et demi du parcours au moins et viendra, en houclant pour la première fois le circuit, franch, en plein vol la ligne de départ. Il continuera ensuite son parcours qu'il terminera en passant la ligne d'arrivée en plein vol et ammerrira sur le circuit.

Rank equivalents

RN:	French	Italian
Captain	Capitaine de vaisseau	Capitano di Vascello
Commander	Capitaine de fregate	Capitano di Fregata
Lt-Commander	Capitaine de corvette	Capitano di Corvetta
Lieutenant	Lieutenant de vaisseau	Tenente di Vascello
Sub-Lt	Enseigne	Soustenente di Vascello
Midshipman	Aspirante	Guardia-marina

Regia Aeronautica	RAF
Colonnello	Group Captain
Tenente Colonnello	Wing Commander
Maggiore	Squadron Leader
Capitano	Flight Lieutenant
Tenente	Flying Officer
Soustenente	Pilot Officer
Maresciallo	Warrant Officer
Sergente maggiore	Flight Sergeant

Bibliography

The Schneider Trophy Contest 1913–31, Meldon, D., AGFA

Schneider Trophy Racers, Hirsch, R. S., Motor Books Intl. 1992

The Schneider Trophy, Mondey, D. Hale 1975

The Schneider Trophy Races, Barker, R., Airlife 1981

Schneider Trophy Aircraft 1913–1931, James, D.N., Putnam 1981

British Piston Aero Engines, Lumsden, A. S., Airlife 1994

Fifty Years of Engineering Learning, Banks, F. R., Air Commodore, *RAeSoc Journal* March 1968

Air International

Aeroplane Monthly

Aeronautical Engineering

Jane's All The World's Aircraft

L'Aeronautique

Flight

Aeronautical Research Committee R & M No. 1575, *British High Speed Aircraft for the 1931 Schneider Trophy Contest*. HMSO 1934

Il Reparto Alta Velocità 1934–1954

I Motori Italiani per gli Apparecchi di Alta Velocità. Pub. Reale Academia D'Italia

Royal Aero Club Souvenir Programme 1929

Technical Aspects of the Schneider Trophy and the World Speed Record for Seaplanes. Bazzochi, Dr. E., 1971, *RAeSoc Journal* Feb 1972

The Wright Navy Racers Part 2 Historical Aviation Album Vol IV, Foxworth, T. G., Matt 1967

Index

Note: Illustrations have *italic* page numbers. There may also be textual references on these pages.